# THE 1997-98 HOCKEY ANNUAL

## MURRAY TOWNSEND

Warwick Publishing

Toronto   Los Angeles

Published by Warwick Publishing Inc.
• 388 King Street, West, Suite 111, Toronto, ON M5V 1K2
• 1424 North Highland Ave., Los Angeles, CA 90027

ISBN: 1 - 895629 - 90 - X

Front cover photograph: Dan Hamilton, Vantage Point Studios
Cover design: Diane Farenick
Text design: Kimberley Davison

Distributed in the United States and Canada by:

Firefly Books Ltd.
3680 Victoria Park Avenue
Willowdale, ON
M2H 3K1

Printed and bound in Canada

# Contents

# Introduction

I was at a game in Maple Leaf Gardens around Christmas time last season watching the lowly Leafs lay a beating on the Detroit Red Wings.

Goalie Mike Vernon looked terrible and had to be pulled in the 6-2 Toronto victory. That was it, I figured, the end of the line for Vernon in Detroit.

Six months later, of course, he was skating around Joe Louis Arena hoisting a Stanley Cup and a Conn Smythe Trophy.

I'd probably rank Vernon's success as my biggest surprise of last year, right up there with the Ottawa Senators, who I had boldly predicted to finish last.

But, hey, that's what makes hockey, and writing this book, so much fun.

There are a few changes in format for this year's *Hockey Annual.*

We have team rankings in goaltending, defence, forward, and coaching and management. These are based on rosters at the time of writing. If a team is weak in goal and then go out and get Martin Brodeur and Dominik Hasek, don't think me an idiot for ranking them 25th.

Also, I've put special teams scoring for each team on its own in each team section. Better to use for pool information.

With each player's individual season stats this year, I've also included their career numbers.

I've added a couple categories in the team sections. "Stat Analysis" is just what it sounds like, and "STUFF," is just, well...stuff. Stuff is just things that I've picked up in the course of writing the book. There is by no means an attempt to make the section complete. Some teams have lots of "STUFF" and some teams have very little.

In the pool section, I've added an analysis of each team in various categories.

A couple things about the text in the book, which shows some of my personal preferences: I rarely mention anything to do with salaries. I don't know why anybody could care less, except for the person putting it in the bank. It doesn't help me enjoy the game in any way I can imagine.

Also, I'm not big on remembering types of injuries. I know a player's injured and won't return until such and such a time, but darned if I can remember why.

Once again, there are a number of people to thank. My daughters, Holly and Heather, didn't do anything in particular to warrant special mention, except be who they are. The same with lady friend Janis, and her kids, Laura and Brad.

My father does deserve special mention for a reason, and he just got it. In fact, he deserves two special mentions.

Thanks again to Nick Pitt, Jim Williamson, Kimberly Davison, and Diane Farenick at Warwick Publishing, and thanks again to the readers.

You can E-Mail me at mtownsend@mailserv.interhop.net if you have any questions, comments or suggestions. You can also find me in *The Hockey News* Online edition, under Townsend's Pool Tips at www.thn.com.

Murray Townsend
July, 1997
Toronto, Canada

# Eastern
# Conference

# Boston Bruins

The Bruins had a very successful season — if the plan was to get the number one draft choice, Joe Thornton.

Otherwise, it was the worst in the league and one the worst in their storied history.

How bad was it?

* they finished dead last in points.

* 47 defeats were the most in franchise history.

* Steve Heinze finished fourth in team goals with 17, and only played 30 games.

* the team leader in game-winning goals only had four, and that was Sheldon Kennedy, who had just eight in total.

* Ray Bourque didn't make an all-star team for the first time in his career.

* the Bruins gave up the most goals against in the league, the only team to allow 300.

* gave up 66 more goals than they scored, the second most behind San Jose at -67

* had the second worst drop in winning percentage, from .555 to .372, for a minus .183. Only Detroit had a bigger drop.

* allowed at least five goals in a game ? times, most in the league.

* gave up 161 goals on the road, most in the league.

* even though it was a relatively low-scoring season around the league, it was the second most goals a Bruins team had ever given up.

* Ray Bourque was -11 in plus-minus stats, the first time in his career that he'd been a minus.

* they scored just 46 power play goals.

* at even strength the Bruins were -56, worst in the league.

* had the league's worst second half record at 10-28-3.

* the Bruins missed the playoffs for the first time in 29 years, had their first losing season in 29 years, and first losing record at home in 29 years.

That's the bad news statistically. It wasn't much better off the ice either. The big news was Oates criticizing management for not getting good enough players. He was right, but Harry Sinden and Mike O'Connell couldn't handle the truth. Oates was traded to Washington.

Coach Steve Kasper also came under heavy criticism. Management couldn't handle that truth either, until the summer when he was replaced by Pat Burns.

There is some good news, however: they can't be any worse than they were last year.

## STUFF

* the Bruins are 8-0-2 in their last 10 season-opening games.
* Bourque became the Bruins all-time leading point scorer last season, with 1,362 points. He passed John Bucyk, who had 1,339.
* Bourque became the third player in NHL history to earn 1,000 assists. Wayne Gretzky leads with 1,843, followed by Paul Coffey (1,063) and Bourque (1,001).
* a 20-game point streak by Adam Oates was the longest in the league last season, and just two short of the Bruins' record of 22 held by Bronco Horvath in 1959-60.
* Oates had a 14-game assist streak with with Boston, the longest in the league.
* in a 4-1 loss in Detroit on March 19, the Bruins managed just 14 shots, and nine of them were in the first period.

* the Bruins had three penalty shots last season, and missed them all. Todd Elik, Brett Harkins and Jason Allison all were stopped.

## STAT ANALYSIS

The Bruins under Harry Sinden have not had a lot of success in the last 10 years at the draft table. That's likely to change this year, however, with Joe Thornton and Sergei Samsanov expected to make immediate impacts.

The chart below shows each of their first round picks since 1988, and what has happened to each.

## TEAM PREVIEW

GOAL: Can Jim Carey rebound back to his Vezina Trophy winning season of two years ago?

The answer is yes...and no.

He's an excellent NHL goalie who lost his way a bit in his second full NHL season. Call it the sophomore jinx if you like. He's not another in a long line of one-year wonders, however. Even one-year wonders don't accomplish what he has.

The "no" part is that he's no longer on a

## FIRST ROUND DRAFT PICKS:

| Year | Overall | Player | Result |
| --- | --- | --- | --- |
| 1988 | 13 | Rob Cimetta | Played 103 NHL games; scored 16 goals |
| 1989 | 17 | Shayne Stevenson | Played 27 NHL games; 0 goals |
| 1990 | 21 | Bryan Smolinski | Traded; is having good NHL career |
| 1991 | 18 | Glen Murray | Traded a couple times; marginal NHLer |
| 1992 | 16 | Dimitri Kvartalnov | Out of NHL; major flop played two years |
| 1993 | 25 | Kevyn Adams | minor-league; no NHL games |
| 1994 | 21 | Evgeny Ryabchikov | could not even find place in minors |
| 1995 | 9 | Kyle McLaren | good NHL defenceman |
| 1996 | 8 | Johnathan Aitken | on his way up |

team that has one of the best and deepest defence groups in the league. That's what he had in Washington when he was making a name for himself.

At least last season he didn't make the playoffs so we didn't have to witness his expected playoff collapse. He didn't do anything to help Boston get there either, though, with a 5-13 record and GAA of 3.82.

The bottom line is that even if he does rebound and play great, it won't much matter on this team, he's still going to have a tough time. But, he's young and when the Bruins become a better team they will have a proven commodity in net.

As for a backup, take your pick. Robbie Tallas played the most with the Bruins last season, but there's also Scott Bailey and Paxton Schafer. None are intended to inspire much confidence.

Hockey Annual Rating: 22 of 26

DEFENCE: Ray Bourque didn't have a banner season, but it's a little unfair to judge him on last year's fiasco. He missed 20 games with injuries and he played for the worst team in the league. He'll be around a couple more years yet, which is good news for the Bruins if they want to rebuild their defence corps with youth. Who better to teach them by example?

After Bourque is Don Sweeney and Kyle McLaren.

After them it's a mess.

That includes free agent signee, Dave Ellett, whose career has been on the down-slope for years. How much of that was the responsibility of playing for the Toronto Maple Leafs is debatable, but obviously his former coach, Pat Burns, liked him enough to get him on board in Boston. He's a big guy who doesn't use the body, doesn't cover the front of the net very well, and doesn't have near the offensive pizzazz he once had. Good enough to be in the top six on Boston, however.

They shored up last season with lots of "whatever" that didn't do the job. The players they've had around for years have pretty much proven themselves unworthy and the castoffs they've picked up from other organizations have shown why they're in that category.

After the first three, it's mostly a minor-league lineup. Many of their defencemen showed promise, but only in short spurts. Steve Staois looked good for a while, and then was eventually lost on waivers to Vancouver. Barry Richter, Dean Chynoweth, and Dean Malkoc have made careers out of travelling up and down from the minors. Many of them filled Sinden's and O'Connell's desire of being American, but that was about it.

Other defencemen, including Mattias Timander, Jon Rohloff, and Anders Myrvold have promise, but not much else. John Gruden, who did a lot of scoring for Providence, didn't even get a call up to the big

| GOALTENDER | GPI | MINS | AVG | W | L | T | EN | SO | GA | SA | SV% |
|---|---|---|---|---|---|---|---|---|---|---|---|
| TIM CHEVELDAE | 2 | 93 | 3.23 | 0 | 1 | 0 | 1 | 0 | 5 | 33 | .848 |
| ROBBIE TALLAS | 28 | 1244 | 3.33 | 8 | 12 | 1 | 1 | 1 | 69 | 587 | .882 |
| BILL RANFORD | 37 | 2147 | 3.49 | 12 | 16 | 8 | 0 | 2 | 125 | 1102 | .887 |
| SCOTT BAILEY | 8 | 394 | 3.65 | 1 | 5 | 0 | 2 | 0 | 24 | 181 | .867 |
| JIM CAREY | 19 | 1004 | 3.82 | 5 | 13 | 0 | 2 | 0 | 64 | 496 | .871 |
| PAXTON SCHAFER | 3 | 77 | 4.68 | 0 | 0 | 0 | 1 | 0 | 6 | 25 | .760 |
| BOS TOTALS | 82 | 4982 | 3.61 | 26 | 47 | 9 | 7 | 3 | 300 | 2431 | .877 |

team, which doesn't bode well for his future, considering just about everyone else did.

Last year's top draft pick, Johnathan Aitken, could be ready to make the grade. He played this season for the Brandon Wheat Kings in the WHL.

Otherwise, the Bruins may try to sign some free agents to shore up the leftover spots. Or try to make minor-leaguers into major-leaguers, which is what Sinden has tried to do in recent years.

Hockey Annual Rating: 18 of 26

FORWARD: The problem with the Bruins' forward situation at the end of last year is that they didn't have a first line...or a second line. Plenty of third and fourth lines, however.

Normally, that would be cause for extreme pessimism, but the Bruins have some great young players who are going to make names for themselves, and eventually lead this team back to respectability.

Pretty exciting if you're a Bruins fan.

Start with the number one draft pick, Joe Thornton, who is the team's number one centre before he ever plays a game, despite what you may hear about having to make the team first.

Josef Stumpel, who is only 25-years-old, is a second or third line centre, and a pretty good one, in that role. He led the Bruins with 76 points, after being thrust into the number one centre role by necessity when Oates was traded. Anson Carter came over in the Oates deal with Washington and made a good first impression. The right winger also joined Canada at the world championships and played an important role in their gold medal win.

Jason Allison, also picked up from Washington, has shown great scoring in the minors and junior, but not yet in the NHL. The knock against him has always been his

skating, but if he can pile up the points that can be overlooked.

Another youngster who will join the team this year is right winger Cameron Mann. He's tabbed as a can't miss prospect and has shown he can take his game to new levels, judging by great playoffs the last couple years with Peterborough of the OHL.

Throw in the eighth overall draft pick this year, Sergei Samsonov. He's small, which is why seven other teams passed on him, but he's considered a great prospect. He didn't exactly set the IHL on first last season, with stats of 29-35-64, but that was as a 17-year-old. Boston hasn't had much success drafting Europeans, but Samsonov could change that.

That's not it for the young talent. Landon Wilson was obtained from Colorado, along with defenceman Anders Myrvold, for a first round pick in 1998. A first rounder himself, in 1993, Wilson is supposed to be a big, tough, power winger. He hasn't shown much of anything yet, but the big guys often take a little longer to come around.

Want more? Randy Robitaille, a speedy free agent signee and Hobey Baker finalist out of Miami of Ohio, is given a good shot at making the team. He signed late last season, went out on the ice for his first shift and promptly separated his shoulder, knocking him out of action for the remainder of the season.

Shawn Bates, a draft pick who played with Boston University is signed and ready for a shot at the big time, as is left winger Per-Johan Axelsson, who played in Sweden last year.

Many of the veterans last year had decent scoring years, but that's because they were playing in more important scoring roles than they probably should have. Ted Donato, for example, set a career high with 25 goals. Steve Heinze was well on his way to a career year with 17 goals, but that was in 30 games which was all he played due to injuries.

Free agent signee Ken Baumgartner will handle the rough stuff.

Other veterans won't include Sheldon Kennedy, who earned much respect when he revealed that he was the target of sexual abuse from coach Graham James. It sent shock waves through the amateur hockey world, and sickened everyone, but it served a much larger purpose. It made people aware that the hockey world wasn't immune from sexual perversity. Since it was such big news, all hockey players in heard about it, and hopefully were talked to by parents and coaches who could discuss appropriate and inappropriate behavior by coaches. For that we all owe Sheldon Kennedy a debt of gratitude. The Bruins chose not to re-sign him at the end of the season.

Back to hockey, other players who won't be back include unrestricted free agents, Troy Mallette, Todd Elik and Tim Sweeney. There are plenty more forwards around, most of whom were up and down from Providence. Almost all of them were able to show something — mostly that they were capable third or fourth line NHLers or AHLers.

Sandy Moger, J-V Roy, Trent McCleary, Brett Harkins, Clayton Beddoes, and others almost too numerous to mention all received playing time last season. Mike Sullivan, in the same boat as the above, was obtained during the summer from Calgary.

There's no point in the Bruins not sticking their good young talent into the lineup. They can't win with what they used last year, so if they're going to lose anyway why waste ice time on players who don't have a future with the team.

Some teams try to play young players, thinking they're going to make them into good players that way. That's not likely to work, but if a team is using youth that is already very talented, as would Boston, that

could be a different story.

At the very least, watching the Bruins young forwards next season will be fun and interesting.

Hockey Annual Rating: 21 of 26

SPECIAL TEAMS: Note to coaching staff: Ted Donato should not be the top goal scoring power play forward. Note also: a defenceman should not lead the team in power play goals. Another note: good luck trying to find someone to score.

Some of the youngsters, such as Thornton and Mann, could provide some sniping ability with the man-advantage. Bourque of course will help out from the point.

There is some cause for optimism, but since it's all unproven, it doesn't add up to much.

Great penalty killing has always been a trademark of Bruin teams, but that was when they played on the tiny ice surface of the Boston Garden. No such advantage anymore.

POWER PLAY

|  | G | ATT | PCT |
|---|---|-----|-----|
| Overall | 46 | 310 | 14.8% (T-16th NHL) |
| Home | 23 | 157 | 14.6% (18th NHL) |
| Road | 23 | 153 | 15.0% (18th NHL) |

6 SHORT HANDED GOALS ALLOWED (3rd NHL)

PENALTY KILLING

|  | G | TSH | PCT |
|---|---|-----|-----|
| Overall | 56 | 308 | 81.8% (21st NHL) |
| Home | 24 | 148 | 83.8% (T-10th NHL) |
| Road | 32 | 160 | 80.0% (T-22nd NHL) |

15 SHORT HANDED GOALS SCORED (T-2nd NHL)

BRUINS SPECIAL TEAMS SCORING

| Power play | G | A | PTS |
|------------|---|---|-----|
| STUMPEL | 6 | 18 | 24 |
| BOURQUE | 8 | 9 | 17 |

| DONATO | 6 | 5 | 11 |
| ALLISON | 2 | 9 | 11 |
| RICHTER | 1 | 6 | 7 |
| HARKINS | 3 | 3 | 6 |
| HEINZE | 4 | 1 | 5 |
| SWEENEY | 2 | 3 | 5 |
| CARTER | 2 | 3 | 5 |
| ROHLOFF | 1 | 3 | 4 |
| MOGER | 3 | 0 | 3 |
| ROY | 2 | 1 | 3 |
| TIMANDER | 0 | 3 | 3 |
| SWEENEY | 0 | 3 | 3 |
| ODGERS | 1 | 1 | 2 |
| ELIK | 1 | 1 | 2 |
| DIMAIO | 0 | 2 | 2 |
| BEERS | 1 | 0 | 1 |
| WILSON | 0 | 1 | 1 |
| PAYNE | 0 | 1 | 1 |
| MYRVOLD | 0 | 1 | 1 |

| Short handed | G | A | PTS |
| --- | --- | --- | --- |
| BOURQUE | 1 | 5 | 6 |
| KENNEDY | 4 | 1 | 5 |
| DIMAIO | 3 | 2 | 5 |
| DONATO | 2 | 1 | 3 |
| HEINZE | 2 | 0 | 2 |
| CARTER | 1 | 0 | 1 |
| SWEENEY | 0 | 1 | 1 |
| MCLAREN | 0 | 1 | 1 |
| MCCLEARY | 0 | 1 | 1 |

## COACHING AND MANAGEMENT:

If Steve Kasper ever gets another NHL coaching job, you would hope he's learned a few things. It's one thing to show everyone who's boss, it's another thing to have people respect the fact that you're the boss.

Kasper alienated his stars, deserving or not, and few players who left the Bruins had nice things to say about him or management. When the boys get together in the bar after the game and spend their time grumbling about the coach, the GM and the assistant GM, it doesn't make for a productive atmosphere.

You could argue in Kasper's defence that he didn't have the horses, and that he had a job to do and did it the best way he knew how. But, you can't argue too much with failure and that's what his term as coach was all about. The Bruins not only fell from prominence they dropped out of sight.

New coach Pat Burns has a reputation for liking his veteran players and having little patience with youngsters. The truth is probably that he has patience with young players, as long as they're talented, a commodity that was in short supply in Toronto. In Montreal, he guided a very young defence to a very successful season. Boston has some very talented youngsters, so there should be no problem.

Harry Sinden was one of the older generation of NHL general managers who fell on hard times last season. Cliff Fletcher, David Poile, and John Muckler were all relieved of their duties after last season.

Sinden's been saying for years that he will retire, and might be saying it for a lot more years. Who knows? For now, Mike O'Connell handles some of the duties and does some of the dirty work.

The two seem to operate on emotion, which isn't a bad thing, but it can cloud the big picture. For example, they tried to build an American team with players from Massachusetts a couple seasons ago. It's not odd thinking, or unusual. They think they're serving the local area but what they're doing is compromising the team as a whole. The Massachusetts boys were almost all gone by the end of the season. At least Sinden didn't become glued to his faulty vision, and made amends for it.

Most American fans and Canadian fans don't care where players come from - they're only interested in winning. Perhaps the exception is Montreal where language and culture are more a factor than anywhere else.

Hockey Annual Rating: 9 of 26

## DRAFT

| Round | Sel. | Player | Pos | Amateur Team |
|-------|------|--------|-----|--------------|
| 1 | 1 | Joe Thornton | C | Sault Ste. Marie (OHL) |
| 1 | 8 | Sergei Samsonov | LW | Detroit (IHL) |
| 2 | 27 | Ben Clymer | D | U. of Minnesota |
| 3 | 54 | Mattias Karlin | C | Sweden |
| 3 | 63 | Leo Goren | RW | North Dakota |
| 4 | 81 | Karol Bartanus | RW | Drummondville (QMJHL) |
| 6 | 135 | Denis Timofeev | D | Russia |
| 7 | 162 | Joel Trottier | RW | Ottawa (OHL) |
| 7 | 200 | Jim Baxter | D | Oshawa (OHL) |
| 8 | 191 | Antti Laaksonen | LW | Denver |
| 9 | 218 | Eric Van Acker | D | Chicoutimi (QMJHL) |
| 9 | 246 | Jay Henderson | LW | Edmonton (WHL) |

The Bruins not only got the consensus best player in the draft, but they got the player who was projected a couple years ago to be the best player.

Thornton is projected as a Lindros-type player, but not to be as good as the big guy in Philadelphia. Samsonov is small at 5-8, but that shouldn't be as big a problem as some think. He made it through an IHL season without coming in contact with many opponents, so he knows how to do it and still score.

Both should be able to stick with the Bruins this year.

## PROGNOSIS

Not all is bad. The Bruins won't finish last overall in the league again this year. They have some good young talent and should be a tough, aggressive young team.

If they can fix up their defence, Carey plays in net like he should, and the young forwards put the puck in the net, a playoff spot is a good possibility.

And for the first time in a while, the Bruins should be exciting to watch.

## PREDICTION

Eastern Conference: 7th
Overall: 13th

## STAT SECTION

| Team Scoring Stats | | | 1996-97 | | | | | CAREER | | | |
|--------------------|-----|-----|---------|------|-----|-----|-----|-------|-----|-------|-------|
| | GP | G | A | PTS | +/- | PIM | SH | Gm | G | A | Pts |
| JOZEF STUMPEL | 78 | 21 | 55 | 76 | 22- | 14 | 168 | 274 | 54 | 122 | 176 |
| TED DONATO | 67 | 25 | 26 | 51 | 9- | 37 | 172 | 372 | 96 | 116 | 212 |
| RAY BOURQUE | 62 | 19 | 31 | 50 | 11- | 18 | 230 | 1,290 | 362 | 1,001 | 1,362 |
| JASON ALLISON | 72 | 8 | 26 | 34 | 6- | 34 | 99 | 105 | 10 | 31 | 41 |

| | | | | | | | | | | |
|---|---|---|---|---|---|---|---|---|---|---|
| ROB DIMAIO | 72 | 13 | 15 | 28 | 21- | 82 | 152 | 348 | 48 | 60 | 108 |
| DON SWEENEY | 82 | 3 | 23 | 26 | 5- | 39 | 113 | 611 | 40 | 142 | 182 |
| STEVE HEINZE | 30 | 17 | 8 | 25 | 8- | 27 | 96 | 306 | 71 | 57 | 128 |
| JEAN-YVES ROY | 52 | 10 | 15 | 25 | 8- | 22 | 100 | 59 | 12 | 16 | 28 |
| TIM SWEENEY | 36 | 10 | 11 | 21 | 0 | 14 | 65 | 235 | 44 | 65 | 109 |
| LANDON WILSON | 49 | 8 | 12 | 20 | 5- | 72 | 83 | 56 | 9 | 13 | 21 |
| ANSON CARTER | 38 | 11 | 7 | 18 | 7- | 9 | 79 | 38 | 11 | 7 | 18 |
| SHELDON KENNEDY | 56 | 8 | 10 | 18 | 17- | 30 | 65 | 310 | 49 | 58 | 107 |
| BARRY RICHTER | 50 | 5 | 13 | 18 | 7- | 32 | 79 | 54 | 5 | 14 | 19 |
| BRETT HARKINS | 44 | 4 | 14 | 18 | 3- | 8 | 52 | 53 | 4 | 18 | 22 |
| TODD ELIK | 31 | 4 | 12 | 16 | 12- | 16 | 72 | 448 | 110 | 219 | 329 |
| JEFF ODGERS | 80 | 7 | 8 | 15 | 15- | 197 | 84 | 414 | 55 | 42 | 97 |
| TROY MALLETTE | 68 | 6 | 8 | 14 | 8- | 155 | 61 | 453 | 51 | 68 | 119 |
| KYLE MCLAREN | 58 | 5 | 9 | 14 | 9- | 54 | 68 | 132 | 10 | 21 | 31 |
| SANDY MOGER | 34 | 10 | 3 | 13 | 12- | 45 | 54 | 132 | 27 | 23 | 50 |
| MATTIAS TIMANDER | 41 | 1 | 8 | 9 | 9- | 14 | 62 | 41 | 1 | 8 | 9 |
| JON ROHLOFF | 37 | 3 | 5 | 8 | 14- | 31 | 69 | 150 | 7 | 25 | 32 |
| TRENT MCCLEARY | 59 | 3 | 5 | 8 | 16- | 33 | 41 | 134 | 7 | 15 | 22 |
| BOB BEERS | 27 | 3 | 4 | 7 | 0 | 8 | 49 | 258 | 28 | 79 | 107 |
| CLAYTON BEDDOES | 21 | 1 | 2 | 3 | 1- | 13 | 11 | 60 | 2 | 8 | 10 |
| DEAN CHYNOWETH | 57 | 0 | 3 | 3 | 12- | 171 | 30 | 239 | 4 | 18 | 22 |
| ANDERS MYRVOLD | 9 | 0 | 2 | 2 | 1- | 4 | 8 | 13 | 0 | 3 | 3 |
| ANDRE ROY | 10 | 0 | 2 | 2 | 5- | 12 | 12 | 13 | 0 | 2 | 2 |
| YEVGENY SHALDYBIN | 3 | 1 | 0 | 1 | 2- | 0 | 5 | 3 | 1 | 0 | 1 |
| DAVIS PAYNE | 15 | 0 | 1 | 1 | 4- | 7 | 8 | 22 | 0 | 1 | 1 |
| CAMERON STEWART | 15 | 0 | 1 | 1 | 2- | 4 | 21 | 83 | 3 | 7 | 10 |
| RANDY ROBITAILLE | 1 | 0 | 0 | 0 | 0 | 0 | 0 | 1 | 0 | 0 | 0 |
| TIM CHEVELDAE | 2 | 0 | 0 | 0 | 0 | 0 | 0 | | | | |
| KEVIN SAWYER | 2 | 0 | 0 | 0 | 0 | 0 | 0 | 10 | 0 | 0 | 0 |
| PAXTON SCHAFER | 3 | 0 | 0 | 0 | 0 | 0 | 0 | | | | |
| P.C. DROUIN | 3 | 0 | 0 | 0 | 1 | 0 | 1 | 3 | 0 | 0 | 0 |
| DAVID EMMA | 5 | 0 | 0 | 0 | 1- | 0 | 3 | 28 | 5 | 6 | 11 |
| SCOTT BAILEY | 8 | 0 | 0 | 0 | 0 | 0 | 0 | | | | |
| ROBBIE TALLAS | 28 | 0 | 0 | 0 | 0 | 0 | 0 | | | | |
| DEAN MALKOC | 33 | 0 | 0 | 0 | 14- | 70 | 7 | 74 | 0 | 2 | 2 |
| JIM CAREY | 59 | 0 | 0 | 0 | 0 | 2 | 0 | | | | |

## TEAM RANKINGS

| | | Conference Rank | League Rank |
|---|---|---|---|
| Record | 26-47-19 | 13 | 26 |
| Home | 14-20-7 | 13 | 25 |
| Away | 12-27-2 | 12 | 24 |
| Versus Own Conference | 19-32-5 | 13 | 26 |
| Versus Other Conference | 7-15-4 | 12 | 24 |
| Team Plus\Minus | -56 | 13 | 26 |
| Goals For | 234 | 7 | 15 |
| Goals Against | 300 | 13 | 26 |
| Average Shots For | 29.5 | 7 | 13 |
| Average Shots Against | 29.6 | 7 | 14 |
| Overtime | 3-3-9 | 6 | 12 |
| One Goal Games | 9-12 | 11 | 21 |
| Times outshooting opponent | 44 | 6 | 12 |
| Versus Teams Over .500 | 11-24-3 | 12 | 22 |
| Versus Teams Under .500 | 15-23-6 | 13 | 26 |
| First Half Record | 16-19-6 | 9 | 16 |
| Second Half Record | 10-28-3 | 13 | 26 |

## PLAYOFFS

- did not make the playoffs.

## ALL-TIME LEADERS

Goals
John Bucyk        545
Phil Esposito     459
Rick Middleton    402

Assists
Ray Bourque       1,001
John Bucyk        794
Bobby Orr         624
Points
Ray Bourque       1,363
John Bucyk        1,339
Phil Esposito     1,012

## BEST INDIVIDUAL SEASONS

Goals
Phil Esposito   70/71   76
Phil Esposito   73/74   68
Phil Esposito   71/72   66

Assists
Bobby Orr       70/71   102
Adam Oates      92/93   97
Bobby Orr       73/74   90
Points
Phil Esposito   70/71   152
Phil Esposito   73/74   145
Adam Oates      92/93   142

## TEAM

Last 3 years

| | GP | W | L | T | Pts | % |
|---|---|---|---|---|---|---|
| 1996-97 | 82 | 26 | 47 | 9 | 61 | .372 |
| 1995-96 | 82 | 40 | 31 | 11 | 91 | .555 |
| 1994-95 | 48 | 27 | 18 | 3 | 57 | .594 |

Best 3 regular seasons

| | | | | | | |
|---|---|---|---|---|---|---|
| 1929-30 | 44 | 38 | 5 | 1 | 77 | .875 |
| 1969-70 | 76 | 57 | 14 | 7 | 121 | .791 |
| 1938-39 | 48 | 36 | 10 | 2 | 74 | .771 |

Worst 3 regular seasons

| | | | | | | |
|---|---|---|---|---|---|---|
| 1924-25 | 30 | 6 | 24 | 0 | 12 | .200 |
| 1961-62 | 70 | 15 | 47 | 8 | 38 | .271 |
| 1960-61 | 70 | 15 | 42 | 13 | 43 | .307 |

Most Goals (min. 70 game schedule)
| 1970-71 | 399 |
|---------|-----|
| 1973-74 | 349 |
| 1974-75 | 345 |

Fewest Goals (min. 70 game schedule)
| 1955-56 | 147 |
|---------|-----|
| 1952-53 | 152 |
| 1951-52 | 162 |

Most Goals Against (min. 70 game schedule)
| 1961-62 | 306 |
|---------|-----|
| 1995-96 | 300 |
| 1985-86 | 288 |

Fewest Goals Against (min. 70 game schedule)
| 1952-53 | 172 |
|---------|-----|
| 1956-57 | 174 |
| 1951-52 | 176 |

# Buffalo Sabres

The way the NHL Awards night went, you would have thought the Buffalo Sabres finished on top of the league and won the Stanley Cup. Mike Peca took the Selke Award for best defensive forward, Ted Nolan won the Adams for best coach, and Dominik Hasek won the Vezina for best goalie as well as the Hart Trophy for most valuable player.

The Sabres were knocked out in the second round of the playoffs, but did manage to do something special during the regular season. Predicted by almost everyone to finish out of the playoffs, they ended up on top of the Northeast Division and third in the conference. If not for a late season slump they would have done even better.

So, who and what was responsible? See the list below.

1. Dominik Hasek

2. Dominik Hasek

3. Dominik Hasek

4. Ted Nolan - the coach of the year is a passionate, emotional coach who apparently has the gift to pass those traits on to his players.

5. John Muckler - *The Hockey News* gave more credit to Muckler than Nolan for the team's success, naming him the Executive of the Year, and leaving Nolan out of the finalists for coach of the year.

6. Feuds - It's amazing how often teams are successful when there's well-publicized off-ice problems. Maybe, for some weird reason, it allows the players to unify their focus on the ice. Or, maybe their own problems with coaches or management become less significant, and they worry about them less. And maybe the players don't know who they're supposed to impress, so they impress everyone. Nolan and Muckler's feud was well known, there were other earlier management fights, and reportedly Nolan didn't get along with all the players, including Hasek.

7. Pat LaFontaine Injury - It's not unusual for teams to rally together when their superstar is out of action. Without LaFontaine, the Sabre skaters knew the only way they could compensate for his absence was to pull together as a team and have all the oars in the water and rowing at the same time.

8. The Sky is Falling - The new scoreboard at the new Marine Midland Centre crashed to the ice one day. That's bound to shake up the players who could have possibly been skating under it. Just kidding here, but they might have put on a little extra speed when they skated through the neutral zone.

9. Toughness - This is an example of one of those things that work...when they work. The Sabres had toughness the previous season and the Sharks had toughness last year, but it didn't help them win. Probably, when there are some other components that make the team win, then toughness can become an additional contributing factor.

10. Dominik Hasek - without him, there would have been none of the above.

## STUFF

* Buffalo's leading scorer, Plante, had the fewest points (53) of any team leading scorer in the league.
* a 12-game undefeated streak was the third longest in Sabres' history, and tied for fourth longest in the league last season.
* 43 power play goals was a team record low. The previous low was 48 in 1972-74.
* a 13.2 percent power play efficiency record was the lowest in team history. The previous low was 17.2% in 1987-88.
* the Sabres' division title was their first since 1980-81.
* Miroslav Satan led the league with a 21.0% shooting percentage (minimum 82 shots).
* Dominik Hasek has led the league in save percentage for four straight seasons. In each of the last three seasons it has been .930.
* Derek Plante's overtime winner in game seven versus Ottawa gave them their first game seven victory in team history. They had previously been 0-3.
* Hasek took over the all-time lead in shutouts, with 19. He passed Don Edwards, who had 14.
* Buffalo will host next summer's entry draft.

## STAT ANALYSIS

The reason Buffalo was able to win so often last year despite being outshot more than any other team had much to do with a certain goaltender. But that still doesn't explain why they were able to be around the middle of the pack in goals scored despite so few shots.

We can't assume they just had accurate shots, although that's what the stats suggests, but rather that they were in position to take quality shots as opposed to quantity.

Fewest Shots Per Game:

| Buffalo | 25.5 |
|---|---|
| NY Islanders | 26.7 |
| Vancouver | 28.1 |
| Anaheim | 28.4 |
| San Jose | 28.8 |

Highest Difference - Shots for and Against:

| | Shots For | Shots Against | Difference Per Game |
|---|---|---|---|
| Buffalo | 25.5 | 33.3 | -7.8 |
| Toronto | 29.3 | 34.4 | -5.1 |
| Los Angeles | 29.0 | 33.9 | -4.9 |
| Pittsburgh | 29.4 | 34.3 | -4.9 |
| Anaheim | 28.4 | 32.8 | -4.4 |

## TEAM PREVIEW

GOAL: Despite everything Hasek did on the ice last season, it will be hard not to remember him for his off-ice antics during the playoffs. Mainly, of course, for an attack on Buffalo News reporter Larry Kelly, who Hasek felt had accused him of over-stating an injury. Hasek was suspended for three games, that he might not have been able to play anyway because of the injury.

Maybe there was something better to remember him by, come to think of it. How about winning the Vezina, the Hart, and the Pearson trophies. That ought to do it. The fact that he deserved them all was just as impressive. Truly one of the great regular seasons in NHL history.

Steve Shields has emerged as the superstar backup. Thrust into the impossible situation of replacing Hasek in the playoffs he did a darn good job. He also guaranteed himself future employment.

That was thanks to Andrei Trefilov, who blew it. Trefilov was upset that he wasn't getting a lot of playing time early in the season, or more to the point, almost no playing time. His point was that he couldn't be expected to play well when he did eventually spell Hasek. He was probably right, too, but nobody much cared because Hasek was winning game after game for them.

So, Trefilov opted to have some minor surgery that could have waited until the end of the year. The reasoning, of course, is that he might as well have it then, since he wasn't playing anyway.

Bad, bad move. Shields got the chance to backup Hasek, got in some games when Hasek was injured, and played well enough to push Trefilov out of the picture. In the playoffs, Trefilov ended up being the backup to Shields when Hasek wasn't playing.

Hockey Annual Rating: 1 of 26

DEFENCE: Maybe the Buffalo defence is okay, but they don't have any depth, and considering the number of shots that Buffalo had last season, they're nothing special.

Competent may be the word. Alexei Zhitnik is a competent mid-range scoring defenceman; Richard Smehlik is a competent defenceman who can score goals and contribute offensively; Darryl Shannon is a competent, reliable workhorse; Bob Boughner is a competent tough-guy; Mike Wilson is developing into a competent NHL defenceman; and Jay McKee will be in just his second year, hoping to become a competent NHL defenceman.

Down on the farm is another tough guy in Rumun Ndur, and the future prospect is Cory Sarich, who played for Canada's world championship junior team. He's considered a two-way defenceman, with a can't miss label.

The Sabres are said to need a quarterback for the power play, but they don't really. Yes, the power play sucks, but it's not the point-men's fault. Zhitnik and Smehlik can handle things back there, but without somebody to put the puck in the net up front, they're not going to look very good.

Adequate, competent, call it what you want. It becomes something considerably less, however, if they begin to have problems with injuries.

Hockey Annual Rating: 12 of 26

| GOALTENDER | GPI | MINS | AVG | W | L | T | EN | SO | GA | SA | SV % |
|---|---|---|---|---|---|---|---|---|---|---|---|
| DOMINIK HASEK | 67 | 4037 | 2.27 | 37 | 20 | 10 | 3 | 5 | 153 | 2177 | .930 |
| STEVE SHIELDS | 13 | 789 | 2.97 | 3 | 8 | 2 | 2 | 0 | 39 | 447 | .913 |
| ANDREI TREFILOV | 3 | 159 | 3.77 | 0 | 2 | 0 | 1 | 0 | 10 | 98 | .898 |
| BUF TOTALS | 82 | 5003 | 2.49 | 40 | 30 | 12 | 6 | 5 | 208 | 2728 | .924 |

FORWARD: This is such a tough call. You see a team whose leading scorer has 53 points, lowest in the league, and it doesn't take much thought to figure out that they need more scoring.

But, you see also a team with six 20-goal scorers and one with 19. They were tied with Colorado for the most 20-goal scorers.

So, what's better? One or two guys scoring 40 or 50 goals, or a bunch of players sharing the load.

If there are more players contributing, it means there's less chance of a breakdown if there's an injury or a slump by a particular individual. That's good. It also means players aren't waiting for the superstar to score all the goals.

But, there's also less chance of a hot sniper carrying the team for a week or two. And it hurts on the power play as evidenced by the fact Buffalo was last in that category.

The ultimate would be one big scorer and lots of little scorers. Or maybe not.

The Sabres don't have a legitimate first line. LaFontaine, of course, if he returns, would be the first line centre, but that's about it.

Derek Plante led the team in scoring, but that was by default. Donald Audette led in goals, with 28, but that was no great feat either. Still, the team would have been in deep trouble if not for them and the players in the next paragraph.

Brian Holzinger had his breakout season, with 22-29-51, quite an improvement over the 10-10-20 he had in his rookie year. Jason Dawe contributed about as expected, and Michal Grosek performed okay in his first full NHL season.

Randy Burridge had an off year because of injuries, and Brad May had a horrendous season, also because of injuries.

The Sabres did come up with three treasures - Mike Peca, Matthew Barnaby and Dixon Ward.

Peca won the award for the league's best defensive forward, but on the Sabres he was also one of their best scorers. He took big faceoffs, killed penalties, and if not for Hasek would have been the team's most valuable player.

Dixon Ward has been around the block, and back. In seven pro seasons he's played with seven different pro teams, including Vancouver, Los Angeles and Toronto, before ending up Buffalo. His inspired play earned him a spot as a Sabres regular, even playing sometimes on the top line.

The Sabres obtained Miroslav Satan at the trade deadline and promptly went into a lengthy slump. They were 3-8-1 at the end of last season. Nobody was blaming Satan personally, because he had eight goals in just 12 games with Buffalo, but he may have upset the team's chemistry. Eventually, Nolan was sitting him out and coming up with excuses.

The three top prospects remain Wayne Primeau, Curtis Brown and Valcav Verada.

Brown started the year in Buffalo but then was sent down to Rochester. Primeau didn't score as much as hoped, but the Sabres are hardly giving up on him. Those two, along with Verada, should get a chance to stick with the Sabres this season.

Hockey Annual Rating: 12 of 26

SPECIAL TEAMS: Not only did they have the worst power play in the league, but the worst in Buffalo Sabres history. The strangest thing is that it didn't seem to hurt them much, considering their record. But, imagine how much better they could have been if they could score with the man-advantage.

Not having a sniper for the power play was the main problem. Their leader, Audette, had eight. And get this, their leader in shorthanded goals had almost as many, Peca with six.

In fact they were first in shorthanded goals scored, and first in fewest shorthanded goals allowed.

So, let's add up the net goals. On the power play it was 43 for and four against for a net of 39. When shorthanded they had 59 against and 16 for, for a net of 43. Using that analysis their special teams were just about even — didn't help and didn't hurt. Much better than it looks when you see that they're ranked 26th.

Strange, but apparently effective.

POWER PLAY

|  | G | ATT | PCT |
|---|---|---|---|
| Overall | 4 | 326 | 13.2% (26th NHL) |
| Home | 24 | 165 | 14.5% (19th NHL) |
| Road | 19 | 161 | 11.8% (25th NHL) |

4 SHORT HANDED GOALS ALLOWED (1st NHL)

PENALTY KILLING

|  | G | TSH | PCT |
|---|---|---|---|
| Overall | 59 | 364 | 83.8% (13th NHL) |
| Home | 31 | 188 | 83.5% (12th NHL) |
| Road | 28 | 176 | 84.1% (16th NHL) |

16 SHORT HANDED GOALS SCORED (1st NHL)

SABRES SPECIAL TEAMS SCORING

| Power play | G | A | PTS |
|---|---|---|---|
| AUDETTE | 8 | 6 | 14 |
| ZHITNIK | 3 | 11 | 14 |
| GALLEY | 1 | 13 | 14 |
| DAWE | 4 | 8 | 12 |
| SATAN | 7 | 4 | 11 |
| PLANTE | 5 | 5 | 10 |
| PECA | 5 | 4 | 9 |
| HOLZINGER | 2 | 5 | 7 |
| SMEHLIK | 2 | 4 | 6 |
| LAFONTAINE | 1 | 5 | 6 |
| GROSEK | 1 | 4 | 5 |
| BURRIDGE | 1 | 4 | 5 |
| BARNABY | 2 | 2 | 4 |
| WARD | 1 | 3 | 4 |
| SHANNON | 1 | 2 | 3 |
| MAY | 1 | 2 | 3 |
| MCKEE | 0 | 3 | 3 |
| SEMENOV | 1 | 0 | 1 |
| PRIMEAU | 1 | 0 | 1 |

| Short handed | G | A | PTS |
|---|---|---|---|
| PECA | 6 | 3 | 9 |
| BURRIDGE | 3 | 1 | 4 |
| WARD | 2 | 2 | 4 |
| HOLZINGER | 2 | 1 | 3 |
| ZHITNIK | 1 | 2 | 3 |
| DAWE | 1 | 1 | 2 |
| GALLEY | 1 | 0 | 1 |
| SHANNON | 0 | 1 | 1 |
| PLANTE | 0 | 1 | 1 |
| BOUGHNER | 0 | 1 | 1 |

COACHING AND MANAGEMENT: Who was better? Muckler or Nolan.

It was Muckler who put the party together, but it was Nolan who made everyone dance.

You decide which is more important.

Some suggest neither was responsible for the team's success, and that it was all Hasek.

Muckler made some good deals for the team, including getting Mike Peca, Mike Wilson and a number one draft choice (Jay McKee) from Vancouver for Alexander Mogilny. He had to work within the confines of a budget, and his philosophy seemed to be to let the young players earn their wings in the NHL. Nolan, apparently, had the opposite view.

Muckler was fired, so the Sabres obviously chose Nolan in the dispute, but then they signed Liny Ruff at presstime, after insulting Nolan, so after a celebrated feud neither one has a job in Buffalo. Wouldn't it be funny if they both ended up in the same place?

The new GM is Darcy Regier, who was the assistant GM for the NY Islanders for five years before Mike Milbury fired him because of personal differences. That means he could fit right into the Buffalo scheme of things. Hopefully, he didn't learn too much in his days with the Islanders, because they haven't exactly been successful in recent years.

Regier seems to place a premium on communication, a good (or bad) quality to have in Buffalo. He had headaches right from his first day on the job, mostly figuring out whether to re-sign Nolan. He had to listen to the fact that Hasek didn't like Nolan. And so and so didn't like so and so, and blah, blah, blah.

He's already made one mistake that makes him look bad. If he had decided on re-hiring Nolan, as apparently he had, why insult him with a one-year contract? Nolan was furious, and ceremoniously turned it down.

Stay tuned. More wackiness to come.

Hockey Annual Rating: 24 of 26

DRAFT

| Round | Sel. | Player | Pos | Amateur Team |
|-------|------|--------|-----|--------------|
| 1 | 21 | Mika Noranen | G | Finland |
| 2 | 48 | Hendrik Tallinder | D | Sweden |
| 3 | 69 | M. Afinoganov | RW | Russia |
| 3 | 75 | Jeff Martin | C | Windsor (OHL) |
| 4 | 101 | Luc Theoret | D | Lethbridge (WHL) |
| 5 | 128 | Torrey DiRoberto | C | Seattle (WHL) |
| 6 | 156 | Brian Campbell | D | Ottawa (OHL) |
| 7 | 184 | Jeremy Adduno | RW | Sudbury (WHL) |
| 8 | 212 | Kamil Piros | C | Czech Rep. |
| 9 | 238 | Dylan Kemp | D | Lethbridge (WHL) |

Goaltending wasn't exactly the position that the Sabres needed the most help at, especially when a Finnish goaltender has never been successful in the NHL. The Sabres think he could be the first.

Second round pick Hendrik Tallinder was also a questionable choice. Taken 48th overall, his Central Scouting Bureau ranking was 30th among Europeans.

PROGNOSIS: Bad news here. The Cinderalla team may turn into pumpkins this season.

They have some good talent and character, but they also set records last year for overachievement. They could run into big problems if Hasek doesn't continue to play like he did last year.

Management is also a mess, worse than it was last season. At press time no coach had been hired, but their best bet would be to hire someone that Hasek doesn't like. He didn't like Nolan and look how well he played last year.

PREDICTION

Eastern Conference: 9th
Overall: 15th

STAT SECTION

| Team Scoring Stats | | 1996-97 | | | | CAREER | | | | | |
|---|---|---|---|---|---|---|---|---|---|---|---|
| | GP | G | A | PTS | +/- | PIM | SH | Gm | G | A | Pts |
| DEREK PLANTE | 82 | 27 | 26 | 53 | 14 | 24 | 191 | 282 | 74 | 113 | 187 |
| BRIAN HOLZINGER | 81 | 22 | 29 | 51 | 9 | 54 | 142 | 143 | 32 | 42 | 74 |
| DONALD AUDETTE | 73 | 28 | 22 | 50 | 6- | 48 | 182 | 334 | 140 | 105 | 245 |
| MICHAEL PECA | 79 | 20 | 29 | 49 | 26 | 80 | 137 | 184 | 37 | 55 | 92 |
| JASON DAWE | 81 | 22 | 26 | 48 | 14 | 32 | 136 | 222 | 60 | 62 | 122 |
| DIXON WARD | 79 | 13 | 32 | 45 | 17 | 36 | 93 | 246 | 49 | 70 | 119 |
| MATTHEW BARNABY | 68 | 19 | 24 | 43 | 16 | 249 | 121 | 201 | 38 | 45 | 83 |
| MIROSLAV SATAN | 76 | 25 | 13 | 38 | 3- | 26 | 119 | 138 | 43 | 30 | 73 |
| GARRY GALLEY | 71 | 4 | 34 | 38 | 10 | 102 | 84 | 889 | 97 | 399 | 496 |
| MICHAL GROSEK | 82 | 15 | 21 | 36 | 25 | 71 | 117 | 132 | 24 | 27 | 51 |
| ALEXEI ZHITNIK | 80 | 7 | 28 | 35 | 10 | 95 | 170 | 351 | 41 | 144 | 185 |
| RANDY BURRIDGE | 55 | 10 | 21 | 31 | 17 | 20 | 85 | 676 | 195 | 245 | 440 |
| RICHARD SMEHLIK | 62 | 11 | 19 | 30 | 19 | 43 | 100 | 265 | 33 | 80 | 113 |
| DARRYL SHANNON | 82 | 4 | 19 | 23 | 23 | 112 | 94 | 314 | 16 | 58 | 74 |
| MIKE WILSON | 77 | 2 | 9 | 11 | 13 | 51 | 57 | 135 | 6 | 17 | 23 |
| ROB RAY | 82 | 7 | 3 | 10 | 3 | 286 | 45 | 506 | 31 | 30 | 61 |
| JAY MCKEE | 43 | 1 | 9 | 10 | 3 | 35 | 29 | 44 | 1 | 10 | 11 |
| PAT LAFONTAINE | 13 | 2 | 6 | 8 | 8- | 4 | 38 | 798 | 445 | 506 | 951 |
| BOB BOUGHNER | 77 | 1 | 7 | 8 | 12 | 225 | 34 | 108 | 1 | 8 | 9 |
| CURTIS BROWN | 28 | 4 | 3 | 7 | 4 | 18 | 31 | 33 | 5 | 4 | 9 |
| BRAD MAY | 42 | 3 | 4 | 7 | 8- | 106 | 75 | 389 | 63 | 82 | 145 |
| ANATOLI SEMENOV | 25 | 2 | 4 | 6 | 3- | 2 | 21 | 362 | 68 | 126 | 194 |
| WAYNE PRIMEAU | 45 | 2 | 4 | 6 | 2- | 64 | 25 | 48 | 3 | 4 | 7 |
| ED RONAN | 18 | 1 | 4 | 5 | 4 | 11 | 10 | 182 | 13 | 23 | 36 |
| DOMINIK HASEK | 67 | 0 | 3 | 3 | 0 | 30 | 0 | | | | |
| CHARLIE HUDDY | 1 | 0 | 0 | 0 | 1- | 0 | 0 | 1,083 | 99 | 354 | 453 |
| RUMUN NDUR | 2 | 0 | 0 | 0 | 1 | 2 | 0 | 2 | 0 | 0 | 0 |
| ANDREI TREFILOV | 3 | 0 | 0 | 0 | 0 | 0 | 0 | | | | |
| VACLAV VARADA | 5 | 0 | 0 | 0 | 0 | 2 | 2 | 6 | 0 | 0 | 0 |
| STEVE SHIELDS | 13 | 0 | 0 | 0 | 0 | 4 | 0 | | | | |

## TEAM RANKINGS

|  |  | Conference Rank | League Rank |
|---|---|---|---|
| Record | 40-30-12 | 3 | 6 |
| Home | 24-11-6 | 3 | 4 |
| Away | 16-19-6 | 5 | 11 |
| Versus Own Conference | 30-19-7 | 2 | 4 |
| Versus Other Conference | 10-11-5 | 8 | 14 |
| Team Plus\Minus | +45 | 2 | 3 |
| Goals For | 237 | 5 | 12 |
| Goals Against | 208 | 3 | 6 |
| Average Shots For | 25.4 | 13 | 26 |
| Average Shots Against | 33.2 | 11 | 22 |
| Overtime | 5-4-12 | 5 | 11 |
| One Goal Games | 13-10 | 3 | 5 |
| Times outshooting opponent | 12 | 13 | 26 |

| Versus Teams Over .500 | 13-14-7 | 5 | 7 |
|---|---|---|---|
| Versus Teams Under .500 | 27-16-5 | 4 | 8 |
| First Half Record | 21-15-5 | 4 | 6 |
| Second Half Record | 19-15-7 | 3 | 7 |

## PLAYOFFS

Results: defeated Ottawa 4-3
            lost to Philadelphia 4-1

Record: 5-7

Home: 2-5

Away: 3-2

Goals For: 27 (2.3/game)

Goals Against: 34 (2.8/game)

Overtime: 2-1

Power play: 15.1% (9th)

Penalty Killing: 81.7% (11th)

|  | GP | G | A | PTS | +/- | PIM | PP | SH | GW | OT | S |
|---|---|---|---|---|---|---|---|---|---|---|---|
| DEREK PLANTE | 12 | 4 | 6 | 10 | 4 | 4 | 1 | 0 | 2 | 1 | 26 |
| DONALD AUDETTE | 11 | 4 | 5 | 9 | 3- | 6 | 3 | 0 | 0 | 0 | 33 |
| BRIAN HOLZINGER | 12 | 2 | 5 | 7 | 3- | 8 | 0 | 1 | 1 | 0 | 20 |
| RANDY BURRIDGE | 12 | 5 | 1 | 6 | 5- | 2 | 3 | 0 | 0 | 0 | 26 |
| MICHAL GROSEK | 12 | 3 | 3 | 6 | 3 | 8 | 0 | 0 | 0 | 0 | 18 |
| GARRY GALLEY | 12 | 0 | 6 | 6 | 2 | 14 | 0 | 0 | 0 | 0 | 22 |
| DARRYL SHANNON | 12 | 2 | 3 | 5 | 1- | 8 | 1 | 0 | 0 | 0 | 8 |
| DIXON WARD | 12 | 2 | 3 | 5 | 2 | 6 | 0 | 1 | 1 | 0 | 23 |
| MATTHEW BARNABY | 8 | 0 | 4 | 4 | 2 | 36 | 0 | 0 | 0 | 0 | 12 |
| JASON DAWE | 11 | 2 | 1 | 3 | 2- | 6 | 0 | 0 | 0 | 0 | 19 |
| BRAD MAY | 10 | 1 | 1 | 2 | 2- | 32 | 0 | 0 | 0 | 0 | 7 |
| MICHAEL PECA | 10 | 0 | 2 | 2 | 3- | 8 | 0 | 0 | 0 | 0 | 20 |
| RICHARD SMEHLIK | 12 | 0 | 2 | 2 | 0 | 4 | 0 | 0 | 0 | 0 | 17 |
| ED RONAN | 6 | 1 | 0 | 1 | 1- | 6 | 0 | 0 | 1 | 1 | 6 |
| ALEXEI ZHITNIK | 12 | 1 | 0 | 1 | 9- | 16 | 0 | 0 | 0 | 0 | 16 |

| | | | | | | | | | | |
|---|---|---|---|---|---|---|---|---|---|---|
| MIKE WILSON | 10 | 0 | 1 | 1 | 3 | 2 | 0 | 0 | 0 | 0 | 8 |
| BOB BOUGHNER | 11 | 0 | 1 | 1 | 0 | 9 | 0 | 0 | 0 | 0 | 1 |
| ROB RAY | 12 | 0 | 1 | 1 | 3- | 28 | 0 | 0 | 0 | 0 | 4 |
| ANDREI TREFILOV | 1 | 0 | 0 | 0 | 0 | 0 | 0 | 0 | 0 | 0 | 0 |
| DOMINIK HASEK | 3 | 0 | 0 | 0 | 0 | 2 | 0 | 0 | 0 | 0 | 0 |
| JAY MCKEE | 3 | 0 | 0 | 0 | 0 | 0 | 0 | 0 | 0 | 0 | 1 |
| MIROSLAV SATAN | 7 | 0 | 0 | 0 | 1- | 0 | 0 | 0 | 0 | 0 | 5 |
| WAYNE PRIMEAU | 9 | 0 | 0 | 0 | 2- | 6 | 0 | 0 | 0 | 0 | 4 |
| STEVE SHIELDS | 10 | 0 | 0 | 0 | 0 | 9 | 0 | 0 | 0 | 0 | 0 |

| GOALTENDER | GPI | MINS | AVG | W | L | EN | SO | GA | SA | SV % |
|---|---|---|---|---|---|---|---|---|---|---|
| ANDREI TREFILOV | 1 | 5 | .00 | 0 | 0 | 0 | 0 | 0 | 4 | 1.000 |
| DOMINIK HASEK | 3 | 153 | 1.96 | 1 | 1 | 0 | 0 | 5 | 68 | .926 |
| STEVE SHIELDS | 10 | 570 | 2.74 | 4 | 6 | 3 | 1 | 26 | 334 | .922 |
| BUF TOTALS | 12 | 734 | 2.78 | 5 | 7 | 3 | 1 | 34 | 409 | .917 |

## ALL-TIME LEADERS

GOALS
Gil Perreault 512
Rick Martin 382
Dave Andreychuk 348

ASSISTS
Gil Perreault 814
Dave Andreychuk 423
Craig Ramsay 420

POINTS
Gil Perreault 1,326
Dave Andreychuk 771
Rick Martin 695

## BEST INDIVIDUAL SEASONS

GOALS
Alexander Mogilny 92-93 76
Danny Gare 79-80 56
Pat LaFontaine 92-93 53

ASSISTS
Pat LaFontaine 92-93 95
Dale Hawerchuk 92-93 80
Dale Hawerchuk 91-92 75

POINTS
Pat LaFontaine 92-93 148
Alexander Mogilny 92-93 127
Gil Perreault 75-76 113

## TEAM

### Last 3 years

|         | GP | W  | L  | T  | Pts | %    |
|---------|----|----|----|----|-----|------|
| 1996-97 | 82 | 40 | 30 | 12 | 92  | .561 |
| 1995-96 | 82 | 33 | 42 | 7  | 72  | .445 |
| 1994-95 | 48 | 22 | 19 | 7  | 51  | .531 |

### Best 3 regular seasons

|         | GP | W  | L  | T  | Pts | %    |
|---------|----|----|----|----|-----|------|
| 1974-75 | 78 | 49 | 16 | 15 | 113 | .724 |
| 1979-80 | 80 | 47 | 17 | 16 | 110 | .688 |
| 1975-76 | 80 | 46 | 21 | 13 | 105 | .656 |

### Worst 3 regular seasons

|         | GP | W  | L  | T  | Pts |
|---------|----|----|----|----|-----|
| 1971-72 | 78 | 16 | 43 | 19 | 51  |
| 1986-87 | 80 | 28 | 44 | 8  | 64  |
| 1991-92 | 80 | 31 | 37 | 12 | 74  |

### Most Goals (min. 70 game schedule)

| 1974-75 | 354 |
|---------|-----|
| 1975-76 | 339 |
| 1992-93 | 335 |

### Fewest Goals (min. 70 game schedule)

| 1971-72 | 203 |
|---------|-----|
| 1996-97 | 237 |
| 1973-74 | 242 |

### Most Goals Against (min. 70 game schedule)

| 1986-87 | 308 |
|---------|-----|
| 1987-88 | 305 |
| 1991-92 | 299 |

### Fewest Goals Against (min. 70 game schedule)

| 1979-80 | 201 |
|---------|-----|
| 1996-97 | 208 |
| 1977-78 | 215 |

# Carolina Hurricanes

One thing Hartford fans won't have to worry about now that their team has moved to Carolina, is reminiscing about the good old days. That's because they didn't have any.

They only made the playoffs eight times in their 18-year run in Hartford. And they won a grand total of one playoff round. That's one, in case you didn't hear.

The year was 1986. The Whalers had finished fourth in the Adams division with a 40-36-4 record. They wiped out the first place Quebec Nordiques in three games and then took Montreal to a seventh game overtime, when none other than Claude Lemieux scored the winner.

The Whalers had a grand total of three winning years in Hartford, and only one excellent regular season. In 1986-87 they had a record of 43-30-7 and finished on top of the Adams Division. They were eliminated in six games in the first round by Quebec.

That takes care of the team highlights. The individual ones won't take as long. No Whaler ever won an individual award, with Mike Liut the only one even coming close, when he was second in Vezina Trophy balloting in 1986-87.

Blaine Stoughton had the best individual season when he tied for the league goal lead with 56 in 1979-80. He also had the only Hartford 50-goal season, with 52 in 1981-82.

Mike Rogers (remember him?) had the two highest point seasons with 105 in 1979-89 and 105 the following year. Ron Francis had 101 in 1989-90.

The Whalers all-time record was 552-740-177, good for 188 games under .500.

In the playoffs they had a 1-8 series record, and were 18-31 in games.

In the Hartford Courant, they ran a fan poll of the best Whalers all-time team. Since there wasn't much to choose from, it wasn't much of a race. Mike Liut got the nod in net, Ulf Samuelsson and Mark Howe on defence, and Ron Francis, Kevin Dineen and Geoff Sanderson at forward.

Not too much argument, except that they should have voted Blaine Stoughton in at a forward spot, and probably left Sanderson off. Sanderson needed a couple more good seasons before he qualified. Sean Burke may still end up being the best franchise goalie.

As for the Whalers' biggest booboo, besides losing their team. How about the trading of Ron Francis, who was traded by GM at the time Ed Johnston, to Pittsburgh along with Ulf Samuelsson and Grant Jennings, for John Cullen, Jeff Parker. *John Cullen?*

## STUFF

* through games of December 12, the Whalers were 14-8-6, first in the Northeast Division, second in the Eastern Conference and fourth overall.

* when Curtis Leschyshyn played his first game with Hartford after being acquired in a trade from Washington, his first shot on net was an overtime game winner. His second shot on net, in his next game, was also a goal.
* the Hurricanes have the longest current non-playoff streak - five years.
* Sean Burke had a streak of 146:58 without allowing a goal, falling just short of the team record of 151:34, set by Mike Liut in 1986-87.
* with 100 career wins, Burke needs just 15 to tie Luit for the all-time franchise lead.
* the fourth place ranking on the power play last season was the best in franchise history.
* 51 power play goals allowed were the fewest in a full season for the Hurricanes.

## STAT ANALYSIS

There's no place like home. Especially when it's new home.

Every team that has changed cities performed better in their first season in their new home, with the exception of the Colorado to New Jersey move, where the records were almost identical.

There are a lot of reasons for the improvements:
* there's a lot of fuss because they're the new game in town and they want to impress the fans.
* better attendance and more enthusiasm from the fans to get the players pumped up during the games.
* more money in the new place, which again, is why they left their last place.
* better atmosphere, with the players and management happier.
* most teams that move usually were losers in their old city (as were the Whalers) so it gives them a chance at a fresh start.

## TEAM PREVIEW

GOAL: If Sean Burke ever played for a winning team, he'd probably be considered one of the best goalies in the game. Not that he isn't one of the best now, but it's tough to get that recognition when you're never in the playoffs. He does get a lot of credit, however, for his international play, including backstopping Canada to the world championship in the spring. Mind you, he was always able to play for his country because the Whalers kept missing the playoffs.

## TEAMS THAT HAVE CHANGED CITIES

| Old Home | Final Season Record | New Home | Year | First Season Record |
|---|---|---|---|---|
| Winnipeg | 36-40-6 | Phoenix | 1996-97 | 38-37-4 |
| Quebec | 30-13-5 | Colorado | 1995-96 | 47-25-10 * |
| Minnesota | 36-38-10 | Dallas | 1993-94 | 42-29-13 |
| Colorado | 18-49-13 | New Jersey | 1982-83 | 17-49-14 |
| Atlanta | 35-32-13 | Calgary | 1980-81 | 39-27-14 |
| Kansas City | 12-56-12 | Colorado | 1976-77 | 20-46-14 |

* won Stanley Cup

No complaints about Burke, and no complaints about Jean-Sebastien Giguere, who is considered one of the best prospects in the league. Jason Muzzatti handled backup chores last season, but could be out of the picture if Gigeure is ready.

Hockey Annual Rating: 10 of 26

DEFENCE: It's always been a priority under the current team's regime to build a good strong stable defence that can play together for a couple years. It took them a while to do, but now they have one, or are close to having one.

Steve Chiasson is one of the better all-round defencemen in the league. Not flashy by any means, but he handles things well in his own zone, and when called upon can play the power play point and contribute offensively.

Jeff Brown is the quarterback for the power play, but only played one game last season due to back surgery. He's strictly offensive, so if he's healthy, he can also improve the point totals of the forwards.

Glen Wesley is also a power play point-man, so the depth allowed the Whalers to fare okay without Brown last season, and the drop in quality isn't high when the second unit goes out.

Fill out the top six with Curtis Leschyshyn, Adam Burt and Kevin Haller, and you have an pretty decent defence corps.

Marek Malik is still young and improving, and other young fill-ins last season included Jason McBain and Nolan Pratt. Veteran Alexander Godynuk also got a lot of playing time, but was traded to St. Louis for Stephen Leach.

The one component the Hurricanes don't have on defence is one of those nutty guys, such as Bryan Marchment or Dave Manson. But, that's a luxury, not a necessity.

Hockey Annual Rating: 9 of 26

FORWARD: The Hurricanes had five 20-goal scorers last year. In today's NHL, with the reduced scoring, that's what passes for good balance because that was tied for second most in the league. In what passes for optimism, they probably should have had a couple more.

Geoff Sanderson led the way with 36 goals, including 12 on the power play. His 67 points were tops on the team, as well, although there's nothing exciting about that.

Robert Kron is counted on for around 20 goals, but had only 10 last season, and Paul Ranheim chipped in with 10 as well. The Grim Reaper, Stu Grimson, is the designated enforcer.

At centre, Andrew Cassels is the playmaker, but threw in 22 goals as a bonus. Keith Primeau is the kind of player every team in the league wants — a big, tough centre, who can score goals. There aren't many of them around.

Jeff O'Neill showed signs of breaking out,

| GOALTENDER | GPI | MINS | AVG | W | L | T | EN | SO | GA | SA | SV % |
| --- | --- | --- | --- | --- | --- | --- | --- | --- | --- | --- | --- |
| SEAN BURKE | 51 | 2985 | 2.69 | 22 | 22 | 6 | 6 | 4 | 134 | 1560 | .914 |
| JASON MUZZATTI | 31 | 1591 | 3.43 | 9 | 13 | 5 | 1 | 0 | 91 | 815 | .888 |
| J SEBASTIEN GIGUE | 8 | 394 | 3.65 | 1 | 4 | 0 | 0 | 0 | 24 | 201 | .881 |
| HFD TOTALS | 82 | 4996 | 3.07 | 32 | 39 | 11 | 7 | 4 | 256 | 2583 | .901 |

but didn't score consistently. This will be his third season in the NHL, so this one or next year is the traditional break out period for young players. If he does it this year, the Whalers line up with one of the better one-two-three punches at centre in the league. Kent Manderville handles fourth centre duties for the time being. He has a history of looking great for a while and then dropping his intensity like a sack of potatoes. He may realize, however, that any drop in intensity now will mean the end of his NHL career.

On the right side, Kevin Dineen had a phenomenal season considering he had been written off as a has-been. The 33-year-old proved to be the heart-and-soul of the team, contributing with great character and even throwing in 19 goals, 48 points and 141 penalty minutes. Steven Rice had his best scoring season with 21 goals, and is probably the prototypical NHL third-line right winger — a big guy who uses his body, knows where both ends of the rink are, can play some on the power play, and can score 20 goals. Unfortunately, he wasn't always playing on the third line, or even the second line, and he's certainly not ideal for the top line. Chris Murray, obtained from Montreal via Phoenix, is a tough right winger, who is expected to contribute more than bloody noses. Also on the right side is Sami Kapanen and Nelson Emerson. Emerson had some great point streaks last season, then some lengthy droughts. That wasn't much different, however, than almost all the Hurricanes — the drought part, that is. Stephen Leach is a right winger obtained in the off-season from St. Louis, and if he's ever healthy enough can make a good offensive contribution.

The team is overloaded on the right side, but in today's NHL they move all around anyway so it isn't a problem. What is a problem is that they have too many small players on the wings. They intend to beef up there as soon as possible.

The Hurricanes don't have dominant players at any forward position, but they have a lot of good players. Is balance better than having one or two guys do all the scoring, such as in Anaheim with Paul Kariya and Teemu Selanne? Tough question. It wasn't last year, but if a couple players raise their games some, and everyone else remains stable, it just could be the difference.

There isn't much in the way of prospects in the Hurricanes' system, so unless deals are made, what you see is what you get. Byron Ritchie is a tough little centre who scored 50-76-126 for Lethbridge in the WHL, good for second in league scoring. That's about it.

Hockey Annual Rating: 21 of 26

SPECIAL TEAMS: Pretty impressive of the Hurricanes to finish fourth overall in power play percentage last season. They have a good setup man in Cassels, an excellent sniper in Sanderson, a good potential sniper in Primeau, and three defencemen who can man the power play points in Brown, Chiasson and Wesley.

Except for maybe Sanderson and Brown, there are no power play superstars, so when they put out the second unit it doesn't drop considerably. A lot of other teams don't have that luxury.

POWER PLAY

|  | G | ATT | PCT | |
| --- | --- | --- | --- | --- |
| Overall | 58 | 321 | 18.1% | (T-4th NHL) |
| Home | 28 | 162 | 17.3% | (8th NHL) |
| Road | 30 | 159 | 18.9% | (5th NHL) |

11 SHORT HANDED GOALS ALLOWED (T-15th NHL)

PENALTY KILLING

|          | G  | TSH | PCT   |            |
|----------|----|-----|-------|------------|
| Overall  | 51 | 332 | 84.6% | (10th NHL) |
| Home     | 24 | 153 | 84.3% | (7th NHL)  |
| Road     | 27 | 179 | 84.9% | (12th NHL) |

12 SHORT HANDED GOALS SCORED (T-7th NHL)

WHALERS SPECIAL TEAMS SCORING

| Power play  | G  | A  | PTS |
|-------------|----|----|-----|
| SANDERSON   | 12 | 11 | 23  |
| CASSELS     | 8  | 14 | 22  |
| CHIASSON    | 4  | 13 | 17  |
| EMERSON     | 2  | 15 | 17  |
| DINEEN      | 8  | 7  | 15  |
| WESLEY      | 3  | 11 | 14  |
| KING        | 6  | 6  | 12  |
| PRIMEAU     | 6  | 4  | 10  |
| RICE        | 5  | 3  | 8   |
| O'NEILL     | 2  | 4  | 6   |
| KRON        | 2  | 4  | 6   |
| LESCHYSHYN  | 1  | 5  | 6   |
| KAPANEN     | 3  | 1  | 4   |
| BURT        | 0  | 3  | 3   |
| HALLER      | 0  | 2  | 2   |
| RANHEIM     | 0  | 1  | 1   |
| BROWN       | 0  | 1  | 1   |

| Short handed | G | A | PTS |
|--------------|---|---|-----|
| PRIMEAU      | 3 | 2 | 5   |
| RANHEIM      | 3 | 1 | 4   |
| CHIASSON     | 2 | 0 | 2   |
| CASSELS      | 0 | 2 | 2   |
| BURT         | 0 | 2 | 2   |
| WESLEY       | 1 | 0 | 1   |
| SANDERSON    | 1 | 0 | 1   |
| O'NEILL      | 1 | 0 | 1   |
| LESCHYSHYN   | 1 | 0 | 1   |
| EMERSON      | 1 | 0 | 1   |
| MANDERVILLE  | 0 | 1 | 1   |
| DINEEN       | 0 | 1 | 1   |

COACHING AND MANAGEMENT: Now that he has some NHL experience Jim Rutherford is developing into an competent General Manager.

He seems to have the smarts to learn from his mistakes. For example, trading three number one choices for Wesley was a mistake, so now he gets number one choices in deals. He got one from Detroit last year in the Shanahan deal and one from Philadelphia in the Coffey deal.

Rutherford has had to deal with some disgruntled players, such as the two in the previous paragraph, so it could have been perceived he was at a disadvantage with the other teams knowing he had to get rid of those guys. He was patient (too patient according to some) however, and waited for what he perceived to be the best deals.

What are you going to do when you have someone who doesn't want to play on your team? Shanahan in particular would have made the team more successful, but if he decides he wants to go elsewhere, what good is it keeping him around. You get rid of him for the sake of the team.

Rutherford's talent appraisal has improved over the years too, which just naturally comes from experience. Instead of getting mediocre players that he hopes will play better than they've shown previously, he's gone out and got good players that he hopes will play the same.

Paul Maurice was the youngest coach in any of the four major professional sports last year in North America. He was 29-years-old until January 30.

Like all coaches, he was perceived to be doing a great job when the team was winning, and not so great when they were losing. He just couldn't get the team out of lengthy slumps no matter what he tried, but at least he tried a lot of things. Maybe no coach could have done anything, who knows.

If the Hurricanes don't show a lot of improvement this year, or at least make the playoffs, Maurice will be the youngest coach in North American sports to be fired.

Hockey Annual Rating: 20 of 26

## DRAFT

| Round | Sel. | Player | Pos | Amateur Team |
|---|---|---|---|---|
| 1 | 22 | Nikos Tselios | D | Belleville (OHL) |
| 2 | 28 | Brad DeFauw | LW | North Dakota |
| 3 | 80 | Francis Lessard | D | Val d'Or (QMJHL) |
| 4 | 88 | Shane Willis | RW | Lethbridge (WHL) |
| 6 | 142 | Kyle Dafoe | D | Owen Sound (OHL) |
| 7 | 169 | Andrew Merrick | C | Michigan |
| 8 | 195 | Niklas Nordgren | LW | Sweden |
| 8 | 199 | Randy Fitzgerald | LW | Detroit (OHL) |
| 9 | 225 | Ken McDonnell | RW | Guelph (OHL) |

Nikos Tselios is a cousin of Chris Chelios. The Chris Chelios family decided to change the spelling, but both are pronounced the same. The only similarity between the two right now is their original name. Tselios is a few years away from making it to the NHL. He's considered to have good raw talent that needs to be developed.

PROGNOSIS: The Whalers were one of the big surprises in the early going of last year and then did a complete reversal in the latter part of the season.

The team has solidified itself from the blue-line back to the net, as long as key players can stay healthy. As for the forwards, there are still question marks. Could improve, could stay the same. Some tinkering has to be done.

A lot of the Hurricanes are in prime-time, meaning their best years are right now. That's usually a good sign.

Last year, I correctly picked the Dallas Stars as one of the surprise success stories of the year. This year, I'm saying the Carolina Hurricanes could be one of the surpises.

## PREDICTION

Eastern Conference: 8th
Overall: 14th

STAT SECTION

| Team Scoring Stats | CAREER | | | | | | | | | | |
|---|---|---|---|---|---|---|---|---|---|---|---|
| | GP | G | A | PTS | +/- | PIM | SH | Gm | G | A | Pts |
| GEOFF SANDERSON | 82 | 36 | 31 | 67 | 9- | 29 | 297 | 439 | 189 | 163 | 352 |
| ANDREW CASSELS | 81 | 22 | 44 | 66 | 16- | 46 | 142 | 498 | 105 | 272 | 377 |
| DEREK KING | 82 | 26 | 33 | 59 | 6- | 22 | 181 | 650 | 214 | 291 | 505 |
| KEITH PRIMEAU | 75 | 26 | 25 | 51 | 3- | 161 | 169 | 438 | 123 | 158 | 281 |
| KEVIN DINEEN | 78 | 19 | 29 | 48 | 6- | 141 | 185 | 871 | 323 | 356 | 679 |

| | | | | | | | | | | |
|---|---|---|---|---|---|---|---|---|---|---|
| NELSON EMERSON | 66 | 9 | 29 | 38 | 21- | 34 | 194 | 443 | 130 | 212 | 342 |
| STEVEN RICE | 78 | 21 | 14 | 35 | 11- | 59 | 159 | 282 | 62 | 57 | 139 |
| GLEN WESLEY | 68 | 6 | 26 | 32 | 0 | 40 | 126 | 721 | 93 | 286 | 379 |
| JEFF O'NEILL | 72 | 14 | 16 | 30 | 24- | 40 | 101 | 137 | 22 | 35 | 57 |
| STEVE CHIASSON | 65 | 8 | 22 | 30 | 21- | 39 | 168 | 657 | 85 | 270 | 355 |
| SAMI KAPANEN | 45 | 13 | 12 | 25 | 6 | 2 | 82 | 80 | 18 | 16 | 34 |
| ROBERT KRON | 68 | 10 | 12 | 22 | 18- | 10 | 182 | 416 | 94 | 109 | 203 |
| CURTIS LESCHYSHYN | 77 | 4 | 18 | 22 | 18- | 38 | 102 | 588 | 38 | 120 | 158 |
| PAUL RANHEIM | 67 | 10 | 11 | 21 | 13- | 18 | 96 | 556 | 120 | 148 | 268 |
| KEVIN HALLER | 62 | 2 | 11 | 13 | 12- | 85 | 77 | 397 | 33 | 76 | 109 |
| ADAM BURT | 71 | 2 | 11 | 13 | 13- | 79 | 85 | 498 | 35 | 92 | 127 |
| KENT MANDERVILLE | 44 | 6 | 5 | 11 | 3 | 18 | 51 | 217 | 17 | 25 | 42 |
| CHRIS MURRAY | 64 | 5 | 3 | 8 | 7- | 124 | 41 | 115 | 8 | 7 | 15 |
| ALEXANDER GODYNYUK | 55 | 1 | 6 | 7 | 10- | 41 | 34 | 223 | 10 | 39 | 49 |
| MAREK MALIK | 47 | 1 | 5 | 6 | 5 | 50 | 33 | 55 | 1 | 6 | 7 |
| STU GRIMSON | 76 | 2 | 2 | 4 | 8- | 218 | 17 | 422 | 6 | 13 | 19 |
| KEVIN BROWN | 11 | 0 | 4 | 4 | 6- | 6 | 12 | 41 | 3 | 7 | 10 |
| NOLAN PRATT | 9 | 0 | 2 | 2 | 0 | 6 | 4 | 9 | 0 | 2 | 2 |
| JEFF DANIELS | 10 | 0 | 2 | 2 | 2 | 0 | 6 | 154 | 8 | 13 | 21 |
| SEAN BURKE | 51 | 0 | 2 | 2 | 0 | 14 | 0 | | | | |
| BRIAN GLYNN | 1 | 1 | 0 | 1 | 2 | 2 | 2 | 431 | 25 | 79 | 104 |
| STEVE MARTINS | 2 | 0 | 1 | 1 | 0 | 0 | 2 | 25 | 1 | 4 | 5 |
| JASON MUZZATTI | 31 | 0 | 1 | 1 | 0 | 18 | 0 | | | | |
| JEFF BROWN | 1 | 0 | 0 | 0 | 0 | 0 | 0 | 687 | 150 | 406 | 556 |
| JASON MCBAIN | 6 | 0 | 0 | 0 | 4- | 0 | 1 | 9 | 0 | 0 | 0 |
| J SEBASTIEN GIGUERE | 8 | 0 | 0 | 0 | 0 | 0 | 0 | | | | |

## TEAM RANKINGS 1995-96

| | | Conference Rank | League Rank |
|---|---|---|---|
| Record | 32-39-11 | 10 | 19 |
| Home | 23-15-3 | 6 | 9 |
| Away | 9-24-8 | 13 | 25 |
| Versus Own Conference | 25-23-8 | 5 | 9 |
| Versus Other | | | |

| | | | |
|---|---|---|---|
| Conference | 7-16-3 | 13 | 25 |
| Team Plus\Minus | -37 | 12 | 23 |
| Goals For | 226 | 9 | 18 |
| Goals Against | 256 | 10 | 19 |
| Average Shots For | 29.6 | 6 | 13 |
| Average Shots Against | 31.5 | 9 | 19 |
| Overtime | 3-4-11 | 9 | 18 |
| One Goal Games | 10-12 | 9 | 19 |

| Times outshooting | | | |
|---|---|---|---|
| opponent | 35 | 9 | 17 |
| Versus Teams | | | |
| Over .500 | 14-20-4 | 7 | 15 |
| Versus Teams | | | |
| Under .500 | 18-19-7 | 9 | 19 |
| First Half Record | 17-17-7 | 7 | 17 |
| Second Half | | | |
| Record | 14-22-4 | 12 | 23 |

## PLAYOFFS

- did not make the playoffs

## ALL-TIME LEADERS

### GOALS
| | |
|---|---|
| Ron Francis | 264 |
| Kevin Dineen | 235 |
| Blaine Stoughton | 219 |

### ASSISTS
| | |
|---|---|
| Ron Francis | 557 |
| Kevin Dineen | 268 |
| Andrew Cassels | 253 |

### POINTS
| | |
|---|---|
| Ron Francis | 821 |
| Kevin Dineen | 503 |
| Pat Verbeek | 403 |

## BEST INDIVIDUAL SEASONS

### GOALS
| | | |
|---|---|---|
| Blaine Stoughton | 1979-80 | 56 |
| Blaine Stoughton | 1981-82 | 52 |
| Geoff Sanderson | 1992-93 | 46 |

### ASSISTS
| | | |
|---|---|---|
| Ron Francis | 1989-90 | 69 |
| Mike Rogers | 1980-81 | 65 |
| Andrew Cassels | 1992-93 | 65 |

### POINTS
| | | |
|---|---|---|
| Mike Rogers | 1979-80 | 105 |
| Mike Rogers | 1980-81 | 105 |
| Ron Francis | 1989-90 | 101 |

## TEAM

### Last 3 years
| | GP | W | L | T | Pts | % |
|---|---|---|---|---|---|---|
| 1996-97 | 82 | 32 | 39 | 11 | 75 | .457 |
| 1995-96 | 82 | 34 | 39 | 9 | 77 | .470 |
| 1994-95 | 48 | 19 | 24 | 5 | 43 | .448 |

### Best 3 regular seasons
| | | | | | | |
|---|---|---|---|---|---|---|
| 1986-87 | 80 | 43 | 30 | 7 | 93 | .600 |
| 1989-90 | 80 | 38 | 33 | 9 | 85 | .531 |
| 1985-86 | 80 | 40 | 36 | 4 | 84 | .525 |

### Worst 3 regular seasons
| | | | | | | |
|---|---|---|---|---|---|---|
| 1982-83 | 80 | 19 | 54 | 7 | 45 | .281 |
| 1992-93 | 84 | 26 | 52 | 6 | 58 | .345 |
| 1993-94 | 84 | 27 | 48 | 9 | 63 | .375 |

### Most Goals (min. 70 game schedule)
| | |
|---|---|
| 1985-86 | 332 |
| 1979-89 | 303 |
| 1988-89 | 299 |

### Fewest Goals (min. 70 game schedule)
| | |
|---|---|
| 1996-97 | 226 |
| 1993-94 | 227 |
| 1995-96 | 237 |

### Most Goals Against (min. 70 game schedule)
| | |
|---|---|
| 1982-83 | 403 |
| 1980-81 | 372 |
| 1992-93 | 369 |

### Fewest Goals Against (min. 70 game schedule)
| | |
|---|---|
| 1996-97 | 256 |
| 1995-96 | 259 |
| 1987-88 | 267 |

# Florida Panthers

If you keep doing the same trick over and over again people are going to catch on to it eventually. Even if it's a good one.

The Florida Panthers weren't able to duplicate their magic of the previous season when they made it to the Stanley Cup finals, but that's not to say their season was a bad one.

They still managed a fourth place finish in the Eastern Conference, they still displayed the work ethic that got them to the finals a year earlier, and they still played an effective, disciplined defensive style.

The thing is, so many teams are playing the same way it's not a mystery to anyone anymore.

In the playoffs, they lost in five games to the Rangers in the opening round, but two of the games were overtime losses, both on goals by Esa Tikkanen, and the other was a one-goal defeat.

During the regular season, the Panthers got off to an amazing start, proving to everyone that they were not going to suffer the expected letdown after making it to the finals the previous season. They were undefeated in their first 12 games with an 8-0-4 record. In those 12 games, they allowed just 20 goals.

After that great opening, the Panthers became ordinary. For the rest of the season they had a 27-28-15 record. Injuries were part of the reason. Many key players, such as Ray Sheppard, Ed Jovanovski, Johan Garpenlov and Brian Skrudland were out for extended periods.

It was also suggested that team chemistry may have suffered a bad reaction when Stu Barnes was traded to Pittsburgh, along with Jason Wooley for big Chris Wells.

A ridiculous schedule didn't help either. During one stretch they played 13 of 16 games on the road, and in another they played 13 of 16 at home.

The main problem, however, was a lack of goal scoring. The Panthers apparently tried to get Adam Oates, Doug Gilmour, Dave Gagner, Robert Reichel, Paul Coffey and Ray Ferraro, all of whom were dealt elsewhere, except Ferraro. They needed more offence and they couldn't get it. It wasn't that the Panthers didn't have some good trading material, it was more like they didn't want to give it up. They did manage to get Kirk Muller, a two-way centre, for one of their top prospects, Jason Podollan. And during the summer, they got free agent Dave Gagner for nothing.

What's next for the Panthers? Naturally, they'll try to continue the same style that's made them successful: tight checking, discipline, hard work, great goaltending, four good lines, and outstanding team play. The thing is, other teams are also using the same recipe and mixing the same ingredients. Some of those other teams also have offence, which means the Panthers better get some more themselves or risk mediocrity.

Florida seems determined to have the proper balance between veterans and youngsters. Sometimes that's walking a pretty high tightrope. With some of the character veterans on their way out, and nothing substantial coming up in the way of prospects, the Panthers could go south this season.

## STUFF

* the Panthers farm team was in Carolina last year, site of the new Carolina Hurricanes. This year, they will share the New Haven team in the AHL with the Hurricanes.
* the Panthers had just 14 shots in a late season game versus Phoenix, tying a team futility record.

## STAT ANALYSIS

The Panthers got off to one of the best starts last year in NHL history. Their 8-0-4 mark out of the gate was only three games shy of the record for the longest undefeated streak from the start of a season.

A 12-game undefeated streak isn't all that unusual. There were seven streaks last year of at least 12 games, and 10 of at least 11 games. Nobody seems to remember them, though, unless they happen at the beginning of the season.

Most every team has a period in which everything goes well for them. And most every team has a spell in which the opposite happens. It's just the nature of the game.

Longest Undefeated Streaks From Start of Season:

| Team | Year | Games |
|------|------|-------|
| Edmonton | 1984-85 | 15 |
| Montreal | 1943-44 | 14 |
| Montreal | 1972-73 | 13 |
| Pittsburgh | 1994-95 | 13 |
| FLORIDA | 1996-97 | 12 |

## TEAM PREVIEW

GOAL: You could say that the Panther style of play means their goaltending is going to be good no matter who they have in net, but that would require a lengthy debate. The Panthers could care less anyway because Vanbiesbrouck has been much more than they ever could have expected when they picked him up in the expansion draft.

It's also nice to know that they don't lose anything when backup Mark Fitzpatrick plays. His goals against average and save percentage were almost identical to Vanbiesbrouck's.

Fitzpatrick was another expansion draft pickup. They drafted another goalie, too that hasn't been too bad, Darren Puppa, but lost him in the secondary phase of that draft.

Kevin Weekes, who was unspectacular with a poor team in Carolina of the AHL last season, is the goalie in waiting.

Hockey Annual Rating: 5 of 26

DEFENCE: Ed Jovanovski is the prize, a future all-star who had a bit of a rough time last season. Big deal. It was his second year in the

| GOALTENDER | GPI | MINS | AVG | W | L | T | EN | SO | GA | SA | SV % |
|------------|-----|------|-----|---|---|---|----|----|-----|------|------|
| J. VANBIESBROUCK | 57 | 3347 | 2.29 | 27 | 19 | 10 | 3 | 2 | 128 | 1582 | .919 |
| MARK FITZPATRICK | 30 | 1680 | 2.36 | 8 | 9 | 9 | 4 | 0 | 66 | 771 | .914 |
| FLA TOTALS | 82 | 5041 | 2.39 | 35 | 28 | 19 | 7 | 2 | 201 | 2360 | .915 |

league, traditionally reserved for such fall-offs. He's far too talented not to be a major impact player for many years to come.

Robert Svelha has been a great find for the Panthers. He provides offence, works the power play, kills penalties and doesn't cower away from physical play.

Rhett Warrener is a defenceman many teams wanted when the Panthers went looking for more offence last year. Obviously, they weren't offered enough to justify trading him, which means they like him a lot.

Paul Laus is the tough guy defenceman and Gord Murphy is another offensive threat. Terry Carkner re-signed after becoming a free agent, and Per Gustafsson was traded to Toronto during the summer when it became obvious he was scared of his own shadow and couldn't contribute enough defensively.

Signed as a free agent during the summer was Dallas Eakins, a interesting statistical case. His career teams and games:

| 1992-93 | Winnipeg | 14 games |
|---------|----------|----------|
| 1993-94 | Florida | 1 game |
| 1994-95 | Florida | 17 games |
| 1995-96 | St. Louis | 16 games |
| | Winnipeg | 2 games |
| 1996-97 | Phoenix | 4 games |
| | NY Rangers | 3 games |

That's not all about Eakins. He has never scored a goal. Currently, he is third on the all-time list for most career games without a goal. In other words, that's from the start of a career to the end of it. His only chance to get off the list is to score. Matt Martin, who played for Toronto last year, is the leader with 76 goal-less games, followed by Chris LiPuma at 72. Lou Marcon, who was with Detroit in the late fifties and early sixties, is third at 60 games, and then there's Eakins at 57 games. But remember (if anybody cares) it's not an official record until a player retires.

The Panthers have built a pretty good top six on defence, which stacks up well against any in the league. They don't have much depth though, so a couple major injuries and it could be trouble. But, then again, that's always been the situation there and they've managed just fine.

Hockey Annual Rating: 7 of 26

FORWARD: You look at the Florida forwards and you wonder how a team like that can even make it to the .500 level. But, that's the Panthers for you.

Their strategy is to put four good lines on the ice. Without any major stars, what choice do they have. Players with puny little scoring totals have to do something to justify their spot on the team, and they do by playing good defence.

Ray Sheppard, Scott Mellanby, free agent pickup Dave Gagner, and Kirk Muller can all score 20-30 goals, but none of those guys are kids and they don't have a major playmaker such as an Adam Oates.

Rob Niedermayer and Radek Dvorak are two rising stars, who can also score, but on the Panthers all the scoring comes in medium to small doses. They don't have a game-breaking dependable scorer who won't go into 20 game slumps.

Johan Garpenlov missed a lot of time last year, so he should score more than 11 goals and 36 points. Scoring from Tom Fitzgerald and Dave Lowry is incidental, the same with Bill Lindsay and Jody Hull. Mike Hough became an unrestricted free agent during the summer, and signed with the Islanders. Brian Skrudland signed with the Rangers.

Martin Straka is gone, with the team buying out his contract. For somebody who's role is to provide goals and points, totals of 7-22-

29 are ridiculous. Steve Washburn had nine points in 18 games before getting injured, so he takes over from Straka.

David Nemirovsky appears to have earned a place on the right side, and if Florida is able to make Chris Wells into an everyday player who can score, they deserve some kind of reward.

Unless changes are made, the Panthers will have Niedermayer, Muller, Gagner, Washburn and Wells at centre. Fitzgerald can also play in the middle.

On the right side are Sheppard, Mellanby, Fitzgerald and Nemirovsky, with Hull as injury replacement.

The left side has Dvorak, Garpenlov, Lindsay and Lowry.

Most of the prospects are a couple years away and none did much of anything last year, unless you count Peter Worrell, who racked up 437 penalty minutes for the Memorial Cup winning Hull team.

The biggest loss will be Skrudland. Their captain was the heart and soul of the team and one of the main reasons for their early franchise success.

Hockey Annual Rating: 16 of 26

SPECIAL TEAMS: No one expected the Panthers to lead the league on the power play, so their ranking was no big surprise. No one expected them to be near the bottom of the league either. They have a power play sniper or two in Sheppard, Mellanby and Niedermayer, and Svehla and Jovanovski can handle the points just fine. A playmaking center is the key. Gagner isn't one of the elite in that area, but he's decent enough.

The oddity about their ranking was that they were last on the road and seventh at home. Only 16 goals in 158 opportunities on the road, which is amazingly poor. They had more than twice as many goals at home. That could be a product of a tendency to play even more defensively on the road. A team can get into such a defensive groove that when they're required to turn on the offence, it just isn't that easy.

Even worse was the amount of shorthanded goals they surrendered with the man advantage. They were second last in the league, with 16 against them. That sort of contradicts the previous statement of being in a defensive mode, which would leave only one possible explanation: their power play sucks.

An secod oddity here is that they scored 50 power play goals and ranked 21st, and they allowed 50 power play goals and ranked seventh in penalty killing.

POWER PLAY

|  | G | ATT | PCT |
|---|---|---|---|
| Overall | 50 | 352 | 14.2% (21st NHL) |
| Home | 34 | 194 | 17.5% (7th NHL) |
| Road | 16 | 158 | 10.1% (26th NHL) |

16 SHORT HANDED GOALS ALLOWED (25th NHL)

PENALTY KILLING

|  | G | TSH | PCT |
|---|---|---|---|
| Overall | 50 | 346 | 85.5% (7th NHL) |
| Home | 25 | 166 | 84.9% (6th NHL) |
| Road | 25 | 180 | 86.1% (T-7th NHL) |

5 SHORT HANDED GOALS SCORED (T-23rd NHL)

PANTHERS SPECIAL TEAMS SCORING

| Power play | G | A | PTS |
|---|---|---|---|
| SHEPPARD | 13 | 9 | 22 |
| SVEHLA | 5 | 14 | 19 |
| MULLER | 10 | 5 | 15 |
| MELLANBY | 9 | 6 | 15 |
| GUSTAFSSON | 2 | 10 | 12 |
| NIEDERMAYER | 3 | 7 | 10 |
| JOVANOVSKI | 3 | 5 | 8 |
| GARPENLOV | 1 | 7 | 8 |
| STRAKA | 2 | 5 | 7 |

| | | | |
|---|---|---|---|
| DVORAK | 2 | 5 | 7 |
| MURPHY | 2 | 4 | 6 |
| LOWRY | 2 | 3 | 5 |
| WARRENER | 1 | 2 | 3 |
| NEMIROVSKY | 1 | 1 | 2 |
| HULL | 0 | 2 | 2 |
| WASHBURN | 1 | 0 | 1 |
| LAUS | 0 | 1 | 1 |
| CARKNER | 0 | 1 | 1 |

| Short handed | G | A | PTS |
|---|---|---|---|
| LINDSAY | 1 | 3 | 4 |
| FITZGERALD | 2 | 1 | 3 |
| MURPHY | 0 | 2 | 2 |
| MULLER | 1 | 0 | 1 |
| MELLANBY | 1 | 0 | 1 |
| HULL | 1 | 0 | 1 |
| NIEDERMAYER | 0 | 1 | 1 |
| LAUS | 0 | 1 | 1 |

COACHING AND MANAGEMENT: Doug MacLean has earned a lot of respect around the NHL. The Panthers had a few letdowns last season, just like every single team in the league, but for the most part he has been able to get his players to compete every night. No small task. Often, a coach's motivation wears off after a year or two, and it's time for a change. No problem in Florida yet.

GM Brian Murray wasn't able to get the playmaking centre the team needed during the stretch drive, but he got one in the summer, in Dave Gagner. Gagner is no Adam Oates, but should be okay.

Murray showed some restraint last year when it was obvious the team needed some offence. There were plenty of rumors, but no deals. Whether or not that's a good thing, he wasn't about to mortgage the future for the present.

A much better plan is to be competitive every year, not just for a couple. To that end, he's trying to fit in the youngsters with the veterans. And he's trying to create more balance between offence and defence.

The Panthers have never had a good team on paper, but they don't play the game on paper.

Hockey Annual Rating: 6 of 26

DRAFT

| Round | Sel. | Player | Pos | Amateur Team |
|---|---|---|---|---|
| 1 | 20 | Mike Brown | C | Red Deer (WHL) |
| 2 | 47 | Kristen Huselius | LW | Sweden |
| 3 | 56 | Vratislav Cech | D | Kitchener (OHL) |
| 3 | 74 | Nick Smith | C | Barrie (OHL) |
| 4 | 95 | Ivan Novoseltsev | RW | Russia |
| 5 | 127 | Pat Parthenais | D | Detroit (OHL) |
| 6 | 155 | Keith Delaney | C | Barrie (OHL) |
| 7 | 183 | Tyler Palmer | D | Lake Superior State |
| 8 | 211 | Doug Schueller | D | Twin Cities (USHL) |
| 9 | 237 | Benoit Cote | C | Shawinigan (QMJHL) |

The Panthers appeared pleased with their drafting. They got Mike Brown, who was considered by some to be the best fighter in junior hockey last year. He had 243 penalty minutes to go along with 19 goals in 70 games for Red Deer in the WHL. Brown is 6-5, 183 pounds.

The Panthers had their second round, Kristen Huselius, ranked as a first rounder, which is pretty much what every team says with their second round pick.

PROGNOSIS: The Panthers look to be about a

.500 hockey team. That's good enough to squeeze into the playoffs, but it's not even a certainty.

They will be without their leader and top defensive player, Brian Skrudland, and even though they acquired free agent Dave Gagner, they're still not strong enough offensively.

Defensively, they're solid in goal, on defence and at forward. That should keep their heads above water but don't be surprised if they slide some and finish out of the playoffs. They could even be this year's disaster team.

## PREDICTION

Eastern Conference: 6th
Overall: 10th

## STAT SECTION

| Team Scoring Stats | | 1996-97 | | | | | | CAREER | | | |
| --- | --- | --- | --- | --- | --- | --- | --- | --- | --- | --- | --- |
| | GP | G | A | PTS | +/- | PIM | SH | Gm | G | A | Pts |
| RAY SHEPPARD | 68 | 29 | 31 | 60 | 4 | 4 | 226 | 625 | 304 | 238 | 542 |
| SCOTT MELLANBY | 82 | 27 | 29 | 56 | 7 | 170 | 221 | 793 | 223 | 267 | 490 |
| ROBERT SVEHLA | 82 | 13 | 32 | 45 | 2 | 86 | 159 | 168 | 22 | 82 | 104 |
| KIRK MULLER | 76 | 21 | 19 | 40 | 25- | 89 | 174 | 962 | 326 | 521 | 847 |
| RADEK DVORAK | 78 | 18 | 21 | 39 | 2- | 30 | 139 | 155 | 31 | 35 | 66 |
| ROB NIEDERMAYER | 60 | 14 | 24 | 38 | 4 | 54 | 136 | 255 | 47 | 130 | 177 |
| JOHAN GARPENLOV | 53 | 11 | 25 | 36 | 10 | 47 | 83 | 433 | 102 | 171 | 273 |
| BILL LINDSAY | 81 | 11 | 23 | 34 | 1 | 120 | 168 | 353 | 45 | 73 | 118 |
| DAVE LOWRY | 77 | 15 | 14 | 29 | 2 | 51 | 96 | 741 | 122 | 132 | 254 |
| MARTIN STRAKA | 55 | 7 | 22 | 29 | 9 | 12 | 94 | 295 | 58 | 112 | 170 |
| PER GUSTAFSSON | 58 | 7 | 22 | 29 | 11 | 22 | 105 | 58 | 7 | 22 | 29 |
| TOM FITZGERALD | 71 | 10 | 14 | 24 | 7 | 64 | 135 | 489 | 69 | 106 | 175 |
| GORD MURPHY | 80 | 8 | 15 | 23 | 3 | 51 | 137 | 632 | 75 | 197 | 272 |
| ED JOVANOVSKI | 61 | 7 | 16 | 23 | 1- | 172 | 80 | 131 | 17 | 27 | 44 |
| BRIAN SKRUDLAND | 51 | 5 | 13 | 18 | 4 | 48 | 57 | 747 | 112 | 210 | 322 |
| JODY HULL | 67 | 10 | 6 | 16 | 1 | 4 | 92 | 477 | 95 | 101 | 196 |
| MIKE HOUGH | 69 | 8 | 6 | 14 | 12 | 48 | 85 | 622 | 95 | 149 | 244 |
| DAVID NEMIROVSKY | 39 | 7 | 7 | 14 | 1 | 32 | 53 | 48 | 7 | 9 | 16 |
| TERRY CARKNER | 70 | 0 | 14 | 14 | 4- | 96 | 38 | 722 | 39 | 172 | 212 |
| RHETT WARRENER | 62 | 4 | 9 | 13 | 20 | 88 | 58 | 124 | 11 | 17 | 28 |
| PAUL LAUS | 77 | 0 | 12 | 12 | 13 | 313 | 63 | 231 | 5 | 25 | 30 |
| STEVE WASHBURN | 18 | 3 | 6 | 9 | 2 | 4 | 21 | 19 | 3 | 7 | 10 |
| CHRIS WELLS | 47 | 2 | 6 | 8 | 5 | 42 | 29 | 101 | 4 | 8 | 12 |

| | | | | | | | | | | | |
|---|---|---|---|---|---|---|---|---|---|---|---|
| J. VANBIESBROUCK | 57 | 0 | 2 | 2 | 0 | 8 | 0 | | | | |
| MARK FITZPATRICK | 30 | 0 | 1 | 1 | 0 | 13 | 0 | | | | |
| CRAIG MARTIN | 1 | 0 | 0 | 0 | 0 | 5 | 1 | 21 | 0 | 1 | 1 |
| GEOFF SMITH | 3 | 0 | 0 | 0 | 1 | 2 | 2 | 443 | 17 | 72 | 89 |
| CRAIG FERGUSON | 3 | 0 | 0 | 0 | 1- | 0 | 5 | 24 | 1 | 1 | 2 |
| CRAIG FISHER | 4 | 0 | 0 | 0 | 2- | 0 | 2 | 12 | 0 | 0 | 0 |

## TEAM RANKINGS

| | | Conference Rank | League Rank |
|---|---|---|---|
| Record | 35-28-19 | 4 | 8 |
| Home | 21-12-8 | 5 | 8 |
| Away | 14-16-11 | 3 | 9 |
| Versus Own Conference | 23-20-13 | 4 | 15 |
| Versus Other Conference | 12-8-6 | 5 | 10 |
| Team Plus\Minus | +20 | 5 | 9 |
| Goals For | 221 | 11 | 21 |
| Goals Against | 201 | 2 | 4 |
| Average Shots For | 29.1 | 10 | 19 |
| Average Shots Against | 28.8 | 5 | 9 |
| Overtime | 3-4-19 | 8 | 17 |
| One Goal Games | 12-10 | 5 | 8 |
| Times outshooting opponent | 41 | 7 | 14 |

| | | | |
|---|---|---|---|
| Versus Teams Over .500 | 15-13-7 | 3 | 5 |
| Versus Teams Under .500 | 20-15-11 | 7 | 14 |
| First Half Record | 21-11-9 | 2 | 3 |
| Second Half Record | 14-17-10 | 7 | 16 |

## PLAYOFFS

Results: lost 4-1 to NY Rangers
Record: 1-4
Home: 1-2
Away: 0-2
Goals For: 10 (2.0/game)
Goals Against: 13 (2.6/game)
Overtime: 0-2
Power play: 24.0% (2nd)
*Penalty Killing: 90.5% (4th)

| | GP | G | A | PTS | +/- | PIM | PP | SH | GW | OT | S |
|---|---|---|---|---|---|---|---|---|---|---|---|
| ROBERT SVEHLA | 5 | 1 | 4 | 5 | 4- | 4 | 1 | 0 | 0 | 0 | 13 |
| GORD MURPHY | 5 | 0 | 5 | 5 | 0 | 4 | 0 | 0 | 0 | 0 | 18 |
| ROB NIEDERMAYER | 5 | 2 | 1 | 3 | 1- | 6 | 1 | 0 | 0 | 0 | 5 |
| KIRK MULLER | 5 | 1 | 2 | 3 | 3- | 4 | 1 | 0 | 0 | 0 | 20 |
| JOHAN GARPENLOV | 4 | 2 | 0 | 2 | 0 | 4 | 2 | 0 | 1 | 0 | 6 |
| RAY SHEPPARD | 5 | 2 | 0 | 2 | 4- | 0 | 1 | 0 | 0 | 0 | 12 |
| SCOTT MELLANBY | 5 | 0 | 2 | 2 | 1- | 4 | 0 | 0 | 0 | 0 | 6 |
| DAVID NEMIROVSKY | 3 | 1 | 0 | 1 | 2- | 0 | 0 | 0 | 0 | 0 | 4 |

| | | | | | | | | | | | |
|---|---|---|---|---|---|---|---|---|---|---|---|
| MIKE HOUGH | 5 | 1 | 0 | 1 | 2- | 2 | 0 | 0 | 0 | 0 | 10 |
| BILL LINDSAY | 3 | 0 | 1 | 1 | 0 | 8 | 0 | 0 | 0 | 0 | 4 |
| TOM FITZGERALD | 5 | 0 | 1 | 1 | 1- | 0 | 0 | 0 | 0 | 0 | 14 |
| PAUL LAUS | 5 | 0 | 1 | 1 | 3- | 4 | 0 | 0 | 0 | 0 | 6 |
| CHRIS WELLS | 3 | 0 | 0 | 0 | 1- | 0 | 0 | 0 | 0 | 0 | 1 |
| RADEK DVORAK | 3 | 0 | 0 | 0 | 0 | 0 | 0 | 0 | 0 | 0 | 1 |
| MARTIN STRAKA | 4 | 0 | 0 | 0 | 2- | 0 | 0 | 0 | 0 | 0 | 2 |
| TERRY CARKNER | 5 | 0 | 0 | 0 | 3- | 6 | 0 | 0 | 0 | 0 | 7 |
| JODY HULL | 5 | 0 | 0 | 0 | 1- | 0 | 0 | 0 | 0 | 0 | 12 |
| DAVE LOWRY | 5 | 0 | 0 | 0 | 3- | 0 | 0 | 0 | 0 | 0 | 8 |
| J. VANBIESBROUCK | 5 | 0 | 0 | 0 | 0 | 0 | 0 | 0 | 0 | 0 | 0 |
| ED JOVANOVSKI | 5 | 0 | 0 | 0 | 4- | 4 | 0 | 0 | 0 | 0 | 7 |
| RHETT WARRENER | 5 | 0 | 0 | 0 | 0 | 0 | 0 | 0 | 0 | 0 | 5 |

| GOALTENDER | GPI | MINS | AVG | W | L | T | EN | SO | GA | SA | SV % |
|---|---|---|---|---|---|---|---|---|---|---|---|
| J. VANBIESBROUCK | 5 | 328 | 2.38 | 1 | 4 | 0 | 1 | 0 | 13 | 184 | .929 |
| FLA TOTALS | 5 | 329 | 2.37 | 1 | 4 | 0 | 1 | 0 | 13 | 184 | .929 |

## ALL-TIME LEADERS

### Goals
| | |
|---|---|
| Scott Mellanby | 102 |
| Jody Hull | 54 |
| Rob Niedermayer | 53 |

### Assists
| | |
|---|---|
| Scott Mellanby | 109 |
| Gord Murphy | 82 |
| Rob Niedermayer | 82 |
| Robert Svehla | 82 |

### Points
| | |
|---|---|
| Scott Mellanby | 211 |
| Rob Niedermayer | 135 |
| Stu Barnes | 121 |

## BEST INDIVIDUAL SEASONS

### Goals
| | | |
|---|---|---|
| Scott Mellanby | 1995-96 | 32 |
| Scott Mellanby | 1993-94 | 30 |
| Ray Sheppard | 1996-97 | 29 |

### Assists
| | | |
|---|---|---|
| Robert Svelha | 1995-96 | 49 |
| Scott Mellanby | 1995-96 | 38 |
| Rob Niedermayer | 1995-96 | 35 |

### Points
| | | |
|---|---|---|
| Scott Mellanby | 1995-96 | 70 |
| Rob Niedermayer | 1995-96 | 61 |
| Scott Mellanby | 1993-94 | 60 |
| Ray Sheppard | 1996-97 | 60 |

## TEAM

### Last 3 years

|         | GP | W  | L  | T  | Pts | %    |
|---------|----|----|----|----|-----|------|
| 1996-97 | 82 | 35 | 28 | 19 | 89  | .549 |
| 1995-96 | 82 | 41 | 31 | 10 | 92  | .561 |
| 1994-95 | 48 | 20 | 22 | 6  | 46  | .479 |

### Best 3 regular seasons

|         | GP | W  | L  | T  | Pts | %    |
|---------|----|----|----|----|-----|------|
| 1995-96 | 82 | 41 | 31 | 10 | 92  | .561 |
| 1996-97 | 82 | 35 | 28 | 19 | 89  | .549 |
| 1993-94 | 84 | 33 | 34 | 17 | 83  | .494 |

### Worst 3 regular seasons

|         | GP | W  | L  | T  | Pts | %    |
|---------|----|----|----|----|-----|------|
| 1994-95 | 48 | 20 | 22 | 6  | 46  | .479 |
| 1993-94 | 84 | 33 | 34 | 17 | 83  | .494 |
| 1996-97 | 82 | 35 | 28 | 19 | 89  | .549 |

### Most Goals (min. 70 game schedule)

| 1995-96 | 254 |
|---------|-----|
| 1993-94 | 233 |
| 1996-97 | 221 |

### Fewest Goals (min. 70 game schedule)

| 1996-97 | 221 |
|---------|-----|
| 1993-94 | 233 |
| 1995-96 | 254 |

### Most Goals Against (min. 70 game schedule)

| 1995-96 | 234 |
|---------|-----|
| 1993-94 | 233 |
| 1996-97 | 201 |

### Fewest Goals Against (min. 70 game schedule)

| 1996-97 | 201 |
|---------|-----|
| 1993-94 | 233 |
| 1995-96 | 234 |

# Montreal Canadiens

They sure know how to have fun during a hockey season in Montreal, don't they?

Here's a partial list of some of the stuff that happened last year, in chronological order.

* Patrice Brisebois' name came up in the early season lottery, and he won the right to be booed every time he touched the puck.

* The Canadiens are playing good old-fashioned pond hockey in the early going, and are scoring lots of goals. Unfortunately for them, their opponents like pond hockey too, and are even better at it. Montreal is last in goals against.

* Pierre Turgeon became the fifth captain in six years to be traded, when he went to St. Louis along with Craig Conroy and Rory Fitzpatrick for Shayne Corson, Murray Baron and a fifth round draft pick.

* Mario Tremblay yells and swears at Donald Brashear at practice, because Tremblay didn't like the way he was doing one of the drills. Brashear is sent off the ice, back to Montreal, and then traded to Vancouver. One Montreal newspaper suggests Tremblay should be fired for using vulgar and abusive language. If that was the case, however, there wouldn't be any coaches in the league left.

* An incredible run of injuries continues with Saku Koviu, Marc Bureau, Benoit Brunet, Terry Ryan and Shayne Corson all out of the lineup at the same time. A little while later, Vladimir Malakhov, Stephane Quintal, Koviu, Bureau, Ryan, Corson, Martin Rucinsky and Scott Thornton all hit the injury list. Most all of their key players, with the exception of Damphousse, Recchi and Savage, would miss time with injuries.

* Rucinsky is accused by a Montreal radio station of faking his shoulder injury and refusing to play in a game versus Dallas. Rucinsky reportedly replied, "That's crazy," which should be the battle cry for everyone on the Canadiens.

* Mario Lemieux plays his final game in his hometown of Montreal and scores four third period goals in a 5-2 win.

* Stephane Richer says Canadiens fans should get a life, and is booed relentlessly in his next game.

* Stephane Richer proves his point by coming to the rescue of a woman lying unconcious in a snowbank in freezing temperatures after breaking her ankle.

* the Habs suffer the ultimate humiliation by

losing 5-1 at home to Toronto, showcasing how two of hockey's proudest franchises have sunk so low.

* the team's failures are getting to some players, including Scott Thornton and Mark Recchi, who suggested that some of their teammates don't come to play every night and just don't care about winning.

* Montreal becomes the last team in the league to record a shutout when Thibault beat Boston 3-0. It was their seventieth game.

* Murray Baron and Chris Murray are traded to Phoenix for tough defenceman Dave Manson.

* the Canadiens clinch a playoff berth, the last one available, on the second last night of the season, with a 3-3 tie against Philadelphia.

* the Canadiens' farm team in Fredericton finishes with the worst record in the AHL.

* New Jersey goalie Martin Brodeur scores a goal against Montreal in the opening game of the playoffs.

* Patrice Brisebois scores in overtime against New Jersey in game four to give the Canadiens their only playoff win.

* Mario Tremblay resigns, before he's fired, and Alain Vigneault is selected as the new coach. Immediately there's more controversy, with assistant Dave King seen as being anti-French with some of his decisions when he was coaching Canada's national team.

## STUFF

* the Canadiens scored three shorthanded goals in a game, October 16 versus Calgary, to tie a team record. The last time they accomplished that was in 1948.
* the Canadiens just missed having a losing home record (17-17-7) which would have made it the first time since the 1939-40 season.

## STAT ANALYSIS

Montreal had the worst combined special teams in the league last season. To determine that, we take each team's power play percentage and each team's penalty killing percentage, and add them. The total for the league is always 100% when you combine the two numbers, so teams whose total is above 100 are better than average, and those less than 100 are below average.

Montreal finished on the bottom, but presumably a new coach and a tactician assistant like Dave King, will have some effect on that.

The index isn't mathematically perfect because it's more weighted on the higher percentage penalty killing side, but it serves the purpose.

Worst Special Teams:

|  | PP% | PK% | Total |
| --- | --- | --- | --- |
| Montreal | 15.7 | 79.5 | 95.3 |
| Boston | 14.8 | 81.8 | 96.7 |
| Buffalo | 13.2 | 83.8 | 97.0 |
| NY Islanders | 13.9 | 83.4 | 97.3 |
| Toronto | 15.5 | 82.0 | 97.5 |

Best Special Teams

|  | | | |
| --- | --- | --- | --- |
| Colorado | 20.6 | 87.6 | 108.2 |
| Detroit | 17.9 | 86.7 | 104.6 |
| Phoenix | 18.1 | 85.9 | 104.0 |
| Pittsburgh | 21.9 | 81.1 | 103.0 |
| Carolina | 18.1 | 84.6 | 102.7 |

## TEAM PREVIEW

GOAL: They love him, they love him not. They love him, they love him not. So goes the career of Jocelyn Thibault, who seems destined (if he's lucky) to get out of the pressure cooker in Montreal.

Pat Jablonski had some good games and some poor ones and was shipped out, while Jose Theodore did pretty much the same, not overly impressing anyone.

There was a call for more experienced, reliable goaltending, which they may get, but the real problem was a team committment to defence. Give Thibault and Theodore some of that and their worries will be reduced considerably.

Hockey Annual Rating: 24 of 26

DEFENCE: They're big and they're bad. Bad in the real sense, however, not the vernacular, "Yeah, we're bad, we're bad" way.

The Montreal defence is one of the biggest in league. That's a good thing to be, except for one thing: a lot of them play half a foot shorter than their listed height.

NHL defence trends seem to change quite frequently. Probably, in just the last 10 years, teams have changed from wanting a lot of offensive power on the blueline, to wanting size, to wanting toughness, to wanting good mobility, to wanting defensive defencemen, to wanting size, to wanting toughness...and so on and so on.

At the moment, teams only need (or can get) one or two offensive threats, so they've tried to load up on big guys who play defence first. Mobility is out at the moment. Toughness is in.

The idea is to make life miserable for opposing forwards. Montreal allowed the third most shots in the NHL last season. That's not the fault of the defencemen. If they're not getting help from the forwards, of course there will be a lot of shots. What the defence can do is keep the front of the net clear and make sure teams don't get second and third helpings. It's always more effective when opposing players are more concerned with what might happen to them if they get the puck instead of what they're going to do with the puck when they get it.

Dave Manson is perfect in that role. But they need more. Brad Brown had 368 penalty minutes in 64 games for Fredericton last year. He would fit in as a regular. Stephane Quintal uses his size, and that's about it for toughness.

The offence from the defence is supposed to be supplied by Vladimir Malakhov, Patrice Brisebois and second-year man, David Wilkie. They all can do that, although none well enough to be termed a quarterback. Brisebois is a likely candidate to be traded, which would probably be best for him.

| GOALTENDER | GPI | MINS | AVG | W | L | T | EN | SO | GA | SA | SV % |
|---|---|---|---|---|---|---|---|---|---|---|---|
| JOCELYN THIBAULT | 61 | 3397 | 2.90 | 22 | 24 | 11 | 5 | 1 | 164 | 1815 | .910 |
| JOSE THEODORE | 16 | 821 | 3.87 | 5 | 6 | 2 | 0 | 0 | 53 | 508 | .896 |
| PAT JABLONSKI | 17 | 754 | 3.98 | 4 | 6 | 2 | 0 | 0 | 50 | 438 | .886 |
| TOMAS VOKOUN | 1 | 20 | 12.0 | 0 | 0 | 0 | 0 | 0 | 4 | 14 | .714 |
| MTL TOTALS | 82 | 5008 | 3.31 | 31 | 36 | 15 | 5 | 1 | 276 | 2780 | .901 |

Peter Popovic (6-6, 235) and Jassen Cullimore (6-5, 225) are two of the big guys, but their size is not used to play a physical game.

Other defencemen who will get a chance to show their stuff are Francois Groleau and Craig Rivet.

Rejean Houle reportedly said that the Canadiens' defence doesn't need any help, and that it's as good as Detroit's was last season. Hmmm...well, not quite. Not nearly. They're one of the worst in the league, but there is some hope.

Hockey Annual Rating: 19 of 26

FORWARD: The Canadiens started out playing firewagon hockey. They were going to have three scoring lines and shoot the lights out. That lasted for a couple weeks and then they tried to achieve some sort of balance to stop the opposing teams from shooting their own lights out.

So many of the Montreal forwards are streaky scorers. But, let's get this straight — almost every forward in the league is streaky. It's just that they seem more so in Montreal, and if you're going to shoot the lights out, the lights have to be on more often.

On paper, the Canadiens' forward lines look to be one of the best in the league. They've got two top centres in Koivu and Damphousse to begin with. Koivu had his coming-out season, although it was slowed somewhat by injuries. With Damphousse, you suffer through the slow times and enjoy the good times, knowing it all balances out in the end. Marc Bureau and Chris Tucker are pencilled in as the other Montreal centres, with Sebastien Bordeleau, Eric Houde and junior Matt Higgins waiting in the wings.

On the right side is Mark Recchi, their top goal scorer mentioned often as trade bait; Benoit Brunet, constantly hampered with

injuries; Stephane Richer, who can never live up to expectations; Turner Stevenson, who's showing signs of coming into his own; and Valeri Bure, coming off a disappointing season.

The left wing lines up with low-scoring but still valuable Corson; the streakiest of goal scorers, Brian Savage; streaky, but effective Martin Rucinsky; defensive winger, Scott Thornton; and junior star Terry Ryan, who missed his chance to play with Montreal last season because of post-concussion syndrome.

Hockey Annual Rating: 9 of 26

SPECIAL TEAMS: With all their supposed offence, the Montreal power play was expected to be good. It was mediocre, with no individual scoring more than seven goals.

The penalty killing was atrocious — worst in the league. Often, it's a criticism of coaching when special teams fail, so the team should expect some improvement under new man Vigneault, and possibly with Dave King assisting with strategy.

Many teams seem to view shorthanded situations as an opportunity to score, or an opportunity to get more playing time out of their high-prized help, but Montreal needs to worry more about stopping opposing scorers.

POWER PLAY

|  | G | ATT | PCT |
|---|---|---|---|
| Overall | 53 | 337 | 15.7% (13th NHL) |
| Home | 28 | 171 | 16.4% (11th NHL) |
| Road | 25 | 166 | 15.1% (17th NHL) |

11 SHORT HANDED GOALS ALLOWED (T-15th NHL)

PENALTY KILLING

|  | G | TSH | PCT |
|---|---|---|---|
| Overall | 71 | 347 | 79.5% (26th NHL) |
| Home | 40 | 181 | 77.9% (26th NHL) |
| Road | 31 | 166 | 81.3% (T-19th NHL) |

10 SHORT HANDED GOALS SCORED (T-13th NHL)

CANADIENS SPECIAL TEAMS SCORING

| Power play | G | A | PTS |
|---|---|---|---|
| DAMPHOUSSE | 7 | 14 | 21 |
| RECCHI | 7 | 13 | 20 |
| KOIVU | 5 | 12 | 17 |
| RUCINSKY | 6 | 9 | 15 |
| MALAKHOV | 5 | 9 | 14 |
| SAVAGE | 5 | 7 | 12 |
| BURE | 4 | 8 | 12 |
| MANSON | 2 | 8 | 10 |
| RICHER | 2 | 4 | 6 |
| QUINTAL | 1 | 5 | 6 |
| WILKIE | 3 | 2 | 5 |
| BRISEBOIS | 0 | 5 | 5 |
| CORSON | 3 | 1 | 4 |
| BRUNET | 2 | 1 | 3 |
| CULLIMORE | 0 | 3 | 3 |
| TUCKER | 1 | 1 | 2 |
| THORNTON | 1 | 1 | 2 |
| STEVENSON | 1 | 1 | 2 |
| BUREAU | 1 | 0 | 1 |

| Short handed | G | A | PTS |
|---|---|---|---|
| DAMPHOUSSE | 2 | 3 | 5 |
| RUCINSKY | 3 | 0 | 3 |
| RECCHI | 2 | 1 | 3 |
| BUREAU | 1 | 1 | 2 |
| BORDELEAU | 0 | 2 | 2 |
| THORNTON | 1 | 0 | 1 |
| CULLIMORE | 1 | 0 | 1 |
| QUINTAL | 0 | 1 | 1 |
| POPOVIC | 0 | 1 | 1 |
| MANSON | 0 | 1 | 1 |
| MALAKHOV | 0 | 1 | 1 |
| KOIVU | | 0 | 1 | 1 |
| CORSON | 0 | 1 | 1 |
| BRUNET | 0 | 1 | 1 |

COACHING AND MANAGEMENT: Few coaches have suffered through as stormy a tenure as coach as did Mario Tremblay in Montreal. He resigned, probably to save him-self from being fired, citing pressure on his and his family from the media. The fiery Tremblay had no coaching experience when he took the job, but walks away from the toughest coaching job in hockey, knowing that he did the best he could. He was expected to provide motivation to win, but that's a tough task for anyone in today's NHL.

There was much player unrest in Montreal with Tremblay. It makes it difficult for the coach to motivate when a number of players are hoping he's fired. That may also account for reports by some players that some of their teammates weren't playing hard every night.

Alain Vigneault moves to the hot seat. He's only 36-years-old, but has a lot of junior coaching experience, and was an assistant in Ottawa when Rick Bowness was coach. Dave King, who has plenty of experience in a number of different places, was hired as his assistant. His best personal trait had better be a thick skin.

Rejean Houle escaped some of the criticism that Tremblay had to endure. He too was inexperienced, and made some questionable trades before last season. His deals last year, however, showed that he is able to recognize problems and make some attempt to fix them. He wasn't, however, able to fix their goaltending woes.

The Canadiens are going to have to show some improvement this year, if Houle wants to keep his job. They're not big on failure, or patience, in Montreal.

Hockey Annual Rating: 22 of 26

DRAFT

| Round | Sel. | Player | Pos | Amateur Team |
|---|---|---|---|---|
| 1 | 11 | Jason Ward | C | Erie (OHL) |
| 2 | 37 | G. Baumgartner | C | Laval (QMJHL) |

| | | | | |
|---|---|---|---|---|
| 3 | 65 | Ilkka Mikkola | D | Finland |
| 4 | 91 | Daniel Tetrault | D | Brandon (WHL) |
| 5 | 118 | Konstantin Sidulov | D | Russia |
| 5 | 122 | Gennady Razin | D | Kamloops (WHL) |
| 6 | 145 | J. Desroches | D | Granby (QMJHL) |
| 7 | 172 | Ben Guite | RW | Maine |
| 8 | 197 | Petr Kubos | D | Czech Rep. |
| 8 | 202 | Andrei Sidyakin | LW | Russia |
| 9 | 228 | Jari-Espen Ygranes | D | Norway |

Much was made of top draft pick Jason Ward's surprise ability to speak fluent French. Of considerable more concern should be his ability to play hockey. He is supposed to be an excellent two-way player, who can score and play defence. The Canadiens said they had Ward rated much higher than 11th, which is what every team says, at least until contract time.

PROGNOSIS: Who knows? Much depends on the influence of new coach Vigneault. If he can get the forwards to play a more rounded game and venture into their own end on occasion, it's going to help the defence and the goalies, and make the Habs a better team.

They're not going to make a run at the Stanley Cup this year, but there's room to maneuver in the Eastern Conference and they shouldn't have too much difficult making the playoffs.

## PREDICTION

Eastern Conference: 5th
Overall: 9th

## TEAM RANKINGS

| | | Conference Rank | League Rank |
|---|---|---|---|
| Record | 33-40-9 | 7 | 16 |
| Home | 17-17-7 | 10 | 18 |
| Away | 14-19-8 | 8 | 14 |
| Versus Own Conference | 18-26-12 | 11 | 22 |
| Versus Other Conference | 13-10-3 | 6 | 10 |
| Team Plus\Minus | -9 | 8 | 15 |
| Goals For | 249 | 4 | 9 |
| Goals Against | 276 | 11 | 23 |
| | | | |
| Average Shots For | 30.2 | 5 | 10 |
| Average Shots Against | 33.9 | 12 | 23 |
| Overtime | 2-4-15 | 11 | 21 |
| One Goal Games | 11-11 | 6 | 10 |
| Times outshooting opponent | 29 | 10 | 20 |
| Versus Teams Over .500 | 8-18-12 | 11 | 20 |
| Versus Teams Under .500 | 23-18-3 | 6 | 12 |
| First Half Record | 15-18-8 | 10 | 17 |
| Second Half Record | 16-18-7 | 6 | 15 |

## PLAYOFFS

Results: lost 4-1 to NY Rangers
Record: 1-4
Home: 1-1
Away: 0-3
Goals For: 11 (2.2/game)
Goals Against: 22 (4.4/game)
Overtime: 1-0
Power play: 0.0% (16th)
Penalty Killing: 67.9% (16th)

## STAT SECTION

| Team Scoring Stats | 1996-97 | | | | | CAREER | | | | | |
|---|---|---|---|---|---|---|---|---|---|---|---|
| | GP | G | A | PTS | +/- | PIM | SH | Gm | G | A | Pts |
| V. DAMPHOUSSE | 82 | 27 | 54 | 81 | 6- | 82 | 244 | 852 | 310 | 511 | 821 |
| MARK RECCHI | 82 | 34 | 46 | 80 | 1- | 58 | 202 | 628 | 285 | 430 | 715 |
| BRIAN SAVAGE | 81 | 23 | 37 | 60 | 14- | 39 | 219 | 196 | 61 | 52 | 113 |
| SAKU KOIVU | 50 | 17 | 39 | 56 | 7 | 38 | 135 | 132 | 37 | 64 | 101 |
| MARTIN RUCINSKY | 70 | 28 | 27 | 55 | 1 | 62 | 172 | 311 | 88 | 133 | 221 |
| STEPHANE RICHER | 63 | 22 | 24 | 46 | 0 | 32 | 126 | 826 | 366 | 326 | 692 |
| VALERI BURE | 64 | 14 | 21 | 35 | 4 | 6 | 131 | 165 | 39 | 42 | 81 |
| V. MALAKHOV | 65 | 10 | 20 | 30 | 3 | 43 | 177 | 306 | 43 | 145 | 188 |
| SHAYNE CORSON | 58 | 8 | 16 | 24 | 9- | 104 | 115 | 747 | 200 | 294 | 494 |
| BENOIT BRUNET | 39 | 10 | 13 | 23 | 6 | 14 | 63 | 265 | 49 | 84 | 133 |
| STEPHANE QUINTAL | 71 | 7 | 15 | 22 | 1 | 100 | 139 | 522 | 32 | 99 | 131 |
| DAVE MANSON | 75 | 4 | 18 | 22 | 26- | 187 | 175 | 763 | 87 | 223 | 310 |
| TURNER STEVENSON | 65 | 8 | 13 | 21 | 14- | 97 | 76 | 189 | 23 | 30 | 53 |
| SCOTT THORNTON | 73 | 10 | 10 | 20 | 19- | 128 | 110 | 315 | 34 | 43 | 77 |
| DARCY TUCKER | 73 | 7 | 13 | 20 | 5- | 110 | 62 | 76 | 7 | 13 | 20 |
| MARC BUREAU | 43 | 6 | 9 | 15 | 4 | 16 | 56 | 359 | 35 | 66 | 101 |
| DAVID WILKIE | 61 | 6 | 9 | 15 | 9- | 63 | 65 | 86 | 7 | 14 | 21 |
| PATRICE BRISEBOIS | 49 | 2 | 13 | 15 | 7- | 24 | 72 | 312 | 29 | 100 | 129 |
| PETER POPOVIC | 78 | 1 | 13 | 14 | 9 | 32 | 82 | 234 | 5 | 42 | 47 |
| S. BORDELEAU | 28 | 2 | 9 | 11 | 3- | 2 | 27 | 32 | 2 | 9 | 11 |
| JASSEN CULLIMORE | 52 | 2 | 6 | 8 | 2 | 44 | 54 | 113 | 4 | 9 | 13 |
| CRAIG RIVET | 35 | 0 | 4 | 4 | 7 | 54 | 24 | 59 | 1 | 9 | 10 |
| ERIC HOUDE | 13 | 0 | 2 | 2 | 1 | 2 | 1 | 13 | 0 | 2 | 2 |
| TOMAS VOKOUN | 1 | 0 | 0 | 0 | 0 | 0 | 0 | | | | |
| DAVID LING | 2 | 0 | 0 | 0 | 0 | 0 | 0 | 2 | 0 | 0 | 0 |
| TERRY RYAN | 3 | 0 | 0 | 0 | 0 | 0 | 0 | 3 | 0 | 0 | 0 |
| FRANCOIS GROLEAU | 5 | 0 | 0 | 0 | 0 | 4 | 3 | 7 | 0 | 1 | 1 |
| BRAD BROWN | 8 | 0 | 0 | 0 | 1- | 22 | 0 | 8 | 0 | 0 | 0 |
| PIERRE SEVIGNY | 13 | 0 | 0 | 0 | 0 | 5 | 1 | 75 | 4 | 5 | 9 |
| JOSE THEODORE | 16 | 0 | 0 | 0 | 0 | 0 | 0 | | | | |
| JOCELYN THIBAULT | 61 | 0 | 0 | 0 | 0 | 0 | 0 | | | | |

## ALL-TIME LEADERS

### Goals
| | |
|---|---|
| Maurice Richard | 544 |
| Guy Lafleur | 518 |
| Jean Beliveau | 507 |

### Assists
| | |
|---|---|
| Guy Lafleur | 728 |
| Jean Beliveau | 712 |
| Henri Richard | 688 |

### Points
| | |
|---|---|
| Guy Lafleur | 1,246 |
| Jean Beliveau | 1,219 |
| Henri Richard | 1,046 |

## BEST INDIVIDUAL SEASONS

### Goals
| | | |
|---|---|---|
| Steve Shutt | 1976-77 | 60 |
| Guy Lafleur | 1977-78 | 60 |
| Guy Lafleur | 1976-77 | 56 |
| Guy Lafleur | 1975-76 | 56 |

### Assists
| | | |
|---|---|---|
| Peter Mahovlich | 1974-75 | 82 |
| Guy Lafleur | 1976-77 | 80 |
| Guy Lafleur | 1978-79 | 77 |

### Points
| | | |
|---|---|---|
| Guy Lafleur | 1976-77 | 136 |
| Guy Lafleur | 1977-78 | 132 |
| Guy Lafleur | 1978-79 | 129 |

## TEAM

### Last 3 years
| | GP | W | L | T | Pts | % |
|---|---|---|---|---|---|---|
| 1996-97 | 82 | 31 | 36 | 15 | 77 | .470 |
| 1995-96 | 82 | 40 | 32 | 10 | 90 | .549 |
| 1994-95 | 48 | 18 | 23 | 7 | 43 | .448 |

### Best 3 regular seasons
| | | | | | | |
|---|---|---|---|---|---|---|
| 1976-77 | 80 | 60 | 8 | 12 | 132 | .825 |
| 1977-78 | 80 | 59 | 10 | 11 | 129 | .806 |
| 1975-76 | 80 | 58 | 11 | 11 | 127 | .794 |

### Worst 3 regular seasons
| | | | | | | |
|---|---|---|---|---|---|---|
| 1939-40 | 48 | 10 | 33 | 5 | 25 | .260 |
| 1925-26 | 36 | 11 | 24 | 1 | 23 | .319 |
| 1935-36 | 48 | 11 | 26 | 11 | 33 | .344 |

### Most Goals (min. 70 game schedule)
| | |
|---|---|
| 1976-77 | 387 |
| 1981-82 | 360 |
| 1977-78 | 359 |

### Fewest Goals (min. 70 game schedule)
| | |
|---|---|
| 1952-55 | 155 |
| 1949-50 | 172 |
| 1950-51 | 173 |

### Most Goals Against (min. 70 game schedule)
| | |
|---|---|
| 1983-84 | 295 |
| 1982-83 | 286 |
| 1992-93 | 280 |
| 1985-86 | 280 |

### Fewest Goals Against (min. 70 game schedule)
| | |
|---|---|
| 1955-56 | 131 |
| 1953-54 | 141 |
| 1952-53 | 148 |

| | GP | G | A | PTS | +/- | PIM | PP | SH | GW | OT | S |
|---|---|---|---|---|---|---|---|---|---|---|---|
| MARK RECCHI | 5 | 4 | 2 | 6 | 2 | 2 | 0 | 0 | 0 | 0 | 18 |
| BENOIT BRUNET | 4 | 1 | 3 | 4 | 4 | 4 | 0 | 1 | 0 | 0 | 8 |
| SAKU KOIVU | 5 | 1 | 3 | 4 | 1 | 10 | 0 | 0 | 0 | 0 | 10 |
| PATRICE BRISEBOIS | 3 | 1 | 1 | 2 | 3 | 24 | 0 | 0 | 1 | 1 | 3 |
| TURNER STEVENSON | 5 | 1 | 1 | 2 | 1 | 2 | 0 | 0 | 0 | 0 | 5 |
| BRIAN SAVAGE | 5 | 1 | 1 | 2 | 1 | 0 | 0 | 0 | 0 | 0 | 6 |
| SHAYNE CORSON | 5 | 1 | 0 | 1 | 5- | 4 | 0 | 1 | 0 | 0 | 8 |
| SCOTT THORNTON | 5 | 1 | 0 | 1 | 1 | 2 | 0 | 0 | 0 | 0 | 11 |
| STEPHANE QUINTAL | 5 | 0 | 1 | 1 | 1- | 6 | 0 | 0 | 0 | 0 | 6 |
| VALERI BURE | 5 | 0 | 1 | 1 | 4- | 2 | 0 | 0 | 0 | 0 | 7 |
| CRAIG RIVET | 5 | 0 | 1 | 1 | 2- | 14 | 0 | 0 | 0 | 0 | 6 |
| JASSEN CULLIMORE | 2 | 0 | 0 | 0 | 1- | 2 | 0 | 0 | 0 | 0 | 0 |
| DAVID WILKIE | 2 | 0 | 0 | 0 | 0 | 2 | 0 | 0 | 0 | 0 | 1 |
| JOSE THEODORE | 2 | 0 | 0 | 0 | 0 | 0 | 0 | 0 | 0 | 0 | 0 |
| PETER POPOVIC | 3 | 0 | 0 | 0 | 3- | 2 | 0 | 0 | 0 | 0 | 1 |
| JOCELYN THIBAULT | 3 | 0 | 0 | 0 | 0 | 0 | 0 | 0 | 0 | 0 | 0 |
| DARCY TUCKER | 4 | 0 | 0 | 0 | 0 | 0 | 0 | 0 | 0 | 0 | 4 |
| V. DAMPHOUSSE | 5 | 0 | 0 | 0 | 5- | 2 | 0 | 0 | 0 | 0 | 7 |
| DAVE MANSON | 5 | 0 | 0 | 0 | 6 | 17 | 0 | 0 | 0 | 0 | 10 |
| STEPHANE RICHER | 5 | 0 | 0 | 0 | 3- | 0 | 0 | 0 | 0 | 0 | 9 |
| V. MALAKHOV | 5 | 0 | 0 | 0 | 3- | 6 | 0 | 0 | 0 | 0 | 12 |
| MARTIN RUCINSKY | 5 | 0 | 0 | 0 | 5- | 4 | 0 | 0 | 0 | 0 | 10 |

| GOALTENDER | GPI | MINS | AVG | W | L | T | EN | SO | GA | SA | SV % |
|---|---|---|---|---|---|---|---|---|---|---|---|
| JOSE THEODORE | 2 | 168 | 2.50 | 1 | 1 | 0 | 0 | 0 | 7 | 108 | .935 |
| JOCELYN THIBAULT | 3 | 179 | 4.36 | 0 | 3 | 2 | 0 | 0 | 13 | 101 | .871 |
| MTL TOTALS | 5 | 348 | 3.79 | 1 | 4 | 2 | 0 | 0 | 21 | 211 | .896 |

# New Jersey Devils

Strange doings with the Devils. At least from a statistical viewpoint. Consider:

Oddity: In three consecutive years, the Devils won the Stanley Cup, finished out of the play-offs, and then earned 104 points, best in the Eastern Conference.
Explanation: The year they won the Cup they finished four games over .500; the year they missed the playoffs they also finished four games over .500. The only reason they didn't make the playoffs was that the Eastern Conference dominated the Western Conference that year and more teams had better records. Also, there probably was a bit of a Stanley Cup letdown. The bottom line was that they were a good team in each of the three years.

Oddity: The Devils are blamed for all the defensive woes which many see as a plague on the NHL. This, despite mid-range goal scoring and the fourth highest shot total in the league.
Explanation: The strict defence thing may be part myth, because they're not that low scoring a team, but the high shot total is interesting. If they're so defensive, how come so many shots? The thing is they have one of the worst team shooting percentages in the league. Only Calgary and Tampa Bay were worse.
Sometimes that means they're shooting from outside the perimeter or getting a lot of low-percentage shots from the point. But, their defencemen don't have extraordinary shot totals, so it must be something else. What? Don't know.

Oddity: The Devils draw the fewest penalties and get the fewest power plays.
Explanation: You'll find on most teams that penalty totals for and against are remarkably similar. There are some big differences, but human nature dictates that referees don't like to give a team eight power plays and the other two. It tends to give the appearance of being unfair, and whether it was deserved or not, players and coaches squawk. On the Devils there are more reasons. One is that they play a disciplined style, which includes not taking dumb penalties. Lyle Odelein, who used to have goon-type numbers, led the team with just 110 minutes. That was easily the lowest total for a team leader in the league. Another reason is that the Devils' defencemen didn't take a lot of penalties. Sufficiently skilled, and still tough, they didn't have to drag people down to stop them. Also, the Devils aren't a particularly speedy team. Speedy teams tend to draw more penalties.

## SHORTS

* Brodeur broke his own team record for con-

secutive shutout minutes in net, with 189:58.

* Brodeur's goal in the playoffs made him the second goalie ever to accomplish that feat. Ron Hextall was the first.

* The Devils allowed just eight shots in a December 18 game versus Vancouver, a team record, and just one more than the NHL record.

* Bill Guerin set a team record when he was plus or even in 29 straight games.

* Ken Daneyko has played in every single franchise playoff game.

* New Jersey prospect, Brendan Morrison, won the Hobey Baker Award last year, as the best U.S. college player.

* 182 goals allowed by the Devils were the fewest in franchise history (for a full season) and the first time they had surrendered less than 200.

* Bob Carpenter played in his 1,000th game last season.

* their road record of 22-14-5 was the best in franchise history, and only the second time they had been over .500.

* Bobby Holik had the team's longest point scoring streak, a 10-gamer.

* Mike Dunham played 41 seconds in a 4-0 win over the Islanders, but was still credited with a shared shutout.

* if Brodeur plays 33 games for the Devils this year, he will take over the all-time team lead in games played by a goalie, passing Chris Terreri, who played 268.

* Brodeur passed Terreri to take over the franchise lead in all-time wins. He has 119 to Terreri's 106.

* a 15-game home undefeated streak by the Devils was the longest in the league last year and set a team record.

## STAT ANALYSIS

When the New Jersey Devils were outshot in games they had a remarkable record of 14-2-4. How do you explain that?

Maybe it's not so complicated. The three teams at the top of the list below were also the teams with the best overall records.

Maybe what it means is absolutely nothing. They won when they outshot their opponents, they won when they were outshot. It didn't matter.

Best Records When Outshot:

| | |
|---|---|
| New Jersey | 14-2-4 |
| Dallas | 17-6-2 |
| Colorado | 19-11-1 |
| NY Rangers | 23-14-6 |

## TEAM PREVIEW

GOAL: If not for Dominik Hasek, Martin Brodeur would be the league's most dominant goalie. He's not all that far behind anyway, leading the league with 10 shutouts, leading with a 1.88 goals against average, and finishing second in save percentage to Hasek. Not bad.

There is little use for a backup in New Jersey, but that job is tentatively held by Mike Dunham.

Dunham and the Devils were involved in some controversy last season. In order to keep Dunham away from unrestricted free agency he had to appear in at least 25 games. Some of his game appearances were for less than a minute, causing some grief for his agent, who has charged the Devils with making a mockery of the rule, and unfairly hurting his client.

What the Devils did was pretty obvious. Of course they wanted Dunham to appear in 25 games, any way they could. Why shouldn't they? Every year, on many teams, players are being paid not to play. They're not good enough anymore or they're injured or something. That doesn't stop them from happily collecting their unearned money for the duration of their contract. Agents don't have a problem with that. Some agents don't even have a problem with having their clients' services withheld unless their contract is renegotiated.

This is the one time a team uses something in the rules to their own advantage — it's a major crime?

Any smart team would have done the same thing. The Devils are smart. Good for them.

Hockey Annual Rating: 2 of 26

DEFENCE: The Devils have perhaps the best top four defencemen in the league in Scott Stevens, Scott Niedermayer, Ken Danyko and Lyle Odelein. The names pretty much speak for themselves. And the four of them missed a total of just 12 games last season.

New Jersey had two other regular defenceman in Shawn Chambers and Dave Ellett. Both free agents, Chambers signed with Dallas and Ellett with Boston.

That leaves just two other defencemen who laced them up for the team last year, Kevin Dean and Jason Smith, who was traded to Toronto.

There are openings on the New Jersey defence. At least one regular spot and one or two backups.

Sheldon Souray, who played in Albany last season, is projected as a regular New Jersey defenceman at some point, so that could begin this year. 1996 top draft pick, Lance Ward, might be a year away, but he might be closer if he can show something in training camp.

The Devils traded away two young defenceman last season, Jason Smith and Chris McAlpine, so obviously they're not too worried. With the top four defencemen they already have in place, filling the other two spots won't be a major problem, whether they sign free agents, bring them up from the minors or trade for them. Fringe veterans on other teams may just get the right dose of playing time in New Jersey.

Hockey Annual Rating: 4 of 26

FORWARD: The Devils knew last year that they desperately needed an offensive centre, so they did one better and got Doug Gilmour, who can also play defence.

Gilmour caught fire as soon as he arrived in New Jersey, and finished with 22 points in 20 games. But, Gilmour, one of the best playoff performers in the league, didn't score any goals in the Devils' 10 post-season games, and had just four assists. It was worth a try anyway by New Jersey, who will keep him around for a while. Gilmour's best days are behind him, but he appears to be a nice fit on this team.

Actually, Gilmour did score a goal in the playoffs, but it was called back after Mark

| GOALTENDER | GPI | MINS | AVG | W | L | T | EN | SO | GA | SA | SV % |
|---|---|---|---|---|---|---|---|---|---|---|---|
| MARTIN BRODEUR | 67 | 3838 | 1.88 | 37 | 14 | 13 | 5 | 10 | 120 | 1633 | .927 |
| MIKE DUNHAM | 26 | 1013 | 2.55 | 8 | 7 | 1 | 1 | 2 | 43 | 456 | .906 |
| JEFF REESE | 3 | 139 | 5.61 | 0 | 2 | 0 | 0 | 0 | 13 | 65 | .800 |
| N.J TOTALS | 82 | 4999 | 2.18 | 45 | 23 | 14 | 6 | 13 | 182 | 2160 | .916 |

Messier complained to the referee after seeing the replay on the big screen. They went upstairs for the instant replay and sure enough somebody had their baby toe in the crease.

The crease rule, which was universally panned, was brought up at the GM meetings and remains exactly the same as it was. Their stand is that once players get used to it, they won't go near the crease, and goalies will be protected. Whatever.

He wasn't the only veteran who played well for New Jersey. John MacLean led the team with 29 goals, and Dave Andreychuk had 27. MacLean is 33-years-old and Andreychuk is 34. Another veteran, Steve Thomas, missed 25 games and didn't have a good scoring season, with only 15.

Age doesn't seem to be as big a factor in the NHL as it was not that long ago. Better conditioning, better money, better everything, makes it more attractive for a player to prolong his career.

A number of Devils had good seasons, or came into their own. Bobby Holik wanted an increased role in the team, instead of fourth line duty, and he had 62 points, the highest for a Devil who was with the team all year. Bill Guerin, long rumored to be an up-and-coming power forward, had his best goal scoring season with 29.

Denis Pederson, another long rumored up-and-comer, up and came last year. Although his stats weren't great, he proved his value to the team in other ways, and should improve his numbers this year. And Brian Rolston, while not exactly having a breakout season, improved dramatically.

Among those not mentioned yet, are Randy McKay, a valuable guy to have around, defensive centre Peter Zezel, and Zelepukin, who has never scored much, but always looked like he could. Jay Pandolfo and

Patrick Elias earned some playing time as rookies, while Sergei Brylin also put in frequent flyer mileage between Albany and New Jersey. Petr Sykora's season was a write-off, mostly because of injuries, but even when he was available he was shipped to the minors. And Reid Simpson earned regular duty later in the season, possibly to compensate for the loss of tough Mike Peluso, who was traded to St. Louis.

Not expected back is Bob Carpenter, who became an unrestricted free agent.

The Devils have a good mixture at forward. They have their dependable veterans who can put the puck in the net, prime time players who put up decent numbers, and young players working their way into the lineup.

College star, Brendan Morrison from Michigan, may be the next rookie to get on the bottom rung with the Devils.

That's almost a perfect situation. That way you have players moving up the ladder and down the ladder at the same time, creating a nice balance.

Hockey Annual Rating: 8 of 26

SPECIAL TEAMS: Near the bottom on the power play, best in penalty killing. Just about what you'd expect.

Only 28 goals allowed shorthanded is almost in the ridiculous category. Colorado allowed the second fewest, and they still let in 42. The Devils were shorthanded the fewest ties in the league, which is part of the reason. They had 174 fewer power plays against than did San Jose, which led with 409. The Devils also had the second fewest power plays for, one more than the Rangers.

The power play was a source of concern for the Devils last year, which is why they picked up Gilmour. He should help improve the ranking, being there from the start of the season. During the playoffs, the power play became one of their bright spots and they finished fourth in the rankings.

POWER PLAY

|        | G  | ATT | PCT              |
|--------|----|-----|------------------|
| Overall | 40 | 288 | 13.9% (T-22nd NHL) |
| Home    | 21 | 138 | 15.2% (16th NHL) |
| Road    | 19 | 150 | 12.7% (22nd NHL) |

9 SHORT HANDED GOALS ALLOWED (T-9th NHL)

PENALTY KILLING

|        | G  | TSH | PCT              |
|--------|----|-----|------------------|
| Overall | 28 | 235 | 88.1% (1st NHL)  |
| Home    | 16 | 112 | 85.7% (5th NHL)  |
| Road    | 12 | 123 | 90.2% (1st NHL)  |

4 SHORT HANDED GOALS SCORED   (26th NHL)

DEVILS SPECIAL TEAMS SCORING

| Power play | G | A | PTS |
|------------|---|---|-----|
| GILMOUR     | 4 | 18 | 22 |
| NIEDERMAYER | 3 | 15 | 18 |
| HOLIK       | 5 | 8  | 13 |
| GUERIN      | 7 | 4  | 11 |
| ANDREYCHUK  | 4 | 5  | 9  |
| ROLSTON     | 2 | 7  | 9  |
| ELLETT      | 1 | 8  | 9  |
| MACLEAN     | 5 | 3  | 8  |
| ZELEPUKIN   | 3 | 3  | 6  |
| CHAMBERS    | 1 | 5  | 6  |
| STEVENS     | 0 | 6  | 6  |
| ODELEIN     | 1 | 4  | 5  |
| PEDERSON    | 3 | 1  | 4  |
| THOMAS      | 1 | 2  | 3  |
| MCKAY       | 0 | 2  | 2  |
| ZEZEL       | 0 | 1  | 1  |
| SYKORA      | 0 | 1  | 1  |
| DEAN        | 0 | 1  | 1  |

| Short handed | G | A | PTS |
|--------------|---|---|-----|
| ELLETT      | 0 | 3 | 3 |
| ROLSTON     | 2 | 0 | 2 |
| GILMOUR     | 1 | 0 | 1 |
| CARPENTER   | 1 | 0 | 1 |
| ANDREYCHUK  | 1 | 0 | 1 |
| DANEYKO     | 0 | 1 | 1 |
| CHAMBERS    | 0 | 1 | 1 |

COACHING AND MANAGEMENT: Not every player loves Jacques Lemaire. But, that's no newsflash. In fact, it's getting old. If there's a team on which everybody loves the coach, it's probably kids in minor atom or peewee.

Big deal anyway. Lemaire makes them winners, which is what they'd all like to be if they weren't already.

Lou Lamoriello runs a good organization in New Jersey. He ensures they will be competitive every year, and unlike some teams, they're competitive in the regular season and the playoffs.

Hockey Annual Rating: 2 of 26

DRAFT

| Round | Sel. | Player | Pos | Amateur Team |
|-------|------|--------|-----|--------------|
| 1 | 24  | J-F Damphousse   | G  | Moncton (QMJHL) |
| 2 | 38  | Stanislav Grohn  | C  | Slovakia |
| 4 | 104 | Lucas Nehriling   | D  | Sarnia (OHL) |
| 5 | 131 | Jiri Bicek        | W  | Slovakia |
| 6 | 159 | Sasha Goc         | D  | Germany |
| 7 | 188 | Mathieu Benoit    | RW | Chicoutimi (QMJHL) |
| 8 | 215 | Scott Clemmensen  | G  | Des Moines (USHL) |
| 9 | 241 | Jan Srdinko       | D  | Czech Rep. |

Weird stuff going on at the New Jersey draft table. First they select goalie J.F. Damphousse, who weighs all of 146 pounds and is still six feet tall. This, when they've already got one of the best three goalies in the game, who is still young.

Then they trade two third round picks for Ottawa's second selection, and take a guy rated so low, he almost wasn't rated.

The size of Damphousse isn't much of a factor in his goaltending skills. He was ranked second behind Robert Luongo by Central Scouting, and nobody would argue the point. That means he must be exceptional to overcome his slight weight.

Grohn was rated 33rd among European players but was the fifth European skater selected.

## PROGNOSIS

The Devils were one of the best teams in the league last year despite a perceived lack of offence. Nothing much has changed, except they have a little more firepower from the start of the season, so there's no reason to expect them not to perform at the same level.

Look for the Devils to be right there to the end.

## PREDICTION

Eastern Conference: 2nd
Overall: 3rd

## STAT SECTION

| Team Scoring Stats | | 1996-97 | | | | | CAREER | | | |
| --- | --- | --- | --- | --- | --- | --- | --- | --- | --- | --- |
| | GP | G | A | PTS | +/- | PIM | SH | Gm | G | A | Pts |
| DOUG GILMOUR | 81 | 22 | 60 | 82 | 2 | 68 | 143 | 1,062 | 368 | 755 | 1,123 |
| BOBBY HOLIK | 82 | 23 | 39 | 62 | 24 | 54 | 192 | 478 | 121 | 151 | 272 |
| DAVE ANDREYCHUK | 82 | 27 | 34 | 61 | 38 | 48 | 233 | 1,082 | 503 | 561 | 1,064 |
| JOHN MACLEAN | 80 | 29 | 25 | 54 | 11 | 49 | 254 | 908 | 344 | 346 | 690 |
| BILL GUERIN | 82 | 29 | 18 | 47 | 2- | 95 | 177 | 361 | 103 | 101 | 204 |
| BRIAN ROLSTON | 81 | 18 | 27 | 45 | 6 | 20 | 237 | 171 | 38 | 49 | 87 |
| VALERI ZELEPUKIN | 71 | 14 | 24 | 38 | 10- | 36 | 111 | 340 | 83 | 125 | 208 |
| S. NIEDERMAYER | 81 | 5 | 30 | 35 | 4- | 64 | 159 | 373 | 38 | 136 | 174 |
| STEVE THOMAS | 57 | 15 | 19 | 34 | 9 | 46 | 124 | 805 | 310 | 362 | 672 |
| DENIS PEDERSON | 70 | 12 | 20 | 32 | 7 | 62 | 106 | 80 | 15 | 21 | 36 |
| RANDY MCKAY | 77 | 9 | 18 | 27 | 15 | 109 | 92 | 500 | 69 | 90 | 159 |
| SCOTT STEVENS | 79 | 5 | 19 | 24 | 26 | 70 | 166 | 1,120 | 162 | 584 | 746 |
| DAVE ELLETT | 76 | 6 | 15 | 21 | 6- | 40 | 105 | 941 | 148 | 381 | 529 |
| SHAWN CHAMBERS | 73 | 4 | 17 | 21 | 17 | 19 | 114 | 503 | 46 | 154 | 200 |

| | | | | | | | | | | | |
|---|---|---|---|---|---|---|---|---|---|---|---|
| BOB CARPENTER | 62 | 4 | 15 | 19 | 6 | 14 | 76 | 1,056 | 309 | 391 | 700 |
| PETER ZEZEL | 53 | 4 | 12 | 16 | 10 | 16 | 62 | 802 | 208 | 366 | 574 |
| LYLE ODELEIN | 79 | 3 | 13 | 16 | 16 | 110 | 93 | 499 | 23 | 88 | 111 |
| JAY PANDOLFO | 46 | 6 | 8 | 14 | 1- | 6 | 61 | 46 | 6 | 8 | 14 |
| KEN DANEYKO | 77 | 2 | 7 | 9 | 24 | 70 | 63 | 873 | 32 | 109 | 141 |
| KEVIN DEAN | 28 | 2 | 4 | 6 | 2 | 6 | 21 | 86 | 2 | 11 | 13 |
| PATRIK ELIAS | 17 | 2 | 3 | 5 | 4- | 2 | 23 | 18 | 2 | 3 | 5 |
| SERGEI BRYLIN | 29 | 2 | 2 | 4 | 13- | 20 | 34 | 105 | 12 | 15 | 27 |
| REID SIMPSON | 27 | 0 | 4 | 4 | 0 | 60 | 17 | 61 | 1 | 9 | 10 |
| MARTIN BRODEUR | 67 | 0 | 4 | 4 | 0 | 8 | 0 | | | | |
| PETR SYKORA | 19 | 1 | 2 | 3 | 8- | 4 | 26 | 82 | 19 | 26 | 45 |
| PASCAL RHEAUME | 2 | 1 | 0 | 1 | 1 | 0 | 5 | 2 | 1 | 0 | 1 |
| KRZYSZTOF OLIWA | 1 | 0 | 0 | 0 | 1- | 5 | 0 | 1 | 0 | 0 | 0 |
| V. SHARIFIJANOV | 2 | 0 | 0 | 0 | 0 | 0 | 4 | 2 | 0 | 0 | 0 |
| JEFF REESE | 3 | 0 | 0 | 0 | 0 | 0 | 0 | | | | |
| MIKE DUNHAM | 26 | 0 | 0 | 0 | 0 | 2 | 0 | | | | |

## TEAM RANKINGS

| | | Conference Rank | League Rank |
|---|---|---|---|
| Record | 45-23-14 | 1 | 3 |
| Home | 23-9-9 | 2 | 3 |
| Away | 22-14-5 | 2 | 4 |
| Versus Own Conference | 29-16-11 | 1 | 3 |
| Versus Other Conference | 16-7-3 | 2 | 3 |
| Team Plus\Minus | +37 | 3 | 4 |
| Goals For | 231 | 8 | 16 |
| Goals Against | 182 | 1 | 1 |
| Average Shots For | 31.6 | 2 | 4 |
| Average Shots Against | 26.3 | 3 | 5 |
| Overtime | 1-2-14 | 10 | 19 |
| One Goal Games | 13-7 | 2 | 3 |
| Times outshooting opponent | 57 | 2 | 3 |

| | | | |
|---|---|---|---|
| Versus Teams Over .500 | 14-15-6 | 4 | 6 |
| Versus Teams Under .500 | 24-8-8 | 1 | 2 |
| First Half Record | 21-15-5 | 5 | 7 |
| Second Half Record | 24-8-9 | 1 | 1 |

## PLAYOFFS

Results: defeated Montreal 4-1
lost to NY Rangers 4-1

Record: 5-5
Home: 4-2
Away: 1-3
Goals For: 27 (2.7/game)
Goals Against: 21 (2.1/game)
Overtime: 0-2
Power play: 22.0 (4th)
Penalty Killing: 91.9 (2nd)

| | GP | G | A | PTS | +/- | PIM | PP | SH | GW | OT | S |
|---|---|---|---|---|---|---|---|---|---|---|---|
| JOHN MACLEAN | 10 | 4 | 5 | 9 | 1 | 4 | 2 | 1 | 1 | 0 | 32 |
| SHAWN CHAMBERS | 10 | 1 | 6 | 7 | 2- | 6 | 1 | 0 | 0 | 0 | 17 |
| S. NIEDERMAYER | 10 | 2 | 4 | 6 | 0 | 6 | 2 | 0 | 1 | 0 | 34 |
| BRIAN ROLSTON | 10 | 4 | 1 | 5 | 0 | 6 | 1 | 2 | 0 | 0 | 45 |
| VALERI ZELEPUKIN | 8 | 3 | 2 | 5 | 3 | 2 | 1 | 0 | 1 | 0 | 13 |
| PATRIK ELIAS | 8 | 2 | 3 | 5 | 0 | 4 | 1 | 0 | 0 | 0 | 18 |
| BOBBY HOLIK | 10 | 2 | 3 | 5 | 1 | 4 | 1 | 0 | 0 | 0 | 29 |
| LYLE ODELEIN | 10 | 2 | 2 | 4 | 3- | 19 | 1 | 0 | 0 | 0 | 27 |
| DOUG GILMOUR | 10 | 0 | 4 | 4 | 2- | 14 | 0 | 0 | 0 | 0 | 21 |
| SCOTT STEVENS | 10 | 0 | 4 | 4 | 2- | 2 | 0 | 0 | 0 | 0 | 27 |
| BILL GUERIN | 8 | 2 | 1 | 3 | 5- | 18 | 1 | 0 | 1 | 0 | 13 |
| BOB CARPENTER | 10 | 1 | 2 | 3 | 2 | 2 | 0 | 0 | 0 | 0 | 15 |
| DAVE ELLETT | 10 | 0 | 3 | 3 | 1- | 10 | 0 | 0 | 0 | 0 | 15 |
| RANDY MCKAY | 10 | 1 | 1 | 2 | 1 | 0 | 0 | 0 | 0 | 0 | 15 |
| STEVE THOMAS | 10 | 1 | 1 | 2 | 6- | 18 | 0 | 0 | 0 | 0 | 25 |
| KEVIN DEAN | 1 | 1 | 0 | 1 | 1 | 0 | 0 | 0 | 1 | 0 | 3 |
| MARTIN BRODEUR | 10 | 1 | 0 | 1 | 0 | 0 | 0 | 0 | 0 | 0 | 1 |
| JAY PANDOLFO | 6 | 0 | 1 | 1 | 2- | 0 | 0 | 0 | 0 | 0 | 11 |
| DAVE ANDREYCHUK | 1 | 0 | 0 | 0 | 0 | 0 | 0 | 0 | 0 | 0 | 5 |
| PETER ZEZEL | 2 | 0 | 0 | 0 | 0 | 10 | 0 | 0 | 0 | 0 | 4 |
| PETR SYKORA | 2 | 0 | 0 | 0 | 1 | 2 | 0 | 0 | 0 | 0 | 10 |
| REID SIMPSON | 5 | 0 | 0 | 0 | 1- | 29 | 0 | 0 | 0 | 0 | 0 |
| DENIS PEDERSON | 9 | 0 | 0 | 0 | 2- | 2 | 0 | 0 | 0 | 0 | 6 |
| KEN DANEYKO | 10 | 0 | 0 | 0 | 1 | 28 | 0 | 0 | 0 | 0 | 8 |

| GOALTENDER | GPI | MINS | AVG | W | L | T | EN | SO | GA | SA | SV % |
|---|---|---|---|---|---|---|---|---|---|---|---|
| MARTIN BRODEUR | 10 | 659 | 1.73 | 5 | 5 | 2 | 2 | 1 | 9 | 268 | .929 |
| N.J TOTALS | 10 | 662 | 1.90 | 5 | 5 | 2 | 2 | 2 | 1 | 270 | .922 |

## ALL-TIME LEADERS

Goals
| | |
|---|---|
| John MacLean | 344 |
| Kirk Muller | 185 |
| Pat Verbeek | 170 |

Assists
| | |
|---|---|
| John MacLean | 346 |
| Kirk Muller | 335 |
| Bruce Driver | 328 |

Points
| | |
|---|---|
| John MacLean | 690 |
| Kirk Muller | 520 |
| Aaron Broten | 469 |

## BEST INDIVIDUAL SEASONS

Goals
| | | |
|---|---|---|
| Pat Verbeek | 1987-88 | 46 |
| John MacLean | 1990-91 | 45 |
| John MacLean | 1988-89 | 42 |

Assists
| | | |
|---|---|---|
| Scott Stevens | 1993-94 | 60 |
| Aaron Broten | 1987-88 | 57 |
| Kirk Muller | 1987-88 | 57 |

Points
| | | |
|---|---|---|
| Kirk Muller | 1987-88 | 94 |
| John MacLean | 1988-89 | 87 |
| Kirk Muller | 1989-90 | 86 |

## TEAM

Last 3 years
| | GP | W | L | T | Pts | % |
|---|---|---|---|---|---|---|
| 1996-97 | 82 | 45 | 23 | 14 | 104 | .634 |
| 1995-96 | 82 | 37 | 33 | 12 | 86 | .524 |
| 1994-95 | 48 | 22 | 18 | 8 | 52 | .542 |

Best 3 regular seasons
| | | | | | | |
|---|---|---|---|---|---|---|
| 1996-97 | 82 | 45 | 23 | 14 | 104 | .634 |
| 1993-95 | 84 | 47 | 25 | 12 | 106 | .631 |
| 1994-95 | 48 | 22 | 18 | 8 | 52 | .542 |

Worst 3 regular seasons
| | | | | | | |
|---|---|---|---|---|---|---|
| 1975-76 | 80 | 12 | 56 | 12 | 36 | .225 |
| 1983-84 | 80 | 17 | 56 | 7 | 41 | .256 |
| 1974-75 | 80 | 15 | 54 | 11 | 41 | .256 |

Most Goals (min. 70 game schedule)
| | |
|---|---|
| 1992-93 | 308 |
| 1993-94 | 306 |
| 1985-86 | 300 |

Fewest Goals (min. 70 game schedule)
| | |
|---|---|
| 1974-75 | 184 |
| 1975-76 | 190 |
| 1978-79 | 210 |

Most Goals Against (min. 70 game schedule)
| | |
|---|---|
| 1985-86 | 374 |
| 1986-87 | 368 |
| 1981-82 | 362 |

Fewest Goals Against (min. 70 game schedule)
| | |
|---|---|
| 1996-97 | 182 |
| 1995-96 | 202 |
| 1993-94 | 220 |

# New York Islanders

Some teams grow up all at once and some teams take baby-steps until they're ready to walk with the big boys.

The Islanders, of course, are still tip-toeing along. There are signs, however, that they are ready to graduate:

* they were outscored by only 10 goals on the season, an improvement of 76 over the previous year's difference of 86.

* after the trading deadline, they had one of the best lines in hockey with Bryan Smolinski, Robert Reichel and Zigmund Palffy.

* have two of the best young goalies in the game in Tommy Salo and Eric Fichaud. Not to mention draft selection Roberto Luongo.

* it appears that rookie defenceman Bryan Berard is going to be one of the better offensive defencemen in the game.

* their second half record was better than Florida's.

* the Islanders were active in the free agent market, signing Sergei Nemchinov, Mike Hough, and Wade Flaherty, as of press time.

There are also signs that they're not necessarily ready to make a jump forward:

* potential is only potential until it becomes realized.

* forwards are small, and the big guys are playing small.

* despite improvements, the Isles were still 22nd overall and only nine points from finishing last.

* the ownership situation is as screwed up as it gets, with John Spano buying the team and then not having the money to pay for it. It makes for a lot of uncertainty around the team.

## STUFF

* Berard was eight points short of the team record for rookie defencemen, held by Stefan Persson in 1977-78 when he had 56.
* at the 30-game mark, the Islandes were 11-11-8.
* Tommy Salo shut out the Washington Capitals three times.
* not that divisions mean much, but the Islanders were 14-14-4 in the Atlantic, which is the best of the divisions. Versus other divisions they were 15-27-8, second worst in the league.

\* Roberto Luongo's was selected fourth over-all by the Islanders, the highest a goalie has ever been drafted.

## STAT ANALYSIS

Wasn't that something, the way that Robert Reichel came over from the Flames and set the league on fire? Yeah, wasn't that something?

Just another quick question, though.

What the heck was he doing in Calgary?

Already have the answer on that one, because it's easy. He was doing nothing.

So, what happened on the plane ride from Calgary?

What happened to Reichel is something that happens frequently. Players traded during the season almost always have better offensive stats with their new team.

There are plenty of reasons for it: a fresh start, a useful role in mind by the team that traded for him, fewer distractions in an unfamiliar city, and a desire to impress.

One important thing to keep in mind, however, is that it usually only lasts for the one season. After the new car smell wears off they revert back to the way they were before.

I selected some traded players from last year and projected their stats over 82 games with their old team and their new team. It works with almost every player traded, but

none as much as Reichel. His projected 82-game total went from 50 to 130.

## TEAM PREVIEW

GOAL: Before last season, Eric Fichaud was the goalie of the future. Then throw in Tommy Salo and the Islanders had two goalies of the future. In the meantime, they discarded Tommy Soderstrom as a goalie of the future, and made him a goalie of the past.

Then at the draft, they selected who some believe is the ultimate goalie of the future, Robert Luongo.

The Islanders also signed Wade Flaherty, ex of the San Jose Sharks, during the summer. What they need with him is anyone's guess, but we may find out if Milbury trades one of the young goalies.

Mark McArthur is in the unenviable position of being next on the Islanders' goalie of the future depth chart. He played in Utah last season, but won't get a chance with the big team unless somebody gets hurt.

Hockey Annual Rating: 18 of 26

DEFENCE: The Islanders have a nucleus of four defencemen around whom to build: Bryan Berard, Bryan McCabe, Kenny Jonsson and Scott Lachance.

Not a bad group, but far from outstanding.

| | Old Team | | | | New Team | | | |
|---|---|---|---|---|---|---|---|---|
| | Team | Gms | Pts | Projected | Team | Gms | Pts | Projected |
| Jason Allison | Wsh | 53 | 22 | 34 | Bos | 19 | 12 | 52 |
| Anson Carter | Wsh | 19 | 5 | 22 | Bos | 19 | 13 | 56 |
| Doug Gilmour | Tor | 61 | 60 | 81 | NJ | 20 | 22 | 90 |
| Dmitri Mironov | Pit | 15 | 6 | 33 | Ana | 62 | 46 | 61 |
| Glen Murray | Pit | 66 | 22 | 27 | LA | 11 | 8 | 60 |
| Ed Olczyk | LA | 67 | 44 | 54 | Pit | 12 | 11 | 75 |
| ROBERT REICHEL | Cgy | 70 | 43 | 50 | NYI | 12 | 19 | 130 |

| GOALTENDER | GPI | MINS | AVG | W | L | T | EN | SO | GA | SA | SV % |
|---|---|---|---|---|---|---|---|---|---|---|---|
| T. SODERSTROM | 1 | 0 | .00 | 0 | 0 | 0 | 0 | 0 | 0 | 0 | .000 |
| TOMMY SALO | 58 | 3208 | 2.82 | 20 | 27 | 8 | 7 | 5 | 151 | 1576 | .904 |
| ERIC FICHAUD | 34 | 1759 | 3.10 | 9 | 14 | 4 | 1 | 0 | 91 | 897 | .899 |
| NYI TOTALS | 82 | 4988 | 3.01 | 29 | 41 | 12 | 8 | 5 | 250 | 2481 | .899 |

Praise was high from Toronto when the Islanders acquired Jonsson, but that's because there was so little else there in the way of defenceman. Jonsson was never as good as suggested, nor will be. But, he can play in the NHL and be a mid-range offensive threat and zero physical threat. He only had 24 penalty minutes in 81 games so you can assume he utilized a hands-off approach to enemy snipers. Five goalies in the league had more penalty minutes.

McCabe, who has not missed a game in two years, is more of a physical type and better offensively than Jonsson, while Lachance is defensive-oriented.

Berard is one of those players where the other parts of his game aren't going to matter, similar to a Phil Housley or Paul Coffey in his prime. His offensive talents are plenty enough so whatever else he contributes is a bonus. So far, he has not been the expected major defensive liability.

The Islanders will fill in the blanks with Rich Pilon and Denis Vaske, and any free agent veterans the team can sign.

Another young defenceman may also be on the way, and he's a giant. Zdeno Charo is 6-8, 231 pounds. Yvegeny Namestnikov was signed out of Vancouver so he can play on the Islanders' farm team.

Jason Holland could get a chance to stick this year. He's an offensive type (14-25-39 with Kentucky in AHL) something not in short supply on the Islanders. Jason Strudwick, who also played in Kentucky, is the opposite of an offensive defenceman and could get a look.

Too much youth here. They can't all play. Some, such as McCabe, are coveted by other teams, so if the Islanders have pressing needs they can trade one or two and still not be lacking in potential.

Defence is the position where you least like to have so many kids. That's because it's the hardest position to learn properly at the NHL level. Inexperience means too many mistakes, so look for free agent veteran signees or trades to provide leadership and experience on the blueline.

Hockey Annual Rating: 11 of 26

FORWARD: When the Islanders made a late-season deal with Calgary to get Robert Reichel, they got more than they bargained for when he combined with Zigmund Pallfy and Bryan Smolinski to form one of the best lines in hockey.

In the Reichel's first five games the Isles were 4-0-1 and scored 27 goals. Reichel has 12 points, Palffy 11 and Smolinski nine.

After that initial burst, things quieted down considerably. The Isles went 1-5-1 for the rest of the season, scoring 19 goals in the seven games.

Overall, with Reichel on the team, the Islanders were 5-5-2 and averaged 4.0 goals per game, compared to 2.7 before he arrived. Goals against per game also increased, however, from 3.0 to 3.5.

Reichel's arrival, then, should be treated as the glass half empty. Traded players almost invariably (see stat analysis) perform well over the short term with their new team. He had 19 points in 12 games for the Islanders.

Reichel performed so horribly with Calgary before he arrived, you have to wonder some about him. Maybe the same thing will happen to him again. Who knows? Can he be trusted?

There are no questions about Palffy. He has emerged as a premier player with back-to-back exceptional seasons. Forty-three and 48 goals, along with 87 and 90 points are evidence of that.

As for that line, it's not that big a deal. They were awesome for a short period, but the chances of them remaining a unit for long is minimal. It just doesn't happen anymore in the NHL. Probably what you'll see is them playing together, then breaking up when they don't score or another line needs help, then with much fanfare they'll return as a line again, and then later they split them up. Got that?

After that first line, there's not much left. Centre Travis Green is a proven commodity, the type of player with an all-round game that any team would like to have. Sergei Nemchinov was signed as a free agent and is expected to also play a strong two-way game. Right winger Todd Bertuzzi is still unproven, and if he doesn't get his act together will be unplayed. The Islanders want him to be a physical presence on the ice and develop into a power forward. He's reluctant to play that way on a consistent basis, so no matter how hard Bertuzzi and the Isles try, he's not going to end up as that type of player. His sophomore season was terrible, mired by long slumps. But, he's a scorer, and this is his third season, so look for a breakout season from him. Or else.

The Isles can put together a checking line ot two, starting with Claude Lapointe at centre. He started off the year in Utah, played great and got the call to the big team, where he also played well as a defensive forward.

Paul Kruse and Dan Plante are checkers as is free agent signee Mike Hough.

Rounding out the forward hopefuls are tough guys Steve Webb and Ken Belanger. Last year's top draft pick, Jean-Pierre Dumont, would have to show an awful lot to make the team this year.

Milbury says he wants the team to get bigger on the wings. That's a no-brainer because they're puny. Almost all of them. So many little fellas. Probably the smallest forward unit in the league. Reichel, Palffy, Andersson, Plante and Lapointe are all key forwards who don't meet the height requirement for a prototypical forward in today's NHL.

A player doesn't have to be big to be successful, but a team probably does.

Hockey Annual Rating: 14 of 26

SPECIAL TEAMS: Can Reichel be the difference between a lousy power play and a good one? He can if the results from his late season acquision are any indication. The Islanders had a 12.9% power play efficiency rate before Reichel, and 19.6% after he joined the team. That's quite a difference, but unproven over a lengthy period.

Palffy didn't score very often with the man-advantage last year for some reason, so he could move back up from just six goals closer to the 17 he had the previous season. Reichel and Smolinski can do well if the trio remains together, and they have an ace in the hole with Green, who led the team with 10 last year.

Penalty killing was decent, right in the middle of the pack, which was a big improvement. At the start of the year, before they called up Lapointe, the Isles were in more familiar territory, down near the bottom of the rankings.

POWER PLAY

|  | G | ATT | PCT |
|---|---|---|---|
| Overall | 48 | 346 | 13.9% (T-22nd NHL) |
| Home | 22 | 167 | 13.2% (T-24th NHL) |
| Road | 26 | 179 | 14.5% (20th NHL) |

9 SHORT HANDED GOALS ALLOWED (T-9th NHL)

PENALTY KILLING

|  | G | TSH | PCT |
|---|---|---|---|
| Overall | 53 | 319 | 83.4% (T-14th NHL) |
| Home | 27 | 151 | 82.1% (21st NHL) |
| Road | 26 | 168 | 84.5% (14th NHL) |

14 SHORT HANDED GOALS SCORED (T-4th NHL)

ISLANDERS SPECIAL TEAMS SCORING

| Power play | G | A | PTS |
|---|---|---|---|
| PALFFY | 6 | 15 | 21 |
| REICHEL | 6 | 14 | 20 |
| BERARD | 3 | 17 | 20 |
| GREEN | 10 | 9 | 19 |
| SMOLINSKI | 9 | 9 | 18 |
| MCCABE | 2 | 4 | 6 |
| ANDERSSON | 1 | 5 | 6 |
| BERTUZZI | 3 | 2 | 5 |
| JONSSON | 1 | 4 | 5 |
| LACHANCE | 1 | 2 | 3 |
| WEBB | 1 | 1 | 2 |
| HOUDA | 0 | 2 | 2 |
| MCLLWAIN | 1 | 0 | 1 |
| ARMSTRONG | 0 | 1 | 1 |

| Short handed | G | A | PTS |
|---|---|---|---|
| PALFFY | 4 | 2 | 6 |
| LAPOINTE | 3 | 0 | 3 |
| WOOD | 1 | 2 | 3 |
| ANDERSSON | 1 | 2 | 3 |
| PLANTE | 2 | 0 | 2 |
| REICHEL | 1 | 0 | 1 |
| MCCABE | 1 | 0 | 1 |

COACHING AND MANAGEMENT: Mike Milbury seems like a guy who's going to explode at any time. He's a tough, in-your-face type of guy who expects nothing less than better than his players are able to provide. If they don't give it they'll hear about it one way or another.

He gave up the coaching reigns partway through last season and handed them over to Rick Bowness. As a GM he's made some of the better trades in the last couple years.

Last year, he got Bryan Smolinski for Darius Kaspairitis and Andreas Johansson. And he got Robert Reichel for Marty McInnis, goalie prospect Tyrone Garner and sixth round pick in 1997. In other words he traded for two-thirds of his top line. That's not something teams can do normally. He stole Eric Fichaud from Toronto and also got their number one pick in this year's draft.

Bowness is a hard-working coach who suffered through the Ottawa Senators worst seasons. If that's preparation for something, than he's got plenty of it.

Hockey Annual Rating: 12 of 26

DRAFT

| Round | Sel. | Player | Pos | Amateur Team |
|---|---|---|---|---|
| 1 | 4 | Roberto Luongo | G | Val d'or (QMJHL) |
| 1 | 5 | Eric Brewer | D | Prince George (WHL) |
| 2 | 31 | Jeff Zehr | LW | Windsor (OHL) |
| 3 | 59 | Jarrett Smith | C | Prince George (WHL) |
| 3 | 79 | Robert Schnabel | D | Czech Rep. |
| 4 | 85 | Petr Mika | C | Czech Rep. |
| 5 | 115 | Adam Edinger | C | Bowling Green |
| 6 | 139 | Bobby Leavins | LW | Brandon (WHL) |

| 7 | 166 | Kris Knoblauch | LW | Edmonton (WHL) |
|---|-----|----------------|----|----------------|
| 8 | 196 | Jeremy Symington | G | Petrolia (WOJHL) |
| 9 | 222 | Ryan Clark | D | Lincoln (USHL) |

Robert Luongo's selection at fourth overall is the highest a goalie has ever been drafted. The Islanders don't have an immediate need at the position, but couldn't pass him up.

Eric Brewer, taken fifth, is expected to be a solid NHL defenceman who will add character and eventually leadership.

PROGNOSIS: With a good run at the end of last season, the Islanders could have made the playoffs. But, they also weren't that far out of last place overall.

This is not a championship team, but if things go right the playoffs aren't out of the question. Much depends on how well they shore up defensively, if youthful underachievers such as Bertuzzi come through, and if Reichel can stay on track and play as well as he did earlier in his career.

Still too many question marks to be able to accent the positive, but a leap in the standings isn't out of the question.

PREDICTION

Eastern Conference: 12th
Overall: 22nd

STAT SECTION

| Team Scoring Stats | | 1996-97 | | | | | CAREER | | | | |
|--------------------|----|----|----|-----|-----|-----|-----|-----|-----|-----|-----|
| | GP | G | A | PTS | +/- | PIM | SH | Gm | G | A | Pts |
| ZIGMUND PALFFY | 80 | 48 | 42 | 90 | 21 | 43 | 292 | 199 | 101 | 93 | 194 |
| TRAVIS GREEN | 79 | 23 | 41 | 64 | 5- | 38 | 177 | 334 | 78 | 133 | 211 |
| ROBERT REICHEL | 82 | 21 | 41 | 62 | 5 | 26 | 214 | 437 | 158 | 215 | 373 |
| BRYAN SMOLINSKI | 64 | 28 | 28 | 56 | 8 | 25 | 183 | 281 | 102 | 104 | 206 |
| BRYAN BERARD | 82 | 8 | 40 | 48 | 1 | 86 | 172 | 82 | 8 | 40 | 48 |
| NIKLAS ANDERSSON | 74 | 12 | 31 | 43 | 4 | 57 | 122 | 124 | 26 | 44 | 70 |
| BRYAN MCCABE | 82 | 8 | 20 | 28 | 2- | 165 | 117 | 164 | 15 | 36 | 51 |
| TODD BERTUZZI | 64 | 10 | 13 | 23 | 3- | 68 | 79 | 140 | 28 | 34 | 62 |
| KENNY JONSSON | 81 | 3 | 18 | 21 | 10 | 24 | 92 | 186 | 9 | 51 | 60 |
| CLAUDE LAPOINTE | 73 | 13 | 5 | 18 | 11- | 49 | 80 | 361 | 31 | 23 | 54 |
| SCOTT LACHANCE | 81 | 3 | 11 | 14 | 7- | 47 | 97 | 328 | 23 | 60 | 83 |
| DEREK ARMSTRONG | 50 | 6 | 7 | 13 | 8- | 33 | 36 | 70 | 7 | 10 | 17 |
| DAN PLANTE | 67 | 4 | 9 | 13 | 6- | 75 | 61 | 267 | 51 | 96 | 147 |
| RANDY WOOD | 65 | 6 | 5 | 11 | 7- | 61 | 96 | 741 | 175 | 159 | 334 |
| BRENT HUGHES | 51 | 7 | 3 | 10 | 4- | 57 | 47 | 357 | 41 | 39 | 80 |

| Name | | | | | | | | | | | |
|---|---|---|---|---|---|---|---|---|---|---|---|
| DOUG HOUDA | 70 | 2 | 8 | 10 | 1 | 99 | 29 | 501 | 17 | 58 | 75 |
| PAUL KRUSE | 62 | 6 | 2 | 8 | 9- | 141 | 49 | 294 | 28 | 31 | 59 |
| STEVE WEBB | 41 | 1 | 4 | 5 | 10- | 144 | 21 | 41 | 1 | 4 | 5 |
| RICHARD PILON | 52 | 1 | 4 | 5 | 4 | 179 | 17 | 372 | 6 | 41 | 47 |
| DENNIS VASKE | 17 | 0 | 4 | 4 | 3 | 12 | 19 | 213 | 5 | 38 | 43 |
| DAVE MCLLWAIN | 4 | 1 | 1 | 2 | 2- | 0 | 3 | 501 | 100 | 107 | 207 |
| KEN BELANGER | 18 | 0 | 2 | 2 | 1- | 102 | 5 | 28 | 0 | 2 | 2 |
| JASON HOLLAND | 4 | 1 | 0 | 1 | 1 | 0 | 3 | 4 | 1 | 0 | 1 |
| MICK VUKOTA | 17 | 1 | 0 | 1 | 2- | 71 | 7 | 510 | 16 | 29 | 45 |
| TOMMY SALO | 58 | 0 | 1 | 1 | 0 | 4 | 0 | | | | |
| TOMMY SODERSTROM | 1 | 0 | 0 | 0 | 0 | 0 | 0 | | | | |
| CHRIS TAYLOR | 1 | 0 | 0 | 0 | 0 | 0 | 1 | 22 | 0 | 4 | 4 |
| NICK VACHON | 1 | 0 | 0 | 0 | 1- | 0 | 0 | 1 | 0 | 0 | 0 |
| JARRETT DEULING | 1 | 0 | 0 | 0 | 0 | 0 | 0 | 1 | 0 | 0 | 0 |
| MIKE DONNELLY | 3 | 0 | 0 | 0 | 0 | 2 | 5 | 465 | 114 | 121 | 235 |
| JIM DOWD | 3 | 0 | 0 | 0 | 1- | 0 | 0 | 96 | 11 | 29 | 40 |
| ANDREI VASILIEV | 3 | 0 | 0 | 0 | 3- | 2 | 1 | 4 | 0 | 0 | 0 |
| DAVID ARCHIBALD | 7 | 0 | 0 | 0 | 4- | 4 | 4 | 323 | 57 | 67 | 124 |
| COREY FOSTER | 7 | 0 | 0 | 0 | 2- | 2 | 1 | 45 | 5 | 6 | 11 |
| ERIC FICHAUD | 34 | 0 | 0 | 0 | 0 | 2 | 0 | | | | |

## TEAM RANKINGS

| | | Conference Rank | League Rank |
|---|---|---|---|
| Record | 29-41-12 | 12 | 22 |
| Home | 19-18-4 | 9 | 17 |
| Away | 10-23-8 | 11 | 23 |
| Versus Own Conference | 22-27-7 | 10 | 18 |
| Versus Other Conference | 7-14-5 | 11 | 23 |
| Team Plus\Minus | -5 | 7 | 14 |
| Goals For | 240 | 6 | 12 |
| Goals Against | 250 | 9 | 18 |
| Average Shots For | 26.6 | 12 | 25 |
| Average Shots Against | 30.2 | 8 | 16 |
| Overtime | 3-2-12 | 4 | 9 |
| One Goal Games | 7-15 | 13 | 26 |
| Times outshooting opponent | 25 | 11 | 21 |
| Versus Teams Over .500 | 14-21-6 | 9 | 18 |
| Versus Teams Under .500 | 15-20-6 | 12 | 24 |
| First Half Record | 12-21-8 | 12 | 25 |
| Second Half Record | 17-20-4 | 7 | 16 |

PLAYOFFS

- did not make the playoffs

ALL-TIME LEADERS

Goals
| | |
|---|---|
| Mike Bossy | 573 |
| Bryan Trottier | 500 |
| Denis Potvin | 310 |

Assists
| | |
|---|---|
| Bryan Trottier | 853 |
| Denis Potvin | 742 |
| Mike Bossy | 553 |

Points
| | |
|---|---|
| Bryan Trottier | 1,153 |
| Mike Bossy | 1,126 |
| Denis Potvin | 1,052 |

BEST INDIVIDUAL SEASONS

Goals
| | | |
|---|---|---|
| Mike Bossy | 1978-79 | 69 |
| Mike Bossy | 1980-81 | 68 |
| Mike Bossy | 1981-82 | 64 |

Assists
| | | |
|---|---|---|
| Bryan Trottier | 1978-79 | 87 |
| Mike Bossy | 1981-82 | 83 |
| Bryan Trottier | 1981-82 | 79 |

Points
| | | |
|---|---|---|
| Mike Bossy | 1981-82 | 147 |
| Bryan Trottier | 1978-79 | 134 |
| Pierre Turgeon | 1992-93 | 132 |

TEAM

Last 3 years
| | GP | W | L | T | Pts | % |
|---|---|---|---|---|---|---|
| 1996-97 | 82 | 29 | 41 | 12 | 70 | .427 |
| 1995-96 | 82 | 22 | 50 | 10 | 54 | .329 |
| 1994-95 | 48 | 15 | 28 | 5 | 35 | .365 |

Best 3 regular seasons
| | | | | | | |
|---|---|---|---|---|---|---|
| 1981-82 | 80 | 54 | 16 | 10 | 118 | .738 |
| 1978-79 | 80 | 51 | 15 | 14 | 116 | .725 |
| 1977-78 | 80 | 48 | 17 | 5 | 111 | .694 |

Worst 3 regular seasons
| | | | | | | |
|---|---|---|---|---|---|---|
| 1972-73 | 78 | 12 | 60 | 6 | 30 | .192 |
| 1995-96 | 82 | 22 | 50 | 10 | 54 | .329 |
| 1973-74 | 78 | 19 | 41 | 18 | 56 | .359 |

Most Goals (min. 70 game schedule)
| | |
|---|---|
| 1981-82 | 385 |
| 1978-79 | 358 |
| 1983-84 | 357 |

Fewest Goals (min. 70 game schedule)
| | |
|---|---|
| 1972-73 | 170 |
| 1973-74 | 185 |
| 1990-91 | 223 |

Most Goals Against (min. 70 game schedule)
| | |
|---|---|
| 1972-73 | 347 |
| 1988-89 | 325 |
| 1995-96 | 315 |

Fewest Goals Against (min. 70 game schedule)
| | |
|---|---|
| 1975-76 | 190 |
| 1976-77 | 193 |
| 1977-78 | 210 |

# New York Rangers

Hey, guess what?

The Rangers are going for the Stanley Cup this year.

Oh...what's that? They were going for it last year, too.

Well, they're not kidding around this time. During the summer they signed free agents Brian Skrudland and Mike Keane.

Assuming they won't miss Mark Messier, they still have Wayne Gretzky, Luc Robitaille, and some others, so there's little reason to hold back. In fact, there's no reason. With a veteran team like this, it's now or never (or maybe next year).

Neil Smith and the Rangers have a fairly simple plan in effect. They have many old stars, veterans of the Stanley Cup wars who know what it takes to win. They have big, tough defenceman and an offensive threat in Brian Leetch that few teams can match, and they have a money goalie in Mike Richter.

Where they've been messing around is with the supporting cast on the forward lines. They have just a couple young regulars, in Niklas Sundstrom, Darren Langdon and Alexei Kovalev. And they've used a couple younger guys, Daniel Goneau and Christian Dube, in smaller doses.

The rest of the supporting cast has been defensive players, such as Mike Eastwood, Pat Flatley, Bill Berg and Esa Tikkanen. Throw in Russ Courtnall for speed and a couple tryouts hoping for miracles, such as David Oliver.

It appears now that the experimentation is over. Skrudland is a top of the line defensive centre who is also a team-leader, and right winger Mike Keane is in the same mold. Two of the best in the league in that role. They're envisioned to make up a third line with Berg on the left side that would absolutely drive opposing teams nuts. And would be a heck of a thing come the playoffs.

There may be a problem or two with the first two lines, but with no time to spare they'll figure those out.

Will it be enough to make the Rangers Stanley Cup champions?

Could be.

## SHORTS

* the Rangers start of 0-3-2 was their worst since the 1958-59 season.
* with goals in five consecutive games, Daniel Goneau was just one short of the team record.
* Mark Messier led the league with 11 short-handed points.
* Messier became the all-time leader in play-off games with 236.
* Messier is just 23 assists away from 1,000.
* Luc Robitaille is just 38 points away from 1,000.
* Brian Leetch moved into second last season on the Rangers all-time assist list, passing Jean Ratelle.

* Wayne Gretzky's 72 assists last year was tied for the third most ever by a Ranger. It was only eight short of the all-time lead of 80, held by Brian Leetch.
* the Ranges were one of only two teams (Anaheim) undefeated in regular season overtime.

## STAT ANALYSIS

We know the Rangers are built for the play-offs and not the regular season. They've got seasoned veterans of the Cup wars whose main desire is to get back there and do it again.

There is strong statistical evidence to support that. Last year, the Rangers came to play in important games, ones that come close to mirroring the playoffs. But, against weaker teams they had a rough time.

Only three teams had better records versus over .500 teams than under .500 teams: NY Rangers, Tampa Bay and Calgary. Nobody came close to the difference of .152 in winning percentage. Tampa Bay was .024 and Calgary .010.

Best Versus Over .500 Teams

|  | W | L | T | % |
|---|---|---|---|---|
| Colorado | 17 | 9 | 8 | .618 |
| NY RANGERS | 19 | 11 | 7 | .608 |
| Philadelphia | 19 | 12 | 5 | .597 |

Same Teams, Versus Under .500

| Colorado | 32 | 15 | 1 | .677 |
| NY RANGERS | 19 | 23 | 3 | .456 |
| Philadelphia | 26 | 12 | 8 | .652 |

## TEAM PREVIEW

GOAL: Mike Richter is coming off a very busy year. He was the MVP in the World Cup for the United States, where he put on one of the best displays of goaltending any time any place.

Little wonder that part of the time during the regular season, he was just ordinary, although he did go through some excellent stretches. And little wonder, also, that once the playoffs rolled around, he was back to his awesome self. It wasn't quite enough to carry them all the way to the finals, but close enough, and they beat out some good teams along the way.

With dependable Glenn Healy lost to free agency, the Rangers will need a backup to Healy. It doesn't seem like too high a priority, because Richter's going to play the majority of the time, but they do want somebody decent in case Richter gets hurt or needs a rest.

A most likely candidate is Dan Cloutier, considered an excellent prospect, despite a poor statistical season with a poor team in Binghamton.

Hockey Annual Rating: 4 of 26

DEFENCE: The Rangers have everything you need in a defence corps. It starts with the best defenceman in the league, Norris Trophy winner Brian Leetch. That's a nice start.

Then, you have the big tough veterans in Jeff Beukeboom and Ulf Samuelsson.

Then you have a couple guys who can contribute offensively in Bruce Driver and

| GOALTENDER | GPI | MINS | AVG | W | L | T | EN | SO | GA | SA | SV % |
|---|---|---|---|---|---|---|---|---|---|---|---|
| GLENN HEALY | 23 | 1357 | 2.61 | 5 | 12 | 4 | 2 | 1 | 59 | 632 | .907 |
| MIKE RICHTER | 61 | 3598 | 2.68 | 33 | 22 | 6 | 9 | 4 | 161 | 1945 | .917 |
| NYR TOTALS | 82 | 4974 | 2.79 | 38 | 34 | 10 | 11 | 5 | 231 | 2588 | .911 |

Alexander Karpovstev. Then there's big prospect Eric Cairns, and possibly veteran Doug Lidster, a free agent, will be re-signed as insurance.

The Rangers don't have any worries at this position at the moment, but if they had a bunch of injuries at the same time, they'd be in an interesting predicament.

With most of the players old, even for defencemen, they're going to have to revamp this position in the next couple years. That's a lot easier to do in this era, however, because of free agency. They don't have much in the way of defence prospects so that may be their only way to go.

For now, however, the focus is this year, and this year alone. That is if they intend to go all the way.

Hockey Annual Rating: 6 of 26

FORWARD: That Wayne Gretzky guy never ceases to amaze. His 97 points tied him for fourth in league scoring. The 36-year-old will let us all know when he can't do it anymore, but he probably doesn't have much more than 10 or so good years left.

Gretzky makes up for Mark Messier, however, who looks like he may be slowing down. He was an unrestricted free agent during the summer, and signed with Vancouver.

One of the problems both Gretzky and Messier had on the Rangers is a lack of dependable scoring from their wingers. At one time, it didn't much matter who their wingers were, and to some extent it still doesn't, but it's getting to be more important.

They can count on Adam Graves, but after that there are question marks. Sundstrom did okay, although not spectacular, and Luc Robitaille, who scored 24 goals isn't going to make Ranger fans happy unless he scored 40.

Kovalev is the other scoring winger, or supposed scoring winger. He has played five years in the league, and has surpassed the statute of limitations for becoming a superstar. If he hasn't got his act together by now, chances are he never will. So, he'll remain the most talented 20-goal scorer in the NHL.

There are likely to be changes in the two top lines, but the third line looks like it will be a keeper for a while, at least until the season starts. Skrudland will centre Berg on the left and Keane on the right. They won't score a heck of a lot, but they won't need to, their value coming in leadership, committment, tenacity, character, dressing room presence and checking ability.

The fourth line should have tough guys like newcomer Mike Peluson, tough guy holdovers Shane Churla and Darren Langdon, checking centre Mike Eastwood, and youngsters Christian Dube and Daniel Goneau.

Even with the loss of Tikkanen, Courtnall and Pat Flatley to free agency, the Rangers still have some depth here. The Ferraro brothers, Chris and Peter, would like to find room on the team for reasons other than injury replacement. The same with Vladimir Vorobiev, who made a big splash for a week or two when he was called up last year.

Goneau was another who made a good first impression but couldn't keep it up. He had five goals in the Rangers' first nine games, all of those in consecutive contests. He was an early contender for rookie of the year, but it didn't last long.

As it stands, the Rangers are still going to score a lot of goals, and with their new players they're going to prevent more of them, too. The missing piece of the puzzle is a Brendan Shanahan or a Claude Lemieux. Forget Shanahan, but offer Kovalev and something else to the Avalanche and they might bite.

Hockey Annual Rating: 4 of 26

SPECIAL TEAMS: Very interesting special teams play on the Rangers last year. They finish first on the power play, and second in fewest shorthanded goals allowed. Then, on the penalty killing they finish second last, but second from the top in shorthanded goals scored. Go figure.

The penalty killing-shorthanded goal thing is sometimes easily explained, and it's not that uncommon these days. Teams put out their high priced offensive talent out when short a man, where as they used to put out the low-priced defensive help. The offensive guys look at penalty killing as an opportunity to score goals, and it changes their thinking. Instead of concentrating solely on stopping goals, they've got something else on their minds.

The power play on the Rangers is easily explained too. Brian Leetch, Wayne Gretzky, and Adam Graves.

POWER PLAY

|  | G | ATT | PCT |
|---|---|---|---|
| Overall | 63 | 287 | 22.0% (1st NHL) |
| Home | 32 | 135 | 23.7% (1st NHL) |
| Road | 31 | 152 | 20.4% (4th NHL) |

5 SHORT HANDED GOALS ALLOWED (2nd NHL)

PENALTY KILLING

|  | G | TSH | PCT |
|---|---|---|---|
| Overall | 69 | 344 | 79.9% (25th NHL) |
| Home | 33 | 166 | 80.1% (25th NHL) |
| Road | 36 | 178 | 79.8% (24th NHL) |

15 SHORT HANDED GOALS SCORED (T-2nd NHL)

RANGERS SPECIAL TEAMS SCORING

| Power play | G | A | PTS |
|---|---|---|---|
| GRETZKY | 6 | 25 | 31 |
| LEETCH | 9 | 21 | 30 |

| | | | |
|---|---|---|---|
| KARPOVTSEV | 6 | 13 | 19 |
| MESSIER | 7 | 11 | 18 |
| GRAVES | 10 | 6 | 16 |
| ROBITAILLE | 5 | 9 | 14 |
| DRIVER | 2 | 12 | 14 |
| TIKKANEN | 4 | 8 | 12 |
| COURTNALL | 2 | 7 | 9 |
| KOVALEV | 1 | 8 | 9 |
| SUNDSTROM | 5 | 2 | 7 |
| GONEAU | 3 | 1 | 4 |
| VOROBIEV | 2 | 1 | 3 |
| DUBE | 1 | 1 | 2 |
| SAMUELSSON | 1 | 0 | 1 |
| OLIVER | 0 | 1 | 1 |
| FLATLEY | 0 | 1 | 1 |
| FERRARO | 0 | 1 | 1 |

| Short handed | G | A | PTS |
|---|---|---|---|
| MESSIER | 5 | 6 | 11 |
| GRAVES | 4 | 2 | 6 |
| TIKKANEN | 2 | 1 | 3 |
| SUNDSTROM | 1 | 2 | 3 |
| BERG | 2 | 0 | 2 |
| COURTNALL | 1 | 1 | 2 |
| LEETCH | 0 | 2 | 2 |
| KARPOVTSEV | 1 | 0 | 1 |
| SAMUELSSON | 0 | 1 | 1 |
| LIDSTER | 0 | 1 | 1 |
| GRETZKY | 0 | 1 | 1 |
| EASTWOOD | 0 | 1 | 1 |
| BEUKEBOOM | 0 | 1 | 1 |

COACHING AND MANAGEMENT: At time, during Colin Campbell's tenure as Ranger coach, you got the impression that he was hanging onto his job by a thread. But, over time that thread has increased to string to a fairly strong rope. He now appears to be one of the most respected coaches around the league.

GM Neil Smith is a fans' general manager. In other words, he wants a shot at winning the championship every year and makes sure he has one. There is no such word as rebuilding in his vocabulary. We talk about him "going for it" any particular year, but the fact is he "goes for it" every year. A nice big budget helps in that respect, but he still has to put the team together.

Hockey Annual Rating: 5 of 26

## DRAFT

| Round | Sel. | Player | Pos | Amateur Team |
|---|---|---|---|---|
| 1 | 19 | Stefan Cherneski | RW | Brandon (WHL) |
| 2 | 46 | Wes Jarvis | D | Kitchener (OHL) |
| 3 | 73 | Burke Henry | D | Brandon (WHL) |
| 4 | 93 | Tomi Kallarsson | D | Finland |
| 5 | 126 | Jason McLean | G | Moose Jaw (WHL) |
| 5 | 134 | Johan Lindbom | W | Sweden |
| 6 | 136 | Michael York | C | Michigan State |
| 6 | 154 | Shawn Degagne | G | Kitchener (OHL) |
| 7 | 175 | Johan Holmqvist | G | Sweden |
| 7 | 182 | Mike Mottau | D | Boston College |
| 8 | 210 | A. Proskurnicki | LW | Sarnia (OHL) |
| 9 | 236 | Richard Miller | D | Providence |

Stefan Cherneski is described as a goal scorer. Some players can do this and that, but he scores goals. In the NHL, the team that scores wins the game. It's easy to forget sometimes when figuring out which players to draft. Goal scoring is pretty darned important.

Second round pick, Wes Jarvis, is a good steady defenceman, who isn't going to be spectacular. The Hockey News had him pegged as a late first rounder.

PROGNOSIS: Don't worry too much about the regular season when it comes to the Rangers. Oh, they're going to have a better record, but when we'll really see what this team is all about is at playoff time.

If Smith does the right tinkering, they'll be legitimate contenders to win the Stanley Cup.

## PREDICTION

Eastern Conference: 3rd
Overall: 5th

## STAT SECTION

| Team Scoring Stats | 1996-97 | | | | | | CAREER | | | |
|---|---|---|---|---|---|---|---|---|---|---|
| | GP | G | A | PTS | +/- | PIM | SH | Gm | G | A | Pts |
| WAYNE GRETZKY | 82 | 25 | 72 | 97 | 12 | 28 | 286 | 1,335 | 862 | 1,843 | 2,705 |
| MARK MESSIER | 71 | 36 | 48 | 84 | 12 | 88 | 227 | 1,272 | 575 | 977 | 1,552 |
| BRIAN LEETCH | 82 | 20 | 58 | 78 | 31 | 40 | 256 | 649 | 147 | 503 | 650 |
| ADAM GRAVES | 82 | 33 | 28 | 61 | 10 | 66 | 269 | 676 | 209 | 204 | 413 |
| NIKLAS SUNDSTROM | 82 | 24 | 28 | 52 | 23 | 20 | 132 | 164 | 33 | 40 | 73 |

| | | | | | | | | | | |
|---|---|---|---|---|---|---|---|---|---|---|
| LUC ROBITAILLE | 69 | 24 | 24 | 48 | 16 | 48 | 200 | 832 | 462 | 500 | 962 |
| A. KARPOVTSEV | 77 | 9 | 29 | 38 | 1 | 59 | 84 | 231 | 18 | 68 | 86 |
| ALEXEI KOVALEV | 45 | 13 | 22 | 35 | 11 | 42 | 110 | 315 | 93 | 122 | 215 |
| RUSS COURTNALL | 61 | 11 | 24 | 35 | 1 | 26 | 125 | 914 | 279 | 428 | 707 |
| ESA TIKKANEN | 76 | 13 | 17 | 30 | 9- | 72 | 133 | 797 | 241 | 365 | 606 |
| BRUCE DRIVER | 79 | 5 | 25 | 30 | 8 | 48 | 154 | 847 | 91 | 375 | 466 |
| PATRICK FLATLEY | 68 | 10 | 12 | 22 | 6 | 26 | 96 | 780 | 170 | 340 | 510 |
| ULF SAMUELSSON | 73 | 6 | 11 | 17 | 3 | 138 | 77 | 887 | 49 | 256 | 305 |
| BILL BERG | 67 | 8 | 6 | 14 | 2 | 37 | 84 | 435 | 52 | 56 | 108 |
| DANIEL GONEAU | 41 | 10 | 3 | 13 | 5- | 10 | 44 | 41 | 10 | 3 | 13 |
| JEFF BEUKEBOOM | 80 | 3 | 9 | 12 | 22 | 167 | 55 | 696 | 30 | 115 | 145 |
| MIKE EASTWOOD | 60 | 2 | 10 | 12 | 1- | 14 | 44 | 264 | 33 | 53 | 86 |
| VLADIMIR VOROBIEV | 16 | 5 | 5 | 10 | 4 | 6 | 42 | 16 | 5 | 5 | 10 |
| DARREN LANGDON | 60 | 3 | 6 | 9 | 1- | 195 | 24 | 142 | 11 | 11 | 22 |
| DOUG LIDSTER | 48 | 3 | 4 | 7 | 10 | 24 | 42 | 844 | 75 | 264 | 339 |
| DAVID OLIVER | 31 | 3 | 3 | 6 | 5- | 8 | 35 | 155 | 39 | 36 | 75 |
| CHRIS FERRARO | 12 | 1 | 1 | 2 | 1 | 6 | 23 | 14 | 2 | 1 | 3 |
| CHRISTIAN DUBE | 27 | 1 | 1 | 2 | 4- | 4 | 14 | 27 | 1 | 1 | 2 |
| R. VANDENBUSSCHE | 11 | 1 | 0 | 1 | 2- | 30 | 4 | 11 | 1 | 0 | 1 |
| ERIC CAIRNS | 40 | 0 | 1 | 1 | 7- | 147 | 17 | 40 | 0 | 1 | 1 |
| SHANE CHURLA | 45 | 0 | 1 | 1 | 10- | 106 | 19 | 488 | 26 | 45 | 71 |
| JEFF NIELSEN | 2 | 0 | 0 | 0 | 1- | 2 | 1 | 2 | 0 | 0 | 0 |
| PETER FERRARO | 2 | 0 | 0 | 0 | 0 | 0 | 3 | 7 | 0 | 1 | 1 |
| SYLVAIN BLOUIN | 6 | 0 | 0 | 0 | 1- | 18 | 1 | 6 | 0 | 0 | 0 |
| DALLAS EAKINS | 7 | 0 | 0 | 0 | 4- | 16 | 4 | 57 | 0 | 4 | 4 |
| GLENN HEALY | 23 | 0 | 0 | 0 | 0 | 4 | 0 | | | | |
| MIKE RICHTER | 61 | 0 | 0 | 0 | 0 | 4 | 0 | | | | |

## TEAM RANKINGS

| | | Conference Rank | League Rank |
|---|---|---|---|
| Record | 38-34-10 | 5 | 8 |
| Home | 21-14-6 | 7 | 11 |
| Away | 17-20-4 | 4 | 10 |
| Versus Own Conference | 24-24-8 | 7 | 14 |
| Versus Other Conference | 14-10-2 | 4 | 8 |
| Team Plus\Minus | +33 | 4 | 6 |
| Goals For | 258 | 3 | 4 |
| Goals Against | 231 | 5 | 9 |
| Average Shots For | 30.8 | 4 | 7 |
| Average Shots Against | 31.6 | 10 | 20 |
| Overtime | 3-0-10 | 1 | 1 |
| One Goal Games | 13-14 | 8 | 14 |
| Times outshooting opponent | 39 | 8 | 15 |
| Versus Teams Over .500 | 19-11-7 | 1 | 2 |
| Versus Teams Under .500 | 19-23-3 | 10 | 21 |
| First Half Record | 20-16-5 | 6 | 9 |
| Second Half Record | 18-18-5 | 5 | 12 |

## PLAYOFFS

Results:   defeated Florida 4-1
defeated New Jersey 4-1
lost to Philadelphia 4-1

Record: 9-6
Home: 4-2
Away: 5-4
Goals For: 36 (2.4/game)
Goals Against: 35 (2.3/game)
Overtime: 3-0
Power play: 15.6% (8th)
Penalty Killing: 79.4% (12th)

| | GP | G | A | PTS | +/- | PIM | PP | SH | GW | OT | S |
|---|---|---|---|---|---|---|---|---|---|---|---|
| WAYNE GRETZKY | 15 | 10 | 10 | 20 | 5 | 2 | 3 | 0 | 2 | 0 | 44 |
| ESA TIKKANEN | 15 | 9 | 3 | 12 | 2 | 26 | 3 | 1 | 3 | 2 | 45 |
| MARK MESSIER | 15 | 3 | 9 | 12 | 2 | 6 | 0 | 0 | 1 | 0 | 43 |
| LUC ROBITAILLE | 15 | 4 | 7 | 11 | 7 | 4 | 0 | 0 | 0 | 0 | 43 |
| BRIAN LEETCH | 15 | 2 | 8 | 10 | 5 | 6 | 1 | 0 | 1 | 0 | 56 |
| RUSS COURTNALL | 15 | 3 | 4 | 7 | 1 | 0 | 1 | 0 | 0 | 0 | 27 |
| DOUG LIDSTER | 15 | 1 | 5 | 6 | 2- | 8 | 0 | 0 | 0 | 0 | 20 |
| NIKLAS SUNDSTROM | 9 | 0 | 5 | 5 | 3 | 2 | 0 | 0 | 0 | 0 | 18 |
| A. KARPOVTSEV | 13 | 1 | 3 | 4 | 2 | 20 | 1 | 0 | 0 | 0 | 10 |
| ADAM GRAVES | 15 | 2 | 1 | 3 | 1 | 12 | 1 | 0 | 2 | 1 | 39 |
| MIKE EASTWOOD | 15 | 1 | 2 | 3 | 0 | 22 | 0 | 0 | 0 | 0 | 19 |
| ULF SAMUELSSON | 15 | 0 | 2 | 2 | 1 | 30 | 0 | 0 | 0 | 0 | 11 |
| JEFF BEUKEBOOM | 15 | 0 | 1 | 1 | 5 | 34 | 0 | 0 | 0 | 0 | 9 |
| BRUCE DRIVER | 15 | 0 | 1 | 1 | 3- | 2 | 0 | 0 | 0 | 0 | 26 |
| MIKE RICHTER | 15 | 0 | 1 | 1 | 0 | 0 | 0 | 0 | 0 | 0 | 0 |

| | | | | | | | | | | | |
|---|---|---|---|---|---|---|---|---|---|---|---|
| PETER FERRARO | 2 | 0 | 0 | 0 | 0 | 0 | 0 | 0 | 0 | 0 | 2 |
| BILL BERG | 3 | 0 | 0 | 0 | 1- | 2 | 0 | 0 | 0 | 0 | 5 |
| DAVID OLIVER | 3 | 0 | 0 | 0 | 0 | 0 | 0 | 0 | 0 | 0 | 0 |
| ERIC CAIRNS | 3 | 0 | 0 | 0 | 0 | 0 | 0 | 0 | 0 | 0 | 0 |
| CHRISTIAN DUBE | 3 | 0 | 0 | 0 | 2- | 0 | 0 | 0 | 0 | 0 | 0 |
| DALLAS EAKINS | 4 | 0 | 0 | 0 | 1- | 4 | 0 | 0 | 0 | 0 | 1 |
| KEN GERNANDER | 9 | 0 | 0 | 0 | 0 | 0 | 0 | 0 | 0 | 0 | 0 |
| DARREN LANGDON | 10 | 0 | 0 | 0 | 1- | 2 | 0 | 0 | 0 | 0 | 1 |
| PATRICK FLATLEY | 11 | 0 | 0 | 0 | 2 | 14 | 0 | 0 | 0 | 0 | 14 |
| SHANE CHURLA | 15 | 0 | 0 | 0 | 3- | 20 | 0 | 0 | 0 | 0 | 6 |

| GOALTENDER | GPI | MINS | AVG | W | L | T | EN | SO | GA | SA | SV % |
|---|---|---|---|---|---|---|---|---|---|---|---|
| MIKE RICHTER | 15 | 939 | 2.11 | 9 | 6 | 2 | 3 | 0 | 33 | 488 | .932 |
| NYR TOTALS | 15 | 943 | 2.23 | 9 | 6 | 2 | 3 | 0 | 36 | 490 | .929 |

## ALL-TIME LEADERS

### Goals

| | |
|---|---|
| Rod Gilbert | 406 |
| Jean Ratelle | 336 |
| Andy Bathgate | 272 |

### Assists

| | |
|---|---|
| Rod Gilbert | 615 |
| Brian Leetch | 503 |
| Jean Ratelle | 481 |

### Points

| | |
|---|---|
| Rod Gilbert | 1,021 |
| Jean Ratelle | 817 |
| Andy Bathgate | 729 |

## BEST INDIVIDUAL SEASONS

### Goals

| | | |
|---|---|---|
| Adam Graves | 1993-94 | 52 |
| Vic Hadfield | 1971-72 | 50 |
| Mike Gartner | 1990-91 | 49 |

### Assists

| | | |
|---|---|---|
| Brian Leetch | 1991-92 | 80 |
| Sergei Zubov | 1993-94 | 77 |
| Wayne Gretzky | 1996-97 | 72 |
| Brian Leetch | 1990-91 | 72 |

### Points

| | | |
|---|---|---|
| Jean Ratelle | 1971-72 | 109 |
| Mark Messier | 1991-92 | 107 |
| Vic Hadfield | 1971-72 | 106 |

## TEAM

### Last 3 years

| | GP | W | L | T | Pts | % |
|---|---|---|---|---|---|---|
| 1996-97 | 82 | 38 | 34 | 10 | 86 | .524 |
| 1995-96 | 82 | 41 | 27 | 14 | 96 | .585 |
| 1994-95 | 48 | 22 | 23 | 3 | 47 | .490 |

Best 3 regular seasons

| | | | | | | |
|---|---|---|---|---|---|---|
| 1970-71 | 78 | 49 | 18 | 11 | 109 | .699 |
| 1971-72 | 78 | 48 | 17 | 13 | 109 | .699 |
| 1993-94 | 84 | 52 | 24 | 8 | 112 | .667 |
| 1939-40 | 48 | 27 | 11 | 10 | 64 | .667 |

Worst 3 regular seasons

| | | | | | | |
|---|---|---|---|---|---|---|
| 1943-44 | 50 | 6 | 39 | 5 | 17 | .170 |
| 1942-43 | 50 | 11 | 31 | 8 | 30 | .300 |
| 1944-45 | 50 | 11 | 29 | 10 | 32 | .320 |

Most Goals (min. 70 game schedule)

| | |
|---|---|
| 1991-92 | 321 |
| 1974-75 | 319 |
| 1971-72 | 317 |

Fewest Goals (min. 70 game schedule)

| | |
|---|---|
| 1954-55 | 150 |
| 1952-53 | 152 |
| 1953-54 | 161 |

Most Goals Against (min. 70 game schedule)

| | |
|---|---|
| 1984-85 | 345 |
| 1975-76 | 333 |
| 1986-87 | 323 |

Fewest Goals Against (min. 70 game schedule)

| | |
|---|---|
| 1970-71 | 177 |
| 1953-54 | 182 |
| 1967-68 | 183 |

# Ottawa Senators

If you're an Ottawa fan, don't get too excited over what happened late last season. It's not going to happen again this year. In fact, it's going to be a long season for the Senators.

Yes, they made tremendous strides from last place laughing-stock status, but don't confuse that with success. As far as they've come from worst to below average, it's just as long a jump from below average to good.

Keep in mind that their 31-36-15 record for 77 points, was only seven points away from 12th place in the conference.

Let's look at the Senators from a positive-negative point of view.

On the positive side:
* they were only outscored on the season by eight goals.
* have two legitimate scoring stars in Alexei Yashin and Daniel Alfredsson.
* have stability in management and coaching.
* Alexandre Daigle still isn't consistent, but he did score 26 goals.
* Steve Duchesne is a premier power play quarterback.
* Wade Redden is going to develop into a premier NHL defenceman.
* were able to compensate when key defencemen Stan Neckar and Sean Hill went down with injuries at the start of the season.
* power play was much improved.
* had a good second half with a mark of 19-15-7

* had a great stretch run with a record of 9-3-2, when they needed to win to make the playoffs.
* showed good character winning when they needed to.
* allowed the fewest shots against per game in the Eastern Conference and the third fewest overall.
* Buddha power
* took the Buffalo Sabres to seven games in the first round of the playoffs and showed a tremendous amount of drive and determination.

Now, the negative picture.
* Every goalie that ever played in the NHL has had the ability to get hot for a spell (okay, not Hardy Aastrom). No goalie remains that hot constantly. So, is Ron Tugnutt for real or not?
* without a hot streak at the right time the Senators would have disappeared back into the basement area.
* seem to be building with Europeans, which has doomed previous teams that tried it.
* there are only a few legitimate stars, and more than a couple legitimate flops.
* teams that make big rises in the standings, often fall back the next year.

## STUFF

* the Senators were the last team to lose on home ice last year, going 3-0-3 in their first six in the Corel Centre.

* the Senators had 71 more power play opportunites than shorthanded situations, which was highest in the league.
* a 36-point increase was the second highest to Dallas (38) last season.
* the Sens allowed 57 fewer goals last season than they did the year before.

## STAT ANALYSIS

It wasn't a banner year for goal scoring. Unless, of course, you were an Ottawa Senator. They were the most improved team offensively. Only seven teams improved, and all are listed below.

| Team | 1995-96 Goals | 1996-97 Goals | Difference |
|---|---|---|---|
| Ottawa | 191 | 226 | +35 |
| Dallas | 227 | 252 | +25 |
| St. Louis | 219 | 236 | +17 |
| New Jersey | 215 | 231 | +16 |
| Edmonton | 240 | 252 | +12 |
| NY Islanders | 229 | 240 | +11 |
| Anaheim | 234 | 245 | +11 |

## TEAM PREVIEW

GOAL: Hey, where did Ron Tugnutt come from? He was pretty much washed-up as an NHLer, destined for Sweden and the minor leagues for the rest of his career. The Senators took a chance on him, signed him as a free agent, and made him a backup to their star Damian Rhodes.

At first, he was a rarely used backup. Rhodes was doing the job and didn't need much help. After 48 games, Rhodes had played in 39 of them and Tugnutt just 12.

Then Tugnutt got into a few games in a row, then a few more, and before you knew it he was playing in almost all of them. During the great stretch run, it was Tugnutt they turned to. And in the playoffs, it was Tugnutt exclusively.

During that stretch run, when the Senators went 9-3-2 to get into the playoffs, Tugnutt had three shutouts, two against Buffalo.

While Tugnutt was an amazing story, don't write Rhodes out of the book just yet. He'll get his chance again, and he's proven himself in the past. Rhodes seems to get down on himself and loses confidence on occasion. But, he always battles back.

Hockey Annual Rating: 15 of 26

DEFENCE: One of the best images of the Senators' playoffs last year was Lance Pitlick running around hitting everything in sight with bruising bodychecks.

Even without that image the Senators' defence was one of the team's brightest spots last year. And almost of it came in the form of surprises.

Early in the year, two regulars Sean Hill and Stan Neckar, were lost for the season after having to undergo knee operations.

Surprise, Pitlick became a regular. Surprise,

| GOALTENDER | GPI | MINS | AVG | W | L | T | EN | SO | GA | SA | SV % |
|---|---|---|---|---|---|---|---|---|---|---|---|
| DAMIAN RHODES | 50 | 2934 | 2.72 | 14 | 20 | 14 | 2 | 1 | 133 | 1213 | .890 |
| RON TUGNUTT | 37 | 1991 | 2.80 | 17 | 15 | 1 | 2 | 3 | 93 | 882 | .895 |
| MIKE BALES | 1 | 52 | 4.62 | 0 | 1 | 0 | 0 | 0 | 0 | 18 | .778 |
| OTT TOTALS | 82 | 5001 | 2.81 | 31 | 36 | 15 | 4 | 4 | 234 | 2117 | .889 |

Janne Laukannen played well and earned a regular spot. Surprise, Wade Redden was solid and better than expected for his first NHL season. Surprise, Jason York played well. Surprise, Radim Bicanek's progress came sooner than expected and he played in every playoff contest.

No surprise was the play of Steve Duchesne, however. And Frank Musil was able to play when needed as well.

This year, however, with Neckar and Hill returning from injuries there is a logjam at this position. There is going to be a fight for jobs and we're not even taking into account Chris Phillips, who may sign or may carry out his threat to go back into the draft next year.

The glut of defencemen could mean trades. It promises to be interesting in the Senators' training camp. Quantity doesn't necessarily mean quality, however.

They could run into trouble also, in the toughness department. They're a fairly tame group that opposing teams can exploit.

As well, the effectiveness of the defence last season was helped in a big way by a system that meant the forwards were committed to helping them out.

Hockey Annual Rating: 15 of 26

FORWARD: It's not that uncommon around the league these days, but what the Senators have is two-thirds of a scoring line — namely Alexei Yashin and Daniel Alfredsson.

Both are coming off excellent seasons, and best of all Yashin lost his title as the league's biggest whiner. Mostly, we just heard from him last year when his name was in the scoring summaries. That was not only better for him, but better for the team.

The rest of the offence is a big question mark. Who knows what Daigle is going to do? He could continue to improve or disappear off the face of the ice.

Radek Bonk has done next to nothing so far, but there's still hope.

Shawn McEachern had 11 lousy goals and long, lousy slumps.

Andreas Dackell looked to be a good rookie, but slumped for extended periods, and is still a question mark. Same with Sergei Zholtok.

Role players include character guy Randy Cunneyworth, Tom Chorske, Shaun Van Allen, toughster Denny Lambert, Mike Prokopec and defensive centre Bruce Gardiner. Gardiner's value is even higher because he was also able to put the puck in the net.

Among the prospects is Magnus Arvedsson, a 25-year-old draft pick from this year. He is signed and the Sens think he can step right into the NHL and play this year. Unlikely.

Overall, the Ottawa forward situation would be good — if it was in the AHL.

Hockey Annual Rating: 18 of 26

SPECIAL TEAMS: Alfredsson is the one who makes the power play work. He's a talented playmaker and scorer, and moves around the ice like he owns it. His 31 power play points tied him with Wayne Gretzky, which is compliment enough.

Yashin is also valuable on the power play, as is quarterback Duchesne. Those three are what count. The other two don't matter so much and are interchangeable. They have a couple defenceman who can man the other point, and different guys can play the other wing.

The Senators weren't shorthanded very often last year, or their season could have been a lot different. Only New Jersey (235) had fewer advantages against them. The league leader, San Jose, had 144 more advantages against. Overall, Ottawa was the least penalized team, averaging only 13.3 penalty minutes per game. The league average was 18.7. Not taking many penalties can be viewed as smart hockey, or as is more often the case, unagressive hockey.

POWER PLAY

|  | G | ATT | PCT |
|---|---|---|---|
| Overall | 56 | 336 | 16.7% (11th NHL) |
| Home | 27 | 175 | 15.4% (15th NHL) |
| Road | 29 | 161 | 18.0% (8th NHL) |

12 SHORT HANDED GOALS ALLOWED (T-19th NHL)

PENALTY KILLING

|  | G | TSH | PCT |
|---|---|---|---|
| Overall | 48 | 265 | 81.9% (20th NHL) |
| Home | 20 | 125 | 84.0% (T-8th NHL) |
| Road | 28 | 140 | 80.0% (T-22nd NHL) |

9 SHORT HANDED GOALS SCORED (T-16th NHL)

SENATORS SPECIAL TEAMS SCORING

| Power play | G | A | PTS |
|---|---|---|---|
| ALFREDSSON | 11 | 20 | 31 |
| YASHIN | 10 | 17 | 27 |
| DUCHESNE | 10 | 10 | 20 |
| DAIGLE | 4 | 14 | 18 |
| CUNNEYWORTH | 6 | 4 | 10 |
| REDDEN | 2 | 8 | 10 |
| ZHOLTOK | 5 | 4 | 9 |
| LAUKKANEN | 2 | 7 | 9 |
| YORK | 1 | 6 | 7 |
| DACKELL | 2 | 1 | 3 |
| OLSSON | 1 | 2 | 3 |
| MCEACHERN | 0 | 3 | 3 |
| VAN ALLEN | 1 | 1 | 2 |
| CHORSKE | 1 | 1 | 2 |
| VON STEFENELLI | 0 | 1 | 1 |
| GARDINER | 0 | 1 | 1 |
| BONK | 0 | 1 | 1 |

| Short handed | G | A | PTS |
|---|---|---|---|
| ALFREDSSON | 1 | 2 | 3 |

| DUCHESNE | 2 | 0 | 2 |
|---|---|---|---|
| VAN ALLEN | 1 | 1 | 2 |
| MCEACHERN | 1 | 1 | 2 |
| HANNAN | 1 | 1 | 2 |
| CHORSKE | 1 | 1 | 2 |
| GARDINER | 1 | 0 | 1 |
| BONK | 1 | 0 | 1 |
| YASHIN | 0 | 1 | 1 |
| REDDEN | 0 | 1 | 1 |
| LAUKKANEN | 0 | 1 | 1 |

COACHING AND MANAGEMENT:

Great work by Pierre Gauthier and Jacques Martin to bring the Senators a level of respectability.

Martin was one of the three finalists for coach of the year, showing an ability to get the players to buy into a defensive system. Not an easy task by any means but that's what brought the team success.

GM Gauthier deserves marks too, for turning around the team from the Randy Sexton era of incompetence.

Good management and good coaching can compensate for a team that lacks talent.

Now for the problem. Gauthier seems to want to turn the Senators into a European type team. Most of the top forwards and some of the defencemen this year will be European.

This has been tried before, and has met only with resounding failure. It doesn't work, and we could make a list of 20 reasons why. For Gauthier to attempt it means he's starting to think he's smarter than everyone else, which often means quite the opposite. European players can fit into NHL teams and can even be their star player, but once you start building your nucleus composed of players from a different culture, understanding, and hockey training, it's trouble.

Hockey Annual Rating: 14 of 26

## DRAFT

| Round | Sel. | Player | Pos | Amateur Team |
|---|---|---|---|---|
| 1 | 12 | Marian Hossa | W | Slovakia |
| 3 | 58 | Jani Hurme | G | Finland |
| 3 | 66 | Josh Langeld | RW | Lincoln (USHL) |
| 5 | 119 | M. Arvedsson | F | Sweden |
| 6 | 146 | Jeff Sullivan | D | Halifax (QMJHL) |
| 7 | 173 | Robin Bacul | LW | Czech Rep. |
| 8 | 203 | Nick Gillis | RW | Cushing Academy (U.S.H.S) |
| 9 | 229 | Karel Rachunek | D | Czech Rep. |

The Ottawa Red Army, er Senators, loaded up on more Europeans at the draft table. Marian Hossa is seen as a one-dimensional player, who doesn't play defence and prefers non-contact hockey. But, he's a goal scorer, so he can fit in with the other Europeans on the Senators (i.e. Bonk) who are supposed to score goals but do nothing.

Fifth round draft pick, 25-year-old Magnus Arvedsson is expected to step into the lineup immediately. He was so good, every other NHL team passed on him for seven years.

## PROGNOSIS

The Senators playoff run last season was so exciting, that it's a shame it's all for naught. It wasn't the stepping stone to success for them, it was more like an anomaly.

They're headed for a major fall, won't make the playoffs, will lose the fans they picked up last year, and will have people screaming for heads before the season is half over.

You'd like to think they could build on last year, but their prospects are suspect and it's not likely to happen.

## PREDICTION

Eastern Conference: 13th
Overall: 23rd

## STAT SECTION

| Team Scoring Stats | 1996-97 | | | | | | | CAREER | | | |
|---|---|---|---|---|---|---|---|---|---|---|---|
| | GP | G | A | PTS | +/- | PIM | SH | Gm | G | A | Pts |
| ALEXEI YASHIN | 82 | 35 | 40 | 75 | 7- | 44 | 291 | 258 | 101 | 136 | 237 |
| DANIEL ALFREDSSON | 76 | 24 | 47 | 71 | 5 | 30 | 247 | 158 | 50 | 82 | 132 |
| ALEXANDRE DAIGLE | 82 | 26 | 25 | 51 | 33- | 33 | 203 | 263 | 67 | 89 | 156 |
| STEVE DUCHESNE | 78 | 19 | 28 | 47 | 9- | 38 | 208 | 765 | 188 | 394 | 582 |
| R. CUNNEYWORTH | 76 | 12 | 24 | 36 | 7- | 99 | 115 | 781 | 185 | 212 | 297 |
| ANDREAS DACKELL | 79 | 12 | 19 | 31 | 6- | 8 | 79 | 79 | 12 | 19 | 31 |
| SHAWN MCEACHERN | 65 | 11 | 20 | 31 | 5- | 18 | 150 | 366 | 96 | 121 | 217 |
| WADE REDDEN | 82 | 6 | 24 | 30 | 1 | 41 | 102 | 82 | 6 | 24 | 30 |
| SERGEI ZHOLTOK | 57 | 12 | 16 | 28 | 2 | 19 | 96 | 82 | 14 | 18 | 32 |
| TOM CHORSKE | 68 | 18 | 8 | 26 | 1- | 16 | 116 | 455 | 102 | 91 | 193 |

| | | | | | | | | | | |
|---|---|---|---|---|---|---|---|---|---|---|
| SHAUN VAN ALLEN | 80 | 11 | 14 | 25 | 8- | 35 | 123 | 273 | 36 | 81 | 117 |
| BRUCE GARDINER | 67 | 11 | 10 | 21 | 4 | 49 | 94 | 67 | 11 | 10 | 21 |
| JASON YORK | 75 | 4 | 17 | 21 | 8- | 67 | 121 | 188 | 9 | 50 | 59 |
| JANNE LAUKKANEN | 76 | 3 | 18 | 21 | 14- | 76 | 109 | 110 | 4 | 23 | 27 |
| DENNY LAMBERT | 80 | 4 | 16 | 20 | 4- | 217 | 58 | 126 | 5 | 27 | 32 |
| RADEK BONK | 53 | 5 | 13 | 18 | 4- | 14 | 82 | 171 | 24 | 30 | 54 |
| LANCE PITLICK | 66 | 5 | 5 | 10 | 2 | 91 | 54 | 109 | 6 | 12 | 18 |
| JASON ZENT | 22 | 3 | 3 | 6 | 5 | 9 | 20 | 22 | 3 | 3 | 6 |
| CHRISTER OLSSON | 30 | 2 | 4 | 6 | 4- | 10 | 26 | 56 | 4 | 12 | 16 |
| DENIS CHASSE | 22 | 1 | 4 | 5 | 3 | 19 | 12 | 132 | 11 | 14 | 25 |
| FRANK MUSIL | 57 | 0 | 5 | 5 | 6 | 58 | 24 | 728 | 33 | 99 | 132 |
| DAVE HANNAN | 34 | 2 | 2 | 4 | 1- | 8 | 16 | 841 | 114 | 191 | 305 |
| DAMIAN RHODES | 50 | 0 | 2 | 2 | 0 | 2 | 0 | | | | |
| P. VONSTEFENELLI | 6 | 0 | 1 | 1 | 3- | 7 | 2 | 43 | 0 | 5 | 5 |
| DENNIS VIAL | 11 | 0 | 1 | 1 | 0 | 25 | 4 | 223 | 8 | 26 | 34 |
| RADIM BICANEK | 21 | 0 | 1 | 1 | 4- | 8 | 27 | 27 | 0 | 1 | 1 |
| PHILIP CROWE | 26 | 0 | 1 | 1 | 0 | 30 | 8 | 73 | 1 | 4 | 5 |
| RON TUGNUTT | 37 | 0 | 1 | 1 | 0 | 0 | 0 | | | | |
| MIKE BALES | 1 | 0 | 0 | 0 | 0 | 0 | 0 | | | | |
| SEAN HILL | 5 | 0 | 0 | 0 | 1 | 4 | 9 | 229 | 17 | 54 | 71 |
| STANISLAV NECKAR | 5 | 0 | 0 | 0 | 2 | 2 | 3 | 135 | 4 | 12 | 16 |

## TEAM RANKINGS

| | | Conference Rank | League Rank |
|---|---|---|---|
| Record | 31-36-15 | 7 | 16 |
| Home | 16-17-8 | 11 | 19 |
| Away | 15-19-7 | 6 | 12 |
| Versus Own Conference | 24-23-9 | 6 | 11 |
| Versus Other Conference | 7-13-6 | 10 | 21 |
| Team Plus\Minus | -16 | 10 | 18 |
| Goals For | 226 | 9 | 18 |
| Goals Against | 234 | 7 | 12 |
| Average Shots For | 29.2 | 9 | 18 |

| | | | |
|---|---|---|---|
| Average Shots Against | 25.8 | 1 | 3 |
| Overtime | 0-2-15 | 12 | 22 |
| One Goal Games | 14-14 | 7 | 13 |
| Times outshooting opponent | 53 | 3 | 5 |
| Versus Teams Over .500 | 9-24-6 | 12 | 25 |
| Versus Teams Under .500 | 22-12-9 | 3 | 7 |
| First Half Record | 12-21-8 | 13 | 26 |
| Second Half Record | 19-15-7 | 4 | 10 |

## PLAYOFFS

Results: lost 4-3 to Buffalo
Record: 3-4
Home: 1-2
Away: 2-2
Goals For: 13 (1.9/game)
Goals Against: 14 (2.0/game)
Overtime: 1-1
Power play: 20.0% (5th)
Penalty Killing: 92.6% (1st)

| | GP | G | A | PTS | +/- | PIM | PP | SH | GW | OT | S |
|---|---|---|---|---|---|---|---|---|---|---|---|
| DANIEL ALFREDSSON | 7 | 5 | 2 | 7 | 1- | 6 | 3 | 0 | 2 | 1 | 23 |
| ALEXEI YASHIN | 7 | 1 | 5 | 6 | 2- | 2 | 1 | 0 | 0 | 0 | 21 |
| STEVE DUCHESNE | 7 | 1 | 4 | 5 | 3- | 0 | 1 | 0 | 1 | 0 | 18 |
| WADE REDDEN | 7 | 1 | 3 | 4 | 4- | 2 | 0 | 0 | 0 | 0 | 11 |
| SHAWN MCEACHERN | 7 | 2 | 0 | 2 | 1- | 8 | 1 | 0 | 0 | 0 | 21 |
| R. CUNNEYWORTH | 7 | 1 | 1 | 2 | 3- | 10 | 0 | 0 | 0 | 0 | 18 |
| SERGEI ZHOLTOK | 7 | 1 | 1 | 2 | 0 | 0 | 1 | 0 | 0 | 0 | 16 |
| ANDREAS DACKELL | 7 | 1 | 0 | 1 | 0 | 0 | 0 | 0 | 0 | 0 | 5 |
| TOM CHORSKE | 5 | 0 | 1 | 1 | 1- | 2 | 0 | 0 | 0 | 0 | 3 |
| DENNY LAMBERT | 6 | 0 | 1 | 1 | 0 | 9 | 0 | 0 | 0 | 0 | 5 |
| SHAUN VAN ALLEN | 7 | 0 | 1 | 1 | 3- | 4 | 0 | 0 | 0 | 0 | 8 |
| BRUCE GARDINER | 7 | 0 | 1 | 1 | 0 | 2 | 0 | 0 | 0 | 0 | 3 |
| JANNE LAUKKANEN | 7 | 0 | 1 | 1 | 1- | 6 | 0 | 0 | 0 | 0 | 7 |
| RADEK BONK | 7 | 0 | 1 | 1 | 1- | 4 | 0 | 0 | 0 | 0 | 4 |
| PHILIP CROWE | 3 | 0 | 0 | 0 | 0 | 16 | 0 | 0 | 0 | 0 | 1 |
| RON TUGNUTT | 7 | 0 | 0 | 0 | 0 | 0 | 0 | 0 | 0 | 0 | 0 |
| LANCE PITLICK | 7 | 0 | 0 | 0 | 1- | 4 | 0 | 0 | 0 | 0 | 2 |
| JASON YORK | 7 | 0 | 0 | 0 | 3- | 4 | 0 | 0 | 0 | 0 | 18 |
| ALEXANDRE DAIGLE | 7 | 0 | 0 | 0 | 5- | 2 | 0 | 0 | 0 | 0 | 16 |
| RADIM BICANEK | 7 | 0 | 0 | 0 | 0 | 8 | 0 | 0 | 0 | 0 | 4 |

| GOALTENDER | GPI | MINS | AVG | W | L | T | EN | SO | GA | SA | SV % |
|---|---|---|---|---|---|---|---|---|---|---|---|
| RON TUGNUTT | 7 | 425 | 1.98 | 3 | 4 | 0 | 1 | 0 | 14 | 169 | .917 |
| OTT TOTALS | 7 | 428 | 1.96 | 3 | 4 | 0 | 1 | 0 | 14 | 169 | .917 |

## ALL-TIME LEADERS

Goals
Alexei Yashin             101
Alexandre Daigle          67
Daniel Alfredsson         50

Assists
Alexei Yashin             143
Alexandre Daigle          89
Daniel Alfredsson         82

Points
Alexei Yashin             237
Alexandre Daigle          156
Daniel Alfredsson         32

## BEST INDIVIDUAL SEASONS

Goals
Alexei Yashin        1996-97    35
Alexei Yashin        1993-94    30
Daniel Alfredsson    1995-96    26
Alexandre Daigle     1996-97    26

Assists
Alexei Yashin        1993-94    49
Daniel Alfredsson    1996-97    47
Norm MacIver         1992-93    46

Points
Alexei Yashin        1993-94    79
Alexei Yashin        1996-97    75
Daniel Alfredsson    1996-97    71

## TEAM

Last 3 years

|         | GP | W  | L  | T  | Pts | %    |
|---------|----|----|----|----|-----|------|
| 1996-97 | 82 | 31 | 36 | 15 | 77  | .470 |
| 1995-96 | 82 | 18 | 59 | 5  | 41  | .250 |
| 1994-95 | 48 | 9  | 34 | 5  | 23  | .240 |

Best 3 regular seasons

| 1996-97 | 82 | 31 | 36 | 15 | 77 | .470 |
|---------|----|----|----|----|----|------|
| 1995-96 | 82 | 18 | 59 | 5  | 41 | .250 |
| 1994-95 | 48 | 9  | 34 | 5  | 23 | .240 |

Worst 3 regular seasons

| 1992-93 | 84 | 10 | 70 | 4 | 24 | .143 |
|---------|----|----|----|---|----|------|
| 1993-94 | 84 | 14 | 61 | 9 | 37 | .220 |
| 1994-95 | 48 | 9  | 34 | 5 | 23 | .240 |

Most Goals (min. 70 game schedule)
1996-97          226
1992-93          202
1993-94          201

Fewest Goals (min. 70 game schedule)
1995-96          191
1993-94          201
1992-93          202

Most Goals Against (min. 70 game schedule)
1993-94          397
1992-93          394
1995-96          291

Fewest Goals Against (min. 70 game schedule)
1996-97          234
1995-96          291
1992-93          394

# Philadelphia Flyers

It's funny what happens to a Stanley Cup finalist which loses in four games straight. They're perceived as losers.

Never mind that 24 other teams failed to make it that far. Never mind that the Flyers dominated all their previous playoff opponents, much tougher competition than Detroit had to face (except for Colorado).

No, they lost, so not only are they losers, but someone has to take the blame. It's human nature.

Ron Hextall and Garth Snow set a playoff record last year for blame. The evil twins were the root of all their problems and amazingly, responsible for every single one of their losses. Even more astounding, they had nothing to do with any of the 12 Flyers' post-season wins.

Before we get too sarcastic, however, they did stink the joint out on occasion. Granted, Snow was carrying a lot of weight on those big shoulders, and Hextall wouldn't get any respect if they put his picture beside the word in the dictionary.

Most goalies had some bad times in the playoffs, but they were perceived to have "just had a bad game". When one of Snow or Hextall had a poor outing, it was more of a case of "See, I told you so." Many observers felt before the playoffs, for the last couple years actually, that the Flyers didn't have good enough goaltending. In other words, those same people were just waiting for the evidence.

Hextall couldn't take the Flyers to the Stanley Cup. Everybody said so. But, didn't everyone also say the same thing about another goalie? His name: Mike Vernon.

GM Bob Clarke obviously thought his netminders could do the job, or he would have made some moves. Now, it's almost a certainty that there will be a change in that position. It may even be a wise move in order to create more confidence among the players.

But, to blame Hextall and Snow for being one of the two best teams in the league? Naaaa. At least not so much.

The next victim up for blame is coach Terry Murray. He officially received his blame notice when he was fired after the season. Just before the final series, Clarke said he could have his job back next year if he wanted it. Oh well, that's how the blame game is played. Murray may have given Clarke an extra excuse when he accused his players of "choking" in the finals. There were some questions about whether there was respect from the players for Murray anyway. He was considered aloof and didn't communicate well. Gee, kind of sounds an awful like Scotty Bowman.

Eric Lindros also received his share of blame for not being dominant in the final series against Detroit. That was true, but the Wings may have had something to do with that, and besides the Flyers wouldn't have been anywhere near the heights they reached if not for Lindros. It's easy to forget sometimes that the big guy is human.

So, the Flyers will go for the Cup again this year, and when they do they'll try to be sure they have no excuses or anyone to blame if they fail.

## STUFF

* goalie Garth Snow has been involved in fights with all three Buffalo netminders - Andrei Trefilov, Dominik Hasek and Steve Shields.
* the Flyers have had the exact same 45-24-13 record each of the last two years.
* a 17-game point streak by Eric Lindros was the second longest in the league last year, behind a 20-game streak by Adam Oates.
* Rod Brind'Amour finished the regular season with a six-game point streak, while Trent Klatt scored in each of the last five games.
* the Flyers tied Dallas for the longest winning streak last year, seven games.
* the Flyers also had the longest undefeated streak of the season, 17 games.
* Philadelphia had the longest road undefeated streak, at 12 games, and the longest home winning streak of eight games.
* Janne Niinimaa, with 13 points, was just one short of the playoff record for rookie defencemen.

## STAT ANALYSIS

The Flyers are hoping to be the first finalist loser to win
the Stanley Cup the following year, since Edmonton in 1983.

A team that makes it to the finals plays four series, giving them plenty of playoff experience. So, how come they lose so often and so early the next season.

Of the 15 teams in the list below, seven of

them lost in the first round, one didn't even make the playoffs, five others lost in the second round, and just one made it to the conference finals. The only club to make it back to the finals was Edmonton, who won the Cup in 1983.

* Stanley Cup Final Loser The Following Year (since Conference setup in 1982):

|      | Final Loser | Next Year |
|------|-------------|-----------|
| 1996 | Florida     | Lost first round |
| 1995 | Detroit     | Lost Conference Semi-Finals |
| 1994 | Vancouver   | Lost Conference Semi-Finals |
| 1993 | Los Angeles | Missed Playoffs |
| 1992 | Chicago     | Lost first round |
| 1991 | Minnesota   | Lost first round |
| 1990 | Boston      | Lost Conference Finals |
| 1989 | Montreal    | Lost Division Finals |
| 1988 | Boston      | Lost Division Finals |
| 1987 | Philadelphia| Lost First Round |
| 1986 | Calgary     | Lost First Round |
| 1985 | Philadelphia| Lost First Round |
| 1984 | NY Islanders| Lost Division Finals |
| 1983 | Edmonton    | WON STANLEY CUP |
| 1982 | Vancouver   | Lost first round |

## TEAM PREVIEW

GOAL: There's not much use speculating on this position for the upcoming season, because it won't look the same by the end of the year. Whether they need it or not, the Flyers are bound to make a change in this position.

Who will it be? One rumor last year had Felix Potvin of the Maple Leafs going to Philadelphia, but aside from Dominik Hasek, Martin Brodeur, Patrick Roy, Mike Richter, and a few others, it's going to be hard to satisfy the Flyers fans.

The other option is to see whether their

top prospect Brian Boucher is ready. The Flyers' first round pick in 1995 was the goalie of the year in the WHL for the Tri-City Americans. He was bombarded with shots on an extremely weak team, which shows you how well he must have played. It's unusual, however, for goalies to play in the NHL right out of junior. Most of the time, they serve their apprenticeship in the minors.

Hockey Annual Rating: 17 of 26

DEFENCE: Janne Niinimaa was not the rookie of the year last season, but he wasn't far away from it. He was only fourth in the balloting, but came on later in the season and didn't get as much publicity as the players in front of him. His point totals were third among rookies, four behind Calder Trophy winner and defenceman, Bryan Berard, and six behind Jarome Iginla. In the playoffs, he led all rookie scorers with 13 points.

Eric Desjardins, one of the best two-way defencemen in the game, had a good offensive year, but the Flyers felt they needed help on the power play point, and picked up Paul Coffey. Coffey was troubled by injuries, and never did contribute much. He's never going to be completely healthy, but if he's at least healthier, the Flyers are in great shape offensively from the blueline. Few teams can match them in that respect.

The Flyers have their big guys back on defence again this year, and they picked up the prize in the free agent lottery. Luke Richardson is going to make a good defence even better. Chris Therien, mentioned often in

trade rumors is 6-4, 230; Karl Dykhuis is 6-3, 205, and Kjell Samuelsson is 6-6, 235, and will be 39-years-old in October.

Petr Svoboda, one of the most frequently injured players in NHL history, also contributes when he's in uniform.

With the additon of Richardson, the Flyers defence is now probably the best in the league.

Hockey Annual Rating: 1 of 26

FORWARD: If Lindros hadn't been hurt last season and missed 30 games, his pro-rated point total would have led the league in scoring with 125 points, two more than Mario Lemieux.

For some reason, Lindros doesn't get the same level of respect that has been given to the other recent superstars, Lemieux and Wayne Gretzky. Instead, people try to pick him apart and find something wrong with him. The only problem Lindros has exhibited, is an in ability to be dominant game in and game out. He's dominant all right, but just not every single shift. When he reaches that level, he can take his place with Lemieux and Gretzky. A Stanley Cup would help and another scoring championship. Both of those goals are within his grasp this season.

Sometimes we suspect a player like John LeClair benefits too much from playing with someone like Lindros. It doesn't hurt him, but LeClair has proven he can do it on his own. When Lindros missed the first 23 games of the season last year, LeClair had 13 goals, a pace that projects to 46 for a season without Lindros. Previously, the Flyers would have

| GOALTENDER | GPI | MINS | AVG | W | L | T | EN | SO | GA | SA | SV % |
|---|---|---|---|---|---|---|---|---|---|---|---|
| GARTH SNOW | 35 | 1884 | 2.52 | 14 | 8 | 8 | 2 | 2 | 79 | 816 | .903 |
| RON HEXTALL | 55 | 3094 | 2.56 | 31 | 16 | 5 | 4 | 5 | 132 | 1285 | .897 |
| PHI TOTALS | 82 | 4995 | 2.61 | 45 | 24 | 13 | 6 | 7 | 217 | 2107 | .897 |

collapsed without Lindros. LeClair was one of four 50-goal scorers in the league last year, and finished fourth in scoring, and second in all-star voting at left wing, behind Paul Kariya.

The Flyers played around a bit with the Legion of Doom line last year. Renberg didn't have a good year, although the line clicked at different times. Oddly enough, it was their 1996 first round draft pick Dainius Zubrus who looked so good in that spot during the playoffs. Zubrus was the only draft selection from last year to play regularly with his team, and many are predicting future stardom.

Another rookie who shone, but in a shorter audition, was Vaclav Prospal. Not considered much of a prospect previously, he turned heads immediately when joining the Flyers and earned 15 points in 18 games. He was doing the job in the playoffs too, before getting injured.

The biggest improvement by a Flyer last year probably came from Trent Klatt, who was close to the edge of being written off. Not only did he play a valuable role as a checker, but he scored a bonus 24 goals, fourth best on the team. Shjon Podein is on the same page. Now, if only they could do the same thing for Pat Falloon.

Rod Brind'Amour is a valuable second-liner who could play on the first line for many teams. Players like him lead to overall team success because he provides balance. He's also important on the power play.

Others expected back are Joel Otto, one of the best defensive centres in the league; Dale Hawerchuk, although his career is winding down quickly; and John Druce, who is a capable fill-in.

They also have the meanest, toughest, orneriest line in the league when they're together, in Scott Daniels (237 PIM), Dan Kordic (210 PIM) and Daniel Lacroix (163 PIM). Opposing players may not look forward to facing the Legion of Doom, but they have nightmares facing these guys. Maybe they should get their own nickname. How about the Legion of Kaboom?

Hockey Annual Rating: 3 of 26

SPECIAL TEAMS: The Flyers should be in the top five in the league on the power play. A ranking of 18th is extremely curious, and perhaps just a fluke. Watch and see if they aren't much better this year.

Penalty killing, as usual, is in good hands, with good penalty killers such as Brind'Amour, Klatt, Otto and Podein.

POWER PLAY

|  | G | ATT | PCT |
|---|---|---|---|
| Overall | 53 | 362 | 14.6% (T-18th NHL) |
| Home | 24 | 180 | 13.3% (T-22nd NHL) |
| Road | 29 | 182 | 15.9% (13th NHL) |

8 SHORT HANDED GOALS ALLOWED (T-4th NHL)

PENALTY KILLING

|  | G | TSH | PCT |
|---|---|---|---|
| Overall | 49 | 342 | 85.7% (6th NHL) |
| Home | 26 | 156 | 83.3% (T-14th NHL) |
| Road | 23 | 186 | 87.6% (3rd NHL) |

11 SHORT HANDED GOALS SCORED (T-9th NHL)

FLYERS SPECIAL TEAMS SCORING

| Power play | G | A | PTS |
|---|---|---|---|
| NIINIMAA | 1 | 23 | 24 |
| LINDROS | 9 | 14 | 23 |
| LECLAIR | 10 | 6 | 16 |
| DESJARDINS | 5 | 11 | 16 |
| BRIND'AMOUR | 8 | 5 | 13 |
| HAWERCHUK | 6 | 5 | 11 |
| RENBERG | 1 | 8 | 9 |
| COFFEY | 1 | 8 | 9 |
| KLATT | 5 | 3 | 8 |
| FALLOON | 2 | 4 | 6 |

| | | | |
|---|---|---|---|
| PROSPAL | 0 | 6 | 6 |
| DYKHUIS | 2 | 3 | 5 |
| ZUBRUS | 1 | 2 | 3 |
| THERIEN | 0 | 3 | 3 |
| SVOBODA | 1 | 1 | 2 |
| PETIT | 0 | 2 | 2 |
| LACROIX | 1 | 0 | 1 |
| DRUCE | 1 | 0 | 1 |
| PODEIN | 0 | 1 | 1 |

| Short handed | G | A | PTS |
|---|---|---|---|
| KLATT | 5 | 0 | 5 |
| BRIND'AMOUR | 2 | 2 | 4 |
| OTTO | 1 | 2 | 3 |
| DESJARDINS | 1 | 1 | 2 |
| THERIEN | 0 | 2 | 2 |
| DARBY | 1 | 0 | 1 |
| COFFEY | 1 | 0 | 1 |
| PODEIN | 0 | 1 | 1 |
| FALLOON | 0 | 1 | 1 |

COACHING AND MANAGEMENT: The new coach of the Flyers is Wayne Cashman, who has been around for a while as an assistant, and has long been rumored as a head coaching prospect. A couple pieces of advice: get Lindros on your side, and don't call the players "chokers".

Clarke will continue to do what he does as well or better than any general manager in the game — build championship teams. He has some talented players, but he's also able to recognize chemistry and character. You can have all the talent in the world, but it won't make you a winner. Clarke's a winner.

He was also able to get some young players in the lineup last year, something he had been accused of neglecting. If he can fit the youngsters in gradually with the veterans it ensures the team will be competitive for a long, long time.

Hockey Annual Rating: 3 of 26

## DRAFT

| Round | Sel. | Player | Pos | Amateur Team |
|---|---|---|---|---|
| 2 | 30 | Jean-Marc Pelletier | G | Cornell |
| 2 | 50 | Pat Kavanagh | RW | Peterborough (OHL) |
| 3 | 62 | Kris Mallette | D | Kelowna (WHL) |
| 4 | 103 | Mikhail Chernov | D | Russia |
| 6 | 158 | Jordon Flodell | D | Moose Jaw (WHL) |
| 7 | 164 | Todd Fedoruk | LW | Kelowna (WHL) |
| 8 | 214 | Marko Kauppinen | D | Finland |
| 9 | 240 | Par Styf | D | Sweden |

The Flyers didn't have a first round pick. They chose Jean-Marc Pelletier in the second round, despite the fact that he was only the ninth rated North American goalie by Central Scouting, and despite the fact that he's just a backup at Cornell University.

*The Hockey News* had him rated considerably higher at 37th overall. They suggest he could be one of the best dark-horse canidates in the draft.

## PROGNOSIS

The Flyers could go *ALL..THE...WAY*.

There are too many variables which determine a Stanley Cup champion, but they are one of the teams this year that can win it.

As for the regular season, it won't matter so much to the Flyers this year, but they're too good not to finish with close to the best record in the league.

## PREDICTION

Eastern Conference: 1st
Overall: 1st

## STAT SECTION

| Team Scoring Stats | 1996-97 | | | | | CAREER | | | | | |
|---|---|---|---|---|---|---|---|---|---|---|---|
| | GP | G | A | PTS | +/- | PIM | SH | Gm | G | A | Pts |
| JOHN LECLAIR | 82 | 50 | 47 | 97 | 44 | 58 | 324 | 425 | 175 | 186 | 361 |
| ERIC LINDROS | 52 | 32 | 47 | 79 | 31 | 136 | 198 | 297 | 193 | 243 | 436 |
| ROD BRIND'AMOUR | 82 | 27 | 32 | 59 | 2 | 41 | 205 | 614 | 213 | 342 | 555 |
| MIKAEL RENBERG | 77 | 22 | 37 | 59 | 36 | 65 | 249 | 258 | 109 | 132 | 241 |
| ERIC DESJARDINS | 82 | 12 | 34 | 46 | 25 | 50 | 183 | 601 | 67 | 228 | 295 |
| TRENT KLATT | 76 | 24 | 21 | 45 | 9 | 20 | 131 | 303 | 61 | 86 | 147 |
| JANNE NIINIMAA | 77 | 4 | 40 | 44 | 12 | 58 | 141 | 77 | 4 | 40 | 44 |
| DALE HAWERCHUK | 51 | 12 | 22 | 34 | 9 | 32 | 102 | 1,188 | 518 | 891 | 1,409 |
| PAUL COFFEY | 57 | 9 | 25 | 34 | 11 | 38 | 110 | 1,211 | 381 | 1,063 | 1,444 |
| SHJON PODEIN | 82 | 14 | 18 | 32 | 7 | 41 | 153 | 273 | 48 | 46 | 94 |
| JOEL OTTO | 78 | 13 | 19 | 32 | 12 | 99 | 105 | 875 | 192 | 309 | 501 |
| CHRIS THERIEN | 71 | 2 | 22 | 24 | 26 | 64 | 107 | 201 | 11 | 49 | 60 |
| PAT FALLOON | 52 | 11 | 12 | 23 | 8- | 10 | 124 | 372 | 109 | 124 | 233 |
| DAINIUS ZUBRUS | 68 | 8 | 13 | 21 | 3 | 22 | 71 | 68 | 8 | 13 | 21 |
| KARL DYKHUIS | 62 | 4 | 15 | 19 | 7 | 35 | 101 | 195 | 12 | 44 | 56 |
| JOHN DRUCE | 43 | 7 | 8 | 15 | 5- | 12 | 73 | 508 | 112 | 124 | 236 |
| VACLAV PROSPAL | 18 | 5 | 10 | 15 | 3 | 4 | 35 | 18 | 5 | 10 | 15 |
| PETR SVOBODA | 67 | 2 | 12 | 14 | 10 | 94 | 36 | 824 | 47 | 282 | 329 |
| MICHEL PETIT | 38 | 2 | 7 | 9 | 11- | 71 | 43 | 795 | 86 | 236 | 322 |
| DANIEL LACROIX | 74 | 7 | 1 | 8 | 1- | 163 | 54 | 127 | 10 | 3 | 13 |
| SCOTT DANIELS | 56 | 5 | 3 | 8 | 2 | 237 | 48 | 122 | 8 | 9 | 17 |
| KJELL SAMUELSSON | 34 | 4 | 3 | 7 | 17 | 47 | 36 | 718 | 47 | 131 | 178 |
| CRAIG DARBY | 9 | 1 | 4 | 5 | 2 | 2 | 13 | 32 | 1 | 8 | 9 |
| DAN KORDIC | 75 | 1 | 4 | 5 | 1- | 210 | 21 | 134 | 3 | 7 | 10 |
| COLIN FORBES | 3 | 1 | 0 | 1 | 0 | 0 | 3 | 3 | 1 | 0 | 1 |
| ARIS BRIMANIS | 3 | 0 | 1 | 1 | 0 | 0 | 1 | 21 | 0 | 3 | 3 |
| JASON BOWEN | 4 | 0 | 1 | 1 | 1 | 8 | 1 | 73 | 2 | 6 | 8 |
| GARTH SNOW | 35 | 0 | 1 | 1 | 0 | 30 | 0 | | | | |
| PAUL HEALEY | 2 | 0 | 0 | 0 | 0 | 0 | 0 | 2 | 0 | 0 | 0 |
| FRANTISEK KUCERA | 4 | 0 | 0 | 0 | 2- | 2 | 5 | 354 | 21 | 75 | 96 |
| DARREN RUMBLE | 10 | 0 | 0 | 0 | 2- | 0 | 9 | 157 | 10 | 22 | 32 |
| RON HEXTALL | 55 | 0 | 0 | 0 | 0 | 43 | 0 | | | | |

## TEAM RANKINGS

| | | Conference Rank | League Rank |
|---|---|---|---|
| Record | 45-24-13 | 2 | 4 |
| Home | 23-12-6 | 4 | 6 |
| Away | 22-12-7 | 1 | 2 |
| Versus Own Conference | 29-19-8 | 3 | 5 |
| Versus Other Conference | 16-5-5 | 1 | 2 |
| Team Plus\Minus | +53 | 1 | 2 |
| Goals For | 274 | 2 | 3 |
| Goals Against | 217 | 4 | 8 |
| Average Shots For | 32.2 | 1 | 2 |
| Average Shots Against | 25.3 | 1 | 1 |
| Overtime | 3-2-13 | 4 | 10 |
| One Goal Games | 18-9 | 1 | 1 |
| Times outshooting opponent | 59 | 1 | 1 |

| | | | |
|---|---|---|---|
| Versus Teams Over .500 | 19-12-5 | 2 | 3 |
| Versus Teams Under .500 | 26-12-8 | 2 | 5 |
| First Half Record | 25-12-4 | 1 | 1 |
| Second Half Record | 20-12-9 | 2 | 5 |

## PLAYOFFS

Results:  defeated Pittsburgh 4-1
defeated Buffalo 4-1
defeated NY Rangers 4-1
lost to Detroit 4-0

Record: 12-7
Home: 6-4
Away: 6-3
Goals For: 67 (3.5/game)
Goals Against: 55 (2.9/game)
Overtime: 0-1
Power play: 19.1% (6th)
Penalty Killing: 78.7% (13th)

| | GP | G | A | PTS | +/- | PIM | PP | SH | GW | OT | S |
|---|---|---|---|---|---|---|---|---|---|---|---|
| ERIC LINDROS | 19 | 12 | 14 | 26 | 7 | 40 | 4 | 0 | 1 | 0 | 71 |
| ROD BRIND'AMOUR | 19 | 13 | 8 | 21 | 9 | 10 | 4 | 2 | 1 | 0 | 65 |
| JOHN LECLAIR | 19 | 9 | 12 | 21 | 5 | 10 | 4 | 0 | 3 | 0 | 79 |
| JANNE NIINIMAA | 19 | 1 | 12 | 13 | 3 | 16 | 1 | 0 | 1 | 0 | 56 |
| MIKAEL RENBERG | 18 | 5 | 6 | 11 | 1 | 4 | 2 | 0 | 0 | 0 | 35 |
| ERIC DESJARDINS | 19 | 2 | 8 | 10 | 9 | 12 | 0 | 0 | 0 | 0 | 49 |
| DAINIUS ZUBRUS | 19 | 5 | 4 | 9 | 3 | 12 | 1 | 0 | 1 | 0 | 28 |
| PAUL COFFEY | 17 | 1 | 8 | 9 | - | 6 | 0 | 0 | 0 | 0 | 37 |
| TRENT KLATT | 19 | 4 | 3 | 7 | 1 | 12 | 0 | 0 | 2 | 0 | 26 |
| SHJON PODEIN | 19 | 4 | 3 | 7 | 4 | 16 | 0 | 0 | 1 | 0 | 52 |
| DALE HAWERCHUK | 17 | 2 | 5 | 7 | 2- | 0 | 1 | 0 | 1 | 0 | 24 |
| CHRIS THERIEN | 19 | 1 | 6 | 7 | 14 | 6 | 0 | 0 | 1 | 0 | 36 |
| JOEL OTTO | 18 | 1 | 5 | 6 | 3 | 8 | 0 | 0 | 0 | 0 | 23 |
| PAT FALLOON | 14 | 3 | 1 | 4 | 1- | 2 | 1 | 0 | 0 | 0 | 32 |
| VACLAV PROSPAL | 5 | 1 | 3 | 4 | 0 | 4 | 0 | 0 | 0 | 0 | 10 |

| PETR SVOBODA | 16 | 1 | 2 | 3 | 4 | 16 | 0 | 0 | 0 | 0 | 9 |
|---|---|---|---|---|---|---|---|---|---|---|---|
| KARL DYKHUIS | 18 | 0 | 3 | 3 | 1 | 2 | 0 | 0 | 0 | 0 | 15 |
| GARTH SNOW | 12 | 0 | 2 | 2 | 0 | 11 | 0 | 0 | 0 | 0 | 0 |
| DAN KORDIC | 12 | 1 | 0 | 1 | 1 | 22 | 0 | 0 | 0 | 0 | 3 |
| JOHN DRUCE | 13 | 1 | 0 | 1 | 2 | 2 | 0 | 1 | 0 | 0 | 10 |
| DANIEL LACROIX | 12 | 0 | 1 | 1 | 0 | 22 | 0 | 0 | 0 | 0 | 4 |
| MICHEL PETIT | 3 | 0 | 0 | 0 | 1- | 6 | 0 | 0 | 0 | 0 | 1 |
| COLIN FORBES | 3 | 0 | 0 | 0 | 0 | 0 | 0 | 0 | 0 | 0 | 3 |
| KJELL SAMUELSSON | 5 | 0 | 0 | 0 | 3- | 2 | 0 | 0 | 0 | 0 | 4 |
| RON HEXTALL | 8 | 0 | 0 | 0 | 0 | 0 | 0 | 0 | 0 | 0 | 0 |

| GOALTENDER | GPI | MINS | AVG | W | L | T | EN | SO | GA | SA | SV % |
|---|---|---|---|---|---|---|---|---|---|---|---|
| GARTH SNOW | 12 | 699 | 2.83 | 8 | 4 | 0 | 0 | 0 | 33 | 305 | .892 |
| RON HEXTALL | 8 | 444 | 2.97 | 4 | 3 | 0 | 0 | 0 | 22 | 203 | .892 |
| PHI TOTALS | 20 | 1146 | 2.88 | 12 | 7 | 0 | 0 | 0 | 55 | 508 | .892 |

## ALL-TIME LEADERS

### Goals
| Bill Barber | 420 |
|---|---|
| Brian Propp | 369 |
| Tim Kerr | 363 |

### Assists
| Bobby Clarke | 852 |
|---|---|
| Brian Propp | 480 |
| Bill Barber | 463 |

### Points
| Bobby Clarke | 1,210 |
|---|---|
| Bill Barber | 883 |
| Brian Propp | 849 |

## BEST INDIVIDUAL SEASONS

### Goals
| Reg Leach | 1975-76 | 61 |
|---|---|---|
| Tim Kerr | 1986-87 | 58 |
| Tim Kerr | 1985-86 | 58 |

### Assists
| Bobby Clarke | 1975-76 | 89 |
|---|---|---|
| Bobby Clarke | 1974-75 | 89 |
| Mark Recchi | 1992-93 | 70 |

### Points
| Mark Recchi | 1992-93 | 123 |
|---|---|---|
| Bobby Clarke | 1975-76 | 119 |
| Bobby Clarke | 1974-75 | 116 |

## TEAM

### Last 3 years
| | GP | W | L | T | Pts | % |
|---|---|---|---|---|---|---|
| 1996-97 | 82 | 45 | 24 | 13 | 103 | .628 |
| 1995-96 | 82 | 45 | 24 | 13 | 103 | .628 |
| 1994-95 | 48 | 28 | 16 | 4 | 60 | .625 |

Best 3 regular seasons

| | | | | | | |
|---|---|---|---|---|---|---|
| 1975-76 | 80 | 51 | 13 | 16 | 118 | .738 |
| 1979-80 | 80 | 48 | 12 | 20 | 116 | .725 |
| 1973-74 | 76 | 51 | 18 | 11 | 113 | .718 |

Worst 3 regular seasons

| | | | | | | |
|---|---|---|---|---|---|---|
| 1969-70 | 76 | 17 | 35 | 24 | 58 | .382 |
| 1968-69 | 76 | 20 | 35 | 21 | 61 | .401 |
| 1971-72 | 78 | 26 | 38 | 14 | 66 | .423 |

Most Goals (min. 70 game schedule)

| | |
|---|---|
| 1983-84 | 350 |
| 1984-85 | 348 |
| 1975-76 | 348 |

Fewest Goals (min. 70 game schedule)

| | |
|---|---|
| 1967-68 | 173 |
| 1968-69 | 174 |
| 1969-70 | 197 |

Most Goals Against (min. 70 game schedule)

| | |
|---|---|
| 1992-93 | 319 |
| 1993-94 | 314 |
| 1981-82 | 313 |

Fewest Goals Against (min. 70 game schedule)

| | |
|---|---|
| 1973-74 | 164 |
| 1967-68 | 179 |
| 1974-75 | 181 |

# Pittsburgh Penguins

So ends an era in Pittsburgh.

Mario Lemieux wasn't the perfect hero, and never pretended to be. He wasn't Wayne Gretzky either, hockey's playing ambassador.

But on the ice he was good, one of the best to ever play the game. These are just some of his many accomplishments.

* had 613 goals, 6th on the all-time list, and first in goals per game.
* had 881 assists, 11th on the all-time list, tied with Phil Esposito.
* had 1,494 points, 6th on the all-time list.
* six scoring championships
* three Hart Trophies as MVP.
* two Conn Smythe trophies as playoff MVP.
* was a first team all star five times, and second team three times.
* at home, Lemieux had stats of 331-478-809 in just 381 games.
* had 39 hat-tricks.
* tied a record for most goals in a period (4) just last year, and has a share of the playoff record, also four goals in one period.
* had 10 four-goal games.
* scored six points in the 1988 all-star game, the most ever by one player. Also tied a record with four goals in that game. His 20 career all-star points are the most by any player.
* scored the final two winning goals, and 11 goals in nine games, to lead Canada to the 1987 Canada Cup championship.

* holds 51 Pittsburgh team records.
* had three five-goal games.
* holds the NHL record for most shorthanded goals in a season, with 13.
* holds the regular season mark for most career overtime goals (9) and most career overtime points (19).
* had a 46-game scoring streak
* won two Stanley Cups.

## STUFF

* the Penguins got off to their worst road start in team history, losing their first eight in a row, and going 0-11-1 in their first 12. The team record for most consecutive road losses is 18, which they did in 1970-71 and 1982-83.
* the Penguins were also 0-12-1 in their final 13 road games, which means between the poor start and the poor finish, they were 13-2-1 on the road.
* the Penguins set a team record when they didn't allow a power play goal in nine straight games.
* Joe Mullen became the first American player to score 500 NHL goals. He retired after the season.
* the Penguins tied an NHL playoff record when Ed Olczyk and Petr Nedved scored shorthanded goals in the same period.
* Lemieux scored on a penalty shot late last

season. In his career he was 7 for 9.

* farmhand Jeff Christian was suspended for 20 games while playing for Cleveland in the IHL, for shooting a puck at a referee.

* Jagr had the longest goal-streak in the league last year of nine games.

* Ron Francis needs 56 assists to reach 1,000 for his career.

## STAT ANALYSIS

The Penguins decided to take the season off after the all-star break, maybe in farewell tribute to Mario Lemieux.

At the break they had a record of 25-15-5, which was fourth best in the league. After the break they reversed themselves and had a 13-21-3 mark, good for fourth worst.

There's not much point trying to figure out the Penguins. They were a strange team. Check their rankings, they were all over the board. First in goals for, second last in goals against. First in home winning percentage, near the bottom on the road.

Just an odd team.

## TEAM PREVIEW

GOAL: No goaltender in history has ever had the start to his career that Patrick Lalime did. He went undefeated in his first 16 NHL games (14-0-2), the longest such streak in the history of the NHL. The previous record was 14 games, held by Ken Dryden of the Montreal Canadiens, and Ross Brooks of Boston.

When his streak ended, he was leading the league with a 1.94 goals against average, and a .938 save percentage.

A funny thing about Lalime, however. Even while he was putting together his amazing streak, some people were puzzled. He hadn't put up good numbers in the minors and he wasn't even considered the top prospect in Pittsburgh. After Ken Wregget and Tom Barrasso, Philippe De Rouville was supposed to be the man next in line. And uneasy with their goaltending situation, the Penguins selected Craig Hillier in the first round of the 1996 draft.

When Lalime came back to earth, he fell with a thud. After that great start his win-loss record was just 7-12-0, and his GAA and save percentage both ballooned. By the end of the season, he was back to where he was before the streak. If nothing else, Lalime will always remember The Streak, and was named to the NHL's all-rookie team.

It's tough to figure out if Barrasso will be able to play this season or if he'll be able last long if he does. He's been overcome by injuries so much in the last couple seasons, and he's not very good for team chemistry, being unpopular with many of his teammates. Wregget should be able to play lots, and of course, Lalime and De Rouville are capable of backing up.

Hockey Annual Rating: 25 of 26

| GOALTENDER | GPI | MINS | AVG | W | L | T | EN | SO | GA | SA | SV % |
|---|---|---|---|---|---|---|---|---|---|---|---|
| PATRICK LALIME | 39 | 2058 | 2.94 | 21 | 12 | 2 | 3 | 3 | 101 | 1166 | .913 |
| P. DE ROUVILLE | 2 | 111 | 3.24 | 0 | 2 | 0 | 1 | 0 | 6 | 66 | .909 |
| KEN WREGGET | 46 | 2514 | 3.25 | 17 | 17 | 6 | 6 | 2 | 136 | 1383 | .902 |
| TOM BARRASSO | 5 | 270 | 5.78 | 0 | 5 | 0 | 1 | 0 | 26 | 186 | .860 |
| PIT TOTALS | 82 | 4969 | 3.38 | 38 | 36 | 8 | 11 | 5 | 280 | 2812 | .900 |

DEFENCE: It wasn't easy playing defence on the Penguins. Kind of like trying to protect yourself from a monsoon with a newspaper over your head.

Things are expected to be different this year with Kevin Constantine as coach. One thing for certain, they couldn't be any worse.

When the opposing teams get tons of shots and tons of goals, it's the defence that gets blamed, but usually at least an equal part of the blame should be handed to the forwards. Many of them on the Penguins last year, couldn't care less what was happening behind their own blueline. Some didn't even know where that was.

One of the problems seen with Pittsburgh's defence was a lack of muscle, especially evident in their playoff series against Philadelphia, when they couldn't handle Lindros and company.

Kevin Hatcher was being touted in the earlier part of last year as a possible Norris candidate, but later in the year people were wondering why he didn't use his size more effectively. The notorious Darius Kasparaitis, obtained from the Islanders last year, is a good guy to have around in that respect. Opposing players are well aware that he's one of the dirtiest players in the game, so it keeps them looking over their shoulder.

Chris Tamer, Francois Leroux and Neil Wilkinson are all big guys and should get some work, as should the smaller, but effective Ian Moran, a rare NHL defenceman under six feet tall.

For offensive purposes only, along with Hatcher, are Jason Wooley and Fredrik Olausson.

The Pens expect to audition a couple new blueliners, including Sven Butenschon and Stefan Bergkvist, who played with Cleveland in the IHL last season. Bergkvist is an interesting story in that he had to undergo surgery last year to remove a benign brain tumor. He was back and playing by the end of the season.

The Penguin defence is going to look better this year, if there's a better committment to help from the forwards, but they're still not very impressive. Patrick will likely make some moves to get guys with size who use it better.

Hockey Annual Rating: 21 of 26

FORWARD: Okay, let's see what's left.

How about Jaromir Jagr, one of the best players in the game?

How about Ron Francis, a Mr. Everything who seems to improve with age.

How about Petr Nedved, a dependable goal scorer.

That's a lot better start than most teams have.

There is also some squawking about the Penguins being weak at centre without Lemieux. Naturally, his leaving creates a hole, but they're still not that weak at the position, just weaker.

Nedved has to be signed, always a difficult task, but with him and Francis they have a good one-two punch. Then there's Stu Barnes, giving them three scoring centres, a rarity in the NHL. Then there's Alex Hicks, Greg Johnson and Ed Olczyk, all of whom play centre or wing. Getting a fourth line centre won't be a difficult task.

They don't have much left for offence, however, and may not need too much if they can fill with good two-way players, or even just defensive players for that matter.

GM Patrick has changed his supporting cast frequently over the years, but to start with there is Gary Valk, Joe Dzeidzic, Dave Roche, and tough guy Alek Stojanov. Jeff Christian scored well in the minors and in a short stay in Pittsburgh, and Roman Oksiuta is one of those guys who scores for two weeks and then takes two months off.

There will be plenty of changes.

One guy the Penguins would like to get signed and in the lineup is Alexei Morozov. He's considered a future star in the NHL. Like most Europeans, however, he looks a lot better before he gets to this side of the Atlantic. The last can't miss superstar the Penguins had was Markus Naslund, who couldn't score in Pittsburgh and was traded to Vancouver for Stojanov.

Sometimes when a big superstar like Lemieux leaves, players rise to the challenge and take up the slack. In the 1994-95 season, all of which Lemieux missed, the Penguins did very well. When a team has a superior star, they sometimes sit back and let him do the work.

It should be interesting, but one footnote to the Penguins season from last year, is how great the line of Lemieux, Francis and Jagr played. Coach Johnston had them apart to try and create some balance, but when he put them together the Penguins went 19-2-4 in their first 25 games. Lemieux had 53 points, Jagr 49 and Francis 31. With all the linemates and want-to-be's Lemieux has endured over his career it was kind of ironic that in his final season he had the best line of his career and probably one of the best (over the short term) in NHL history.

Hockey Annual Rating: 19 of 26

SPECIAL TEAMS: Absolutely no surprise that the Penguins power play was rated second and that their penalty killing was 23rd.

Even this season, without Lemeiux, it will be among the best in the game. Not that Lemieux wasn't the perfect power play performer, because he was one of the best in the history of the game.

Jagr, Francis and Nedved can handle things quite nicely, as can Kevin Hatcher on the point.

As for the penalty killing, it's getting rather silly, not just with the Penguins but with many teams. The idea should be to stop the other team from scoring, not to try and score themselves.

POWER PLAY

|         | G  | ATT | PCT              |
|---------|----|-----|------------------|
| Overall | 74 | 338 | 21.9% (2nd NHL)  |
| Home    | 33 | 169 | 19.5% (T-2nd NHL)|
| Road    | 41 | 169 | 24.3% (1st NHL)  |

12 SHORT HANDED GOALS ALLOWED (T-19th NHL)

PENALTY KILLING

|         | G  | TSH | PCT              |
|---------|----|-----|------------------|
| Overall | 64 | 338 | 81.1% (23rd NHL) |
| Home    | 28 | 169 | 83.4% (13th NHL) |
| Road    | 36 | 169 | 78.7% (25th NHL) |

10 SHORT HANDED GOALS SCORED (T-13th NHL)

PENGUINS SPECIAL TEAMS SCORING

| Power play  | G  | A  | PTS |
|-------------|----|----|-----|
| LEMIEUX     | 15 | 22 | 37  |
| FRANCIS     | 10 | 24 | 34  |
| NEDVED      | 12 | 14 | 26  |
| JAGR        | 11 | 14 | 25  |
| HATCHER     | 9  | 16 | 25  |
| OLCZYK      | 5  | 13 | 18  |
| OLAUSSON    | 3  | 13 | 16  |
| WOOLLEY     | 2  | 13 | 15  |
| BARNES      | 5  | 7  | 12  |
| MULLEN      | 1  | 4  | 5   |
| JOHNSON     | 1  | 4  | 5   |
| ROCHE       | 2  | 1  | 3   |
| OKSIUTA     | 2  | 0  | 2   |
| JOHANSSON   | 1  | 1  | 2   |
| MORAN       | 0  | 2  | 2   |
| BERANEK     | 1  | 0  | 1   |
| KASPARAITIS | 0  | 1  | 1   |

| Short handed | G | A | PTS |
|---|---|---|---|
| LEMIEUX | 2 | 3 | 5 |
| NEDVED | 3 | 0 | 3 |
| JAGR | 2 | 1 | 3 |
| FRANCIS | 1 | 1 | 2 |
| KASPARAITIS | 0 | 2 | 2 |
| JOHNSON | 0 | 2 | 2 |
| TAMER | 1 | 0 | 1 |
| OLCZYK | 1 | 0 | 1 |
| VALK | 0 | 1 | 1 |
| MUNI | 0 | 1 | 1 |
| HICKS | 0 | 1 | 1 |
| HATCHER | 0 | 1 | 1 |
| BARNES | 0 | 1 | 1 |

COACHING AND MANAGEMENT: When new Pittsburgh coach Kevin Constantine was fired from the San Jose Sharks, there were plenty of horror stories about his tenure there. He was considered a tyrant, a staunch disciplinarian, and extemely intense. And that was the good stuff.

But, for a Penguins team that ranked last in spirit, intensity and discipline, that makes Constantine a good choice. He is sort of the opposite of Ed Johnston, who was fired last year and replaced by GM Craig Patrick. Johnston just let them play, which sometimes is good enough.

There's always the danger, of course, that a lax team like the Penguins may rebel against Constantine.

But, maybe not. Constantine served as an assistant coach in Calgary last year. His hiring upset the players, who threatened a revolt. But, by the end of the season, the players apparently loved him.

It's a big difference, however, between being an assistant and a head coach. Constantine will attempt to bring a bigger committment to defence, which has been a dirty word around the Penguins for a while.

Coaches learn from their mistakes when they're fired and get re-hired. Maybe Constantine has done that.

General Manager Craig Patrick has worked some miracles in the past with this team. He's not afraid to make changes, and when things aren't going well, he's active on the trading front.

One thing that Patrick hasn't seemed too concerned about, however, is bringing in players with character. If they can play the game, the rest didn't matter. It's worked for him in the past, but now he doesn't have Lemieux. With Constantine around, character, tenaciousness and attitude may be a bigger consideration.

Hockey Annual Rating: 10 of 26

DRAFT

| Round | Sel. | Player | Pos | Amateur Team |
|---|---|---|---|---|
| 1 | 17 | Robert Dome | F | Las Vegas (IHL) |
| 2 | 44 | Brian Gaffaney | D | Northern Iowa (USHL) |
| 3 | 71 | Josef Metichar | D | Czech Rep. |
| 4 | 97 | A. Mathieu | C | Halifax (QMJHL) |
| 5 | 124 | Harlan Pratt | D | Prince Albert (WHL) |
| 6 | 152 | Petr Havelka | LW | Czech Rep. |
| 7 | 179 | Mark Moore | D | Harvard |
| 8 | 208 | Andrew Ference | D | Portland (WHL) |
| 9 | 234 | Eric Lind | D | Avon Old Farms (USHS) |

Robert Dome played with three different IHL teams last year, didn't get a lot of playing time, and didn't score much. Highly touted at one time, his stock dropped and dropped. But, the Penguins like what he could become, which they think is a big-time goal scorer.

## PROGNOSIS:

It doesn't look very good for the Penguins. Everything will depend on what Constantine is able to do with this bunch. If they can maintain a good offence and have some defence at the same time, they will do okay.

They have some good talent on this team, but they're not big in character. That may not be big in the standings, either.

Look for the Penguins to miss the playoffs.

## PREDICTION

Eastern Conference: 10
Overall: 18th

## STAT SECTION

| Team Scoring Stats | 1996-97 | | | | | CAREER | | | | | |
|---|---|---|---|---|---|---|---|---|---|---|---|
| | GP | G | A | PTS | +/- | PIM | SH | Gm | G | A | Pts |
| MARIO LEMIEUX | 76 | 50 | 72 | 122 | 27 | 65 | 327 | 745 | 613 | 881 | 1,494 |
| JAROMIR JAGR | 63 | 47 | 48 | 95 | 22 | 40 | 234 | 504 | 266 | 367 | 633 |
| RON FRANCIS | 81 | 27 | 63 | 90 | 7 | 20 | 183 | 1,166 | 403 | 944 | 1,347 |
| PETR NEDVED | 74 | 33 | 38 | 71 | 2- | 66 | 189 | 441 | 158 | 179 | 337 |
| ED OLCZYK | 79 | 25 | 30 | 55 | 14- | 51 | 195 | 881 | 319 | 424 | 743 |
| KEVIN HATCHER | 80 | 15 | 39 | 54 | 11 | 103 | 199 | 886 | 189 | 361 | 550 |
| STU BARNES | 81 | 19 | 30 | 49 | 23- | 26 | 176 | 355 | 89 | 117 | 206 |
| FREDRIK OLAUSSON | 71 | 9 | 29 | 38 | 16 | 32 | 110 | 711 | 106 | 329 | 435 |
| JASON WOOLLEY | 60 | 6 | 30 | 36 | 4 | 30 | 86 | 183 | 17 | 71 | 88 |
| GREG JOHNSON | 75 | 13 | 19 | 32 | 18- | 26 | 108 | 209 | 40 | 57 | 97 |
| ALEX HICKS | 73 | 7 | 21 | 28 | 5- | 90 | 78 | 137 | 17 | 32 | 49 |
| D. KASPARAITIS | 75 | 2 | 21 | 23 | 17 | 100 | 58 | 289 | 8 | 56 | 64 |
| JOE MULLEN | 54 | 7 | 15 | 22 | 0 | 4 | 63 | 1,062 | 502 | 571 | 1,073 |
| GARRY VALK | 70 | 10 | 11 | 21 | 8- | 78 | 100 | 435 | 67 | 91 | 158 |
| JOE DZIEDZIC | 59 | 9 | 9 | 18 | 4- | 63 | 85 | 128 | 14 | 14 | 28 |
| ROMAN OKSIUTA | 35 | 6 | 7 | 13 | 16- | 26 | 58 | 153 | 46 | 37 | 83 |
| A. JOHANSSON | 42 | 4 | 9 | 13 | 12- | 20 | 59 | 45 | 4 | 10 | 14 |
| DAVE ROCHE | 61 | 5 | 5 | 10 | 13- | 155 | 53 | 132 | 12 | 12 | 24 |
| IAN MORAN | 36 | 4 | 5 | 9 | 11- | 22 | 50 | 87 | 5 | 6 | 11 |
| CHRIS TAMER | 45 | 2 | 4 | 6 | 25- | 131 | 56 | 163 | 8 | 14 | 22 |
| ALEK STOJANOV | 35 | 1 | 4 | 5 | 3 | 79 | 11 | 107 | 2 | 5 | 7 |

| | | | | | | | | | | | |
|---|---|---|---|---|---|---|---|---|---|---|---|
| JOSEF BERANEK | 8 | 3 | 1 | 4 | 1- | 4 | 15 | 324 | 77 | 88 | 165 |
| JEFF CHRISTIAN | 11 | 2 | 2 | 4 | 3- | 13 | 18 | 17 | 2 | 2 | 4 |
| TYLER WRIGHT | 45 | 2 | 2 | 4 | 7- | 70 | 30 | 86 | 5 | 3 | 8 |
| CRAIG MUNI | 64 | 0 | 4 | 4 | 6- | 36 | 19 | 779 | 27 | 118 | 145 |
| DAN QUINN | 16 | 0 | 3 | 3 | 6- | 10 | 16 | 805 | 266 | 419 | 685 |
| FRANCOIS LEROUX | 59 | 0 | 3 | 3 | 3- | 81 | 5 | 199 | 2 | 18 | 20 |
| KEN WREGGET | 46 | 0 | 1 | 1 | 0 | 6 | 0 | | | | |
| DOMENIC PITTIS | 1 | 0 | 0 | 0 | 1- | 0 | 0 | | | | |
| PHILIPPE DE ROUVILLE | 2 | 0 | 0 | 0 | 0 | 0 | 0 | | | | |
| TOM BARRASSO | 5 | 0 | 0 | 0 | 0 | 0 | 0 | | | | |
| STEFAN BERGKVIST | 5 | 0 | 0 | 0 | 1- | 7 | 0 | 7 | 0 | 0 | 0 |
| ED PATTERSON | 6 | 0 | 0 | 0 | 0 | 8 | 2 | 68 | 3 | 3 | 6 |
| NEIL WILKINSON | 23 | 0 | 0 | 0 | 12- | 36 | 16 | 402 | 14 | 63 | 77 |
| PATRICK LALIME | 39 | 0 | 0 | 0 | 0 | 0 | 0 | | | | |

## TEAM RANKINGS

| | | Conference Rank | League Rank |
|---|---|---|---|
| Record | 38-36-8 | 6 | 10 |
| Home | 25-11-5 | 1 | 2 |
| Away | 13-25-3 | 10 | 20 |
| Versus Own Conference | 23-26-7 | 9 | 16 |
| Versus Other Conference | 15-10-1 | 3 | 7 |
| Team Plus\Minus | -5 | 6 | 13 |
| Goals For | 285 | 1 | 1 |
| Goals Against | 280 | 12 | 25 |
| Average Shots For | 29.4 | 8 | 16 |
| Average Shots Against | 34.3 | 13 | 25 |
| Overtime | 1-4-8 | 13 | 25 |
| One Goal Games | 5-9 | 12 | 25 |
| Times outshooting opponent | 24 | 12 | 23 |
| Versus Teams Over .500 | 13-20-1 | 10 | 19 |
| Versus Teams Under .500 | 25-16-7 | 5 | 9 |
| First Half Record | 22-15-4 | 3 | 5 |
| Second Half Record | 16-21-4 | 11 | 21 |

## PLAYOFFS

Results: Lost 4-1 to Philadelphia
Record: 1-4
Home: 1-1
Away: 0-3
Goals For: 13 (2.6/game)
Goals Against: 20 (4.0/game)
Overtime: 0-0
Power play: 17.4% (7th)
Penalty Killing: 86.2% (6th)

| | GP | G | A | PTS | +/- | PIM | PP | SH | GW | OT | S |
|---|---|---|---|---|---|---|---|---|---|---|---|
| JAROMIR JAGR | 5 | 4 | 4 | 8 | 4- | 4 | 2 | 0 | 0 | 0 | 18 |
| MARIO LEMIEUX | 5 | 3 | 3 | 6 | 4- | 4 | 0 | 0 | 0 | 0 | 19 |
| RON FRANCIS | 5 | 1 | 2 | 3 | 7- | 2 | 1 | 0 | 0 | 0 | 6 |
| PETR NEDVED | 5 | 1 | 2 | 3 | 2- | 12 | 0 | 1 | 0 | 0 | 10 |
| IAN MORAN | 5 | 1 | 2 | 3 | 1 | 4 | 0 | 0 | 0 | 0 | 8 |
| JASON WOOLLEY | 5 | 0 | 3 | 3 | 1- | 0 | 0 | 0 | 0 | 0 | 9 |
| KEVIN HATCHER | 5 | 1 | 1 | 2 | 5- | 4 | 1 | 0 | 0 | 0 | 12 |
| ED OLCZYK | 5 | 1 | 0 | 1 | 2- | 12 | 0 | 1 | 1 | 0 | 11 |
| GREG JOHNSON | 5 | 1 | 0 | 1 | 1- | 2 | 0 | 0 | 0 | 0 | 2 |
| F. OLAUSSON | 4 | 0 | 1 | 1 | 1- | 0 | 0 | 0 | 0 | 0 | 5 |
| STU BARNES | 5 | 0 | 1 | 1 | 0 | 0 | 0 | 0 | 0 | 0 | 4 |
| JOE DZIEDZIC | 5 | 0 | 1 | 1 | 1- | 4 | 0 | 0 | 0 | 0 | 5 |
| ALEX HICKS | 5 | 0 | 1 | 1 | 1- | 2 | 0 | 0 | 0 | 0 | 2 |
| JOE MULLEN | 1 | 0 | 0 | 0 | 0 | 0 | 0 | 0 | 0 | 0 | 0 |
| FRANCOIS LEROUX | 3 | 0 | 0 | 0 | 0 | 0 | 0 | 0 | 0 | 0 | 0 |
| CRAIG MUNI | 3 | 0 | 0 | 0 | 0 | 0 | 0 | 0 | 0 | 0 | 0 |
| CHRIS TAMER | 4 | 0 | 0 | 0 | 1- | 4 | 0 | 0 | 0 | 0 | 3 |
| NEIL WILKINSON | 5 | 0 | 0 | 0 | 2- | 4 | 0 | 0 | 0 | 0 | 1 |
| KEN WREGGET | 5 | 0 | 0 | 0 | 0 | 2 | 0 | 0 | 0 | 0 | 0 |
| JOSEF BERANEK | 5 | 0 | 0 | 0 | 4- | 2 | 0 | 0 | 0 | 0 | 17 |
| D. KASPARAITIS | 5 | 0 | 0 | 0 | 4- | 6 | 0 | 0 | 0 | 0 | 7 |

| GOALTENDER | GPI | MINS | AVG | W | L | T | EN | SO | GA | SA | SV % |
|---|---|---|---|---|---|---|---|---|---|---|---|
| KEN WREGGET | 5 | 297 | 3.64 | 1 | 4 | 2 | 0 | 0 | 18 | 211 | .915 |
| PIT TOTALS | 5 | 300 | 4.00 | 1 | 4 | 2 | 0 | 0 | 20 | 213 | .906 |

## ALL-TIME LEADERS

### Goals
| | |
|---|---|
| Mario Lemieux | 613 |
| Jean Pronovost | 316 |
| Rick Kehoe | 312 |

### Assists
| | |
|---|---|
| Mario Lemieux | 867 |
| Ron Francis | 387 |
| Jaromir Jagr | 370 |

### Points
| | |
|---|---|
| Mario Lemieux | 1,494 |
| Rick Kehoe | 636 |
| Jaromir Jagr | 633 |

## BEST INDIVIDUAL SEASONS

### Goals
| | | |
|---|---|---|
| Mario Lemieux | 1988-89 | 85 |
| Mario Lemieux | 1987-88 | 70 |
| Mario Lemieux | 1992-93 | 69 |
| Mario Lemieux | 1995-96 | 69 |

### Assists
| | | |
|---|---|---|
| Mario Lemieux | 1988-89 | 114 |
| Mario Lemieux | 1987-88 | 98 |
| Mario Lemieux | 1985-86 | 93 |

### Points
| | | |
|---|---|---|
| Mario Lemieux | 1988-89 | 199 |
| Mario Lemieux | 1987-88 | 168 |
| Mario Lemieux | 1995-96 | 161 |

## TEAM

### Last 3 years
| | GP | W | L | T | Pts | % |
|---|---|---|---|---|---|---|
| 1996-97 | 82 | 38 | 36 | 8 | 84 | .561 |
| 1995-96 | 82 | 49 | 29 | 4 | 102 | .622 |
| 1994-95 | 48 | 29 | 16 | 3 | 61 | .635 |

### Best 3 regular seasons
| | | | | | | |
|---|---|---|---|---|---|---|
| 1993-94 | 84 | 56 | 21 | 7 | 119 | .708 |
| 1994-95 | 48 | 29 | 16 | 3 | 61 | .635 |
| 1995-96 | 82 | 49 | 29 | 4 | 102 | .622 |

### Worst 3 regular seasons
| | | | | | | |
|---|---|---|---|---|---|---|
| 1983-84 | 80 | 16 | 58 | 6 | 38 | .238 |
| 1982-83 | 80 | 18 | 53 | 9 | 45 | .281 |
| 1984-85 | 80 | 24 | 51 | 5 | 53 | .331 |

### Most Goals (min. 70 game schedule)
| | |
|---|---|
| 1992-93 | 367 |
| 1995-96 | 362 |
| 1988-89 | 347 |

### Fewest Goals (min. 70 game schedule)
| | |
|---|---|
| 1969-70 | 182 |
| 1968-69 | 189 |
| 1967-68 | 195 |

### Most Goals Against (min. 70 game schedule)
| | |
|---|---|
| 1982-83 | 394 |
| 1983-84 | 390 |
| 1984-85 | 385 |

### Fewest Goals Against (min. 70 game schedule)
| | |
|---|---|
| 1967-68 | 216 |
| 1969-70 | 238 |
| 1970-71 | 240 |

# Tampa Bay Lightning

When *The Hockey News* featured a mid-season scouting talent report on all teams last year, in which the Lightning placed 25th out of 26. The only team ranked below them was Boston, which did eventually finish last overall.

Tampa Bay finished last in team size (how size is used, not height and weight), last in team skating, and last in team spirit.

Well, that just wouldn't do, so GM Phil Esposito gave me a call (not really) over the summer to come up with some ideas of how to fix this team.

My first question (not really) was how well did he get along with his coach, Terry Crisp. Just fine, was the answer despite 500 or so reports to the contrary.

Is that important, to get along with your coach, I wondered. If you're winning, he replied (not really) then whatever relationship you have with your coach is the right one. When you're losing, it's the wrong one.

How true. Except in Buffalo, where John Muckler and Ted Nolan won and didn't get along, and then both were looking for work.

Okay, next question Phil, before I tell you how to fix things. How come the team failed to make the playoffs? He answered (not really) that they were in the playoff race right up to the last minute, and if not for an injury to Daren Puppa and bad seasons by Roman Hamrlik and Alexander Selivanov, they would have surely picked up a couple more points throughout the season.

How true.

Now, let me see if I understand this right, Phil. Last year was the team's fifth season ever, so the plan has been to build through the system with good young players and fill in with interchangeable veterans until the kids emerge. Hamrlik emerged, two years ago, although he fell back some last season, and then Gratton has a break out season. You're still waiting for Jason Wiemer, but Daymond Langkow showed signs of being a good scorer, Jeff Toms a good centre, and you have some young defencemen on the way up. You also have some top-line role players like Rob Zamuner, who added scoring to his role last season. You also seem to think good goaltending is important, and you have a good one there in Puppa. Two years ago you went over .500 and made the playoffs. Last year, you fell back a bit.

Is that about the size of it, I asked (not really).

Very perceptive, he answered (not really).

Okay, then I said (not really), my advice to you would be, don't change a thing, you're on the right track. Don't panic, just make a few moves as you see fit and stick to the plan. If you're going to trade underachievers such as Hamrlik or son-in-law Selivanov wait for their market value to move back up. But, if they start playing better you probably won't want to trade them anyway.

Esposito breathed a sigh of relief (not really) and thanked me profusely (not really) knowing that everything was going to be okay.

No problem, just doing my job.

## STUFF

* the Lightning scored the fewest goals in their five year existence, but also allowed the fewest.
* Dino Ciccarelli moved into the all-time goal scoring top 10 last season, passing John Bucyk, Guy Lafleur and Mike Bossy, with 586, ninth on the list.
* 47 power play goals were 10 less than their previous season low.
* the Lightning surrendered 48 shots to Vancouver in a March 15 home game, the most they've ever had against at home, and tied for the most anywhere.

## STAT ANALYSIS

Breakout seasons for forwards usually happen in his third or fourth season.

They could look like dogs in their first two or three, and it may appear as if they're never going to be useful NHLers. Then, all of a sudden, Boom! Everything starts working for them.

Why the third or fourth year? Don't know, but that's when it happens.

One note, if we can back up a bit. That's when it happens...if it's ever going to happen.

Chris Gratton had a breakout season last year. He went from 17 goals and 32 points to 30 goals and a team leading 62 points. It was his fourth year.

I could go through a list of players and show you how the above is true, but I don't have time. The book deadline is yesterday. Just take my word for it.

All that said and done, this is Jason Wiemer's fourth season. He fits the profile almost exactly. If it's going to happen for him, this is his year. It will be interesting to watch.

## TEAM PREVIEW

GOAL: The Lightning is counting on Daren Puppa's recovery from back surgery. The star goalie missed almost all of last season, but is signed and ready to go.

The team tried to compensate for Puppa's absence by using rookies Corey Schwab and Derek Wilkinson. Schwab played quite well for a while, but then it became obvious that the Lightning needed something more.

Rick Tabaracci came over from Calgary and did an outstanding job. Maybe the most underrated goalie in the league, he has now played for five NHL teams. Calgary didn't know what to do with him because he was better than their other two goalies, Trevor Kidd and Dwayne Roloson. The problem was that he wasn't supposed to be. So, they got

| GOALTENDER | GPI | MINS | AVG | W | L | T | EN | SO | GA | SA | SV % |
|---|---|---|---|---|---|---|---|---|---|---|---|
| DAREN PUPPA | 6 | 325 | 2.58 | 1 | 1 | 2 | 1 | 0 | 14 | 150 | .907 |
| RICK TABARACCI | 55 | 3012 | 2.75 | 20 | 25 | 6 | 5 | 4 | 138 | 1415 | .902 |
| COREY SCHWAB | 31 | 1462 | 3.04 | 11 | 12 | 1 | 2 | 2 | 74 | 719 | .897 |
| DEREK WILKINSON | 5 | 169 | 4.26 | 0 | 2 | 1 | 1 | 0 | 12 | 72 | .833 |
| T.B TOTALS | 82 | 4984 | 2.97 | 32 | 40 | 10 | 9 | 6 | 247 | 2365 | .896 |

him out of their sight. Then, they realized their mistake and got him back at the end of the season from Tampa Bay. Presumably, if Puppa isn't healthy, Calgary will trade him back to the Lightning.

DEFENCE: Hamrlik was supposed to be the cornerstone of the defence for the next decade or so. It has now been downgraded to day-to-day basis. The Lightning might not mind getting rid of him, but they won't do anything rash. They'd still need a quarterback for the powerplay if they didn't have him. (And might even if they still had him.) He dropped from 65 points to just 40 last season, and did complete disappearing acts at times.

Cory Cross, who played for Team Canada at the world championships, is a big boy who can be a regular, but after him are journeyman NHL defencemen who can play, but are the types that teams use just to fill out their rosters - fifth and sixth defencemen.

Igor Ulanov, Jeff Norton and David Shaw all fit into that category, along with Jamie Huscroft. Regular, Bill Houlder, was a free agent, and signed with San Jose.

Norton did provide some stability to the power play when he came over from Edmonton late last season, and Huscroft provided some toughness.

The status of Rudy Poeschek and Jay Wells has not been finalized. Wells may retire while the Lightning may elect not to re-sign Poeschek.

A couple rookies will be given a chance to make the team. Mike McBain is a character player who makes a contribution at both ends of the rink, while Mario Larocque is more of an offensive threat. Ryan Brown may be given a shot, and 25-year-old draft selection Andrei Skopintsev may get a chance right away.

FORWARD: For a team that almost scored the fewest goals in the league last season, they have some good forward talent.

Gratton had his breakout season with 30 goals, and lines up as one of the top three centres, along with Brian Bradley and Jeff Toms.

Bradley was injured for most of last season and only got into 35 games. Toms was a pleasant surprise as a strong defensive centre.

John Cullen was also having an excellent season at centre before being felled with lymphoma. He had a cancerous lump removed from his chest, and was taking treatment over the summer. He promised he would fight it off and vowed to return. The cure rate for non-Hodgkin's lymphoma is 92%.

Dino Ciccarelli heads up the right side and is the designated sniper on the power play. The 37-year-old scored 35 goals, tops on the team, and his best total since 1991-92.

Also on the right side is Selivanov, who was supposed to hit Ciccarelli-like numbers but just couldn't get it going. He has a chance to return to the 31-goal form he had the previous season in Tampa Bay, and should do it if he works hard and stops floating. Patrick Poulin, who can play the left side, only had 12 goals, and time is up on the promise he had as an NHL rookie in 1992-93. In other words, he's expendable, but nobody is likely to want him. Daymond Langkow is a centreman, but could move to the wing, depending on who's playing centre. Myhres and Andersson also can play on the right side.

On the left side is the talented Zamuner, Shawn Burr, Paul Ysebeart, and Jason Wiemer, who could be ready for a breakout season.

If you figure on a couple players increasing scoring, such as Wiemer, Langkow, Selivanov, and a healthy Bradley, an improvement in this area seems assured.

Hockey Annual Rating: 17 of 26

SPECIAL TEAMS: The Lightning dropped from fourth on the power play in 1995-96 to 24th last year. They fell from 83 power play goals to just 47. Their power play percentage went from 20.8% to 13.8%.

So what was the difference? Ciccarelli came in to take over the sniper role with the extra man, but he's one of the best at that in NHL history. Bradley was injured, which didn't help, and two other key power play performers, Hamrlik (dropped from 42 to 22 power play points) and Selivanov (dropped from 13 to 3 power play goals) had lousy seasons.

With Gratton emerging as a sniper there's no reason why the power play shouldn't be considerably higher. Hamrlik, if not traded, will have to get back on track, and others will have to pick up the slack.

Penalty killing isn't a problem as long as one of the best defensive forwards in the league, Zamuner, is around. Toms also impressed in that area. The Lightning have ranked eighth and fifth the last two seasons.

POWER PLAY

|  | G | ATT | PCT |
|---|---|---|---|
| Overall | 47 | 340 | 13.8% (24th NHL) |
| Home | 28 | 186 | 15.1% (17th NHL) |
| Road | 19 | 154 | 12.3% (23rd NHL) |

9 SHORT HANDED GOALS ALLOWED (T-9th NHL)

PENALTY KILLING

|  | G | TSH | PCT |
|---|---|---|---|
| Overall | 55 | 360 | 84.7% (T-8th NHL) |
| Home | 23 | 187 | 87.7% (2nd NHL) |
| Road | 32 | 173 | 81.5% (18th NHL) |

13 SHORT HANDED GOALS SCORED (6th NHL)

LIGHTNING SPECIAL TEAMS SCORING

| Power play | G | A | PTS |
|---|---|---|---|
| CULLEN | 5 | 18 | 23 |
| HAMRLIK | 6 | 16 | 22 |
| CICCARELLI | 12 | 6 | 18 |
| GRATTON | 9 | 9 | 18 |
| SELIVANOV | 3 | 5 | 8 |
| BRADLEY | 1 | 7 | 8 |
| LANGKOW | 3 | 3 | 6 |
| NORTON | 0 | 6 | 6 |
| BURR | 1 | 4 | 5 |
| YSEBAERT | 2 | 2 | 4 |
| POULIN | 2 | 2 | 4 |
| HOULDER | 0 | 4 | 4 |
| SHAW | 0 | 3 | 3 |
| WIEMER | 2 | 0 | 2 |
| ULANOV | 0 | 1 | 1 |

| Short handed | G | A | PTS |
|---|---|---|---|
| ZAMUNER | 4 | 4 | 8 |
| ANDERSSON | 3 | 2 | 5 |
| POULIN | 3 | 1 | 4 |
| BRADLEY | 2 | 0 | 2 |
| LANGKOW | 1 | 0 | 1 |
| WIEMER | 0 | 1 | 1 |
| NORTON | 0 | 1 | 1 |
| HOULDER | 0 | 1 | 1 |
| HAMRLIK | 0 | 1 | 1 |

COACHING AND MANAGEMENT: Whether or not Esposito and Crisp are getting along hardly seems worrisome, unless it is causing a distraction within the team, as may have been alluded to by Ciccarelli after the season. Unless, of course, he was alluding to other distractions. In any event, there's no proof that in-house wrangling translates to losing hockey.

There's a possible change in ownership in Tampa, which could mean both Esposito's and Crisp's jobs are in peril. Even if they're not, however, this season will be telling. If they don't improve over last year and make the playoffs they both could be out of a job.

Hockey Annual Rating: 11 of 26

## DRAFT

| Round | Sel. | Player | Pos | Amateur Team |
|---|---|---|---|---|
| 1 | 7 | Paul Mara | D | Sudbury (OHL) |
| 2 | 33 | Kyle Kos | D | Red Deer (WHL) |
| 3 | 61 | Matt Elich | RW | Windsor (OHL) |
| 5 | 108 | Mark Thompson | D | Regina (WHL) |
| 5 | 109 | Jan Sulc | C | Czech Rep. |
| 5 | 112 | Karel Betik | D | Kelowna (WHL) |
| 6 | 153 | Andrei Skopintsev | D | Finland |
| 7 | 168 | Justin Jack | RW | Kelowna (WHL) |
| 7 | 170 | Eero Somervuori | W | Finland |
| 7 | 185 | Samuel St. Pierre | RW | Victoriaville (QMJHL) |
| 8 | 198 | Shawn Skolney | D | Seattle (WHL) |
| 9 | 224 | Paul Comrie | C | Denver U. |

One thing is for certain, negotiations between Paul Mara's agent and Phil Esposito should be interesting. Mara's agent is Bobby Orr.

Mara looks like an excellent prospect. He's big, showed some offence with 43 points in 44 games, and had to overcome some adversity when he didn't immediately live up to his billing as a big U.S. high school star coming to save the Sudbury Wolves.

PROGNOSIS: Things are looking up, if only slightly. A lot of teams have a worse prognosis than the Lightning. At least Tampa has some young players with good potential for improvement.

It's just tough to say if they'll make it over the hump and back to respectability. Maybe they will ... *maybe*.

## PREDICTION

Eastern Conference: 11th
Overall: 19th

## STAT SECTION

| Team Scoring Stats | 1996-97 | | | | | | | CAREER | | | |
|---|---|---|---|---|---|---|---|---|---|---|---|
| | GP | G | A | PTS | +/- | PIM | SH | Gm | G | A | Pts |
| CHRIS GRATTON | 82 | 30 | 32 | 62 | 28- | 201 | 230 | 294 | 67 | 102 | 169 |
| DINO CICCARELLI | 77 | 35 | 25 | 60 | 11- | 116 | 229 | 1,156 | 586 | 574 | 1,160 |
| JOHN CULLEN | 70 | 18 | 37 | 55 | 14- | 95 | 116 | 617 | 187 | 363 | 550 |
| ROB ZAMUNER | 82 | 17 | 33 | 50 | 3 | 56 | 216 | 349 | 63 | 95 | 158 |
| ROMAN HAMRLIK | 79 | 12 | 28 | 40 | 29- | 57 | 238 | 340 | 49 | 121 | 170 |
| SHAWN BURR | 74 | 14 | 21 | 35 | 5 | 106 | 128 | 814 | 175 | 250 | 425 |

| Player | | | | | | | | | | |
|---|---|---|---|---|---|---|---|---|---|---|
| A. SELIVANOV | 69 | 15 | 18 | 33 | 3- | 61 | 187 | 191 | 56 | 45 | 111 |
| DAYMOND LANGKOW | 79 | 15 | 13 | 28 | 1 | 35 | 170 | 83 | 15 | 14 | 29 |
| PATRICK POULIN | 73 | 12 | 14 | 26 | 16- | 56 | 124 | 313 | 68 | 83 | 151 |
| BILL HOULDER | 79 | 4 | 21 | 25 | 16 | 30 | 116 | 372 | 34 | 105 | 139 |
| BRIAN BRADLEY | 35 | 7 | 17 | 24 | 2 | 16 | 93 | 637 | 180 | 316 | 496 |
| MIKAEL ANDERSSON | 70 | 5 | 14 | 19 | 1 | 8 | 102 | 587 | 85 | 148 | 233 |
| JEFF NORTON | 75 | 2 | 16 | 18 | 7- | 58 | 81 | 535 | 42 | 265 | 307 |
| PAUL YSEBAERT | 39 | 5 | 12 | 17 | 1 | 4 | 91 | 440 | 136 | 159 | 295 |
| JASON WIEMER | 63 | 9 | 5 | 14 | 13- | 134 | 103 | 165 | 19 | 18 | 37 |
| DAVID SHAW | 57 | 1 | 10 | 11 | 1 | 72 | 59 | 755 | 41 | 151 | 192 |
| JEFF TOMS | 34 | 2 | 8 | 10 | 2 | 10 | 53 | 35 | 2 | 8 | 10 |
| CORY CROSS | 72 | 4 | 5 | 9 | 6 | 95 | 75 | 195 | 7 | 24 | 31 |
| IGOR ULANOV | 59 | 1 | 7 | 8 | 2 | 108 | 56 | 302 | 9 | 60 | 69 |
| RUDY POESCHEK | 60 | 0 | 6 | 6 | 3- | 120 | 30 | 286 | 5 | 18 | 23 |
| JAMIE HUSCROFT | 52 | 0 | 5 | 5 | 2- | 151 | 40 | 257 | 5 | 27 | 32 |
| BRANTT MYHRES | 47 | 3 | 1 | 4 | 1 | 136 | 13 | 62 | 5 | 1 | 6 |
| BRENT PETERSON | 17 | 2 | 0 | 2 | 4- | 4 | 11 | 17 | 2 | 0 | 2 |
| COREY SCHWAB | 31 | 0 | 1 | 1 | 0 | 10 | 0 | | | | |
| RICK TABARACCI | 62 | 0 | 1 | 1 | 0 | 12 | 0 | | | | |
| ALAN EGELAND | 4 | 0 | 0 | 0 | 3- | 5 | 1 | 9 | 0 | 0 | 0 |
| DEREK WILKINSON | 5 | 0 | 0 | 0 | 0 | 0 | 0 | | | | |
| DAREN PUPPA | 6 | 0 | 0 | 0 | 0 | 2 | 0 | | | | |
| PAUL BROUSSEAU | 6 | 0 | 0 | 0 | 4- | 0 | 3 | 14 | 1 | 1 | 2 |
| JAY WELLS | 21 | 0 | 0 | 0 | 3- | 13 | 16 | 1,098 | 47 | 216 | 263 |

## TEAM RANKINGS

| | | Conference Rank | League Rank |
|---|---|---|---|
| Record | 32-40-10 | 11 | 20 |
| Home | 15-18-8 | 12 | 22 |
| Away | 17-22-2 | 7 | 13 |
| Versus Own Conference | 20-29-7 | 12 | 24 |
| Versus Other Conference | 12-11-3 | 7 | 12 |
| Team Plus\Minus | -22 | 11 | 20 |

| | | | |
|---|---|---|---|
| Goals For | 217 | 12 | 22 |
| Goals Against | 247 | 8 | 16 |
| Average Shots For | 31.4 | 3 | 5 |
| Average Shots Against | 28.8 | 6 | 10 |
| Overtime | 4-2-10 | 3 | 6 |
| One Goal Games | 13-10 | 3 | 5 |
| Times outshooting opponent | 48 | 4 | 8 |
| Versus Teams Over .500 | 16-19-6 | 6 | 8 |

| Versus Teams | | | |
|---|---|---|---|
| Under .500 | 16-21-4 | 11 | 23 |
| First Half Record | 16-20-5 | 11 | 18 |
| Second Half Record | 16-20-5 | 10 | 19 |

## PLAYOFFS

- did not make playoffs

## ALL-TIME LEADERS

Goals
Brian Bradley 102
Petr Klima 63
John Tucker 49

Assists
Brian Bradley 167
Roman Hamrlik 93
John Tucker 82

Points
Brian Bradley 269
Petr Klima 133
Roman Hamrlik 130

## BEST INDIVIDUAL SEASONS

Goals
Brian Bradley 1992-93 43
Dino Ciccarelli 1996-97 35
Alexander Selivanov 1995-96 31

Assists
Brian Bradley 1995-96 56
Roman Hamrlik 1995-96 49
Brian Bradley 1992-93 44

Points
Brian Bradley 1992-93 86
Brian Bradley 1995-96 79
Roman Hamrlik 1995-96 65

## TEAM

Last 3 years

| | GP | W | L | T | Pts | % |
|---|---|---|---|---|---|---|
| 1996-97 | 82 | 32 | 40 | 10 | 74 | .451 |
| 1995-96 | 82 | 38 | 32 | 12 | 88 | .543 |
| 1994-95 | 48 | 17 | 28 | 3 | 37 | .385 |

Best 3 regular seasons
| 1995-96 | 82 | 38 | 32 | 12 | 88 | .543 |
| 1996-97 | 82 | 32 | 40 | 10 | 74 | .451 |
| 1993-94 | 84 | 30 | 43 | 11 | 71 | .423 |

Worst 3 regular seasons
| 1992-93 | 84 | 23 | 54 | 7 | 53 | .315 |
| 1994-95 | 48 | 17 | 28 | 3 | 37 | .385 |
| 1993-94 | 84 | 30 | 43 | 11 | 71 | .423 |

Most Goals (min. 70 game schedule)
1992-93 245
1995-96 238
1993-94 224

Fewest Goals (min. 70 game schedule)
1996-97 217
1993-94 224
1995-96 238

Most Goals Against (min. 70 game schedule)
1992-93 332
1993-94 251
1995-96 248

Fewest Goals Against (min. 70 game schedule)
1996-97 247
1995-96 248
1993-94 251

# Washington Capitals

Washington — a place where promise invariably equals disappointment; where dreams can come true, but never do; where nothing quite works according to plan.

Rather a cynical viewpoint, but what we're talking about here is the Capitals, not the capital.

Maybe things will be different now. And maybe they won't.

The David Poile era ended not with a whimper, but with a bang. As in bang, bang, you're fired. This, after 14 years of the same thing - great regular season, poor playoffs - and then finally one year of not even making the playoffs.

The past season was the worst since Poile took over the team in 1982-83. The thing of it is that if not for all their injury problems and the collapse of Jim Carey in net, they probably would have made the playoffs again, probably would have been defeated again in the first round, and probably Poile would still have his job.

In last year's Hockey Annual we went through possible reasons why the Caps folded so often after promising so much, as well as if it was possible that Poile was at fault. So, we won't do it again.

We know what Poile didn't do during his tenure, but how about what he did do?

What he did do was write a blueprint for building a successful (regular season) hockey team.

He showed a lot of patience while developing an excellent system with loads of prospects. He promoted from within, which provides incentive for those in the system, and he didn't discard home-grown players easily. He ensured his team had an excellent defence and top-notch goaltending. And he didn't fire his coaches without giving them a sporting chance.

The only problem with his bluepint was that he was always building and planning and building and planning, but was never able to get to the point where he had put the finishing touches in place and could sit back and enjoy the view.

Sometimes a general manager with job security is as worried about the future of his team as its current state. Sometimes they get to thinking more about potential than they would if their job was on the line.

When the Caps got into trouble last year, it appeared Poile tried putting those finishing touches on the team all at once. That's not to say acquiring Oates, Tocchet and Ranford from the Bruins wasn't a good deal at the right time, just that it hadn't been his style in the past.

There's no general manager in the league without faults, but few can measure up to Poile in terms of the good things he's been able to do. During the summer he signed on as the first general manager of the new Nashville expansion entry.

## SHORTS

* Adam Oates needs four points to reach 1,000 for his career.
* Dale Hunter needs 17 points to reach 1,000 for his career.
* Phil Housley needs just 10 more points to reach 1,000 for his career.
* Kelly Miller became the Caps all-time games played leader last season with 802, passing Rod Langway (726) and Mike Gartner (758).
* Michal Pivonka took over the Caps' all-time lead in assists with 406, when he passed Mike Gartner (392) last season.
* the Caps were shut out nine times last year, the most in team history.

## STAT ANALYSIS

Peter Bondra just missed leading the league in scoring the highest percentage of his team's goals for the third straight season. It's a nice individual accomplishment, but it reflects poorly on the team. If they had more goal scorers then the team would have more goals as a whole, and Bondra wouldn't stand out so much.

The charts below show the top three in this category for the last three years.

1996-97 - Highest Percentage of Team Goals:

|  | Team | Goals | Team Goals | % |
|---|---|---|---|---|
| Keith Tkachuk | Pho | 52 | 240 | 21.7% |
| PETER BONDRA | Wsh | 46 | 214 | 21.5% |
| Teemu Selanne | Ana | 51 | 245 | 20.8% |

1995-96 - Highest Percentage of Team Goals:

|  | Team | Goals | Team Goals | % |
|---|---|---|---|---|
| PETER BONDRA | Wsh | 52 | 234 | 22.2% |
| Paul Kariya | Ana | 50 | 234 | 21.4% |
| A.Mogilny | Van | 55 | 278 | 19.7% |

1994-95 - Highest Percentage of Team Goals:

| PETER BONDRA | Wsh | 34 | 25.0% |
|---|---|---|---|
| Eric Lindros | Phi | 29 | 19.3% |
| Alexei Yashin | Ott | 30 | 19.1% |

## TEAM PREVIEW

GOAL: Last year, Jim Carey's goaltending stock fell faster than you can say Blaine Lacher or Steve Penney. He went from being the Net Detective to needing one to find the puck. He went from Vezina Trophy winner to whipping boy. Then he just went.

Bill Ranford, eight years older, but with a Conn Smythe trophy and two Stanley Cups under his belt, replaced him after the trade with Boston. The Caps had themselves a playoff goalie — a good one. All they needed next was to make the playoffs, which of course they didn't.

Ranford compiled remarkably similar stats to Carey in Washington, but then he was still in a state of shellshock from playing with the lowly Bruins.

Look for Ranford to be up among the league goaltending leaders this year. He's never had a defence like they have in Washington, which if it can just stay healthy, is going to make him look good.

Olaf Kolzig is a quality NHL goalie and if he's a backup he's one of the better ones in the league. Olie the Goalie's role in Washington was to play once in a while in order to give the number one man a rest, and to take over when Carey flopped in the play-offs. He missed the first month or so of the season with mononucleosis but then came on to do another excellent job.

Kolzig seems to be the type of goalie that other teams might consider for their number one job. And the Caps could trade him because he won't get as much time in net as he probably deserves.

Either way, barring injuries, they have one of the best goaltending tandems in the league. But, then again, we thought that at the start of last year when they had Carey instead of Ranford.

Hockey Annual Rating: 6 of 26

DEFENCE: The Caps had the best defence in the league at the start of last season, at least in terms of numbers and depth. And Poile kept getting more of them, stockpiling for the rainy days.

They were so good, Poile couldn't bear to part with them. They were so good, Sylvain Cote was a healthy scratch on opening night.

So, how come if they were so good they were so bad?

Well, injuries for one thing. Lots of them. Regulars Sergei Gonchar and Sylvain Cote only played 57 games, Mark Tinordi was in 56, Calle Johansson 65, and Joe Reekie 65. Only Ken Klee, who's also a winger, and Phil Housley, who had the worst offensive production of his career, didn't miss a lot of time.

Housley earned just 40 points. In the labor-shortened 1994-95 season he had 43 points in just 43 games. His style doesn't suit the Capitals, but they needed help on the power play and he was supposed to provide it. Of course, it's not his fault that few players can score on this team. Give him some production from the forwards and his points should return to normal. He's 33-years-old,

but doesn't play a physical style so age shouldn't be too much of a factor.

Brendan Witt needed more seasoning, so he was sent down to Portland to get some. Give him some time and he should develop into a good NHL defenceman. Same with Nolan Baumgartner, who missed almost all of last season with injuries. Just around the corner, they have yet another outstanding prospect in Nicholas Boynton, who was drafted this year.

The Caps have plenty of fill-ins for the injuries. Stewart Malgunas and Eric Charron have experience, and they can call up Patrick Boileau from Portland.

The Capitals have to get some scoring from their forwards, so since they're deepest at defense, look for them to trade some. A lot of teams would like a bruiser like Witt, and any playoff bound team would like Tinordi for the stretch drive and playoffs.

The Capitals' defence is still among the deepest and best in the league so it's not a worry area. They just have to make sure to keep a good balance with the softees and offensive types such as Housley, Gonchar, Cote and Johansson, and the more physical defensive types, such Tinordi, Reekie, Witt and Baumgartner.

Hockey Annual Rating: 3 of 26

FORWARD: There's no shortage of players who can play forward for the Capitals, but there's a definite shortage of players who can

| GOALTENDER | GPI | MINS | AVG | W | L | T | EN | SO | GA | SA | SV % |
|---|---|---|---|---|---|---|---|---|---|---|---|
| OLAF KOLZIG | 29 | 1645 | 2.59 | 8 | 15 | 4 | 6 | 2 | 71 | 758 | .906 |
| BILL RANFORD | 18 | 1009 | 2.74 | 8 | 7 | 2 | 1 | 0 | 46 | 412 | .888 |
| JIM CAREY | 40 | 2293 | 2.75 | 17 | 18 | 3 | 2 | 1 | 105 | 984 | .893 |
| WSH TOTALS | 82 | 4977 | 2.78 | 33 | 40 | 9 | 9 | 3 | 231 | 2163 | .893 |

put the puck in the net. They scored 214 goals, only three more than San Jose, the lowest scoring team in the league.

Let's see now, who can score goals. Hmmm...one to be exact. Peter Bondra.

Adam Oates is a setup man, Dale Hunter is a setup man, Joe Juneau is a setup man. But, just who are they all going to set up?

Bondra scored 46 goals, followed by Oates with 22 and Rick Tocchet with 21. The latter two scored most of their goals with Boston. Among those who played for Washington all season, Steve Konowalchuk had 17.

The reason the Caps didn't catch fire when they got Oates was that he was filling a job that didn't need filling. Bondra was going to score no matter who was feeding him.

There aren't a lot of pure goal scorers in today's NHL. Maybe only a handful and Bondra is certainly one of them. Washington's problem is that they skip the next level, which is mid-range goal scorers.

At centre, they have a number one man in 35-year-old Oates, which is far better than the undependable Michal Pivonka. Maybe Pivonka will score 81 points as he did two years ago, or maybe he'll get 23, his total from last season. Even though he'd probably be willing, 37-year-old Dale Hunter can't play forever. He hasn't missed a game in either of the last two seasons. Andrei Nikolishin also plays centre, as does part-time Kevin Kaminski and checker Mike Eagles. Joe Juneau can play centre or wing, as can Pivonka, Nikolishin and Kaminski.

Wingers, as well as centres, tend to move around a lot on the Caps, but Peter Bondra does all the scoring, leaving the toughness to Chris Simon, and enforcer Craig Berube. Trying to score, or at least trying to stop other teams from scoring, are Steve Konowalchuk, Kelly Miller and Pat Peake, who missed most of the season with injuries, same as he does every year.

Otherwise they have a lot of proven scoring. Minor league proven that is. Left winger Yogi Svejkovsky looks like a keeper and should be a regular in the lineup this year. In the Capitals' final game of the season he scored four goals. Andrew Brunette has put points on the board wherever he has played, and Richard Zednik and Stefan Ustorf are in and out of the lineup. Todd Krygier is still hanging in there as well.

Rick Tocchet was an unrestricted free agent, and signed with Phoenix.

The offensive prize is supposed to be Alexandre Volkov, the fourth pick overall in the 1996 draft. He was 29-53-82 in scoring for Barrie in the OHL, third on the team. First on that team was Jan Bullis (42-61-103), another Washington draft choice. Volkov has had some attitude problems in the past, so he'll need a good training camp to stick with the team at the start of the year. If they do send him down to the AHL you can bet he'll be up with the big team sometime this year. They need scoring, if you haven't heard.

The Caps have size, toughness, character players, and playmakers. The only thing they need is somebody besides Bondra to score. But, then, we've made that point already, haven't we.

Hockey Annual Rating: 15 of 26

SPECIAL TEAMS: Special teams should get a boost from having Oates around for a full season. He can set them up with the best of them on the power play and is good when the team is short.

POWER PLAY

|  | G | ATT | PCT |
|---|---|---|---|
| Overall | 51 | 322 | 15.8% (12th NHL) |
| Home | 27 | 167 | 16.2% (12th NHL) |
| Road | 24 | 155 | 15.5% (16th NHL) |

10 SHORT HANDED GOALS ALLOWED (14th NHL)

PENALTY KILLING

|  | G | TSH | PCT |
|---|---|---|---|
| Overall | 54 | 354 | 84.7% (T-8th NHL) |
| Home | 29 | 166 | 82.5% (T-18th NHL) |
| Road | 25 | 188 | 86.7% (6th NHL) |

8 SHORT HANDED GOALS SCORED (22nd NHL)

CAPITALS SPECIAL TEAMS SCORING

| Power play | G | A | PTS |
|---|---|---|---|
| BONDRA | 10 | 10 | 20 |
| HOUSLEY | 3 | 17 | 20 |
| OATES | 3 | 16 | 19 |
| JUNEAU | 9 | 9 | 18 |
| HUNTER | 3 | 9 | 12 |
| GONCHAR | 3 | 7 | 10 |
| COTE | 2 | 7 | 9 |
| KONOWALCHUK | 2 | 5 | 7 |
| TOCCHET | 4 | 2 | 6 |
| PIVONKA | 2 | 4 | 6 |
| JOHANSSON | 2 | 4 | 6 |
| NIKOLISHIN | 1 | 5 | 6 |
| BRUNETTE | 2 | 3 | 5 |
| KRYGIER | 1 | 4 | 5 |
| SIMON | 3 | 0 | 3 |
| SVEJKOVSKY | 2 | 1 | 3 |
| ZEDNIK | 1 | 0 | 1 |
| KAMINSKI | 0 | 1 | 1 |

| Short handed | G | A | PTS |
|---|---|---|---|
| OATES | 2 | 4 | 6 |
| BONDRA | 4 | 0 | 4 |
| MILLER | 1 | 1 | 2 |
| KONOWALCHUK | 1 | 1 | 2 |
| PIVONKA | 0 | 2 | 2 |
| JUNEAU | 1 | 0 | 1 |
| HOUSLEY | 1 | 0 | 1 |
| TINORDI | 0 | 1 | 1 |
| REEKIE | 0 | 1 | 1 |
| KLEE | 0 | 1 | 1 |
| GONCHAR | 0 | 1 | 1 |
| EAGLES | 0 | 1 | 1 |

COACHING AND MANAGEMENT: New coach Ron Wilson and new GM are going to make an interesting pair. Neither are shy types and neither have strayed too far from controversy.

McPhee was the assistant general manager in Vancouver, and over the years was involved in strange controversies (none of which I can remember now).

Hockey Annual Rating: 13 of 26

DRAFT

| Round | Sel. | Player | Pos | Amateur Team |
|---|---|---|---|---|
| 1 | 9 | Nicholas Boynton | D | Ottawa (OHL) |
| 2 | 35 | J. Fortin | D | Sherbrooke (QMJHL) |
| 4 | 89 | Curtis Cruickshank | G | Kingston (OHL) |
| 5 | 116 | Kevin Caulfield | RW | Boston College |
| 6 | 143 | Henrik Petre | D | Sweden |
| 9 | 226 | Matt Oikawa | RW | St. Lawrence U. |

Nick Boynton, the pride and joy of Nobleton, Ontario, is going to be a good NHL defenceman. He's solid in every aspect of the game. Not only can he play defence, but he can contribute offensively as well. His plus-minus was the best in all of the Canadian Junior Leagues last season.

PROGNOSIS: The Caps will experience only a short hiatus from the playoffs. If not for injuries alone they would have been there last year.

They have a lot of talent on this team, and more on the way. Poile builds teams to last. So, even though he's gone, his legacy will remain for a while yet.

Defence and goaltending is solid and there's a lot of talent up front. The number one priority of a new general manager will be how to generate more goals. If they can't find them on their own team they'll get them somewhere. That's because it's the only thing standing in their way.

Not only will the Caps be back in the playoffs, they'll be back in the upper echelon of the Eastern Conference. And while we knew what would happen before when they made the playoffs, it's a new era in Washington, so anything can happen now.

## PREDICTION

Eastern Conference: 4th
Overall: 8th

## STAT SECTION

| Team Scoring Stats | 1996-97 | | | | | Career | | | | | |
|---|---|---|---|---|---|---|---|---|---|---|---|
| | GP | G | A | PTS | +/- | PIM | Sh | Gm | G | A | Pts |
| ADAM OATES | 80 | 22 | 60 | 82 | 5- | 14 | 160 | 826 | 258 | 738 | 996 |
| PETER BONDRA | 77 | 46 | 31 | 77 | 7 | 72 | 314 | 468 | 233 | 179 | 412 |
| DALE HUNTER | 82 | 14 | 32 | 46 | 2- | 125 | 110 | 1,263 | 313 | 670 | 983 |
| S. KONOWALCHUK | 78 | 17 | 25 | 42 | 3- | 67 | 155 | 293 | 67 | 82 | 149 |
| JOE JUNEAU | 58 | 15 | 27 | 42 | 11- | 8 | 124 | 354 | 90 | 265 | 355 |
| RICK TOCCHET | 53 | 21 | 19 | 40 | 3- | 98 | 157 | 841 | 359 | 417 | 776 |
| PHIL HOUSLEY | 77 | 11 | 29 | 40 | 10- | 24 | 167 | 1,067 | 285 | 705 | 990 |
| SERGEI GONCHAR | 57 | 13 | 17 | 30 | 11- | 36 | 129 | 166 | 30 | 48 | 78 |
| ANDREI NIKOLISHIN | 71 | 9 | 19 | 28 | 3 | 32 | 98 | 171 | 31 | 66 | 97 |
| KELLY MILLER | 77 | 10 | 14 | 24 | 4 | 33 | 95 | 919 | 172 | 270 | 442 |
| SYLVAIN COTE | 57 | 6 | 18 | 24 | 11 | 28 | 131 | 806 | 95 | 219 | 314 |
| MICHAL PIVONKA | 54 | 7 | 16 | 23 | 15- | 22 | 83 | 756 | 173 | 406 | 579 |
| CHRIS SIMON | 42 | 9 | 13 | 22 | 1- | 165 | 89 | 188 | 33 | 45 | 88 |
| CALLE JOHANSSON | 65 | 6 | 11 | 17 | 2- | 16 | 133 | 710 | 77 | 303 | 380 |
| TODD KRYGIER | 47 | 5 | 11 | 16 | 10- | 37 | 121 | 498 | 98 | 131 | 229 |
| ANDREW BRUNETTE | 23 | 4 | 7 | 11 | 3- | 12 | 23 | 34 | 7 | 10 | 17 |
| KEN KLEE | 80 | 3 | 8 | 11 | 5- | 115 | 108 | 169 | 14 | 12 | 26 |
| J. SVEJKOVSKY | 19 | 7 | 3 | 10 | 1- | 4 | 30 | 19 | 7 | 3 | 10 |
| JOE REEKIE | 65 | 1 | 8 | 9 | 8 | 107 | 65 | 573 | 19 | 99 | 118 |
| MARK TINORDI | 56 | 2 | 6 | 8 | 3 | 118 | 53 | 568 | 44 | 133 | 177 |
| MIKE EAGLES | 70 | 1 | 7 | 8 | 4- | 42 | 38 | 730 | 67 | 117 | 184 |
| CRAIG BERUBE | 80 | 4 | 3 | 7 | 11- | 218 | 55 | 645 | 41 | 69 | 110 |

| | | | | | | | | | | | |
|---|---|---|---|---|---|---|---|---|---|---|---|
| BRENDAN WITT | 44 | 3 | 2 | 5 | 20- | 88 | 41 | 92 | 5 | 5 | 10 |
| RICHARD ZEDNIK | 11 | 2 | 1 | 3 | 5- | 4 | 21 | 12 | 2 | 1 | 3 |
| KEVIN KAMINSKI | 38 | 1 | 2 | 3 | 0 | 130 | 12 | 139 | 3 | 10 | 13 |
| ERIC CHARRON | 25 | 1 | 1 | 2 | 1 | 20 | 11 | 95 | 2 | 6 | 8 |
| BILL RANFORD | 55 | 0 | 1 | 1 | 0 | 7 | 0 | | | | |
| PATRICK BOILEAU | 1 | 0 | 0 | 0 | 0 | 0 | 0 | 1 | 0 | 0 | 0 |
| PAT PEAKE | 4 | 0 | 0 | 0 | 1 | 4 | 9 | 133 | 28 | 41 | 69 |
| STEWART MALGUNAS | 6 | 0 | 0 | 0 | 2 | 2 | 3 | 107 | 1 | 4 | 5 |
| STEFAN USTORF | 6 | 0 | 0 | 0 | 3- | 2 | 7 | 54 | 7 | 10 | 17 |
| OLAF KOLZIG | 29 | 0 | 0 | 0 | 0 | 4 | 0 | | | | |

## TEAM RANKINGS

| | | Conference Rank | League Rank |
|---|---|---|---|
| Record | 33-40-9 | 9 | 18 |
| Home | 19-17-5 | 8 | 15 |
| Away | 14-23-4 | 9 | 18 |
| Versus Own Conference | 23-25-8 | 8 | 15 |
| Versus Other Conference | 10-15-1 | 9 | 18 |
| Team Plus\Minus | -14 | 9 | 17 |
| Goals For | 214 | 13 | 23 |
| Goals Against | 231 | 5 | 9 |
| Average Shots For | 28.9 | 11 | 21 |
| Average Shots Against | 26.3 | 4 | 6 |
| Overtime | 2-2-9 | 7 | 14 |
| One Goal Games | 11-14 | 10 | 20 |
| Times outshooting opponent | 46 | 5 | 10 |
| Versus Teams Over .500 | 14-21-6 | 8 | 18 |
| Versus Teams Under .500 | 19-19-3 | 8 | 18 |
| First Half Record | 17-20-4 | 10 | 17 |
| Second Half Record | 16-20-5 | 9 | 18 |

## PLAYOFFS

- did not make the playoffs

## ALL-TIME LEADERS

Goals
| | |
|---|---|
| Mike Gartner | 397 |
| Peter Bondra | 233 |
| Mike Ridley | 218 |

Assists
| | |
|---|---|
| Michal Pivonka | 406 |
| Mike Gartner | 392 |
| Bengt Gustafsson | 359 |

Points
| | |
|---|---|
| Mike Gartner | 789 |
| Michal Pivonka | 579 |
| Bengt Gustafsson | 555 |

## BEST INDIVIDUAL SEASONS

Goals
| | | |
|---|---|---|
| Dennis Maruk | 1981-82 | 60 |
| Bob Carpenter | 1984-85 | 53 |
| Peter Bondra | 1995-96 | 52 |

Assists
| | | |
|---|---|---|
| Dennis Maruk | 1981-82 | 76 |
| Michal Pivonka | 1995-96 | 65 |
| Scott Stevens | 1988-89 | 61 |

Points
| | | |
|---|---|---|
| Dennis Maruk | 1981-82 | 136 |
| Mike Gartner | 1984-85 | 102 |
| Dennis Maruk | 1980-81 | 97 |

## TEAM

Last 3 years
| | GP | W | L | T | Pts | % |
|---|---|---|---|---|---|---|
| 1996-97 | 82 | 33 | 40 | 9 | 75 | .457 |
| 1995-96 | 82 | 39 | 32 | 11 | 89 | .543 |
| 1994-95 | 48 | 22 | 18 | 8 | 52 | .542 |

Best 3 regular seasons
| | | | | | | |
|---|---|---|---|---|---|---|
| 1985-86 | 80 | 50 | 23 | 7 | 107 | .669 |
| 1983-84 | 80 | 48 | 27 | 5 | 101 | .631 |
| 1984-85 | 80 | 46 | 25 | 9 | 101 | .631 |

Worst 3 regular seasons
| | | | | | | |
|---|---|---|---|---|---|---|
| 1974-75 | 80 | 8 | 67 | 5 | 21 | .131 |
| 1975-76 | 80 | 11 | 59 | 10 | 32 | .200 |
| 1977-78 | 80 | 17 | 49 | 14 | 48 | .333 |

Most Goals (min. 70 game schedule)
| | |
|---|---|
| 1991-92 | 330 |
| 1992-93 | 325 |
| 1984-85 | 322 |

Fewest Goals (min. 70 game schedule)
| | |
|---|---|
| 1974-75 | 181 |
| 1977-78 | 195 |
| 1996-97 | 214 |

Most Goals Against (min. 70 game schedule)
| | |
|---|---|
| 1974-75 | 446 |
| 1975-76 | 394 |
| 1981-82 | 338 |

Fewest Goals Against (min. 70 game schedule)
| | |
|---|---|
| 1995-96 | 204 |
| 1983-84 | 226 |
| 1996-97 | 231 |

# Western Conference

# Anaheim Mighty Ducks

Everybody knows you can't win with a one-man team. But a two-man team?

Maybe.

Teemu Selanne and Paul Kariya, who finished two-three in scoring behind Mario Lemieux, were magical last season, as good a two-man team as Penn and Teller. Actually, Penn and Teller are kind of irritating, but you get the point.

They managed to finish in fourth place in the Western Conference, win a round of the playoffs, and took the eventual Stanley Cup champions to three overtime games.

Not bad.

So, what do you do when you have a two-man team?

You fill in the blanks, of course.

If two guys are doing all the scoring, then you need some big, tough defensive defencemen who can move the puck to them; an offensive defenceman or two to man the points on the power play; grinders and checkers on the wings to make sure the other team doesn't score more than your two guys; maybe a veteran or two for leadership; tough guys for star protection; and you finish off with decent goaltending. Eventually, you build toward a second scoring line to take the heat off the top line.

Judging by that criteria the Ducks are on the right flight path. They have all of the above in varying degrees, except the all-important sec-

ond scoring line. That they can win now without all the pieces in place is a bonus; that many of the players who fill in the blanks are no-name interchangeable parts isn't.

Kariya might be the top scorer this year, and combined with Selanne they make up the top line in the league, no matter who they put in the middle. That's the good news...and the bad news.

One problem is that it can cause trouble when they play on the road. Home teams get last line change, and since they know the key to beating the Ducks is stopping Selanne and Kariya, naturally they'll try to do just that. Opposing coaches just have to tell their top checkers: "Stop this line and our team wins."

It shows up in the stats too, with Anaheim 23-12-6 at home (third best in conference) and 13-21-7 on the road (ninth best in conference).

Kariya wasn't exactly a dog on the road, with stats of 19-21-41 compared to 25-33-58 at home, but if teams can put their checkers against him then it frees up their own scoring line. If the scoring line doesn't have to worry about stopping the big guns they can do some firing of their own.

****

One other noteworty item of the Ducks' season was that they put together a remarkable run at the end of the year just to get into the playoffs. They were 10-3-6 from March

1, and in their last 14 home games were undefeated.

Good late season runs are becoming a tradition in Anaheim. The previous year they were 12-4-3 after March 1.

While management is building the team, success is building confidence.

All that said and done, one fact still remains: the Ducks suck without Kariya.

## STUFF

* allowed three shorthanded goals versus San Jose (Oct. 18) to set a club record.
* in a 6-6 tie with Colorado (Oct. 10) the Ducks came back from a 6-2 deficit with less than 10 minutes remaining in the third period to tie the game 6-6. With 2:47 remaining, the score was still 6-3.
* the Ducks started the season without Kariya and compiled a record of 1-8-2 before he returned to the lineup.
* Kariya scored eight seconds into a game versus Colorado (March 9) to break a team record.
* the Ducks set a team record with a 12-game undefeated streak that ended in late March.
* had power play goals in 10 straight games, a team record.
* the only team Anaheim hadn't beaten before the start of last season was Detroit (0-9-3), but they were 3-0-1 against them last season. In the playoffs, however, they were 0-4.
* were one of only two teams not to lose an overtime game (NY Rangers was the other).
* since Selanne joined the Ducks they are 50-29-11 when both he and Kariya are in the lineup
* finished off the season with a 14-game home undefeated streak.
* were swept in their Western Conference semi-final series by Detroit, but three of the four games went into overtime.

* will open the 1997-98 regular season in Tokyo, Japan with two games against Vancouver.

## STAT ANALYSIS

Was Paul Kariya the most valuable player to his team last year?

If you don't count Buffalo goalie Dominik Hasek, then the answer is yes. In fact, nobody even comes close.

The chart below shows key players on teams around the league and the team's record when they were out of the lineup, and when they were in the lineup. Of the players listed below, Kariya's difference is the biggest. Jaromir Jagr's absence from Pittsburgh's lineup was second.

### KEY PLAYERS OUT OF THE LINEUP:

| Player | Team | Record Without | Record With |
|---|---|---|---|
| Paul Kariya | Ana | 1-10-2 | 35-23-11 |
| Jaromir Jagr | Pit | 4-12-3 | 34-24-5 |
| Saku Koivu | Mtl | 10-15-7 | 21-21-8 |
| Eric Lindros | Phi | 16-13-1 | 29-11-12 |
| Trevor Linden | Van | 13-16-4 | 22-24-3 |
| Pavel Bure | Van | 7-7-5 | 28-33-2 |
| Ray Bourque | Bos | 7-10-3 | 19-37-6 |
| Joe Sakic | Col | 11-4-2 | 38-20-7 |
| Peter Forsberg | Col | 11-2-4 | 38-22-5 |
| Alexander Mogilny | Van | 4-0-2 | 31-40-5 |

## TEAM PREVIEW

**GOAL:** Whenever you hear an analysis of a player's abilities, in any sport, it's always that he's above average this, above average that, below average this. You rarely hear a player described as average, even though that should be the most common classification. Average, somehow, has taken on a negative connotation.

So, perhaps Guy Hebert is an average goalie, in the real sense. Above average if "average" doesn't mean good to you.

The Ducks finished in 11th place in team goals against average. Hebert was fifth in save percentage, however, definitely "above average" and 16th in goals against average among qualified goalies.

At times Hebert's play is way "above average" and sometimes it falls way "below average". The rest of the time he's "average".

One thing for certain is that Hebert played too often last year. He started 42 of 43 games during one stretch, including 23 games in a row. He suffered from exhaustion and dehydration towards the end of the season.

As for Mikail Shtalenkov — he's an "average" backup.

Overall, the Ducks' goaltending is average, because as we know, average is good.

Hockey Annual Rating: 13 of 26

**DEFENCE:** You know that old complaint everyone has when looking for a job for the first time? "How am I supposed to get experience if nobody gives me a chance to get some?"

That's one objection you won't hear on the Ducks. Darren Van Impe, Jason Marshall, and Dan Trebil were all regulars at the end of the season, and none had played 30 NHL games previously. Nikolai Tsulygin and Ruslan Salei were other inexperienced players with on the job training.

Veterans included Bobby Dollas, Dave Karpa and trade acquisitions J.J. Daigneault and Dimitri Mironov.

Mironov and Daigneault handle the offense from the defense and the points on the power play. Both are the latest in a slew of rent-an-offensive-defenseman moves by the Ducks. Prior to last year they had Fredrik Olausson, and before him was Tom Kurvers and Bill Houlder. By the end of this season look for two different offensive defensemen manning the points. Mironov is one of those players who looks good playing on other teams, and on your own team - for a while. Then, he becomes good trade bait for a team looking for help on the power play. Daigneault is an unrestricted free agent, but he'd be wise to sign there again with the situation suited to him perfectly.

Van Impe is the only other offensive defensman of note. He showed a definite flair when given an opportunity to play the power play. He has some impressive minor league stats (58 points in 63 games for Baltimore in 1995-96) and junior stats (20-64-84 in his best junior season at Red Deer). In one 20-game stretch last season he scored 16 points, accounting for 70 percent (16 of 23) of his production for the year.

Whether or not the young defensemen would have even been given a chance to play

| GOALTENDER | GPI | MINS | AVG | W | L | T | EN | SO | GA | SA | SV % |
|---|---|---|---|---|---|---|---|---|---|---|---|
| GUY HEBERT | 67 | 3863 | 2.67 | 29 | 25 | 12 | 2 | 4 | 172 | 2133 | .919 |
| M. SHTALENKOV | 24 | 1079 | 2.89 | 7 | 8 | 1 | 4 | 2 | 52 | 539 | .904 |
| MICHAEL O'NEILL | 1 | 31 | 5.81 | 0 | 0 | 0 | 0 | 0 | 3 | 10 | .700 |
| ANA TOTALS | 82 | 4994 | 2.80 | 36 | 33 | 13 | 6 | 6 | 233 | 2688 | .913 |

on most other teams is a question that can easily be answered. No. But, since they did play, they'll be better for it. The players that is.

Hockey Annual Rating: 17 of 26

**FORWARD:** The cushiest job in hockey is:
a: goal judge since the advent of video replay
b: backup to Patrick Roy in the playoffs
c: championship banner hanger in Washington
d: centreman for Paul Kariya and Teemu Selanne

Any of the above would be an appropriate answer, but "d" has the added attraction of being the most coveted job in hockey.

So, if they could put anyone in that position that they wanted, who would it be? Well, somebody too good and they'd run into the law of diminishing returns. Ideally, he would be big, defensive-minded, tough, a good corner-digger, and be able to hand the puck over quickly to one of the other two guys when it came on his stick.

Actually, it probably doesn't matter all that much. Whomever they put there is going to do well on the scoresheet and Kariya and Selanne are going to do well no matter who it is. Last year, it was mostly Steve Rucchin, but Jari Kurri spent some time there as did Kevin Todd. Todd later suffered from Kariya-Selanne withdrawal and went through a 27-game goal scoring drought, playing himself out of a regular spot. Richard Park, who must have thought he was dreaming, also got some time there when Rucchin was injured during the playoffs.

After the top line the Anaheim forward situation can be described as:
a: pathetic
b: pathetic
c: pathetic
d: pathetic

The only chance the Ducks have is to try and get a decent unrestricted free agent as a stopgap.

They have an option to pick up Kurri's contract for another season, but at an inflated price with a low return, they decided against it. The 37-year-old scored 13 goals and 35 points, and was the only Duck to play in all 82 games. The 35 points were exactly 100 fewer than his best season, in 1984-85 with Edmonton.

Another oldtimer, Brian Bellows, is an unrestricted free agent, as is old-time tough guy Ken Baumgartner, who has signed on with Boston.

Baumgartner played on an intriguing line during the playoffs, combining with Warren Rychel and Mark Janssens to make probably the toughest line in the league.

Rychel equaled his career goal high when he popped in 10 during the reular season. That's the equivalent of about 70 goals from Eric Lindros.

Janssens is one of the rarest breeds in the NHL. He's a tough guy who plays centre and rarely scores. He's had exactly two goals in each of the last four seasons. Despite that, he'd probably rate highly in a ranking of fourth line centres, because of the fact he contributes everywhere but on the scoresheet.

That's not so unusual on the Ducks, however, because almost no one after the first line does score. And there's no help in sight.

At centre, there is Rucchin, Janssens, Sean Pronger, Richard Park, and Todd. Maybe the worst centre lineup in the league, and easily the lowest scoring.

Other wingers, not already mentioned, include Joe Sacco and Ted Drury, who also can play centre. J-F Jomphe also plays wing and centre.

Also in the wings are three more tough guys, something they already have in abundance - Shawn Antoski (coming off abdominal surgery) Peter Leboutillier and Barry Nieckar.

As for help on the way, the pickings are pretty slim. Frank Banham was a big-time junior scorer who suffered through injuries last season. Mike LeClerc, another big junior scorer also got the call for a short while. Craig Reichert led Baltimore of the AHL in scoring, and Matt Cullen put in a short apprenticeship in Baltimore after a good college career at St. Cloud.

The Ducks have one first line and then a bunch of third or fourth lines. Of course, that first line is going to be one of the best in the league, but their third and fourth lines are nowhere near the best. And remember, they don't have a second scoring line.

Hockey Annual Rating: 7 of 26

## SPECIAL TEAMS:

When you have Kariya and Selanne you can't help but have a good power play. Any two offensive defensemen on the points will help - Mironov and Daigneault by the end of the year. And the other guy doesn't much matter.

Penalty killing was weak, which is a bit of a surprise considering they had some good defensive talent on board. But, that's not the way it works anymore. Teams, such as Anaheim, will put out their offensive stars, such as Kariya and Selanne, when shorthanded, in part because of their skating ability and in part just to give them more ice-time. It helps to score the odd shorthanded goal, but not enough to compensate for defensive weaknesses.

### POWER PLAY

|         | G  | ATT | PCT                |
|---------|----|-----|--------------------|
| Overall | 56 | 333 | 16.8% (T-9th NHL)  |
| Home    | 28 | 168 | 16.7% (9th NHL)    |
| Road    | 28 | 165 | 17.0% (11th NHL)   |

11 shorthanded goals allowed (T-15th NHL)

PENALTY KILLING

|         | G  | TSH | PCT                |
|---------|----|-----|--------------------|
| Overall | 62 | 336 | 81.5% (22nd NHL)   |
| Home    | 28 | 160 | 82.5% (T-18th NHL) |
| Road    | 34 | 176 | 80.7% (21st NHL)   |

9 Shorthanded goals scored (T-16th NHL)

MIGHTY DUCKS SPECIAL TEAMS SCORING

| Power play | G  | A  | PTS |
|------------|----|----|-----|
| KARIYA     | 15 | 19 | 34  |
| SELANNE    | 11 | 21 | 32  |
| MIRONOV    | 3  | 21 | 24  |
| RUCCHIN    | 6  | 10 | 16  |
| BELLOWS    | 8  | 3  | 11  |
| DAIGNEAULT | 0  | 11 | 11  |
| VAN IMPE   | 2  | 8  | 10  |
| KURRI      | 3  | 4  | 7   |
| DOLLAS     | 1  | 3  | 4   |
| TODD       | 0  | 4  | 4   |
| SACCO      | 1  | 1  | 2   |
| PRONGER    | 1  | 1  | 2   |
| JOMPHE     | 0  | 2  | 2   |
| RYCHEL     | 1  | 0  | 1   |
| DRURY      | 1  | 0  | 1   |
| MARSHALL   | 0  | 1  | 1   |
| KARPA      | 0  | 1  | 1   |
| JANSSENS   | 0  | 1  | 1   |

| Short handed | G | A | PTS |
|--------------|---|---|-----|
| KARIYA       | 3 | 1 | 4   |
| RUCCHIN      | 1 | 2 | 3   |
| SACCO        | 1 | 1 | 2   |
| JOMPHE       | 1 | 1 | 2   |
| SELANNE      | 1 | 0 | 1   |
| RYCHEL       | 1 | 0 | 1   |
| MIRONOV      | 1 | 0 | 1   |
| VAN IMPE     | 0 | 1 | 1   |
| TREBIL       | 0 | 1 | 1   |
| KURRI        | 0 | 1 | 1   |

COACHING AND MANAGEMENT:

Ron Wilson was a good coach for the Ducks, and had the second longest tenure (Terry Crisp) when he was fired. But, since he wasn't paying his own salary he had to get in line with the people who were.

At the press conference when the firing was announced, GM Jack Ferreira claimed philisophical differences, and added: "Ron Wilson is a good coach, but he's also a good quote." That's as much as he would say on the subject or needs to.

Obviously, Wilson didn't keep his mouth shut when he should have, and the bosses didn't like it. And also, quite obviously he had been warned enough times.

General Manager Jack Ferreira is establishing himself as a top-notch GM. At the time, many scoffed at the trade in which he sent Oleg Tverdovsky and Chad Kilger to Winnipeg for Selanne, but few would dispute that it has turned out heavily in favor of Anaheim.

Ferreira also isn't afraid to admit his mistakes and seems to back coaching decisions. Getting rid of Roman Oksuita is a good example of that. Wilson didn't play him, because he didn't deserve to be played, and so despite signing him to a hefty contract after a holdout, Ferreira dumped him off to Pittsburgh.

He also showed good sense in shoring up weaknesses by acquiring Mironov and Daigneault to help the power play points. Since there isn't much talent in the system, Ferreira has to work harder than others to make the team competitive.

Competitive he can do, but his next job is to take the Ducks to the next level and that won't be near as easy.

Note: no coach had been hired to replace Wilson at press time.

Hockey Annual Rating: 15 of 26

DRAFT

| Round | Sel. | Player | Pos | Amateur Team |
|---|---|---|---|---|
| 1 | 18 | Mikael Holmqvist | C | Sweden |
| 2 | 45 | M. Balmochnykh | LW | Russia |
| 3 | 72 | Jay Legault | LW | London (OHL) |
| 5 | 125 | Luc Vaillancourt | G | Beauport (QMJHL) |
| 7 | 178 | Tony Mohagen | LW | Seattle (WHL) |
| 7 | 181 | Mat Snesrud | D | N. Iowa (USHL) |
| 8 | 209 | Rene Stussi | C | Switzerland |
| 9 | 235 | Tommi Degerman | W | Boston U. |

Could Mikael Holmqvist be a future centre for Kariya and Selanne? Scoring isn't a problem, and his style of play would fit right in with the other two. They could call it the Lady Byng Line. Kariya and Selanne are regular candidates for the most gentlemanly players, and Holmqvist reportedly has a strict rule against any kind of physical contact. That's the knock against Holmqvist, who GM Ferreira described as a one-iron - long and skinny. He's 6-3, 183 pounds. Anaheim fans aren't likely to see the talented Swede in their lineup for a few years. In the meantime, he should eat his Wheaties.

PROGNOSIS

On one hand it would seem that the Ducks can't be much more than a mediocre team until they fluff up the pillows around their two stars. Their defence is mediocre, their goaltending inconsistent and their forward situation gruesome. If Kariya missed the whole season they'd finish in last place. If Kariya and Selanne missed the whole season they'd finish in last place in the AHL.

On the other hand, assuming no major injuries, the Ducks had a record of 35-23-11 when Kariya was in the lineup, so it would figure that they could continue to do that.

Since we're running out of hands, there doesn't appear to be another option. The thing of it is, a lot of teams don't have what the Ducks have in Kariya and Selanne. No one else, to be more concise.

For now, they're a .500 plus playoff team because Kariya and Selanne are just too good. The supporting cast isn't going to hurt them because they're not important yet. But, they're not going to help them either. Within two or three years, however, if things go right, the Ducks can be a championship calibre team.

PREDICTION
Western Conference: 4th
Overall: 7th

## STAT SECTION

| Team Scoring Stats | | 1996-97 | | | | Career | | | | | |
|---|---|---|---|---|---|---|---|---|---|---|---|
| | GP | G | A | PTS | +/- | PIM | Sh | Gm | G | A | Pts |
| TEEMU SELANNE | 78 | 51 | 58 | 109 | 28 | 34 | 327 | 214 | 23 | 7 | 451 |
| PAUL KARIYA | 69 | 44 | 55 | 99 | 36 | 6 | 198 | 112 | 134 | | 246 |
| STEVE RUCCHIN | 79 | 19 | 48 | 67 | 26 | 24 | 186 | 44 | 84 | | 128 |
| DMITRI MIRONOV | 77 | 13 | 39 | 52 | 16 | 101 | 324 | 38 | 133 | | 171 |
| JARI KURRI | 82 | 13 | 22 | 35 | 13- | 12 | 1,181 | 596 | 780 | | 1,376 |
| BRIAN BELLOWS | 69 | 16 | 15 | 31 | 15- | 22 | 1,101 | 462 | 500 | | 962 |
| KEVIN TODD | 65 | 9 | 21 | 30 | 7- | 44 | 356 | 66 | 126 | | 192 |
| JOE SACCO | 77 | 12 | 17 | 29 | 1 | 35 | 338 | 65 | 70 | | 135 |
| J.J. DAIGNEAULT | 66 | 5 | 23 | 28 | 0 | 58 | 704 | 48 | 161 | | 209 |
| DARREN VAN IMPE | 74 | 4 | 19 | 23 | 3 | 90 | 91 | 5 | 22 | | 27 |
| JEAN-FRANCOIS JOMPHE | 64 | 7 | 14 | 21 | 9- | 53 | 95 | 9 | 26 | 35 | |
| TED DRURY | 73 | 9 | 9 | 18 | 9- | 54 | 199 | 27 | 34 | 61 | |
| BOBBY DOLLAS | 79 | 4 | 14 | 18 | 17 | 55 | 453 | 34 | 74 | 108 | |
| WARREN RYCHEL | 70 | 10 | 7 | 17 | 6 | 218 | 307 | 33 | 31 | 64 | |
| SEAN PRONGER | 39 | 7 | 7 | 14 | 6 | 20 | 46 | 7 | 8 | 15 | |
| DAVE KARPA | 69 | 2 | 11 | 13 | 11 | 210 | 245 | 11 | 45 | 56 | |
| KEN BAUMGARTNER | 67 | 0 | 11 | 11 | 0 | 182 | 545 | 12 | 37 | 49 | |
| JASON MARSHALL | 73 | 1 | 9 | 10 | 6 | 140 | 100 | 2 | 10 | 12 | |
| MARK JANSSENS | 66 | 2 | 6 | 8 | 13- | 137 | 513 | 34 | 60 | 94 | |
| DANIEL TREBIL | 29 | 3 | 3 | 6 | 5 | 23 | 29 | 3 | 3 | 6 | |
| MIKE LECLERC | 5 | 1 | 1 | 2 | 2 | 0 | 5 | 1 | 1 | 2 | |
| RICHARD PARK | 12 | 1 | 1 | 2 | 1- | 10 | 69 | 5 | 8 | 13 | |

| VALERI KARPOV | 9 | 1 | 0 | 1 | 2- | 16 | 76 | 14 | 15 | 29 |
|---|---|---|---|---|---|---|---|---|---|---|
| PETER LEBOUTILLIER | 23 | 1 | 0 | 1 | 0 | 121 | 23 | 1 | 0 | 1 |
| NIKOLAI TSULYGIN | 22 | 0 | 1 | 1 | 5- | 8 | 22 | 0 | 1 | 1 |
| RUSLAN SALEI | 30 | 0 | 1 | 1 | 8- | 37 | 30 | 0 | 1 | 1 |
| GUY HEBERT | 67 | 0 | 1 | 1 | 0 | 4 | | | | |
| MICHAEL O'NEILL | 1 | 0 | 0 | 0 | 0 | 0 | | | | |
| BARRY NIECKAR | 2 | 0 | 0 | 0 | 0 | 5 | 7 | 0 | 0 | 0 |
| FRANK BANHAM | 3 | 0 | 0 | 0 | 2- | 0 | 3 | 0 | 0 | 0 |
| CRAIG REICHERT | 3 | 0 | 0 | 0 | 2- | 0 | 3 | 0 | 0 | 0 |
| JEREMY STEVENSON | 5 | 0 | 0 | 0 | 1- | 14 | 8 | 0 | 1 | 1 |
| ADRIAN PLAVSIC | 6 | 0 | 0 | 0 | 5- | 2 | 214 | 15 | 56 | 71 |
| SHAWN ANTOSKI | 15 | 0 | 0 | 0 | 1 | 51 | 174 | 2 | 5 | 7 |
| M. SHTALENKOV | 24 | 0 | 0 | 0 | 0 | 4 | | | | |

## TEAM RANKINGS

| | | Conference Rank | League Rank |
|---|---|---|---|
| Record | 36-33-13 | 4 | 9 |
| Home | 23-12-6 | 3 | 6 |
| Away | 13-21-7 | 9 | 17 |
| Versus Own Conference | 24-22-10 | 5 | 10 |
| Versus Other Conference | 12-11-3 | 6 | 12 |
| Team Plus\Minus | +18 | 5 | 10 |
| Goals For | 245 | 6 | 10 |
| Goals Against | 233 | 5 | 11 |
| Average Shots For | 28.4 | 12 | 23 |
| Average Shots Against | 32.7 | 11 | 21 |
| Overtime | 3-0-13 | 2 | 3 |
| One Goal Games | 12-12 | 6 | 10 |
| Times outshooting opponent | 21 | 12 | 24 |
| Versus Teams Over .500 | 11-16-6 | 8 | 14 |
| Versus Teams Under .500 | 25-18-7 | 6 | 11 |
| First Half Record | 15-21-5 | 9 | 20 |
| Second Half Record | 21-12-8 | 3 | 4 |

## PLAYOFFS

Results:    defeated Phoenix 4-3
            lost to Detroit 4-0

Record: 4-7

Home: 3-3

Away: 1-4

Goals For: 25 (2.3/game)

Goals Against: 30 (2.7/game)

Overtime: 1-3

Power play: 25.6% (1st)

Penalty Killing: 86.7% (5th)

# AHAHEIM MIGHTY DUCKS

| | GP | G | A | PTS | +/- | PIM | PP | SH | GW | OT | S |
|---|---|---|---|---|---|---|---|---|---|---|---|
| PAUL KARIYA | 11 | 7 | 6 | 13 | 2- | 4 | 4 | 0 | 1 | 1 | 61 |
| DMITRI MIRONOV | 11 | 1 | 10 | 11 | 0 | 10 | 1 | 0 | 0 | 0 | 36 |
| TEEMU SELANNE | 11 | 7 | 3 | 10 | 3- | 4 | 3 | 0 | 1 | 0 | 38 |
| J.J. DAIGNEAULT | 11 | 2 | 7 | 9 | 6- | 16 | 1 | 0 | 1 | 0 | 24 |
| BRIAN BELLOWS | 11 | 2 | 4 | 6 | 7- | 2 | 1 | 0 | 0 | 0 | 36 |
| STEVE RUCCHIN | 8 | 1 | 2 | 3 | 2- | 10 | 0 | 0 | 0 | 0 | 8 |
| JARI KURRI | 11 | 1 | 2 | 3 | 2 | 4 | 0 | 0 | 0 | 0 | 18 |
| JOE SACCO | 11 | 2 | 0 | 2 | 4- | 2 | 0 | 0 | 0 | 0 | 20 |
| DAVE KARPA | 8 | 1 | 1 | 2 | 2- | 20 | 0 | 0 | 1 | 0 | 13 |
| SEAN PRONGER | 9 | 0 | 2 | 2 | 0 | 4 | 0 | 0 | 0 | 0 | 7 |
| DARREN VAN IMPE | 9 | 0 | 2 | 2 | 3- | 16 | 0 | 0 | 0 | 0 | 11 |
| WARREN RYCHEL | 11 | 0 | 2 | 2 | 2- | 19 | 0 | 0 | 0 | 0 | 16 |
| TED DRURY | 10 | 1 | 0 | 1 | 2- | 4 | 0 | 0 | 0 | 0 | 17 |
| JASON MARSHALL | 7 | 0 | 1 | 1 | 1 | 4 | 0 | 0 | 0 | 0 | 3 |
| DANIEL TREBIL | 9 | 0 | 1 | 1 | 6- | 6 | 0 | 0 | 0 | 0 | 10 |
| KEN BAUMGARTNER | 11 | 0 | 1 | 1 | 0 | 11 | 0 | 0 | 0 | 0 | 0 |
| RICHARD PARK | 11 | 0 | 1 | 1 | 2- | 2 | 0 | 0 | 0 | 0 | 10 |
| MIKE LECLERC | 1 | 0 | 0 | 0 | 0 | 0 | 0 | 0 | 0 | 0 | 0 |
| IGOR NIKULIN | 1 | 0 | 0 | 0 | 0 | 0 | 0 | 0 | 0 | 0 | 1 |
| KEVIN TODD | 4 | 0 | 0 | 0 | 3- | 2 | 0 | 0 | 0 | 0 | 3 |
| M. SHTALENKOV | 4 | 0 | 0 | 0 | 0 | 2 | 0 | 0 | 0 | 0 | 0 |
| GUY HEBERT | 9 | 0 | 0 | 0 | 0 | 0 | 0 | 0 | 0 | 0 | 0 |
| BOBBY DOLLAS | 11 | 0 | 0 | 0 | 2- | 4 | 0 | 0 | 0 | 0 | 10 |
| MARK JANSSENS | 11 | 0 | 0 | 0 | 3- | 15 | 0 | 0 | 0 | 0 | 13 |

| GOALTENDER | GPI | MINS | AVG | W | L | EN | SO | GA | SA | SV % |
|---|---|---|---|---|---|---|---|---|---|---|
| GUY HEBERT | 9 | 534 | 2.02 | 4 | 4 | 1 | 1 | 18 | 255 | .929 |
| M. SHTALENKOV | 4 | 211 | 2.84 | 0 | 3 | 1 | 0 | 10 | 162 | .938 |
| ANA TOTALS | 11 | 747 | 2.41 | 4 | 7 | 2 | 1 | 30 | 419 | .928 |

## ALL-TIME LEADERS

Goals
| Paul Kariya | 112 |
| Teemu Selanne | 67 |
| Joe Sacco | 54 |

Assists
| Paul Kariya | 134 |
| Steve Rucchin | 84 |
| Teemu Selanne | 78 |

Points
| Paul Kariya | 246 |
| Shaun Van Allen | 145 |
| Steve Rucchin | 128 |

## BEST INDIVIDUAL SEASONS

Goals
| Teemu Selanne | 1996-97 | 51 |
| Paul Kariya | 1995-96 | 50 |
| Paul Kariya | 1996-97 | 44 |

Assists
| Paul Kariya | 1995-96 | 58 |
| Teemu Selanne | 1996-97 | 58 |
| Paul Kariya | 1996-97 | 55 |

Points
| Teemu Selanne | 1996-97 | 109 |
| Paul Kariya | 1995-96 | 108 |
| Paul Kariya | 1996-96 | 99 |

TEAM

Last 3 years

|  | GP | W | L | T | Pts | % |
|---|---|---|---|---|---|---|
| 1996-97 | 82 | 36 | 33 | 13 | 85 | .518 |
| 1995-96 | 82 | 35 | 39 | 8 | 78 | .476 |
| 1994-95 | 48 | 16 | 27 | 5 | 37 | .385 |

Best 3 regular seasons

| 1996-97 | 82 | 36 | 33 | 13 | 85 | .518 |
| 1995-96 | 82 | 35 | 39 | 8 | 78 | .476 |
| 1993-94 | 84 | 33 | 46 | 5 | 71 | .423 |

Worst 3 regular seasons

| 1994-95 | 48 | 16 | 27 | 5 | 37 | .385 |
| 1993-94 | 84 | 33 | 46 | 5 | 71 | .423 |
| 1995-96 | 82 | 35 | 39 | 8 | 78 | .476 |

Most Goals (min. 70 game schedule)
| 1996-97 | 245 |
| 1995-96 | 234 |
| 1993-94 | 229 |

Fewest Goals (min. 70 game schedule)
| 1993-94 | 229 |
| 1995-96 | 234 |
| 1996-97 | 245 |

Most Goals Against (min. 70 game schedule)
| 1995-96 | 247 |
| 1993-94 | 251 |
| 1996-97 | 233 |

Fewest Goals Against (min. 70 game schedule)
| 1996-97 | 233 |
| 1993-94 | 251 |
| 1995-96 | 247 |

# Calgary Flames

The Flames won't be doing any bragging over it, but they may very well have finished on top of the NHL in one category last season: most problems.

These are just 10 of them, with an added bonus, at no extra charge, of how they can be fixed.

1. Poor Goaltending. Trevor Kidd and Dwayne Roloson were inconsistent. Goaltenders were pulled in 11 Calgary games last season. The Flames may have already fixed the problem when they re-acquired Rick Tabaracci from Tampa Bay. He's been their best goalie over the last two years, but the team was stuck on Kidd. They may not be anymore.

2. No scoring. Only San Jose scored fewer goals, and that was just three fewer. Enough said. What to do? Duh... get more scorers.

3. No offence from defence. The leading point scorer among defencemen was Yves Racine, who had just 16. Either they have to get a proven offensive defenceman, or they have to let the young ones they have develop into one.

4. Reichel bombed. This guy was supposed to provide the offence for the Flames after his return from Germany. He did next to nothing before being traded to the Islanders, where he decided to start playing for real.

5. Off-year for Fleury. It was an off-year for a lot of players, with scoring down around the league. Fleury can return to form — no problem — but he can't shoulder the entire load. During the summer he relinquished the captaincy, taking off some of the weight.

6. Couldn't win on the road. Only 11-23-7 away from Calgary, it shows that the defensive system the Flames had in place was not working. Good defensive teams often perform well on the road, where they can play their game without fear of boring their fans.

7. Bad stretches. The Flames were 7-5-1 in October; 3-9-1 in November; 3-7-3 in December; 5-5-1 in January; 8-5-1 in February; 6-5-1 in March; and 0-5-1 in April. All over the place. They showed they could play well at times, but they also showed they could play poorly.

8. Couldn't win when they needed it most. Up to the last couple games of the season the Flames were right in the playoff race. How did they respond? In the last seven games they were 0-6-1.

9. Couldn't beat weak teams. The Flames were actually better against teams over .500 than versus teams under .500. That's often an indication that a team is talented enough,

but only motivates itself to play big games.

10. Young defence. For the most part they were very good. Injuries to veterans meant they were thrust into major responsibility. It wasn't really until later in the season that they struggled.

## STUFF

* 23 road losses was tied for the most in Flames history.
* 41 losses were a franchise record.
* the Flames had 14 rookies play at least one game.
* a 10-1 loss to Edmonton was the worst home defeat in team history.
* Fleury is seven goals behind Joe Nieuwendyk, who is the all-time team leader with 314.
* the Flames had the worst April regular season record at 0-5-1.

## Stat Analysis

When a team outshoots the other, there's a high probability that that team was the winner of the game. Right?

Wrong.

Last year, 16 of the 26 teams had losing records when they outshot their opponents. Overall, teams that outshot their opponents only had a very slight 448-437-142 edge.

Calgary had a record of 16-27-6 when they outshot their opponents. When they were outshot by their opponents, they had a considerably better mark of 13-14-3.

The stats show that it's not the quantity of shots taken, but the quality.

Calgary had the worst team shooting percentage in the league. That doesn't necessarily mean that they can't shoot very well, but more so that they were not able to get their shots from high percentage scoring areas.

## WORST SHOOTING PERCENTAGES:

| | |
|---|---|
| Calgary | 8.3% |
| Tampa Bay | 8.4% |
| New Jersey | 8.9% |
| San Jose | 8.9% |
| | |
| League Average | 9.8% |
| League High | 11.8% (Pittsburgh) |

## TEAM PREVIEW

GOAL: Two was company, but three was a crowd in the Flames' net last season. They were forced to keep three goalies at the start of the season so that they wouldn't lose Dwayne Roloson on waivers when he was sent to the minors.

Tabaracci was better, but the Flames wanted Kidd as number one, so Tabaracci was traded to Tampa Bay for Aaron Gavey.

Tabaracci may be one of the most underrated players in the league. He wasn't protected in the waiver draft, but still nobody bit.

Both Tabaracci and Kidd admitted tension between them because both were vying for the number one job. It was tough for them to cheer the other one on when they knew they could take playing time away from themselves. That's something more common than you'd think, but few players are going to admit it in interviews. There was trouble with the same thing in Chicago last year with Ed Belfour and Jeff Hackett.

Kidd might have been better off with the competition anyway. After Tabaracci left he had some bad spells. He has had a number of stretches of poor play since he's joined the Flames, so it has gotten to be a habit. There's nothing to say that he won't develop consistency and become the goaltender the Flames want, but there's also nothing to suggest he will.

Rumors suggest he may be traded before the season starts. Inconsistency and perceived poor conditioning are the reasons.

Roloson handled backup duties, and also got the call when Kidd got in a funk. He did a decent job, with the predictable good and bad times. In the last couple games of the season when the Flames desperately needed a win to make the playoffs, Roloson started.

But, wait a minute, guess what? The Flames reacquired Tabaracci in the off-season. All is well again. Right back where they started from.

Hockey Annual Rating: 21 of 26

DEFENCE: Hey, the kids were all right. Rookie pairing, Todd Simpson and Joel Bouchard performed best and most consistently, and were asked to join Team Canada at the end of the season for the world championships.

Simpson, who was never drafted, is a tough, aggressive defenceman who can play the game. Those players are like gold in the NHL today.

At times, because of injuries during the season the Flames had five rookie defencemen in the lineup, and six played for them during the season. Chris O'Sullivan, Cale Hulse and Jamie Allison were three more rookie defencemen who played regularly at various points during the season, while Sami Helenius got the call for a couple games.

With injuries to veterans such as Zarley Zalapski (played two games) James Patrick (played 19 games) Tommy Albelin and Steve Chiasson before he was traded to Hartford, there was no choice.

The good news is that most of them won't be rookies this year. They have experience under their belts, and for defencemen, experience is everything. More important than at any other position.

Also, none of the rookies, except O'Sullivan, were just thrown into the lineup. They all had minor pro experience. O'Sullivan later went down to Saint John.

The Flames didn't have anything in the way of an offensive defenseman. Racine had 16 points to lead all rearguards, which made the Flames worst in the league. O'Sullivan looks to be a definite possibility in that area, while some of the other youngsters have good offensive junior stats in their background.

Zalapski and Patrick are coming off knee surgery, but should be back in the lineup this year. Figure on Bouchard and Simpson remaining together, and add in two more veterans in Albelin and Featherstone. Racine, who has played for six NHL teams in the last five years, will continue on his tour of NHL cities. That leaves the youngsters fighting for playing time. Hulse, O'Sullivan, and Allison have shown they can play in the NHL.

And wouldn't you know it, the best Flames prospects are defencemen.

Derek Morris is a possible future offensive defenceman. The top selection (13th overall) for the Flames in 1996, he led the WHL in

| GOALTENDER | GPI | MINS | AVG | W | L | T | EN | SO | GA | SA | SV % |
|---|---|---|---|---|---|---|---|---|---|---|---|
| RICK TABARACCI | 7 | 361 | 2.33 | 2 | 4 | 0 | 0 | 1 | 14 | 155 | .910 |
| TREVOR KIDD | 55 | 2979 | 2.84 | 21 | 23 | 6 | 4 | 4 | 141 | 1416 | .900 |
| DWAYNE ROLOSON | 31 | 1618 | 2.89 | 9 | 14 | 3 | 2 | 1 | 78 | 760 | .897 |
| CGY TOTALS | 82 | 4990 | 2.87 | 32 | 41 | 9 | 6 | 6 | 239 | 2337 | .898 |

scoring by defencemen with 18-57-75 in 67 games. Called up to Saint John after his season was over he made a positive impression.

Denis Gauthier, the team's first rounder in 1995 (20th overall) is coming along slower than expected, but the team still has high hopes for him.

Hockey Annual Rating: 14 of 26

FORWARD: The Flames were three goals away from being the lowest scoring team in the NHL last season. With Dave Gagner, their second top pointman, lost to free agency, improving on those totals will be difficult.

With the grand total of one proven good scorer (Fleury), one proven mid-range scorer (Titov), one decent scoring hope for the future (Jarome Iginla) and one recycled flop (Mikael Nylander) just what's the idea?

Unless they're planning on having four checking lines, of course.

Expect a comeback season for Fleury. He's had too many good ones to let one bad one decide his fate. Titov is a good power play sniper, as long as the other components are in place with the man-advantage. Nylander may get enough regular season points to make up for the loss of Gagner, but at playoff time he usually finds a home in the press box when the team can't abide his one-dimensional offensive play. Iginla can improve his scoring in his second year but only if he has some decent linemates.

Marty McInnis's style of play has become more valuable in recent years. He's a decent scorer who also plays defence and works the penalty killing units. Down the middle you can start with Nylander and McInnis, followed by defensive centre Aaron Gavey; Corey Stillman, who has suffered through some incredibly long scoring slumps; and Hnat Dominicelli, if he can get his scoring

going. Not a bad unit, but not a particularly good one either. Fleury, of course, can play centre as well.

On the right side are Fleury, Iginla, Sandy McCarthy and tough guy Ronnie Stern, who can contribute with some goals.

On the left side are Titov, Jonas Hoglund, and take your pick of Ed Ward, or Todd Hlushko.

Prospects include Steve Begin, a tough defensive style centre, who played with Val d'or in the QMJHL last season. And Marty Murray is still waiting for his chance to score at the NHL level.

Despite stinky stats from last season, the Flames have some promising youth, some (but not much) size, some good tough players, and guys who have the potential to score. All of this is in moderation, of course, so they need guys to step from the back of the line to the front of it.

At best, Gagner's departure won't be a monumental loss if Fleury and some of the youngsters step up. At worst, the Flames won't score any goals again this year.

There's one other ray of hope. Gary Roberts wants to make a comeback. He says he's undergone intensive therapy for his neck problems and is clear to play. The Flames made him a qualifying offer, but Roberts wants to play for an eastern team that doesn't travel quite so much. That means he'll probably be traded.

Hockey Annual Rating: 22 of 26

SPECIAL TEAMS: Pretty decent power play for such a lousy team, and for one without a quarterback on the point. Good snipers is the reason, or at least part of it. Titov led the team with 12 power play markers, and with only 10 at even strength, it shows where his talents are. Over the last two seasons, exactly half (25 of 50) of his goals have been on the power play. Still, it's not a bad skill to have. Players who can pump them in with the extra man isn't as common a commodity as it once was. Fleury, Gagner and Igilna were no slouches either.

The good power play was offset to some degree by their inability to stop the other team from scoring shorthanded. They were last in the league, allowing 19 shorthanded goals, two shy of the team record. A full season of McInnis killing penalties should contribute to a major improvement in that area.

POWER PLAY

|  | G | ATT | PCT |
|---|---|---|---|
| Overall | 61 | 361 | 16.9% (8th NHL) |
| Home | 35 | 184 | 19.0% (4th NHL) |
| Road | 26 | 177 | 14.7% (19th NHL) |

19 SHORT HANDED GOALS ALLOWED (26th NHL)

PENALTY KILLING

|  | G | TSH | PCT |
|---|---|---|---|
| Overall | 58 | 345 | 83.2% (17th NHL) |
| Home | 31 | 169 | 81.7% (22nd NHL) |
| Road | 27 | 176 | 84.7% (13th NHL) |

11 SHORT HANDED GOALS SCORED (T-9th NHL)

FLAMES SPECIAL TEAMS SCORING

| Power play | G | A | PTS |
|---|---|---|---|
| TITOV | 12 | 13 | 25 |
| FLEURY | 9 | 15 | 24 |
| GAGNER | 9 | 12 | 21 |
| IGINLA | 8 | 9 | 17 |
| HOGLUND | 3 | 11 | 14 |
| MCINNIS | 5 | 7 | 12 |
| STILLMAN | 2 | 8 | 10 |
| RACINE | 1 | 9 | 10 |
| ALBELIN | 2 | 7 | 9 |
| O'SULLIVAN | 1 | 6 | 7 |
| MILLEN | 1 | 6 | 7 |
| FEATHERSTONE | 0 | 5 | 5 |

|  | | | |
|---|---|---|---|
| GAVEY | 3 | 1 | 4 |
| DOMENICHELLI | 1 | 1 | 2 |
| PATRICK | 1 | 0 | 1 |
| MCCARTHY | 1 | 0 | 1 |
| BOUCHARD | 0 | 1 | 1 |

| Short handed | G | A | PTS |
|---|---|---|---|
| IGINLA | 1 | 3 | 4 |
| SULLIVAN | 3 | 0 | 3 |
| FLEURY | 2 | 1 | 3 |
| MCINNIS | 1 | 2 | 3 |
| GAGNER | 0 | 3 | 3 |
| STERN | 1 | 1 | 2 |
| HULSE | 1 | 1 | 2 |
| BOUCHARD | 1 | 0 | 1 |
| PATRICK | 0 | 1 | 1 |
| HLUSHKO | 0 | 1 | 1 |
| FEATHERSTONE | 0 | 1 | 1 |

COACHING AND MANAGEMENT: Pierre Page couldn't get an extension on his coaching contract, so he up and quit. Strange for him to make such a stand, because he's certainly not considered among the elite coaches in the game. He's rumored to be going to Anaheim.

Stern taskmaster, Brian Sutter, is going to give it another go. He's a no-nonsense guy who won't bother to try and motivate the troops with psychology like Page. Sutter is more likely to use a hammer.

Al Coates is showing signs of being a decent GM. It wasn't his fault that Reichel played like a stiff, but he was able to get something of value for him. This year will be a more telling season. If he can find the players to improve this club, and all the young defencemen on board continue to make a difference, then he will have earned his pay.

Hockey Annual Rating: 18 of 26

## DRAFT

| Round | Sel. | Player | Pos | Amateur Team |
|---|---|---|---|---|
| 1 | 6 | Daniel Tkachuk | C | Barrie (OHL) |
| 2 | 32 | Evan Lindsay | G | Prince Albert (WHL) |
| 2 | 42 | John Tripp | RW | Oshawa (OHL) |
| 2 | 51 | Dimitri Kokorev | D | Russia |
| 3 | 60 | Derek Schultz | C | Spokane (WHL) |
| 3 | 70 | Erik Andersson | C | Denver U. |
| 4 | 92 | Chris St. Croix | D | Kamloops (WHL) |
| 4 | 100 | Ryan Ready | LW | Belleville (OHL) |
| 5 | 113 | Martin Moise | LW | Beauport (QMJHL) |
| 6 | 140 | Ilga Demidov | D | Russia |
| 7 | 167 | Jeremy Rondeau | LW | Swift Current (WHL) |
| 9 | 223 | Dustin Paul | RW | Moose Jaw (WHL) |

Daniel Tkachuk (no relation to Keith) is considered to be an all-round player. He can score, he can play defensively, he can kill penalties, and he's considered an excellent character player and leader. That'll just about do it.

The top second round selection, Evan Lindsay, was ranked the third best North American goalie by Central Scouting. His stock rose considerably last year when he got a chance to be the number one in Prince Albert.

## PROGNOSIS

Things aren't all bad here. If not for injuries last season and slumps by their top scorers they probably would have slipped into the playoffs. Scoring is still going to be a problem this year, unless they get it from somewhere unexpected. But, on the defence they have lots of good players and lots of prospects pushing on the door.

They will likely have their good days and bad days. Predicting how many of each will be tough. Rule out a championship run, but a playoff spot is a good possibility.

## PREDICTION

Western Conference: 10
Overall: 21 of 26

## STAT SECTION

| Team Scoring Stats | 1996-97 | | | | | | | Career | | | |
|---|---|---|---|---|---|---|---|---|---|---|---|
| | GP | G | A | PTS | +/- | PIM | SH | Gm | G | A | Pts |
| THEOREN FLEURY | 81 | 29 | 38 | 67 | 12- | 104 | 336 | 649 | 307 | 376 | 683 |
| DAVE GAGNER | 82 | 27 | 33 | 60 | 2 | 48 | 228 | 799 | 292 | 351 | 643 |
| GERMAN TITOV | 79 | 22 | 30 | 52 | 12- | 36 | 192 | 277 | 89 | 119 | 208 |
| JAROME IGINLA | 82 | 21 | 29 | 50 | 4- | 37 | 169 | 82 | 21 | 29 | 50 |
| MARTY McINNIS | 80 | 23 | 26 | 49 | 8- | 22 | 182 | 347 | 82 | 123 | 205 |
| JONAS HOGLUND | 68 | 19 | 16 | 35 | 4- | 12 | 189 | 68 | 19 | 16 | 35 |

| Player | | | | | | | | | | |
|---|---|---|---|---|---|---|---|---|---|---|
| COREY MILLEN | 61 | 11 | 15 | 26 | 19- | 32 | 82 | 335 | 90 | 119 | 209 |
| CORY STILLMAN | 58 | 6 | 20 | 26 | 6- | 14 | 112 | 142 | 22 | 41 | 63 |
| AARON GAVEY | 57 | 8 | 11 | 19 | 12- | 46 | 62 | 130 | 16 | 15 | 31 |
| TODD HLUSHKO | 58 | 7 | 11 | 18 | 2- | 49 | 76 | 66 | 8 | 12 | 20 |
| RONNIE STERN | 79 | 7 | 10 | 17 | 4- | 157 | 98 | 493 | 64 | 72 | 136 |
| YVES RACINE | 46 | 1 | 15 | 16 | 4 | 24 | 82 | 448 | 37 | 186 | 223 |
| TOMMY ALBELIN | 72 | 4 | 11 | 15 | 8- | 14 | 103 | 545 | 33 | 146 | 179 |
| TODD SIMPSON | 82 | 1 | 13 | 14 | 14- | 208 | 85 | 88 | 1 | 13 | 14 |
| ED WARD | 40 | 5 | 8 | 13 | 3- | 49 | 33 | 90 | 10 | 14 | 24 |
| MIKE SULLIVAN | 67 | 5 | 6 | 11 | 11- | 10 | 64 | 376 | 36 | 49 | 85 |
| GLEN FEATHERSTONE | 54 | 3 | 8 | 11 | 1- | 106 | 67 | 384 | 19 | 61 | 80 |
| CHRIS O'SULLIVAN | 27 | 2 | 8 | 10 | 0 | 2 | 41 | 27 | 2 | 8 | 10 |
| JOEL BOUCHARD | 76 | 4 | 5 | 9 | 23- | 49 | 61 | 82 | 4 | 5 | 9 |
| SANDY MCCARTHY | 33 | 3 | 5 | 8 | 8- | 113 | 38 | 224 | 22 | 20 | 42 |
| CALE HULSE | 63 | 1 | 6 | 7 | 2- | 91 | 58 | 74 | 1 | 6 | 7 |
| HNAT DOMENICHELLI | 23 | 3 | 3 | 6 | 3- | 9 | 30 | 23 | 3 | 3 | 6 |
| JAMES PATRICK | 19 | 3 | 1 | 4 | 2 | 6 | 22 | 875 | 120 | 428 | 548 |
| DALE MCTAVISH | 9 | 1 | 2 | 3 | 4- | 2 | 14 | 9 | 1 | 2 | 3 |
| TREVOR KIDD | 55 | 0 | 2 | 2 | 0 | 16 | 0 | | | | |
| SAMI HELENIUS | 3 | 0 | 1 | 1 | 1 | 0 | 1 | 3 | 0 | 1 | 1 |
| SASHA LAKOVIC | 19 | 0 | 1 | 1 | 1- | 54 | 10 | 19 | 0 | 1 | 1 |
| PAXTON SCHULTE | 1 | 0 | 0 | 0 | 1 | 2 | 1 | 2 | 0 | 0 | 0 |
| ZARLEY ZALAPSKI | 2 | 0 | 0 | 0 | 1- | 0 | 7 | 562 | 96 | 271 | 367 |
| MARTY MURRAY | 2 | 0 | 0 | 0 | 0 | 4 | 2 | 17 | 3 | 3 | 6 |
| MARKO JANTUNEN | 3 | 0 | 0 | 0 | 1- | 0 | 7 | 3 | 0 | 0 | 0 |
| JAMIE ALLISON | 20 | 0 | 0 | 0 | 4- | 35 | 8 | 21 | 0 | 0 | 0 |
| DWAYNE ROLOSON | 31 | 0 | 0 | 0 | 0 | 2 | 0 | | | | |

## TEAM RANKINGS

| | | Conference Rank | League Rank |
|---|---|---|---|
| Record | 32-41-9 | 10 | 21 |
| Home | 21-18-2 | 6 | 13 |
| Away | 11-23-7 | 12 | 22 |
| Versus Own Conference | 22-29-5 | 9 | 19 |
| Versus Other Conference | 10-12-4 | 7 | 15 |
| Team Plus\Minus | -28 | 11 | 22 |
| Goals For | 214 | 11 | 23 |
| Goals Against | 239 | 6 | 13 |
| Average Shots For | 31.3 | 3 | 6 |
| Average Shots Against | 28.5 | 4 | 8 |
| Overtime | 3-4-9 | 10 | 20 |
| One Goal Games | 12-14 | 9 | 17 |
| Times outshooting opponent | 49 | 3 | 6 |
| Versus Teams Over .500 | 14-19-5 | 5 | 11 |
| Versus Teams Under .500 | 18-22-4 | 12 | 22 |
| First Half Record | 14-22-5 | 12 | 24 |
| Second Half Record | 18-19-4 | 9 | 14 |

## PLAYOFFS

- did not make the playoffs

## All-Time Leaders

### Goals
Joe Nieuwendyk 314
Theoren Fleury 307
Gary Roberts 257

### Assists
Al MacInnis 609
Gary Suter 437
Theoren Fleury 376

### Points
Al MacInnis 822
Theoren Fleury 683
Joe Nieuwendyk 616

## BEST INDIVIDUAL SEASONS

### Goals
Lanny McDonald 1982-83 66
Gary Roberts 1991-92 53
Joe Nieuwendyk 1987-88 51
Joe Mullen 1988-89 51
Joe Nieuwendyk 1988-89 51
Theoren Fleury 1990-91 51

### Assists
Kent Nilsson 1980-81 82
Al MacInnis 1990-91 75
Bob MacMillen 1978-79 71

### Points
Kent Nilsson 1980-81 131
Joe Mullen 1988-89 110
Joe Mullen 1978-79 108

## TEAM

### Last 3 years
| | GP | W | L | T | Pts | % |
|---|---|---|---|---|---|---|
| 1996-97 | 82 | 32 | 41 | 9 | 73 | .445 |
| 1995-96 | 82 | 34 | 37 | 11 | 79 | .482 |
| 1994-95 | 48 | 24 | 17 | 7 | 55 | .573 |

### Best 3 regular seasons
| | GP | W | L | T | Pts | % |
|---|---|---|---|---|---|---|
| 1988-89 | 80 | 54 | 17 | 9 | 117 | .731 |
| 1987-88 | 80 | 48 | 23 | 9 | 105 | .656 |
| 1990-91 | 80 | 46 | 26 | 8 | 100 | .625 |

### Worst 3 regular seasons
| | GP | W | L | T | Pts | % |
|---|---|---|---|---|---|---|
| 1972-73 | 78 | 25 | 38 | 15 | 65 | .416 |

| | | | | | | |
|---|---|---|---|---|---|---|
| 1996-97 | 82 | 32 | 41 | 9 | 73 | .445 |
| 1991-92 | 80 | 31 | 37 | 12 | 74 | .463 |

Most Goals (min. 70 game schedule)
| | |
|---|---|
| 1987-88 | 397 |
| 1984-85 | 363 |
| 1988-89 | 354 |
| 1985-86 | 354 |

Fewest Goals (min. 70 game schedule)
| | |
|---|---|
| 1972-73 | 191 |
| 1996-97 | 214 |
| 1973-74 | 214 |

Most Goals Against (min. 70 game schedule)
| | |
|---|---|
| 1981-82 | 345 |
| 1982-83 | 317 |
| 1985-86 | 315 |

Fewest Goals Against (min. 70 game schedule)
| | |
|---|---|
| 1988-89 | 226 |
| 1974-75 | 233 |
| 1975-76 | 237 |

# Chicago Blackhawks

Because of the great Blackhawks tradition, it's difficult to think of them as a team that could be out of the running this season. Somehow, they have always manage to look better on the ice than they do on paper.

Take last year, for instance. They had little going for them early in the season — no offence at all. Roenick was gone and they didn't have Alexei Zhamnov signed yet. Their top line was Murray Craven between Tony Amonte and James Black. We can't even legally talk about their second and third lines.

Somehow they managed to escape relatively unscathed, however, when Tony Amonte, the hero for the U.S. in the World Cup, turned on the red light all over the league. If not for Amonte, it would have been very ugly.

They recovered some later, with Zhamnov coming aboard, but still finished one game under .500.

So, is this the year they plummet to the dregs of the Western Conference, or do they stay the same, or do they improve? Oddly enough, there are signs that point to all three possibilities.

We'll start with the argument that says the Blackhawks are going to fall further in the standings, out of the playoffs.
* Amonte isn't likely to duplicate the season he had last year. His 41 goals were like 50 in another season, and he's a 30-35 goal man.
* There is too little in the way of goal scoring.

Only Amonte, Daze and Zhamnov had more than 15 goals. And except for Amonte, none of the three had an easy time getting the totals they did.
* Aging players. It's always been a trademark of a Pulford team to have the older veterans around, although it hasn't hurt them much in the past. He has a knack of moving them in and moving them out. Now, there's Murray Craven, Ulf Dahlen, Kevin Miller, Bob Probert, Brent Sutter, Eric Weinrich and Gary Suter all on the wrong side of 30. Some of them are way over the line. So is Chelios for that matter, but he doesn't count.
* Pulford has always been able to get the players the team needed to be competitive. Will new GM Bob Murray have the same magic?

There is no optimism that the team could go way up, but there is some that they could be an improved team to some degree this year.
* Zhamnov, Daze and Suter are proven offensive performers who can do better than they did last season.
* the Hawks lost 17 games by one goal last season, most in the league.
* the Hawks had a terrible time at home last season, but that's an area in which there's often a turnaround by the next year.
* with Pulford retiring, a new GM could shake things up.
* Chris Chelios.

And reasons why the Hawks could stay the same, around the .500 mark:
* no goal scoring has been added.
* solid defence.
* solid goaltending.
* veteran leadership.

## SHORTS

* the Hawks tied a team record when they went undefeated in their first five games of the season away from home.
* the Blackhawks have been in the playoffs for 28 straight years, the longest such current streak in North American professional sports.
* Murray Craven needs 58 games to reach 1,000 for his career, and Chris Chelios needs 80.
* Chicago's losing home record was the first since 1958-59.
* Gary Suter's 3.1 shooting percentage was the lowest for all players with at least 200 shots on net.
* Denis Savard's number 18 will be retired, making him the fifth Blackhawk to be so honored. Glenn Hall - 1, Bobby Hull - 9, Stan Mikita - 21, and Tony Esposito - 35, are the others.
* it has been 36 years since the Blackhawks last won the Stanley Cup.

## STAT ANALYSIS

The Blackhawks lost 17 games by one goal last season, the most in the league. They won 11.

Losing a lot of games by that margin suggests one thing: they're not that far away from winning them. That means a turnaround is more of a possibility than if they didn't lose so many close games.

The season before, Buffalo and Ottawa were tied for the league lead in one-goal losses. They were the second and third most improved teams, behind Dallas.

## TEAM PREVIEW

GOAL: Jeff Hackett certainly has come a long way since holding the distinction of having the worst win-loss record in the history of the NHL. Last season, he was third in goals against average and third in save percentage.

This from a guy who was "nothing more than a back-up" according to dethroned number one goalie, Ed Belfour, who was traded to San Jose.

That's not to diminish the contributions of Ed Belfour, who has been another in a line of great Chicago goalies.

The Blackhawks have themselves a pretty fair backup too, in Chris Terreri, obtained in the Belfour deal with San Jose. Terreri probably can't even be termed a back-up, giving the Hawks two number one goalies, which is something few teams can claim.

Hockey Annual Rating: 9 of 26

| GOALTENDER | GPI | MINS | AVG | W | L | T | EN | SO | GA | SA | SV % |
|---|---|---|---|---|---|---|---|---|---|---|---|
| JEFF HACKETT | 41 | 2473 | 2.16 | 19 | 18 | 4 | 2 | 2 | 89 | 1212 | .927 |
| CHRIS TERRERI | 7 | 429 | 2.66 | 4 | 1 | 2 | 1 | 0 | 19 | 192 | .901 |
| ED BELFOUR | 33 | 1966 | 2.69 | 11 | 15 | 6 | 4 | 1 | 88 | 946 | .907 |
| JIM WAITE | 2 | 105 | 4.00 | 0 | 1 | 1 | 0 | 0 | 7 | 58 | .879 |
| CHI TOTALS | 82 | 5000 | 2.52 | 34 | 35 | 13 | 7 | 3 | 210 | 2415 | .913 |

DEFENCE: When you have the best all-round blueliner in the game in Chris Chelios, then you know your defence can't be too bad.

They have a supporting cast of solid NHL players to go with him: Eric Weinrich, Keith Carney, and Michal Sykora.

The question marks are Gary Suter, Steve Smith and Cam Russell. None of those players, of course, were question marks when healthy and in their prime. Smith was expected to retire.

Youngsters who could move up include Tuomas Gronman and Christian Laflamme. Remi Royer, the team's top draft pick in 1996, finished off the season in Indianapolis.

Suter's collapse was particularly immense. In The Hockey News Online edition, there is a hockey pool section called Townsend's Tips (yes, that's me) in which among other things, I list players who are hot and players who are cold. The cold players have to be among those expected to score. In other words, if Enrico Ciccone didn't have any points in 20 straight games, he still wouldn't make the list. But, Gary Suter made the list — almost every week. In fact, if I had to pick one person as the coldest player of the year, it would Suter, easily.

The best thing about the Chicago defence, excluding Chelios, is that they don't have hands of stone. They can play their position and still contribute offensively and move the puck up. Weinrich didn't even get to play the power play all that often, so 32 points for him, four more than Suter, who did play the power play, is a good offensive total. If Suter bounces back, Weinrich's offensive value still remains high; if he doesn't Weinrich can play on the power play more often.

Another thing in their favor is that most of them have played together for a number of years. That's extemely rare in the NHL these days, but defencemen mostly would benefit from knowing what their partner is going to do in a certain situation. You'd think it would help forwards too, but teams rarely keep lines together anymore.

Hockey Annual Rating: 8 of 26

FORWARD: Somebody is going to have to put the puck in the net besides Tony Amonte. And if he doesn't score at the same rate as he did last year there's even more trouble.

Alexei Zhamnov is a premier NHL centre, although many considered his 62 points a disappointment. He was a holdout at the start of the season, but he did some scoring in bunches, and 62 points in last year's NHL isn't all that bad anyway.

The same is true with Eric Daze. He popped in 22, a drop from the 30 he had in his rookie season, but he can score in the 30 range again quite easily. Nine of his goals came in the last 13 games.

That's pretty much it for the offensive firepower, if you can call it that. No second scoring line, no third.

A second line centre would be nice. Second line scoring wingers would be a bonus too.

Maybe Dimitri Nabakov is ready to make the jump. He's a centre, who played well for Regina in the WHL last season, scoring 95 points in 50 games. If he can move up to the NHL and contribute offensively, the Hawks will be in much better shape.

As for the rest of the offence, look toward Ulf Dahlen, who can be hot and cold; Murray Craven, coming off a horrendous season; Kevin Miller, who should be contributing more; and Ethan Moreau, who had a decent rookie season with 15 goals, fourth on the team.

Jeff Shantz and Brent Sutter are your defensive centremen, and fill in with Sergei Krivokrasov, tough guys Bob Probert and Jim Cummins, and minor-league low scorers Steve

Dubinsky, Jean-Yves Leroux, Craig Mills and Denis Chasse. Those minor-leaguers, however, can contribute in ways other than scoring goals. Denis Savard retired during the summer.

Dan Cleary might be ready to step up to the NHL, even though he had a relatively poor junior season. The thinking was that he had been in the OHL so long, he was getting bored and wasn't challenged. That's his own fault, if that's true, but his negligence could be to Chicago's advantage if he's ready to play in the NHL.

The Hawks have to make changes and get more offence, whether they get it from trades, free agent signings, or players in the system.

Hockey Annual Rating: 23 of 26

SPECIAL TEAMS: The Blackhawks were shorthanded 72 more times last season than they had the man-advantage. That tends to be the case with defensive teams, such as the Hawks, because the other team has the puck more often, and the team with the puck is most likely to draw penalties.

Amonte, Zhamnov and Daze make a pretty good forward unit with the extra man, but Chelios and especially Suter were expected to contribute more offensively. Two years ago they were probably the top one-two power play pointman team. Suter went long, long periods without even getting a point last season. You don't want to write him off yet though, because he's looked like he was winding down once before and came back with a vengeance.

POWER PLAY

|          | G   | ATT | PCT                |
|----------|-----|-----|--------------------|
| Overall  | 45  | 304 | 14.8% (T-16th NHL) |
| Home     | 23  | 165 | 13.9% (21st NHL)   |
| Road     | 22  | 139 | 15.8% (14th NHL)   |

9 SHORT HANDED GOALS ALLOWED (T-9th NHL)

PENALTY KILLING

|         | G  | TSH | PCT               |
|---------|----|-----|-------------------|
| Overall | 59 | 374 | 84.2% (11th NHL)  |
| Home    | 28 | 175 | 84.0% (T-8th NHL) |
| Road    | 31 | 199 | 84.4% (15th NHL)  |

5 SHORT HANDED GOALS SCORED (T-23rd NHL)

BLACKHAWKS SPECIAL TEAMS SCORING

| Power play  | G  | A  | PTS |
|-------------|----|----|-----|
| ZHAMNOV     | 6  | 16 | 22  |
| CHELIOS     | 2  | 18 | 20  |
| DAZE        | 11 | 4  | 15  |
| AMONTE      | 9  | 6  | 15  |
| SUTER       | 3  | 11 | 14  |
| MILLER      | 5  | 4  | 9   |
| CRAVEN      | 2  | 7  | 9   |
| DAHLEN      | 4  | 4  | 8   |
| SAVARD      | 2  | 6  | 8   |
| WEINRICH    | 1  | 6  | 7   |
| KRIVOKRASOV | 2  | 1  | 3   |
| SYKORA      | 1  | 2  | 3   |
| CARNEY      | 0  | 3  | 3   |
| SHANTZ      | 0  | 2  | 2   |
| PROBERT     | 1  | 0  | 1   |
| BLACK       | 0  | 1  | 1   |

| Short handed | G | A | PTS |
|--------------|---|---|-----|
| AMONTE       | 2 | 1 | 3   |
| ZHAMNOV      | 1 | 2 | 3   |
| SHANTZ       | 1 | 1 | 2   |
| MILLER       | 1 | 0 | 1   |
| CHELIOS      | 0 | 1 | 1   |

COACHING AND MANAGEMENT: How could you say that Craig Hartsburg didn't do a good job last year, considering the tools he was given. Without any offence, he made them play good defence, which was the only thing that helped keep their heads above water. He has to manage a group of veterans and young players together, and it often isn't easy keeping veterans happy.

Pulford isn't the type of guy to sit around and watch a weakness fester, but uncharacteristically didn't do anything of consequence last season when the team needed more scoring. Unless you count obtaining Ulf Dahlen.

With Pulford retiring, it's up to Bob Murray, his former assistant, to make things happen. He's new on the job and won't likely have a lot of patience. For sure, he won't want to see a weakness go unfixed, or it will make him look weak.

Hockey Annual Rating: 19 of 26

## DRAFT

| Round | Sel. | Player | Pos | Amateur Team |
|---|---|---|---|---|
| 1 | 13 | Daniel Cleary | LW | Belleville (OHL) |
| 1 | 16 | Ty Jones | RW | Spokane (WHL) |
| 2 | 39 | Jeremy Reich | C | Seattle (WHL) |
| 3 | 67 | Mike Souza | LW | U. of New Hampshire |
| 5 | 110 | Benjamin Simon | C | Notre Dame |
| 5 | 120 | Peter Gardiner | RW | RPI |
| 5 | 130 | Kyle Calder | C | Regina (WHL) |
| 6 | 147 | Heath Gordon | LW | Green Bay (USHL) |
| 7 | 174 | Jerad Smith | D | Portland (WHL) |
| 8 | 204 | Sergei Shikhanov | RW | Russia |
| 9 | 230 | Chris Feil | D | Ohio State |

At one time, Daniel Cleary was projected as a sure-fire top three draft pick. He was putting up good numbers for Belleville in the OHL at the age of 15. He had 80 points that season, then rose to 53-62-115, then fell to 32-48-80 last season. As his points dropped, so did his ranking.

He was accused of being in poor condition at the start of the season, although he counters that by saying he couldn't find ice during the summer in his home in Newfoundland. Some say his points dropped because he wasn't challenged. That means there are two knocks against his character. Another reason they fell, however, is that Belleville did not have a particularly good team, so he wasn't getting a lot of points off his teammates.

Cleary's best bet would be to show everyone that they made a mistake in knocking him down in the rankings. A theory that draft expert Bob McKenzie, of *The Sports Network* and *The Hockey News* (and former writer of this book) adheres to is that when a player is around as long as Cleary, scouts get tired of looking at all his good points, and start looking for the bad. Maybe that's what happened to Cleary.

Chicago's other first round pick, Ty Jones, is everybody's dream winger — big, rough, tough, and can score goals. Twenty goals in the WHL, however, doesn't translate to much in the NHL, but it's the same number that Bob Probert had in his last year of junior.

PROGNOSIS: There's a temptation to write off the Blackhawks and suggest they'll slide down out of the playoffs. They were only four points out of missing them last year, but only four points away from fourth overall.

They have some very easily identified weaknesses, however, which can be fixed. If they are, the Hawks are in; if not, the Hawks are out. Simple as that.

## PREDICTION

Western Conference: 6th
Overall: 12th

## STAT SECTION

| Team Scoring Stats | | 1996-97 | | | | CAREER | | | | | |
|---|---|---|---|---|---|---|---|---|---|---|---|
| | GP | G | A | PTS | +/- | PIM | SH | Gm | G | A | Pts |
| TONY AMONTE | 81 | 41 | 36 | 77 | 35 | 64 | 266 | 451 | 172 | 190 | 362 |
| ALEXEI ZHAMNOV | 74 | 20 | 42 | 62 | 18 | 56 | 208 | 309 | 123 | 206 | 329 |
| CHRIS CHELIOS | 72 | 10 | 38 | 48 | 6 | 112 | 194 | 920 | 153 | 567 | 720 |
| ERIC DAZE | 71 | 22 | 19 | 41 | 4- | 16 | 176 | 155 | 53 | 43 | 96 |
| MURRAY CRAVEN | 75 | 8 | 27 | 35 | 0 | 12 | 122 | 942 | 250 | 464 | 714 |
| ULF DAHLEN | 73 | 14 | 19 | 33 | 2- | 18 | 131 | 686 | 231 | 249 | 480 |
| ERIC WEINRICH | 81 | 7 | 25 | 32 | 19 | 62 | 115 | 520 | 39 | 164 | 203 |
| ETHAN MOREAU | 82 | 15 | 16 | 31 | 13 | 123 | 114 | 90 | 15 | 17 | 32 |
| KEVIN MILLER | 69 | 14 | 17 | 31 | 10- | 41 | 139 | 537 | 142 | 169 | 311 |
| JEFF SHANTZ | 69 | 9 | 21 | 30 | 11 | 28 | 86 | 244 | 24 | 60 | 84 |
| GARY SUTER | 82 | 7 | 21 | 28 | 4- | 70 | 225 | 845 | 167 | 535 | 702 |
| DENIS SAVARD | 64 | 9 | 18 | 27 | 10- | 60 | 82 | 1,196 | 473 | 865 | 1,138 |
| S. KRIVOKRASOV | 67 | 13 | 11 | 24 | 1- | 42 | 104 | 167 | 32 | 28 | 60 |
| JAMES BLACK | 64 | 12 | 11 | 23 | 6 | 20 | 122 | 134 | 23 | 24 | 47 |
| BOB PROBERT | 82 | 9 | 14 | 23 | 3- | 326 | 111 | 634 | 142 | 180 | 322 |
| KEITH CARNEY | 81 | 3 | 15 | 18 | 26 | 62 | 77 | 262 | 16 | 43 | 59 |
| MICHAL SYKORA | 63 | 3 | 14 | 17 | 4 | 69 | 77 | 176 | 8 | 38 | 46 |
| BRENT SUTTER | 39 | 7 | 7 | 14 | 10 | 18 | 62 | 1,059 | 361 | 460 | 821 |
| JIM CUMMINS | 65 | 6 | 6 | 12 | 4 | 199 | 61 | 188 | 14 | 14 | 28 |
| ENRICO CICCONE | 67 | 2 | 2 | 4 | 1- | 233 | 65 | 272 | 7 | 13 | 20 |
| ADAM CREIGHTON | 19 | 1 | 2 | 3 | 2- | 13 | 20 | 708 | 187 | 216 | 403 |
| CAM RUSSELL | 44 | 1 | 1 | 2 | 8- | 65 | 19 | 313 | 7 | 18 | 25 |
| C. LAFLAMME | 4 | 0 | 1 | 1 | 3 | 2 | 3 | 4 | 0 | 1 | 1 |
| T. GRONMAN | 16 | 0 | 1 | 1 | 4- | 13 | 9 | 16 | 0 | 1 | 1 |
| JEFF HACKETT | 41 | 0 | 1 | 1 | 0 | 6 | 0 | | | | |
| S. KLIMOVICH | 1 | 0 | 0 | 0 | 0 | 2 | 0 | 1 | 0 | 0 | 0 |
| JIM WAITE | | 2 | 0 | 0 | 0 | 0 | 0 | 0 | | | |
| STEVE DUBINSKY | 5 | 0 | 0 | 0 | 2 | 0 | 4 | 91 | 4 | 9 | 13 |
| MIKE PROKOPEC | 6 | 0 | 0 | 0 | 1- | 6 | 2 | 15 | 0 | 0 | 0 |
| DAVE CHYZOWSKI | 8 | 0 | 0 | 0 | 1 | 6 | 6 | 126 | 15 | 16 | 31 |
| BASIL MCRAE | 8 | 0 | 0 | 0 | 2- | 12 | 1 | 576 | 53 | 83 | 136 |

| | | | | | | | | | | | |
|---|---|---|---|---|---|---|---|---|---|---|---|
| STEVE SMITH | 21 | 0 | 0 | 0 | 4 | 29 | 7 | 702 | 71 | 283 | 354 |
| CHRIS TERRERI | 29 | 0 | 0 | 0 | 0 | 0 | 0 | | | | |

## TEAM RANKINGS

| | | Conference Rank | League Rank |
|---|---|---|---|
| Record | 34-35-13 | 8 | 14 |
| Home | 16-21-4 | 12 | 24 |
| Away | 18-14-9 | 5 | 7 |
| Versus Own Conference | 22-26-8 | 8 | 17 |
| Versus Other Conference | 12-9-5 | 5 | 11 |
| Team Plus\Minus | +27 | 4 | 8 |
| Goals For | 223 | 10 | 20 |
| Goals Against | 210 | 4 | 7 |
| Average Shots For | 30.3 | 5 | 9 |
| Average Shots Against | 29.4 | 6 | 12 |
| Overtime | 1-5-13 | 11 | 23 |
| One Goal Games | 11-17 | 12 | 23 |

Times outshooting

| | | | |
|---|---|---|---|
| opponent | 46 | 6 | 11 |
| Versus Teams Over .500 | 16-20-7 | 3 | 9 |
| Versus Teams Under .500 | 18-15-6 | 8 | 15 |
| First Half Record | 15-20-6 | 8 | 19 |
| Second Half Record | 19-15-7 | 5 | 8 |

## PLAYOFFS

Results: lost to Colorado 4-2
Record: 2-4
Home: 2-1
Away: 0-3-1
Goals For: 14 (2.3/game)
Goals Against: 28 (4.7/game)
Overtime: 1-0
Power play: 3.7% (15th)
Penalty Killing: 73.3% (15th)

| | GP | G | A | PTS | +/- | PIM | PP | SH | GW | OT | S |
|---|---|---|---|---|---|---|---|---|---|---|---|
| TONY AMONTE | 6 | 4 | 2 | 6 | 2 | 8 | 0 | 2 | 0 | 0 | 24 |
| GARY SUTER | 6 | 1 | 4 | 5 | 1 | 8 | 0 | 0 | 0 | 0 | 12 |
| JEFF SHANTZ | 6 | 0 | 4 | 4 | 4 | 6 | 0 | 0 | 0 | 0 | 7 |
| BOB PROBERT | 6 | 2 | 1 | 3 | 4- | 41 | 1 | 0 | 1 | 0 | 10 |
| ERIC DAZE | 6 | 2 | 1 | 3 | 1- | 2 | 0 | 0 | 0 | 0 | 15 |
| JAMES BLACK | 5 | 1 | 1 | 2 | 1 | 2 | 0 | 0 | 0 | 0 | 8 |
| KEITH CARNEY | 6 | 1 | 1 | 2 | 2- | 2 | 0 | 0 | 0 | 0 | 7 |
| DENIS SAVARD | 6 | 0 | 2 | 2 | 3- | 2 | 0 | 0 | 0 | 0 | 14 |
| STEVE DUBINSKY | 4 | 1 | 0 | 1 | 0 | 4 | 0 | 0 | 0 | 0 | 6 |
| SERGEI KRIVOKRASOV | 6 | 1 | 0 | 1 | 2- | 4 | 0 | 0 | 1 | 1 | 11 |
| ETHAN MOREAU | 6 | 1 | 0 | 1 | 3 | 9 | 0 | 0 | 0 | 0 | 10 |
| ULF DAHLEN | 5 | 0 | 1 | 1 | 0 | 0 | 0 | 0 | 0 | 0 | 2 |

| | | | | | | | | | | | |
|---|---|---|---|---|---|---|---|---|---|---|---|
| CHRIS CHELIOS | 6 | 0 | 1 | 1 | 2- | 8 | 0 | 0 | 0 | 0 | 18 |
| KEVIN MILLER | 6 | 0 | 1 | 1 | 0 | 0 | 0 | 0 | 0 | 0 | 10 |
| ERIC WEINRICH | 6 | 0 | 1 | 1 | 1- | 4 | 0 | 0 | 0 | 0 | 8 |
| MICHAL SYKORA | 1 | 0 | 0 | 0 | 2- | 0 | 0 | 0 | 0 | 0 | 1 |
| MURRAY CRAVEN | 2 | 0 | 0 | 0 | 4- | 2 | 0 | 0 | 0 | 0 | 5 |
| BRENT SUTTER | 2 | 0 | 0 | 0 | 2- | 6 | 0 | 0 | 0 | 0 | 3 |
| CHRIS TERRERI | 2 | 0 | 0 | 0 | 0 | 2 | 0 | 0 | 0 | 0 | 0 |
| STEVE SMITH | 3 | 0 | 0 | 0 | 0 | 4 | 0 | 0 | 0 | 0 | 3 |
| CAM RUSSELL | 4 | 0 | 0 | 0 | 0 | 4 | 0 | 0 | 0 | 0 | 1 |
| ENRICO CICCONE | 4 | 0 | 0 | 0 | 0 | 18 | 0 | 0 | 0 | 0 | 6 |
| JEFF HACKETT | 6 | 0 | 0 | 0 | 0 | 0 | 0 | 0 | 0 | 0 | 0 |
| JIM CUMMINS | 6 | 0 | 0 | 0 | 5- | 24 | 0 | 0 | 0 | 0 | 3 |

| GOALTENDER | GPI | MINS | AVG | W | L | T | EN | SO | GA | SA | SV % |
|---|---|---|---|---|---|---|---|---|---|---|---|
| CHRIS TERRERI | 2 | 44 | 4.09 | 0 | 0 | 0 | 0 | 0 | 3 | 28 | .893 |
| JEFF HACKETT | 6 | 345 | 4.35 | 2 | 4 | 0 | 0 | 0 | 25 | 190 | .868 |
| CHI TOTALS | 6 | 391 | 4.30 | 2 | 4 | 0 | 0 | 0 | 28 | 218 | |

## ALL-TIME LEADERS

Goals
Bobby Hull        604
Stan Mikita       541
Steve Larmer      406

Assists
Stan Mikita       926
Denis Savard      719
Doug Wilson       554

Points
Stan Mikita     1,467
Bobby Hull      1,153
Denis Savard    1,096

## BEST INDIVIDUAL SEASONS

Goals
Bobby Hull   1968-69   58
Al Secord    1982-83   54
Bobby Hull   1965-66   54

Assists
Denis Savard 1987-88   87
Denis Savard 1981-82   87
Denis Savard 1982-83   86

Points
Denis Savard 1987-88   131
Denis Savard 1982-83   121
Denis Savard 1981-82   119

## TEAM

### Last 3 years

|         | GP | W  | L  | T  | Pts | %    |
|---------|----|----|----|----|-----|------|
| 1996-97 | 82 | 34 | 35 | 13 | 81  | .494 |
| 1995-96 | 82 | 40 | 28 | 14 | 94  | .573 |
| 1994-95 | 48 | 24 | 19 | 5  | 53  | .552 |

### Best 3 regular seasons

| 1970-71 | 78 | 49 | 20 | 6  | 107 | .686 |
|---------|----|----|----|----|-----|------|
| 1971-72 | 78 | 46 | 17 | 5  | 107 | .686 |
| 1973-74 | 78 | 41 | 14 | 23 | 105 | .673 |

### Worst 3 regular seasons

| 1927-28 | 44 | 7  | 34 | 3  | 17  | .193 |
|---------|----|----|----|----|-----|------|
| 1953-54 | 70 | 12 | 51 | 7  | 31  | .221 |
| 1928-29 | 44 | 7  | 29 | 8  | 22  | .250 |

### Most Goals (min. 70 game schedule)

| 1985-86 | 351 |
|---------|-----|
| 1982-83 | 338 |
| 1981-82 | 332 |

### Fewest Goals (min. 70 game schedule)

| 1953-54 | 133 |
|---------|-----|
| 1955-56 | 155 |
| 1951-52 | 158 |

### Most Goals Against (min. 70 game schedule)

| 1981-82 | 363 |
|---------|-----|
| 1985-86 | 349 |
| 1988-89 | 335 |

### Fewest Goals Against (min. 70 game schedule)

| 1973-74 | 164 |
|---------|-----|
| 1971-72 | 166 |
| 1963-64 | 169 |

# Colorado Avalanche

So the Avalanche didn't win the Stanley Cup last year. Big Deal.

They can't do it every time. But they can consistently be in position to win and that's why Colorado is a favorite this season.

It takes a lot to go right for a team to win a Stanley Cup. Sometimes, it's just little things. An injury here or there, some luck here or there, the moon and stars in the right positions. Whatever.

There hasn't been a repeat champion in six years, and many people believe dynasties aren't possible in professional sports anymore.

One of the reasons is free agency. A player can up and go, under special circumstances, and sell his services to the highest bidder. A team can become good overnight, or weak overnight. They can plug a weakness without giving anything up in return.

Also, while we're talking money, teams sometimes can't afford to be too good. Strange but true. With too many top-line players all clammering for the big dough, the payroll becomes too high and moves have to be made with respect to budget considerations.

Another strike against dynasties is that there are too many teams now, too many trying to reach the same objective. Those that are close usually don't mess around, they go for it. If they're missing one or two pieces they fill them and whatever it takes they make their club strong for that particular run for the roses.

For a team to be dominant every year is improbable, but for them to be an exceptional team and win the Cup a couple times isn't. The Avalanche are one of the few teams that fit that description. Many of the other top challengers are two old, or have already made their run and fallen short.

Nobody in the league has a young nucleus of stars that include two of the best forwards in the game, in Peter Forsberg and Joe Sakic; one of the best offensive defencemen in Sandis Ozolinsh, one of the best defencemen in Adam Foote, and a cast of even more stars.

That's just the prime time players. There's a secondary list as well of younger players, starting with Adam Deadmarsh. And some future superstars, such as goaltender Marc Denis.

We're not even taking into account older guys like Patrick Roy, Claude Lemieux, Jari Kurri (signed as a free agent) and Valeri Kamensky, whose expiry dates are still a ways off.

Sure, the Avalanche can be a dynasty, but if they don't sign Joe Sakic (they hadn't at press time) or do sign him and then have to trade him, forget all of the above.

## STUFF

* Patrick Roy broke the team's shutout record with seven, breaking the old mark of four by Clint Malarchuk in 1985-86.

* Ozolinsh led the league with 42 power play points.
* 107 points were a franchise high, but the winning percentage of .652 wasn't. In the labor-shortened 48-game season in 1994-95, they earned 65 points for a winning percentage of .677.
* 205 goals allowed was 35 goals lower than the previous low of 240 in 1995-96.
* a 12-game undefeated streak was a team record, beating the old mark of 11, set earlier last season and in 1980-81.
* the Avalanche farm team in Hershey won the AHL championship.

## STAT ANALYSIS

The Avalanche have two of the best playoff performers of all-time — Claude Lemieux and Patrick Roy, not to mention Jari Kurri, whom they added during the summer. And for that matter, not to mention Joe Sakic, who has established a reputation as a great playoff player.

Anyway, Lemieux is one of the few players who has won Stanley Cups with three teams, as well as consecutive Cups with two different clubs. While he may have an ordinary regular season, his play in the post-season is remarkable, and for whatever reason, he's one of the best ever.

The same with Roy. His star shines brightest in the playoffs, making him arguably the best playoff goaltender of all time.

### CLAUDE LEMIEUX:

Most Playoff Game Winning Goals - All-Time

| | |
|---|---|
| Wayne Gretzky | 24 |
| CLAUDE LEMIEUX | 18 |
| Rocket Richard | 18 |
| Mike Bossy | 17 |
| Glenn Anderson | 17 |

Most Playoff Goals - Last Three Years (previous two years plus this year):

| | |
|---|---|
| CLAUDE LEMIEUX | 31 |
| Joe Sakic | 26 |
| Jaromir Jagr | 25 |
| Slava Kozlov | 22 |
| Eric Lindros | 22 |
| Rod Brind'Amour | 21 |

### PATRICK ROY:

Most Playoff Wins by a Goaltender

| | |
|---|---|
| PATRICK ROY | 96 |
| Billy Smith | 88 |
| Ken Dryden | 80 |
| Grant Fuhr | 80 |

Most Playoff Games by a Goaltender

| | |
|---|---|
| Patrick Roy | 153 |
| Billy Smith | 132 |
| Grant Fuhr | 127 |
| Andy Moog | 123 |

## TEAM PREVIEW

GOAL: Even Patrick Roy can't win the Stanley Cup every year. But, he's still the guy you'd want if you had your choice of goalies for a Cup run.

There's little people don't know about Roy, and one day there's going to be little that people don't know about Marc Denis. *The Hockey News*, for example, selected him last year as its number one prospect. That's high praise, considering their previous three top prospects were Bryan Berard, Ed Jovanovski and Peter Forsberg.

Who better to serve an apprenticeship under than Roy. Denis won't be the rookie of the year, and probably won't play all that often, but he will be well on his way to becoming the next Patrick Roy. Or perhaps, the first Marc Denis.

Craig Billington has been re-signed, but it's unclear what his role will be, unless it's emergency backup, or insurance in case Denis isn't ready.

Hockey Annual Rating: 3 of 26

DEFENCE: The Colorado defence is a thing of beauty. It has almost the perfect mix of the type of players any team would want.

They have one of the premier offensive talents in Sandis Ozolinsh whose 68 points were second only to Brian Leetch. They have two of the top defensive defencemen in the game in Adam Foote and Sylvain Lefebvre. They have Uwe Krupp, a good all-round player, and they have solid performers in Jon Klemm, Alexei Gusarov and Aaron Miller. The tough guy is Brent Severyn, although he also plays forward.

Down in the minors they have players who can play when called up, such as Eric Messier and Wade Belak.

Ozolinsh led the league in goals by defencemen with 23. Twenty goals were a good number by forwards this past year, so that many by a defenceman is exceptional. Ozolinsh's goal, of course, is to score goals. That's why he's a threat to grab the puck and go, or especially to move up from his point position when the puck is in the opposing end. The tradeoff is that he can get caught out of position, but it might not be such a bad tradeoff.

The Avalanche would like a little more toughness at this position, but took care of that at the draft when they chose some of the roughest, meanest hombres east or west of the Rockies.

Hockey Annual Rating: 2 of 26

FORWARD: The offensive numbers for Joe Sakic and Peter Forsberg weren't extraordinary last season, but that's because each of them missed 17 games.

Even so, it was quite a drop for Sakic from 51 goals to just 22. But, it was just a blip on the radar screen. Once the playoffs rolled around he was back to being his dominant self. Even though the Avalanche only made it to the conference finals, he was still second in playoff scoring with 25 points, one fewer than leader Eric Lindros.

Everybody else was pretty dependable, with nobody having an off-year for scoring. That's keeping in mind, of course, the reduced scoring league-wide.

A breakthrough season for Adam Deadmarsh was the big news. He led the team with 33 goals, while still playing it tough, and establishing himself as a premier power forward. Twenty-five goals from Keith Jones may have been a bit of a surprise too.

The only loss of significance from last year will be Mike Keane, who signed on with the Rangers as an unrestricted free agent. He's a leader and good all-round influence, but the Avalanche have a number of players of his ilk, so it won't hurt them much. And they replaced him during the summer by signing free agent Jari Kurri.

| GOALTENDER | GPI | MINS | AVG | W | L | T | EN | SO | GA | SA | SV % |
|---|---|---|---|---|---|---|---|---|---|---|---|
| PATRICK ROY | 62 | 3698 | 2.32 | 38 | 15 | 7 | 3 | 7 | 143 | 1861 | .923 |
| CRAIG BILLINGTON | 23 | 1200 | 2.65 | 11 | 8 | 2 | 2 | 1 | 53 | 584 | .909 |
| MARC DENIS | 1 | 60 | 3.00 | 0 | 1 | 0 | 1 | 0 | 3 | 26 | .885 |
| COL TOTALS | 82 | 4980 | 2.47 | 49 | 24 | 9 | 6 | 8 | 205 | 2477 | .917 |

Forsberg between Kamensky and Lemieux is good for line 1-A, and Sakic between Jones and Deadmarsh is good for line 1-B, or some mix of the two. Mike Ricci, Eric Lacroix, Rene Corbet, Jari Kurri and Stephane Yelle are parts of the third and fourth line, along with Scott Young, unless he gets traded as the rumors have been suggesting for some time.

We should see at least one new regular on the forward unit. GM Lacroix lamented the loss of Chris Simon last season, traded to Washington when his contract demands were deemed unreasonable, and the lack of an enforcer was seen as the only problem with the Avalanche lineup. Brent Severyn, a defenceman, sometimes played up front to compensate, but Colorado is likely to find someone before the season starts.

Among the prospects who could get a shot this year are centre Josef Marha (23-49-72 in 67 games for Hershey) who led the AHL in playoff scoring for the championship Hershey team, and Christian Matte (18-18-36 in 49 game with Hersey).

Hockey Annual Rating: 1 of 26

SPECIAL TEAMS: You'd have to nitpick to find a problem with the Avalanche special teams, so we'll do just that. They tend to give up a lot of shorthanded goals. Two years ago, they were the worst in the league with 20 shorthanded markers against, and last year they let in 12, good for 19th worst.

But, really, that's not so bad anyway. When you take the 83 power play goals they scored and substract 12, it gives them a net of 71. Their net was only three behind Pittsburgh's gross, and they were next to Colorodo in power play goals.

POWER PLAY

|  | G | ATT | PCT |
| --- | --- | --- | --- |
| Overall | 83 | 403 | 20.6% (3rd NHL) |
| Home | 42 | 215 | 19.5% (T-2nd NHL) |
| Road | 41 | 188 | 21.8% (2nd NHL) |
| 12 SHORT HANDED GOALS ALLOWED (T-19th NHL) | | | |

PENALTY KILLING

|  | G | TSH | PCT |
| --- | --- | --- | --- |
| Overall | 42 | 339 | 87.6% (2nd NHL) |
| Home | 20 | 167 | 88.0% (1st NHL) |
| Road | 22 | 172 | 87.2% (4th NHL) |
| 14 SHORT HANDED GOALS SCORED (T-4th NHL) | | | |

AVALANCHE SPECIAL TEAMS SCORING

| Power play | G | A | PTS |
| --- | --- | --- | --- |
| OZOLINSH | 13 | 29 | 42 |
| SAKIC | 10 | 26 | 36 |
| KAMENSKY | 8 | 18 | 26 |
| FORSBERG | 5 | 21 | 26 |
| DEADMARSH | 10 | 14 | 24 |
| JONES | 14 | 6 | 20 |
| YOUNG | 7 | 13 | 20 |
| RICCI | 5 | 8 | 13 |
| LEMIEUX | 5 | 8 | 13 |
| KRUPP | 2 | 3 | 5 |
| LACROIX | 2 | 1 | 3 |
| KLEMM | 1 | 2 | 3 |
| CORBET | 1 | 2 | 3 |
| LEFEBVRE | 1 | 1 | 2 |
| FOOTE | 0 | 2 | 2 |
| MILLER | 0 | 1 | 1 |
| GUSAROV | 0 | 1 | 1 |

| Short handed | G | A | PTS |
| --- | --- | --- | --- |
| FORSBERG | 4 | 3 | 7 |
| DEADMARSH | 3 | 1 | 4 |
| SAKIC | 2 | 1 | 3 |
| YELLE | 1 | 2 | 3 |
| KLEMM | 2 | 0 | 2 |
| LEFEBVRE | 0 | 2 | 2 |
| KRUPP | 0 | 2 | 2 |

| | | | |
|---|---|---|---|
| FOOTE | 0 | 2 | 2 |
| KEANE | 1 | 0 | 1 |
| JONES | 1 | 0 | 1 |
| OZOLINSH | 0 | 1 | 1 |

COACHING AND MANAGEMENT: When you've been as successful a coach as Marc Crawford it can get kind of boring. So, when there's the slightest chink in his armor, everybody jumps all over him.

In the playoffs he lost it in a game versus Detroit, going balistic and trying to get at Scotty Bowman. For that he was fined $10,000 and chastised from every corner of the media.

Big Deal. So he had a fit. He wouldn't be the first and he won't be the last. Disgraceful behavior? Not in the least. More like good entertainment. Hockey's an emotional game. If you want to watch robots, watch tennis.

GM Pierre Lacroix hasn't been nearly so controversial in nature. He has quietly gone about assembling the best team in hockey. Not that he just sits back and enjoys the ride. He's constantly doing little things to help the big picture.

Hockey Annual Rating: 1 of 26

DRAFT

| Round | Sel. | Player | Pos | Amateur Team |
|---|---|---|---|---|
| 1 | 26 | Kevin Grimes | D | Kingston (OHL) |
| 2 | 53 | Graham Belak | D | Edmonton (WHL) |
| 3 | 55 | Rick Berry | D | Seattle (WHL) |
| 3 | 78 | Ville Nieminen | W | Finland |
| 4 | 87 | Brad Larsen | LW | Swift Current (WHL) |
| 5 | 133 | Aaron Miskovich | C | Green Bay (USHL) |
| 6 | 161 | David Aebischer | G | Switzerland |
| 8 | 217 | Doug Schmidt | D | Waterloo (USHL) |
| 9 | 243 | Kyle Kidney | LW | Salisbury (USHL) |
| 9 | 245 | Stephen Lafleur | D | Belleville (OHL) |

Kevin Grimes is a big, rough and tumble defenceman, one of the toughest available in the draft. He earned 188 penalty minutes with Kingston last year.

With their second round pick, they selected another big, tough guy. Graham Belak, whose brother Wade was a first round pick for the Avalanche in 1994, earned 246 PIM for Edmonton in the WHL.

Fourth round pick Brad Larsen was a third round pick in 1995 by Ottawa and then traded to Colorado. When the Avalanche and Larsen failed to come to a contract agreement, Larsen went back into the draft. Presumably, he was not happy when the Avalanche selected him again. Presumably, the Avalanche were.

PROGNOSIS

The Avalanche will be on a mission this year. They didn't like losing to Detroit in the Western Conference finals, and by the time the playoffs roll around they'll have their war paint on.

During the regular season don't look for them to set any records. They had some down times last year and it wasn't unusual for a dog team to beat them. And so what if they do? They need a challenge, so they save their best efforts. It's probably not even such a bad thing. Even while taking it easy at times, they still finished with the best record in the league.

A Stanley Cup again for the Avalanche this year?

There's a good possibility.

PREDICTION
Western Conference: 1st
Overall: 2nd

STAT SECTION

| Team Scoring Stats | | 1996-97 | | | | CAREER | | | | | |
|---|---|---|---|---|---|---|---|---|---|---|---|
| | GP | G | A | PTS | +/- | PIM | SH | Gm | G | A | Pts |
| PETER FORSBERG | 65 | 28 | 58 | 86 | 31 | 73 | 188 | 194 | 73 | 179 | 252 |
| JOE SAKIC | 65 | 22 | 52 | 74 | 10- | 34 | 261 | 655 | 307 | 513 | 820 |
| SANDIS OZOLINSH | 80 | 23 | 45 | 68 | 4 | 88 | 232 | 319 | 79 | 155 | 234 |
| VALERI KAMENSKY | 68 | 28 | 38 | 66 | 5 | 38 | 165 | 320 | 126 | 178 | 304 |
| ADAM DEADMARSH | 78 | 33 | 27 | 60 | 8 | 136 | 198 | 204 | 63 | 62 | 125 |
| KEITH JONES | 78 | 25 | 23 | 48 | 3 | 118 | 170 | 325 | 85 | 85 | 170 |
| SCOTT YOUNG | 72 | 18 | 19 | 37 | 5- | 14 | 164 | 599 | 173 | 239 | 412 |
| ERIC LACROIX | 81 | 18 | 18 | 36 | 16 | 26 | 141 | 201 | 43 | 41 | 84 |
| MIKE RICCI | 63 | 13 | 19 | 32 | 3- | 59 | 74 | 479 | 132 | 189 | 321 |
| CLAUDE LEMIEUX | 45 | 11 | 17 | 28 | 4- | 43 | 168 | 758 | 272 | 275 | 547 |
| RENE CORBET | 76 | 12 | 15 | 27 | 14 | 67 | 128 | 126 | 16 | 25 | 41 |
| MIKE KEANE | 81 | 10 | 17 | 27 | 2 | 63 | 91 | 642 | 110 | 206 | 316 |
| STEPHANE YELLE | 79 | 9 | 17 | 26 | 1 | 38 | 89 | 150 | 22 | 31 | 53 |
| JON KLEMM | 80 | 9 | 15 | 24 | 12 | 37 | 103 | 151 | 13 | 28 | 41 |
| UWE KRUPP | 60 | 4 | 17 | 21 | 12 | 48 | 107 | 617 | 57 | 187 | 244 |
| ADAM FOOTE | 78 | 2 | 19 | 21 | 16 | 135 | 60 | 358 | 15 | 60 | 75 |
| AARON MILLER | 56 | 5 | 12 | 17 | 15 | 15 | 47 | 71 | 5 | 15 | 20 |
| ALEXEI GUSAROV | 58 | 2 | 12 | 14 | 4 | 28 | 33 | 396 | 29 | 100 | 129 |
| SYLVAIN LEFEBVRE | 71 | 2 | 11 | 13 | 12 | 30 | 77 | 559 | 24 | 96 | 120 |
| BRENT SEVERYN | 66 | 1 | 4 | 5 | 6- | 193 | 55 | 261 | 8 | 25 | 33 |
| YVES SARAULT | 28 | 2 | 1 | 3 | 0 | 6 | 41 | 61 | 4 | 3 | 7 |
| CHRISTIAN MATTE | 5 | 1 | 1 | 2 | 1 | 0 | 6 | 5 | 1 | 1 | 2 |
| CRAIG BILLINGTON | 23 | 0 | 2 | 2 | 0 | 2 | 0 | | | | |
| JOSEF MARHA | 6 | 0 | 1 | 1 | 0 | 0 | 6 | 8 | 0 | 2 | 2 |
| PATRICK ROY | 62 | 0 | 1 | 1 | 0 | 15 | 1 | | | | |
| MARC DENIS | 1 | 0 | 0 | 0 | 0 | 0 | 0 | | | | |
| RICHARD BRENNAN | 2 | 0 | 0 | 0 | 0 | 0 | 0 | 2 | 0 | 0 | 0 |

| | | | | | | | | | | |
|---|---|---|---|---|---|---|---|---|---|---|
| WADE BELAK | 5 | 0 | 0 | 0 | 1- | 11 | 1 | 5 | 0 | 0 | 0 |
| ERIC MESSIER | 21 | 0 | 0 | 0 | 7 | 4 | 11 | 21 | 0 | 0 | 0 |

## TEAM RANKINGS

| | | Conference Rank | League Rank |
|---|---|---|---|
| Record | 49-24-9 | 1 | 1 |
| Home | 26-10-5 | 1 | 1 |
| Away | 23-14-4 | 2 | 3 |
| Versus Own Conference | 35-17-4 | 1 | 1 |
| Versus Other Conference | 14-7-5 | 3 | 5 |
| Team Plus\Minus | +31 | 3 | 7 |
| Goals For | 277 | 1 | 2 |
| Goals Against | 205 | 3 | 5 |
| Average Shots For | 31.9 | 2 | 3 |
| Average Shots Against | 30.2 | 7 | 14 |
| Overtime | 3-3-9 | 7 | 12 |
| One Goal Games | 17-9 | 1 | 2 |
| Times outshooting opponent | 49 | 4 | 7 |

| | | | |
|---|---|---|---|
| Versus Teams Over .500 | 17-9-8 | 3 | 4 |
| Versus Teams Under .500 | 32-15-1 | 3 | 4 |
| First Half Record | 24-10-7 | 1 | 1 |
| Second Half Record | 25-14-2 | 2 | 3 |

## PLAYOFFS

Results: defeated Chicago 4-2
defeated Edmonton 4-1
lost to Detroit 4-2

Record: 10-7
Home: 8-1
Away: 2-6
Goals For: 59 (3.5/game)
Goals Against: 41 2.4/game)
Overtime: 1-1
Power play: 22.1% (3rd)
Penalty Killing: 91.9% (3rd)

| | GP | G | A | PTS | +/- | PIM | PP | SH | GW | OT | S |
|---|---|---|---|---|---|---|---|---|---|---|---|
| JOE SAKIC | 17 | 8 | 17 | 25 | 5 | 14 | 3 | 0 | 0 | 0 | 50 |
| CLAUDE LEMIEUX | 17 | 13 | 10 | 23 | 7 | 32 | 4 | 0 | 4 | 1 | 73 |
| VALERI KAMENSKY | 17 | 8 | 14 | 22 | 1- | 16 | 5 | 0 | 2 | 0 | 49 |
| PETER FORSBERG | 14 | 5 | 12 | 17 | 6- | 10 | 3 | 0 | 0 | 0 | 35 |
| SANDIS OZOLINSH | 17 | 4 | 13 | 17 | 1- | 24 | 2 | 0 | 1 | 0 | 39 |
| ADAM DEADMARSH | 17 | 3 | 6 | 9 | 6- | 24 | 1 | 0 | 1 | 0 | 39 |
| STEPHANE YELLE | 12 | 1 | 6 | 7 | 5 | 2 | 0 | 0 | 0 | 0 | 19 |
| SCOTT YOUNG | 17 | 4 | 2 | 6 | 1- | 14 | 2 | 0 | 0 | 0 | 21 |
| KEITH JONES | 6 | 3 | 3 | 6 | 2 | 4 | 1 | 0 | 0 | 0 | 16 |
| MIKE RICCI | 17 | 2 | 4 | 6 | 1 | 17 | 0 | 0 | 1 | 0 | 21 |
| ERIC LACROIX | 17 | 1 | 4 | 5 | 2 | 19 | 0 | 0 | 0 | 0 | 15 |

| | | | | | | | | | | | |
|---|---|---|---|---|---|---|---|---|---|---|---|
| MIKE KEANE | 17 | 3 | 1 | 4 | 2 | 24 | 0 | 0 | 1 | 0 | 17 |
| RENE CORBET | 17 | 2 | 2 | 4 | 0 | 27 | 0 | 0 | 0 | 0 | 31 |
| ADAM FOOTE | 17 | 0 | 4 | 4 | 3 | 62 | 0 | 0 | 0 | 0 | 17 |
| AARON MILLER | 17 | 1 | 2 | 3 | 3 | 10 | 0 | 0 | 0 | 0 | 8 |
| ALEXEI GUSAROV | 17 | 0 | 3 | 3 | 3 | 14 | 0 | 0 | 0 | 0 | 9 |
| JON KLEMM | 17 | 1 | 1 | 2 | 1- | 6 | 0 | 0 | 0 | 0 | 20 |
| CRAIG BILLINGTON | 1 | 0 | 0 | 0 | 0 | 0 | 0 | 0 | 0 | 0 | 0 |
| YVES SARAULT | 5 | 0 | 0 | 0 | 0 | 2 | 0 | 0 | 0 | 0 | 2 |
| ERIC MESSIER | 6 | 0 | 0 | 0 | 0 | 4 | 0 | 0 | 0 | 0 | 1 |
| BRENT SEVERYN | 8 | 0 | 0 | 0 | 1 | 12 | 0 | 0 | 0 | 0 | 3 |
| SYLVAIN LEFEBVRE | 17 | 0 | 0 | 0 | 1- | 25 | 0 | 0 | 0 | 0 | 15 |
| PATRICK ROY | 17 | 0 | 0 | 0 | 0 | 12 | 0 | 0 | 0 | 0 | 0 |

| GOALTENDER | GPI | MINS | AVG | W | L | EN | SO | GA | SA | SV % |
|---|---|---|---|---|---|---|---|---|---|---|
| PATRICK ROY | 17 | 1034 | 2.21 | 10 | 7 | 2 | 3 | 38 | 559 | .932 |
| CRAIG BILLINGTON | 1 | 20 | 3.00 | 0 | 0 | 0 | 0 | 1 | 13 | .923 |
| COL TOTALS | 17 | 1060 | 2.32 | 10 | 7 | 2 | 3 | 41 | 574 | .929 |

## ALL-TIME LEADERS

### Goals
| | |
|---|---|
| Michel Goulet | 456 |
| Peter Stastny | 380 |
| Joe Sakic | 360 |

### Assists
| | |
|---|---|
| Peter Stastny | 668 |
| Joe Sakic | 512 |
| Michel Goulet | 489 |

### Points
| | |
|---|---|
| Peter Stastny | 1,048 |
| Michel Goulet | 945 |
| Joe Sakic | 820 |

## BEST INDIVIDUAL SEASONS

### Goals
| | | |
|---|---|---|
| Michel Goulet | 1982-83 | 57 |
| Michel Goulet | 1983-84 | 56 |
| Michel Goulet | 1984-85 | 55 |

### Assists
| | | |
|---|---|---|
| Peter Stastny | 1981-82 | 93 |
| Peter Forsberg | 1995-96 | 86 |
| Peter Stastny | 1985-86 | 81 |

### Points
| | | |
|---|---|---|
| Peter Stastny | 1981-82 | 139 |
| Peter Stastny | 1982-83 | 124 |
| Peter Stastny | 1985-86 | 122 |

## TEAM

Last 3 years

|         | GP | W  | L  | T  | Pts | %    |
|---------|----|----|----|----|-----|------|
| 1996-97 | 82 | 49 | 24 | 9  | 107 | .652 |
| 1995-96 | 82 | 47 | 25 | 10 | 104 | .634 |
| 1994-95 | 48 | 30 | 13 | 5  | 65  | .677 |
| 1993-94 | 84 | 34 | 42 | 8  | 76  | .452 |

Best 3 regular seasons

|         | GP | W  | L  | T  | Pts | %    |
|---------|----|----|----|----|-----|------|
| 1994-95 | 48 | 30 | 13 | 5  | 65  | .677 |
| 1996-97 | 82 | 49 | 24 | 9  | 107 | .652 |
| 1995-96 | 82 | 47 | 25 | 10 | 104 | .634 |

Worst 3 regular seasons

|         | GP | W  | L  | T  | Pts | %    |
|---------|----|----|----|----|-----|------|
| 1989-90 | 80 | 12 | 61 | 7  | 31  | .194 |
| 1990-91 | 80 | 16 | 50 | 14 | 46  | .288 |
| 1991-92 | 80 | 20 | 48 | 12 | 52  | .325 |

Most Goals (min. 70 game schedule)

| 1983-84 | 360 |
|---------|-----|
| 1981-82 | 356 |
| 1992-93 | 351 |

Fewest Goals (min. 70 game schedule)

| 1990-91 | 236 |
|---------|-----|
| 1989-90 | 240 |
| 1979-80 | 248 |

Most Goals Against (min. 70 game schedule)

| 1989-90 | 407 |
|---------|-----|
| 1990-91 | 354 |
| 1981-82 | 345 |

Fewest Goals Against (min. 70 game schedule)

| 1996-97 | 205 |
|---------|-----|
| 1995-96 | 240 |
| 1984-85 | 275 |

# Dallas Stars

That was some season for the Dallas Stars. They went from 66 points and out of the playoffs, to 104 points and second best overall in the league.

Big surprise? To some, but if you read last year's Hockey Annual, it was predicted that Dallas would be the surprise team of the year.

Often, however, when a team takes a big leap in the standings, they fall back the next season. That shouldn't be the case with the Stars, however, because there was no luck involved in their turnaround, it was all carefully choreographed.

How did they have such a great year?

Like all the other successful teams it starts with defence. They managed to allow the third fewest goals, while still being one of the top offensive teams. Not an easy task. In fact, their numbers were almost identical to Detroit. Dallas scored 252 and gave up 198, while Detroit scored 253 and surrendered 197. The difference between the two, besides the fact that the Red Wings went on to win the Stanley Cup, is that Dallas had a record of 48-26-8 and Detroit was 38-26-18.

Coaching and management were major components of their success. Ken Hitchcock has always been a winner, and earned recognition by *The Hockey News* as coach of the year. He was also a close second to Ted Nolan of Buffalo in the NHL's Jack Adams award voting.

Aside from Mike Modano, nobody had a great offensive season on the Stars, which is unusual for such a successful team. Joe Nieuwendyk had a good comeback season, with 30 goals in 66 games, but none of the other forwards had anything close to resembling career years.

That's not what made them winners anyway. Hitchcock brought them together in an all-for-one, one-for-all atmosphere in which they were believing in themselves and the team. They bought into a system that didn't completely stifle their offensive instincts. And as one player suggested, they were no longer "afraid to win". That's one way of saying that they had confidence and expected not to lose.

There was one blip on the screen, however. In the playoffs they lost their opening round series in seven games to Edmonton. Three of the games were overtime defeats, but they still lost them.

It's not unusual for a team that makes a major jump during the regular season to have a tough time in the playoffs. What happens is that they put everything they have into the regular season, sort of like playoff hockey every night. The winning is new to them and they want to do it all the time. After all, that's what you're supposed to do.

The playoffs are a different season. Teams and individuals elevate their game. The Stars had nothing more to give because they'd already given everything. It's not that they were tired, just that their playoff game was the same as the regular season game, and other teams became better.

It's a tough concept to swallow, because you don't want a team to hold back during the regular season. It's probably more of a psychological thing. Take Detroit, for example. They had the best season in NHL history two years ago, but it didn't get them the Cup. In fact, they almost got knocked out in the first round, going to overtime in game seven versus St. Louis. Last season, their regular season was far inferior, dropping 37 points. But, when the playoffs came, they had more to give and they won the Stanley Cup.

You don't want teams thinking that the regular season isn't important, especially now when it's more difficult to get past it, but there's also no point knocking yourself out for a meaningless extra home game in the play-offs. That's an incentive that just isn't worth it.

Maybe a coach could ease up in the last month of the season, if that's possible. Then, when the playoffs come, the players know they have to give something extra and know they have something more give. Awfully difficult to put into practice, however, and it goes against conventional thinking too much.

Teams learn something from the experience, however, as the Stars surely did. It's going to prey on their minds. They'll be thinking more about the playoffs this year and less about the regular season.

Dallas might have a worse record this season, during the regular season, but watch out for them in the playoffs.

## SHORTS

* the Stars opened the season with a 6-0 record, the best start in franchise history.
* Pat Verbeek played in his 1,000th NHL game.

* Mike Modano was second in the league with a +43.
* Modano had nine game winning goals, tying the team record set by Brian Bellows in 1989-90.
* 23 road wins was four more than their previous record of 19, set in 1993-94.
* 13 goals by Zubov was the most ever by a defenceman on the Stars.
* Neal Broten became the all-time leading American in games played, when he passed Gordie Roberts last season.
* 104 points were a franchise high, and the only time they've earned at least 100 points in a season.
* Jamie Langenbrunner's six-game assist streak was the longest of any rookie, and the longest for the Stars.
* the Stars tied Philadelphia for the longest winning streak in the league last year, seven games. It also tied a team record.
* Modano has 38 career game-winning goals, two behind the all-time franchise leader, Brian Bellows. Modano's nine GWG last season tied him for the best single-season franchise mark, with Brian Bellows in 1989-90.

## STAT ANALYSIS

Keep an eye this season on the teams in the following list. It's not unusual for teams that make big point increases to fall back the next season. Some of them make the list of biggest point decreases the next year.

With the exception of perhaps the NY Islanders, who have made a lot of off-season changes, and maybe San Jose, look for each of these teams to have fewer points in 1997-98.

## Most Improved Teams

| | 1995-96 Points | 1996-97 Points | Increase |
|---|---|---|---|
| Dallas | 66 | 104 | +38 |
| Ottawa | 41 | 77 | +36 |
| Buffalo | 73 | 92 | +19 |
| New Jersey | 86 | 104 | +18 |
| NY Islanders | 54 | 70 | +16 |
| San Jose | 47 | 62 | +15 |

## TEAM PREVIEW

GOAL: The Stars didn't have a problem in net last season, but they did when both Andy Moog and Arturs Irbe became unrestricted free agents in the summer. They didn't waste any time fixing it though, when they signed Ed Belfour.

Belfour is no kid, but he's still five years younger than Moog. He's coming off a bit of a rough season, too. He had trouble in Chicago, both on the ice and in the dressing room, and was traded to San Jose where he was not very good at all.

That should prove to be nothing more than a bad season. You don't go from being one of the best goalies in the game to lousy that quickly. Injuries were also a part of it. He should bounce back in a big way this season and don't be surprised if he's among the Vezina candidates.

As for the backup, it could be time for Roman Turek. He's 27-years-old, so another season in the minors isn't going to help. In fact, he was outplayed there by Manny Fernandez, but that won't count for anything.

When he did get the chance to play in Dallas last season, he played well.

Hockey Annual Rating: 11 of 26

DEFENCE: The Stars had just the right mix of defencemen last year. They had offence from surprise Darryl Sydor and Sergei Zubov. They had leadership and all-round play from Derian Hatcher. They had solid defenders Craig Ludwig, Grant Ledyard, Mike Lalor and Richard Mativichuk.

They had size and they had depth, with veterans able to get rest by going in and out of the lineup.

It will be a little different this year Ledyard and Lalor gone to free agency.

They did sign free agent Shawn Chambers, who will join Hatcher, Sydor, Zubov and Matvichuk to give them one of the better defences in the league. And they wisely re-signed Ludwig. Dan Keczmer was re-signed also, to give them some insurance. Sergei Gusev might have a shot at sticking around, too.

They have size, experience, mobility, toughness, and offence, all to varying degrees.

Petr Buzek is a prospect in waiting, as is Richard Jackman, last year's top pick.

Buzek's story is interesting because he was expected to be a high pick in 1995, but got into a car accident that shattered his knee cap and left him more suspect than prospect. The Stars took a chance, however, and he is coming along after a full season with Michigan in the IHL.

| GOALTENDER | GPI | MINS | AVG | W | L | T | EN | SO | GA | SA | SV % |
|---|---|---|---|---|---|---|---|---|---|---|---|
| ROMAN TUREK | 6 | 263 | 2.05 | 3 | 1 | 0 | 0 | 0 | 9 | 129 | .930 |
| ANDY MOOG | 48 | 2738 | 2.15 | 28 | 13 | 5 | 0 | 3 | 98 | 1121 | .913 |
| ARTURS IRBE | 35 | 1965 | 2.69 | 17 | 12 | 3 | 3 | 3 | 88 | 825 | .893 |
| DAL TOTALS | 82 | 4979 | 2.39 | 48 | 26 | 8 | 3 | 6 | 198 | 2078 | .905 |

Jackman took a step back last season. He was suspended by the Sault Ste. Marie Greyhounds in the OHL, for showing up late to practise. That's a black mark against him, which means he will have to work extra hard to show that he has the discipline to play in the NHL.

Hockey Annual Rating: 5 of 26

FORWARD: Mike Modano had two more points last year than he did the year before, but it might as well have been 50 more. That's how much better he played.

His play was the impetus behind the Stars' improvement. If he was willing to accept Hitchcock's way of doing things, then so would everyone else.

Some of the players were more than the sum of their point totals. Pat Verbeek fits into that category. His 17 goals were a dramatic drop from the previous season when he had 41 in just 69 games, but goal scoring was down all over the league, and he's made a career out of having big scoring seasons after poor ones. It wasn't that important, anyway, because he still was a fiery competitor.

That's the kind of thing they went on Dallas, which was why Todd Harvey kept playing, despite poor stats, and why Jamie Langenbrunner could score 13 goals as a rookie and still be a valuable member of the team. Expect both of those players to increase their scoring by a big margin. Grant Marshall is another in their category.

Dave Reid almost scored 20 goals again, a magnificent year for him. Nineteen goals for him is like a double bonus. He's one of the better defensive players in the game who rarely is accorded proper respect.

In fact, it was Jere Lehtenin who finished among the three finalists for the Selke Award as best defensive forward. Incredibly, Modano

was fourth in the voting. Nothing against those guys, who had the big plus-minuses, but it's a little silly when they weren't even the best defensive players on the Stars.

It's a funny award, anyway. People judge it on those plus-minuses, and reputation. It's not an award that you can use stats for and some voters don't get a chance to see the players they're voting for that often. As valuable a player as Modano is, he's not one of the top four defensive forwards in the game, even though his defensive game was better than it had ever been before.

Nieuwendyk missed 16 games, but still managed 30 goals, providing the Stars with some missing offence. Benoit Hogue can score, but does it in bunches. His long slumps may not be enough to compensate for his scoring binges. Greg Adams is still a 20-goal scorer, but he's also 34-years-old.

The Stars have a few old-timers, including 37-year-old Guy Carbonneau. He's the oldest of a group forwards over 30, including Reid, Verbeek, Nieuwendyk, Hogue, Bob Bassen, Bill Huard and Adams. Almost all their forwards to be exact, but that's the way Gainey likes it. The youngsters are moved into the lineup slowly, just like they were in Gainey's day with the Canadiens.

At least one rookie you can expect to see this year is left winger Jason Botterill. The Michigan star had 37 goals in 42 college games. Tough guy, Patrick Cote (237 PIM with Michigan of IHL) could get a look as well. Finn Juha Lind is also a possibility.

On some teams, a lot of players have good scoring years and the team goes up in the standings. On Dallas, there is so much room for improvement, that it should be a scary thought for opposing goaltenders this season.

Hockey Annual Rating: 6 of 26

SPECIAL TEAMS: For such a special team, the Dallas special teams were nothing special. They have some good potential snipers up front and good pointmen so they should have scored more often. Verbeek, for example only scored five power play goals, a drop from 17 the previous year. He has a history of going up and down in scoring, so look for an improvement there.

Modano and Nieuwendyk were the top power play goal scorers, but the big surprise was Sydor, who led the team in power play points and came into his own finally as an offensive threat. You might have thought Zubov, previously thought of as an offence-only type defenceman, would have scored more, but the Stars had him paying more attention to proceedings in his own zone.

At home, the Stars were dead last on the power play and 23rd in penalty killing. That just defies explanation.

Or does it?

Okay, a team comes into Dallas and they're totally frustrated because they can do nothing at even strength. They have to wait for their opportunities on the power play. Once they get one they're more desperate than they might otherwise be because they know that their only chance to win is by scoring with the man-advantage. While killing penalties, they also realize giving up goals to Dallas with the man-advantage are just bonus goals for the Stars, so they work that much harder.

On the other side of the coin, the Stars were usually winning anyway at home, so special team play wasn't going to determine the outcome. There's proof in that because despite poor play with or without the man-advantage, they still had one of the best records in the league at home.

Just some theories, but another fact is that most teams go up and down from year to year on special team rankings, which means the Stars are probably headed up.

### POWER PLAY

|  | G | ATT | PCT |
|---|---|---|---|
| Overall | 46 | 314 | 14.6% (T-18th NHL) |
| Home | 20 | 157 | 12.7% (26th NHL) |
| Road | 26 | 157 | 16.6% (12th NHL) |

9 SHORT HANDED GOALS ALLOWED (T-9th NHL)

### PENALTY KILLING

|  | G | TSH | PCT |
|---|---|---|---|
| Overall | 51 | 308 | 83.4% (T-14th NHL) |
| Home | 28 | 151 | 81.5% (T-23rd NHL) |
| Road | 23 | 157 | 85.4% (T-9th NHL) |

11 SHORT HANDED GOALS SCORED (T-9th NHL)

## STARS SPECIAL TEAMS SCORING

| Power play | G | A | PTS |
|---|---|---|---|
| SYDOR | 2 | 21 | 23 |
| NIEUWENDYK | 8 | 10 | 18 |
| MODANO | 9 | 8 | 17 |
| VERBEEK | 5 | 9 | 14 |
| HOGUE | 5 | 6 | 11 |
| ADAMS | 5 | 6 | 11 |
| ZUBOV | 1 | 9 | 10 |
| LANGENBRUNNER | 3 | 6 | 9 |
| LEHTINEN | 3 | 3 | 6 |
| GILCHRIST | 2 | 3 | 5 |
| LEDYARD | 0 | 4 | 4 |
| BROTEN | 1 | 2 | 3 |
| REID | 1 | 1 | 2 |
| HARVEY | 1 | 1 | 2 |
| MATVICHUK | 0 | 1 | 1 |
| HATCHER | 0 | 1 | 1 |

| Short handed | G | A | PTS |
|---|---|---|---|
| MODANO | 5 | 2 | 7 |
| LEHTINEN | 1 | 3 | 4 |
| REID | 1 | 2 | 3 |
| MATVICHUK | 2 | 0 | 2 |
| BROTEN | 1 | 1 | 2 |
| ZUBOV | 0 | 2 | 2 |

| CARBONNEAU | 1 | 0 | 1 |
|---|---|---|---|
| LUDWIG | 0 | 1 | 1 |
| LALOR | 0 | 1 | 1 |
| HATCHER | 0 | 1 | 1 |

**COACHING AND MANAGEMENT:** Ken Hitchcock deserves all the credit we can give him. Truly an outstanding job. He brought the team together on the ice and convinced them to play his style. Not an easy task for anyone, and it earned him *The Hockey News* coach of the year award.

Bob Gainey made a lot of smart moves as GM, one of which was firing himself and hiring Hitchcock to coach. He also has done about the best job in the area of signing free agents, finding those unselfish players who can get with the program and are interested in the team over themselves.

Gainey also did a good job balancing the Stars through trades. He was able to bring offence to the team, an area in which they were lacking.

Toronto Maple Leaf's new president Ken Dryden thought enough of Gainey during the summer that he was willing to give up Mathieu Schneider as compensation to Dallas if he would go to Toronto. Part of that was inexperience on Dryden's part, but still. The Stars granted him permission to talk, but Gainey decided he liked where he was well enough.

Hockey Annual Rating: 4 of 26

## DRAFT

| Round | Sel. | Player | Pos | Amateur Team |
|---|---|---|---|---|
| 1 | 25 | Brendan Morrow | LW | Portland (WHL) |
| 2 | 52 | Roman Lyashenko | C | Russia |
| 3 | 77 | Steve Gainey | C | Kamloops (WHL) |
| 4 | 105 | Marcus Kristofferson | W | Sweden |
| 5 | 132 | Teemo Elomo | W | Finland |
| 6 | 160 | Alexi Timkin | W | Russia |
| 7 | 189 | Jeff McKercher | D | Barrie (OHL) |
| 8 | 216 | Alexi Komarov | D | Russia |
| 9 | 242 | Brett McLean | C | Kelowna (WHL) |

Brendan Morrow isn't big in height, but he's solid, and is projected as a smart two-way player, who can handle the rough stuff (178 PIM for Portland in WHL). He was never even selected in the WHL bantam draft, so he's had to work his way up from nothing to a top prospect. That's the kind of character that interests the Stars.

Steve Gainey, Bob's son, was selected in the third round at pick number 77. Central Scouting had him tabbed at 173.

## PROGNOSIS

What the Stars accomplished last year was no fluke. It was the result of hard work, discipline, good coaching and talented, character hockey players.

Their motivation this year will be to atone for their early exit from the playoffs at the hands of the Oilers. While they may not put up the same number of points on the board, they will be more playoff-ready this year, which is where it all counts anyway.

Are the Stars legitimate contenders for the Stanley Cup?

Most definitely.

## PREDICTION

Western Conference: 2nd
Overall: 4th

## STAT SECTION

| Team Scoring Stats | 1996-97 | | | | | | | CAREER | | | |
|---|---|---|---|---|---|---|---|---|---|---|---|
| | GP | G | A | PTS | +/- | PIM | SH | Gm | G | A | Pts |
| MIKE MODANO | 80 | 35 | 48 | 83 | 43 | 42 | 291 | 581 | 256 | 339 | 595 |
| PAT VERBEEK | 81 | 17 | 36 | 53 | 3 | 128 | 172 | 1,065 | 430 | 444 | 874 |
| JOE NIEUWENDYK | 66 | 30 | 21 | 51 | 5- | 32 | 173 | 695 | 368 | 341 | 709 |
| DARRYL SYDOR | 82 | 8 | 40 | 48 | 37 | 51 | 142 | 396 | 30 | 131 | 161 |
| BENOIT HOGUE | 73 | 19 | 24 | 43 | 8 | 54 | 131 | 617 | 191 | 263 | 454 |
| JERE LEHTINEN | 63 | 16 | 27 | 43 | 26 | 2 | 134 | 120 | 22 | 49 | 71 |
| SERGEI ZUBOV | 78 | 13 | 30 | 43 | 19 | 24 | 133 | 307 | 54 | 211 | 265 |
| DAVE REID | 82 | 19 | 20 | 39 | 12 | 10 | 135 | 685 | 141 | 165 | 306 |
| J. LANGENBRUNNER | 76 | 13 | 26 | 39 | 2- | 51 | 112 | 90 | 15 | 28 | 43 |
| GREG ADAMS | 50 | 21 | 15 | 36 | 27 | 2 | 113 | 803 | 292 | 307 | 599 |
| TODD HARVEY | 71 | 9 | 22 | 31 | 19 | 142 | 99 | 180 | 29 | 51 | 80 |
| BRENT GILCHRIST | 67 | 10 | 20 | 30 | 6 | 24 | 116 | 556 | 112 | 138 | 250 |
| DERIAN HATCHER | 63 | 3 | 19 | 22 | 8 | 97 | 96 | 378 | 40 | 91 | 131 |
| GUY CARBONNEAU | 73 | 5 | 16 | 21 | 9 | 36 | 99 | 1,098 | 239 | 368 | 607 |
| NEAL BROTEN | 42 | 8 | 12 | 20 | 4- | 12 | 55 | 1,099 | 289 | 634 | 923 |
| GRANT LEDYARD | 67 | 1 | 15 | 16 | 31 | 61 | 99 | 795 | 77 | 238 | 315 |
| CRAIG LUDWIG | 77 | 2 | 11 | 13 | 17 | 62 | 59 | 1,096 | 36 | 171 | 207 |
| BOB BASSEN | 46 | 5 | 7 | 12 | 5 | 41 | 50 | 639 | 83 | 135 | 218 |
| RICHARD MATVICHUK | 57 | 5 | 7 | 12 | 1 | 87 | 83 | 222 | 13 | 31 | 44 |
| BILL HUARD | 40 | 5 | 6 | 11 | 5 | 105 | 34 | 189 | 16 | 17 | 33 |
| GRANT MARSHALL | 56 | 6 | 4 | 10 | 5 | 98 | 62 | 83 | 7 | 5 | 12 |
| MIKE KENNEDY | 24 | 1 | 6 | 7 | 3 | 13 | 26 | 129 | 16 | 35 | 41 |
| MIKE LALOR | 55 | 1 | 1 | 2 | 3 | 42 | 32 | 687 | 17 | 88 | 105 |
| ARTURS IRBE | 35 | 0 | 2 | 2 | 0 | 8 | 0 | | | | |
| DAN KECZMER | 13 | 0 | 1 | 1 | 3 | 6 | 10 | 156 | 7 | 30 | 37 |
| ANDY MOOG | 48 | 0 | 1 | 1 | 0 | 12 | 0 | | | | |
| PATRICK COTE | 3 | 0 | 0 | 0 | 0 | 27 | 1 | 5 | 0 | 0 | 0 |
| SERGEI MAKAROV | 4 | 0 | 0 | 0 | 2- | 0 | 0 | 424 | 134 | 250 | 384 |
| ROMAN TUREK | 6 | 0 | 0 | 0 | 0 | 0 | 0 | | | | |
| MARC LABELLE | 9 | 0 | 0 | 0 | 4- | 46 | 2 | 9 | 0 | 0 | 0 |

## TEAM RANKINGS

|  | | Conference Rank | League Rank |
|---|---|---|---|
| Record | 48-26-8 | 2 | 2 |
| Home | 25-13-3 | 2 | 5 |
| Away | 23-13-5 | 1 | 1 |
| Versus Own Conference | 32-18-6 | 2 | 2 |
| Versus Other Conference | 16-8-2 | 2 | 4 |
| Team Plus\Minus | +59 | 1 | 1 |
| Goals For | 252 | 4 | 7 |
| Goals Against | 198 | 2 | 3 |
| Average Shots For | 29.7 | 7 | 12 |
| Average Shots Against | 25.3 | 2 | 2 |
| Overtime | 4-3-8 | 5 | 7 |
| One Goal Games | 20-12 | 2 | 4 |

| Times outshooting opponent | 54 | 2 | 4 |
|---|---|---|---|
| Versus Teams Over .500 | 18-15-4 | 2 | 4 |
| Versus Teams Under .500 | 30-11-4 | 1 | 1 |
| First Half Record | 23-15-3 | 2 | 2 |
| Second Half Record | 25-11-5 | 1 | 2 |

## PLAYOFFS

Results: lost 4-3 to Edmonton
Record: 3-4
Home: 1-3
Away: 2-1
Goals For: 18 (2.6/game)
Goals Against: 21 (3.0/game)
Overtime: 0-3
Power play: 7.5% (14th)
Penalty Killing: 82.4% (10th)

| | GP | G | A | PTS | +/- | PIM | PP | SH | GW | OT | S |
|---|---|---|---|---|---|---|---|---|---|---|---|
| MIKE MODANO | 7 | 4 | 1 | 5 | 2 | 0 | 1 | 1 | 2 | 0 | 27 |
| BOB BASSEN | 7 | 3 | 1 | 4 | 3 | 4 | 0 | 0 | 0 | 0 | 12 |
| BRENT GILCHRIST | 6 | 2 | 2 | 4 | 0 | 2 | 0 | 0 | 0 | 0 | 20 |
| BENOIT HOGUE | 7 | 2 | 2 | 4 | 1- | 6 | 1 | 0 | 0 | 0 | 16 |
| JOE NIEUWENDYK | 7 | 2 | 2 | 4 | 1- | 6 | 0 | 0 | 0 | 0 | 21 |
| JERE LEHTINEN | 7 | 2 | 2 | 4 | 1 | 0 | 0 | 0 | 0 | 0 | 15 |
| PAT VERBEEK | 7 | 1 | 3 | 4 | 2- | 16 | 1 | 0 | 0 | 0 | 19 |
| SERGEI ZUBOV | 7 | 0 | 3 | 3 | 4 | 2 | 0 | 0 | 0 | 0 | 9 |
| J. LANGENBRUNNER | 5 | 1 | 1 | 2 | 1 | 14 | 0 | 0 | 1 | 0 | 15 |
| GRANT MARSHALL | 5 | 0 | 2 | 2 | 2 | 8 | 0 | 0 | 0 | 0 | 4 |
| GRANT LEDYARD | 7 | 0 | 2 | 2 | 3- | 0 | 0 | 0 | 0 | 0 | 8 |
| CRAIG LUDWIG | 7 | 0 | 2 | 2 | 1 | 18 | 0 | 0 | 0 | 0 | 5 |
| DERIAN HATCHER | 7 | 0 | 2 | 2 | 1 | 20 | 0 | 0 | 0 | 0 | 7 |
| DARRYL SYDOR | 7 | 0 | 2 | 2 | 2- | 0 | 0 | 0 | 0 | 0 | 24 |
| DAVE REID | 7 | 1 | 0 | 1 | 2- | 4 | 0 | 0 | 0 | 0 | 10 |

| | | | | | | | | | | |
|---|---|---|---|---|---|---|---|---|---|---|
| NEAL BROTEN | 2 | 0 | 1 | 1 | 0 | 0 | 0 | 0 | 0 | 0 | 3 |
| GREG ADAMS | 3 | 0 | 1 | 1 | 2 | 0 | 0 | 0 | 0 | 0 | 4 |
| GUY CARBONNEAU | 7 | 0 | 1 | 1 | 3- | 6 | 0 | 0 | 0 | 0 | 9 |
| ANDY MOOG | 7 | 0 | 1 | 1 | 0 | 0 | 0 | 0 | 0 | 0 | 0 |
| R. MATVICHUK | 7 | 0 | 1 | 1 | 1- | 20 | 0 | 0 | 0 | 0 | 8 |
| TODD HARVEY | 7 | 0 | 1 | 1 | 2- | 10 | 0 | 0 | 0 | 0 | 15 |
| ARTURS IRBE | 1 | 0 | 0 | 0 | 0 | 0 | 0 | 0 | 0 | 0 | 0 |

## ALL-TIME LEADERS

### Goals
| | |
|---|---|
| Brian Bellows | 342 |
| Dino Ciccarelli | 332 |
| Bill Goldsworthy | 267 |

### Assists
| | |
|---|---|
| Neal Broten | 586 |
| Brian Bellows | 380 |
| Bobby Smith | 369 |

### Points
| | |
|---|---|
| Neal Broten | 852 |
| Brian Bellows | 722 |
| Dino Ciccarelli | 651 |

## BEST INDIVIDUAL SEASONS

### Goals
| | | |
|---|---|---|
| Brian Bellows | 1989-90 | 55 |
| Dino Ciccarelli | 1981-82 | 55 |
| Mike Modano | 1993-94 | 50 |

### Assists
| | | |
|---|---|---|
| Neal Broten | 1985-86 | 76 |
| Bobby Smith | 1981-82 | 71 |
| Tim Young | 1976-77 | 66 |

### Points
| | | |
|---|---|---|
| Bobby Smith | 1981-82 | 114 |
| Dino Ciccarelli | 1981-82 | 106 |
| Neal Broten | 1985-86 | 105 |

## TEAM

### Last 3 years
| | GP | W | L | T | Pts | % |
|---|---|---|---|---|---|---|
| 1996-97 | 82 | 48 | 26 | 8 | 104 | .634 |
| 1995-96 | 82 | 26 | 42 | 14 | 66 | .402 |
| 1994-95 | 48 | 17 | 23 | 8 | 42 | .438 |

### Best 3 regular seasons
| | | | | | | |
|---|---|---|---|---|---|---|
| 1996-97 | 82 | 48 | 26 | 8 | 104 | .634 |
| 1982-83 | 80 | 40 | 24 | 16 | 96 | .600 |
| 1982-82 | 80 | 37 | 23 | 20 | 94 | .588 |

### Worst 3 regular seasons
| | | | | | | |
|---|---|---|---|---|---|---|
| 1977-78 | 80 | 18 | 53 | 9 | 45 | .281 |
| 1975-76 | 80 | 20 | 53 | 7 | 47 | .293 |
| 1987-88 | 80 | 19 | 48 | 13 | 51 | .319 |

### Most Goals (min. 70 game schedule)
| | |
|---|---|
| 1981-82 | 346 |
| 1983-84 | 345 |
| 1985-86 | 327 |

### Fewest Goals (min. 70 game schedule)
| | |
|---|---|
| 1968-69 | 189 |
| 1970-71 | 191 |
| 1967-68 | 191 |

Most Goals Against (min. 70 game schedule)
1987-88          349
1983-84          344
1974-75          341

Fewest Goals Against (min. 70 game schedule)
1971-72          191
1996-97          198
1970-71          223

# Detroit Red Wings

The only thing of real value that comes from tragedy is that it gives you a a unwelcome dose of reality. Vladimir Konstantinov's car crash so soon after Detroit won the Stanley Cup illustrates that a person fighting for their life is infinitely more important than fighting for a Stanley Cup.

This is a hockey book, however, so we'll carry on.

How did the Red Wings win the Stanley Cup last season, when they were so outmatched the previous season in the conference finals against Colorado? Many reasons. These are the top five.

1. Brendan Shanahan — without him the Wings would not have the Cup, it's that simple. He was exactly what they needed — a big, tough, goal scoring power forward with determination, fire and leadership abilities.

2. Scotty Bowman — some people think he's only been able to win Stanley Cups only with extremely talented teams. That may be so, but there are lots of talented teams that don't win anything. He has the coaching ability to bring them to the final level.

3. The Russians — if they're going to take the blame for failure, which they did previously, then they're going to have to get some credit for success. Sergei Fedorov, who had a lousy regular season, was dynamite in the playoffs. There were suggestions he would have won the Conn Smythe Trophy as MVP if he weren't a Russian. Huh? Do those people know that Fedorov has already won four major awards?

4. Steve Yzerman — Renewed determination from the Detroit captain, knowing that perhaps it could be his only stab at the big prize.

5. Mike Vernon — Every team needs great goaltending to win the Cup, and Vernon supplied it. As simple as that.

## STUFF

* Steve Yzerman played in his 1,000th game.
* this will be Yzerman's 11th year as captain. Only Alex Delvecchio, with 12 years has been captain longer for the Wings.

## STAT ANALYSIS

Okay, which team do you think had the biggest drop in winning percentage last year?

Time's up. But, being a smart person (we know, because you bought this book) you would have figured out that it was Detroit. That's right, the Stanley Cup champions fell the furthest during the regular season.

Of course, there was lots of room to drop after their record breaking 1995-96 season.

So, by getting worse they got better. Interesting, huh?

It's a fairly simple explanation. The Wings gave it their all in 1995-96, every single game of the year. Great stuff, but it didn't do them any good in the playoffs where they were wiped out by Colorado in the conference championship.

Last year, they saved their "all" for the playoffs where it counted.

Largest Decreases in Winning Percentage:

|  | 1995-96 | 1996-96 | Decrease |
|---|---|---|---|
| Detroit | .799 | .573 | -.226 |
| Boston | .555 | .372 | -.183 |
| Pittsburgh | .622 | .512 | -.110 |
| Tampa Bay | .537 | .451 | -.086 |
| Washington | .543 | .457 | -.086 |

## TEAM PREVIEW

GOAL: In its infinite wisdom, the Hockey Annual informed you last year that Mike Vernon was finished. And he was — for that season anyway.

Vernon's biggest believer was Scotty Bowman. When Vernon played poorly, Bowman stuck him right back out there. When it came time for the playoffs, Bowman had his man, and stuck with him.

The odd thing is that Chris Osgood clearly outplayed Vernon during the regular season. He had six shutouts to Vernon's zero. He had a far superior win-loss record, and better goals against average and save percentage.

Osgood can be excused if he was wondering what the heck was going on. He wasn't the only one. The Wings may have still won the Cup with Osgood in net, but we'll never know.

Hockey Annual Rating: 16 of 26

DEFENCE: The defending Stanley Cup champions could have a problem in this area. Konstantinov, of course, won't be playing, and Sergei Fetisov was a free agent.

That leaves Nicklas Lidstrom as their only premier defenceman. Bob Rouse is the likely top defensive defenceman, and he's been accustomed to sitting out games the last couple years.

Larry Murphy came over to Detroit after he was booed out of Toronto, and had an excellent playoffs. Red Wings fans will learn during the regular season, however, why fans disliked his play in Toronto.

That leaves mainly a group of youngsters to make their mark, although it's a good bet the Wings will shore up this position. Jamie Pushor played a full season as a rookie, while Aaron Ward and Anders Eriksson got their feet wet.

Bowman tried a couple forwards at defence last year, including Mathieu Dandenault and Sergei Federov. Fedorov looked good at times, but not at others, and the only purpose it seemed to achieve was to distract Fedorov from his poor regular season.

Overall, the Wings may be too young this year with too little depth.

| GOALTENDER | GPI | MINS | AVG | W | L | T | EN | SO | GA | SA | SV % |
|---|---|---|---|---|---|---|---|---|---|---|---|
| KEVIN HODSON | 6 | 294 | 1.63 | 2 | 2 | 1 | 0 | 1 | 8 | 114 | .930 |
| CHRIS OSGOOD | 47 | 2769 | 2.30 | 23 | 13 | 9 | 3 | 6 | 106 | 1175 | .910 |
| MIKE VERNON | 33 | 1952 | 2.43 | 13 | 11 | 8 | 1 | 0 | 79 | 782 | .899 |
| DET TOTALS | 82 | 5031 | 2.35 | 38 | 26 | 18 | 4 | 7 | 197 | 2075 | .905 |

Hockey Annual Rating: 13 of 26

FORWARD: Things should be pretty much the same this year at forward for the Wings. Igor Larionov became an unrestricted free agent, but it's a good bet he'll re-sign. The Wings want him back, and he fits in there nicely.

Joey Kocur, who played great on a playoff line with Kirk Maltby and Kris Draper, is also a free agent, but probably won't be back. One player sure not to return is Tomas Sandstrom. He went AWOL during the playoffs, scoring zero goals in 20 games.

One addition will be free agent signee Brent Gilchrist, who was with Dallas last year. He should effectively replace Sandstrom, although he won't score much. As well, Mike Knuble is expected to get a shot at full-time work, and Tomas Holmstrom will get another try. It's not certain where Mathieu Dandenault, a forward/defenceman, will fit in.

If Larionov signs, they've also got Yzerman, Federov, and Draper at centre. Tim Taylor got into 44 games last season, so he's in the mix as well. Not that positions are too important if Bowman is coaching.

On the left side is Shanahan, Slava Kozlov, Maltby and Gilchrist.

At right wing are Darren McCarty, who is coming off an excellent season; Martin Lapointe, who came into his own; Doug Brown, and a third or fourth liner to be determined.

The thing that makes it work is that they've got good balance. They can put together two good scoring lines, and two good checking lines. They've got as much toughness up front, from players who also score, as most any team, in Shanahan, McCarty, and Lapointe. They've got character and leadership, starting with Captain Yzerman. They've got talented scorers and playmakers in Larionov and Kozlov. Federov, who is in a category of his own, should improve off a

poor regular season, (for him). That leaves the grinders and checkers, with few teams able to match the likes of Maltby, Draper, Gilchrist, and Brown.

Hockey Annual Rating: 2 of 26

SPECIAL TEAMS: Shanahan tied for the league lead in power play goals. He and Ryan Smyth of the Oilers each had 20. That was just one short of the Detroit power play goal record. Shanahan is the one who made the power play tick, and should continue to do so.

No problems with penalty killing either, and guess who makes a big difference there. That's right, Shanahan again.

POWER PLAY

|  | G | ATT | PCT |
|---|---|---|---|
| Overall | 66 | 368 | 17.9% (7th NHL) |
| Home | 26 | 181 | 14.4% (20th NHL) |
| Road | 40 | 187 | 21.4% (3rd NHL) |

8 SHORT HANDED GOALS ALLOWED (T-4th NHL)

PENALTY KILLING

|  | G | TSH | PCT |
|---|---|---|---|
| Overall | 46 | 346 | 86.7% (4th NHL) |
| Home | 20 | 159 | 87.4% (T-3rd NHL) |
| Road | 26 | 187 | 86.1% (T-7th NHL) |

10 SHORT HANDED GOALS SCORED (T-13th NHL)

RED WINGS SPECIAL TEAMS SCORING

| Power play | G | A | PTS |
|---|---|---|---|
| SHANAHAN | 20 | 15 | 35 |
| LIDSTROM | 8 | 22 | 30 |
| YZERMAN | 8 | 18 | 26 |
| MURPHY | 5 | 18 | 23 |
| LARIONOV | 2 | 15 | 17 |
| MCCARTY | 5 | 11 | 16 |
| FEDOROV | 9 | 6 | 15 |
| LAPOINTE | 5 | 5 | 10 |
| KOZLOV | 3 | 6 | 9 |

| | G | A | PTS |
|---|---|---|---|
| SANDSTROM | 1 | 7 | 8 |
| KONSTANTINOV | 0 | 7 | 7 |
| HOLMSTROM | 3 | 2 | 5 |
| FETISOV | 0 | 3 | 3 |
| BROWN | 1 | 1 | 2 |
| DRAPER | 1 | 0 | 1 |
| WARD | 0 | 1 | 1 |
| TAYLOR | 0 | 1 | 1 |

| Short handed | G | A | PTS |
|---|---|---|---|
| SHANAHAN | 3 | 2 | 5 |
| ROUSE | 2 | 1 | 3 |
| FEDOROV | 2 | 1 | 3 |
| SANDSTROM | 2 | 0 | 2 |
| LARIONOV | 1 | 1 | 2 |
| YZERMAN | 0 | 2 | 2 |
| KONSTANTINOV | 0 | 2 | 2 |
| TAYLOR | 1 | 0 | 1 |
| LAPOINTE | 1 | 0 | 1 |
| WARD | 0 | 1 | 1 |
| MALTBY | 0 | 1 | 1 |
| LIDSTROM | 0 | 1 | 1 |
| DRAPER | 0 | 1 | 1 |
| BROWN | 0 | 1 | 1 |

**COACHING AND MANAGEMENT:** He will be back...he won't be back...he will be back...he won't....

So much goes on behind the scenes in Detroit, and there are so many different versions of the same story, that it's tough to figure out what's going on. At press time, Bowman had said both that he would be back and that he wouldn't be back. Nobody knows. There was also speculation that Bowman might shuffle off to Buffalo. At press time the Sabres still hadn't hired a coach, and Bowman lives there. Stay tuned.

Ken Holland takes over as GM this year, and there are already reports of power struggle problems. Bowman had a major say in player movements last season, but who knows what he will have with Holland as GM. Stay tuned.

Hockey Annual Rating: 7 of 26

**DRAFT**

| Round | Sel. | Player | Pos | Amateur Team |
|---|---|---|---|---|
| 2 | 49 | Yuri Butsayev | C | Russia |
| 3 | 76 | Petr Sykora | C | Czech Rep. |
| 4 | 102 | Quintin Laing | LW | Kelowna (WHL) |
| 5 | 129 | John Wikstrom | D | Sweden |
| 6 | 157 | B.J. Young | RW | Red Deer (WHL) |
| 7 | 186 | Mike Laceby | C | Kingston (OHL) |
| 8 | 213 | Steve Wilejto | C | Prince Albert (WHL) |
| 9 | 239 | Greg Willers | D | Kingston (OHL) |

Not much happening here with no first round pick. Yuri Busayev is projected as a possible checker. Teams don't usually draft checkers because it doesn't make any sense. There are a ton of them already out there, usually veterans who have learned the game at the NHL level.

The Wings are one of the worst drafting teams in the NHL anyway, so write another year off.

**PROGNOSIS:** No Stanley Cup this season. But, that's okay, they waited 42 years for the last one.

The Wings won't have the same drive and committment that carried them to the championship last year. They had a number of older players who gave everything they had for that one big push. Nowadays, a lot of things have to go a team's way to win the Cup. Doing it twice in a row is too difficult.

That's not to say they need to do any rebuilding. They've been bringing along some younger players and they still have some very good ones in their prime. They will likely have another good regular season, but more playoff success is another story.

PREDICTION

Western Conference: 3rd
Overall: 6th

STAT SECTION

| Team Scoring Stats | 1996-97 | | | | | CAREER | | | | | |
|---|---|---|---|---|---|---|---|---|---|---|---|
| | GP | G | A | PTS | +/- | PIM | SH | Gm | G | A | Pts |
| BRENDAN SHANAHAN | 81 | 47 | 41 | 88 | 32 | 131 | 336 | 713 | 335 | 351 | 686 |
| STEVE YZERMAN | 81 | 22 | 63 | 85 | 22 | 78 | 232 | 1,023 | 539 | 801 | 1,339 |
| SERGEI FEDOROV | 74 | 30 | 33 | 63 | 29 | 30 | 273 | 506 | 242 | 350 | 592 |
| NICKLAS LIDSTROM | 79 | 15 | 42 | 57 | 11 | 30 | 214 | 451 | 70 | 237 | 307 |
| IGOR LARIONOV | 64 | 12 | 42 | 54 | 31 | 26 | 95 | 440 | 107 | 243 | 350 |
| DARREN MCCARTY | 68 | 19 | 30 | 49 | 14 | 126 | 171 | 229 | 48 | 69 | 117 |
| VYACHESLAV KOZLOV | 75 | 23 | 22 | 45 | 21 | 46 | 211 | 304 | 110 | 121 | 231 |
| LARRY MURPHY | 81 | 9 | 36 | 45 | 3 | 20 | 158 | 1,315 | 254 | 797 | 1,051 |
| TOMAS SANDSTROM | 74 | 18 | 24 | 42 | 6 | 69 | 139 | 848 | 370 | 437 | 807 |
| VLAD. KONSTANTINOV | 77 | 5 | 33 | 38 | 38 | 151 | 141 | 446 | 47 | 128 | 175 |
| MARTIN LAPOINTE | 78 | 16 | 17 | 33 | 14- | 167 | 149 | 232 | 34 | 35 | 69 |
| VIACHESLAV FETISOV | 64 | 5 | 23 | 28 | 26 | 76 | 95 | 488 | 34 | 180 | 214 |
| KRIS DRAPER | 76 | 8 | 5 | 13 | 11- | 73 | 85 | 223 | 25 | 28 | 53 |
| DOUG BROWN | 49 | 6 | 7 | 13 | 3- | 8 | 69 | 583 | 113 | 151 | 264 |
| BOB ROUSE | 70 | 4 | 9 | 13 | 8 | 58 | 70 | 894 | 36 | 158 | 194 |
| MATHIEU DANDENAULT | 65 | 3 | 9 | 12 | 10- | 28 | 81 | 99 | 8 | 16 | 24 |
| JAMIE PUSHOR | 75 | 4 | 7 | 11 | 1 | 129 | 63 | 80 | 4 | 8 | 12 |
| TOMAS HOLMSTROM | 47 | 6 | 3 | 9 | 10- | 33 | 53 | 47 | 6 | 3 | 9 |
| KIRK MALTBY | 66 | 3 | 5 | 8 | 3 | 75 | 62 | 236 | 25 | 22 | 47 |
| TIM TAYLOR | 44 | 3 | 4 | 7 | 6- | 52 | 44 | 139 | 15 | 22 | 37 |
| AARON WARD | 49 | 2 | 5 | 7 | 9- | 52 | 40 | 55 | 3 | 6 | 9 |
| ANDERS ERIKSSON | 23 | 0 | 6 | 6 | 5 | 10 | 27 | 24 | 0 | 6 | 6 |
| JOEY KOCUR | 34 | 2 | 1 | 3 | 7- | 70 | 38 | 718 | 72 | 72 | 144 |
| CHRIS OSGOOD | 47 | 0 | 2 | 2 | 0 | 6 | 0 | | | | |
| MICHAEL KNUBLE | 9 | 1 | 0 | 1 | 1- | 0 | 10 | 9 | 1 | 0 | 1 |
| KEVIN HODSON | 6 | 0 | 1 | 1 | 0 | 0 | 0 | | | | |

| | | | | | | | | | | | |
|---|---|---|---|---|---|---|---|---|---|---|---|
| MIKE RAMSEY | 2 | 0 | 0 | 0 | 0 | 0 | 3 | 1,070 | 79 | 266 | 345 |
| MARK MAJOR | 2 | 0 | 0 | 0 | 0 | 5 | 0 | 2 | 0 | 0 | 0 |
| MIKE VERNON | 33 | 0 | 0 | 0 | 0 | 35 | 0 | | | | |

## TEAM RANKINGS

| | | Conference Rank | League Rank |
|---|---|---|---|
| Record | 38-26-8 | 3 | 6 |
| Home | 20-12-9 | 4 | 10 |
| Away | 18-14-9 | 5 | 7 |
| Versus Own Conference | 21-20-15 | 6 | 12 |
| Versus Other Conference | 17-16-3 | 1 | 1 |
| Team Plus\Minus | +36 | 2 | 5 |
| Goals For | 253 | 3 | 6 |
| Goals Against | 197 | 1 | 2 |
| Average Shots For | 33.2 | 1 | 1 |
| Average Shots Against | 25.3 | 1 | 1 |
| Overtime | 7-2-18 | 3 | 4 |
| One Goal Games | 8-9 | 8 | 16 |
| Times outshooting opponent | 59 | 1 | 1 |

| | | | |
|---|---|---|---|
| Versus Teams Over .500 | 13-17-7 | 6 | 12 |
| Versus Teams Under .500 | 25-9-11 | 2 | 3 |
| First Half Record | 20-14-7 | 3 | 8 |
| Second Half Record | 18-12-11 | 4 | 6 |

## PLAYOFFS

Results:    defeated St. Louis 4-2
defeated Anaheim 4-0
defeated Colorado 4-2
defeated Philadelphia 4-0

Record: 16-4
Home: 9-1
Away: 7-3
Goals For: 58 (2.9/game)
Goals Against: 38 (1.9/game)
Overtime: 3-0
Power play: 14.5% (11th)
Penalty Killing: 86.7% (5th)

| | GP | G | A | PTS | +/- | PIM | PP | SH | GW | OT | S |
|---|---|---|---|---|---|---|---|---|---|---|---|
| SERGEI FEDOROV | 20 | 8 | 12 | 20 | 5 | 12 | 3 | 0 | 4 | 0 | 79 |
| BRENDAN SHANAHAN | 20 | 9 | 8 | 17 | 8 | 43 | 2 | 0 | 2 | 1 | 82 |
| VYACHESLAV KOZLOV | 20 | 8 | 5 | 13 | 3 | 14 | 4 | 0 | 2 | 1 | 58 |
| STEVE YZERMAN | 20 | 7 | 6 | 13 | 3 | 4 | 3 | 0 | 2 | 0 | 65 |
| IGOR LARIONOV | 20 | 4 | 8 | 12 | 8 | 8 | 3 | 0 | 1 | 0 | 29 |
| MARTIN LAPOINTE | 20 | 4 | 8 | 12 | 8 | 60 | 1 | 0 | 1 | 1 | 37 |
| LARRY MURPHY | 20 | 2 | 9 | 11 | 16 | 8 | 1 | 0 | 1 | 0 | 51 |
| NICKLAS LIDSTROM | 20 | 2 | 6 | 8 | 12 | 2 | 0 | 0 | 0 | 0 | 79 |
| KIRK MALTBY | 20 | 5 | 2 | 7 | 6 | 24 | 0 | 1 | 1 | 0 | 35 |
| DARREN MCCARTY | 20 | 3 | 4 | 7 | 1 | 34 | 0 | 0 | 2 | 0 | 34 |

| | | | | | | | | | | | |
|---|---|---|---|---|---|---|---|---|---|---|---|
| DOUG BROWN | 14 | 3 | 3 | 6 | 4 | 2 | 0 | 0 | 0 | 0 | 23 |
| KRIS DRAPER | 20 | 2 | 4 | 6 | 5 | 12 | 0 | 1 | 0 | 0 | 30 |
| JOEY KOCUR | 19 | 1 | 3 | 4 | 5 | 22 | 0 | 0 | 0 | 0 | 16 |
| VIACHESLAV FETISOV | 20 | 0 | 4 | 4 | 2 | 42 | 0 | 0 | 0 | 0 | 27 |
| TOMAS SANDSTROM | 20 | 0 | 4 | 4 | 3- | 24 | 0 | 0 | 0 | 0 | 36 |
| VLAD. KONSTANTINOV | 20 | 0 | 4 | 4 | 1- | 29 | 0 | 0 | 0 | 0 | 29 |
| JAMIE PUSHOR | 5 | 0 | 1 | 1 | 1- | 5 | 0 | 0 | 0 | 0 | 3 |
| MIKE VERNON | 20 | 0 | 1 | 1 | 0 | 12 | 0 | 0 | 0 | 0 | 0 |
| TOMAS HOLMSTROM | 1 | 0 | 0 | 0 | 1- | 0 | 0 | 0 | 0 | 0 | 0 |
| TIM TAYLOR | 2 | 0 | 0 | 0 | 1- | 0 | 0 | 0 | 0 | 0 | 0 |
| CHRIS OSGOOD | 2 | 0 | 0 | 0 | 0 | 2 | 0 | 0 | 0 | 0 | 0 |
| AARON WARD | 19 | 0 | 0 | 0 | 1 | 17 | 0 | 0 | 0 | 0 | 9 |
| BOB ROUSE | 20 | 0 | 0 | 0 | 8 | 55 | 0 | 0 | 0 | 0 | 14 |

| GOALTENDER | GPI | MINS | AVG | W | L | T | EN | SO | GA | SA | SV % |
|---|---|---|---|---|---|---|---|---|---|---|---|
| MIKE VERNON | 20 | 1229 | 1.76 | 16 | 4 | 0 | 1 | 0 | 36 | 494 | .927 |
| CHRIS OSGOOD | 2 | 47 | 2.55 | 0 | 0 | 0 | 0 | 0 | 2 | 21 | .905 |
| DET TOTALS | 20 | 1280 | 1.78 | 16 | 4 | 0 | 1 | 0 | 38 | 515 | .926 |

## ALL-TIME LEADERS

Goals
| Gordie Howe | 786 |
|---|---|
| Steve Yzerman | 539 |
| Alex Delvecchio | 456 |

Assists
| Gordie Howe | 1,023 |
|---|---|
| Alex Delvecchio | 825 |
| Steve Yzerman | 801 |

Points
| Gordie Howe | 1,809 |
|---|---|
| Steve Yzerman | 1,339 |
| Alex Delvecchio | 1,281 |

## BEST INDIVIDUAL SEASONS

Goals
| Steve Yzerman | 1988-89 | 65 |
|---|---|---|
| Steve Yzerman | 1989-90 | 62 |
| Steve Yzerman | 1992-93 | 58 |

Assists
| Steve Yzerman | 1988-89 | 90 |
|---|---|---|
| Steve Yzerman | 1992-93 | 79 |
| Marcel Dionne | 1974-75 | 74 |

Points
| Steve Yzerman | 1988-89 | 155 |
|---|---|---|
| Steve Yzerman | 1992-93 | 137 |
| Steve Yzerman | 1989-90 | 127 |

## TEAM

### Last 3 years

|         | GP | W  | L  | T  | Pts | %    |
|---------|----|----|----|----|-----|------|
| 1996-97 | 82 | 38 | 26 | 18 | 94  | .573 |
| 1995-96 | 82 | 62 | 13 | 7  | 131 | .799 |
| 1994-95 | 48 | 33 | 11 | 4  | 70  | .729 |

### Best 3 regular seasons

|         | GP | W  | L  | T  | Pts | %    |
|---------|----|----|----|----|-----|------|
| 1995-96 | 82 | 62 | 13 | 7  | 131 | .799 |
| 1994-95 | 48 | 33 | 11 | 4  | 70  | .729 |
| 1950-51 | 70 | 44 | 13 | 13 | 101 | .721 |

### Worst 3 regular seasons

|         | GP | W  | L  | T | Pts | %    |
|---------|----|----|----|---|-----|------|
| 1985-86 | 80 | 17 | 57 | 6 | 40  | .250 |
| 1976-77 | 80 | 16 | 55 | 9 | 41  | .256 |
| 1926-77 | 44 | 12 | 28 | 4 | 28  | .318 |

### Most Goals (min. 70 game schedule)

| 1992-83 | 369 |
|---------|-----|
| 1993-94 | 356 |
| 1995-96 | 325 |

### Fewest Goals (min. 70 game schedule)

| 1958-59 | 167 |
|---------|-----|
| 1957-58 | 176 |
| 1976-77 | 183 |

### Most Goals Against (min. 70 game schedule)

| 1985-86 | 415 |
|---------|-----|
| 1984-85 | 357 |
| 1981-82 | 351 |

### Fewest Goals Against (min. 70 game schedule)

| 1953-54 | 132 |
|---------|-----|
| 1952-53 | 133 |
| 1951-52 | 133 |

# Edmonton Oilers

So, you think it's the start of a new era of success in Edmonton?

Think again.

They're not nearly as good as all that gushing about them in the playoffs last year would have you believe.

What they are, is a .500 hockey team. Maybe a little better, maybe a little worse.

How much over or under .500 will be determined by a number of factors:

Over .500 - if Curtis Joseph continues to play like one of the best goalies in the game.
Under .500 - if Joseph is injured for any extended period, and he does have a injury-riddled past. That's the danger when your goalie is your best player.

Over .500 - if the power play remains as effective as it was last year.
Under .500 - if they don't play better at even strength. The Oilers scored 29% of their goals on the power play, second highest in the league. Power play efficiencies fluctuate, from game to game and season to season. If you depend on it too much you can get into trouble.

Over .500 - if players such as Andrei Kovalenko and Mariusz Czercawski can maintain the level of play they established last season.

Under .500 - if those players revert to the inconsistency that made it possible for the Oilers to obtain in the first place.

Over .500 - if the rookies who showed so much last season, continue to improve.
Under .500 - if they suffer the sophomore jinx.

Over. 500 - if some of the younger defence prospects make the jump and effectively replace Richardson, who departed to free agency.
Under .500 - if they have to use too many young defencemen. It usually means trouble if the guys learning their craft are using each other as teachers.

Over .500 - if they can go on some nice rolls like they did last year when they went 13-4-1 during one stretch.
Under .500 - if they don't continue to prey on weak teams. That roll, described in the previous sentence, involved 10 games at home out of the 15, and 11 games versus under .500 bottom feeders.

Over .500 - if their playoff success against Dallas last year can provide encouragement and confidence.
Under .500 - if their playoff defeat, handily to Colorado, discourages them.

## STUFF

* the Oilers set a team record when they scored five goals in 6:44, in an 8-2 win over Los Angeles on October 24.
* Kevin Lowe played in his 1,000th game as an Oiler last season. Only 27 players in NHL history have played 1,000 games with the same team.
* Curtis Joseph set a team record with six shutouts. Grant Fuhr held the old mark with four, in 1987-88.
* Doug Weight led the league with 35 power play assists.
* 242 goals allowed were 30 fewer than their previous low of 272, in 1990-91.

## STAT ANALYSIS

While impressive, the Oilers defeat of Dallas in the first round of the playoffs was not that unusual. In 11 seasons since all first round series went to seven games, there have been nine upsets where a team was at least 18 points behind the other during the regular season.

What is revealing is what happened to those teams after their big upset. Nine of them lost in the second round.

What that tells is that the first round win was a fluke. Oh, maybe they deserved to win it, but that they were playing so far over their heads they couldn't continue that way. It could also have been that their first round opponents took them lightly, considering how much stronger they were during the regular season. Their next opponent wasn't going to make the same mistake. (See the chart below.)

## TEAM PREVIEW

GOAL: No problems here, unless of course, Joseph gets hurt, but that's the same with every team and their number one goalie. Bob Essensa did well in a back-up role, but nobody's going to be too excited if he has to take over the top job. He was an unrestricted free agent at the end of the season, but there won't be a bidding war, so he may come back.

On deck is Steve Passmore, who overcame a medical problem stemming from a chemical imbalance. He was a big factor in Edmonton's farm team, the Hamilton Bulldogs, making it to the finals of the AHL championship.

There's a bit of a chemical imbalance on the Oilers as well, because they depend too much on Joseph for their wins. If he's not tending the nets, then there's trouble.

Joseph becomes an unrestricted free agent

LARGEST POINT DIFFERENCE - First Round Upsets (since 1987)

| Year | Winner | Pts | Loser | Pts | Difference | Next Series |
|------|--------|-----|-------|-----|------------|-------------|
| 1991 | Minnesota | 68 | Chicago | 106 | 38 | Won |
| 1990 | Los Angeles | 75 | Calgary | 99 | 24 | Lost |
| 1997 | EDMONTON | 81 | Dallas | 104 | 23 | Lost |
| 1993 | Buffalo | 86 | Boston | 109 | 23 | Lost |
| 1993 | St. Louis | 85 | Chicago | 106 | 21 | Lost |
| 1987 | Quebec | 72 | Hartford | 93 | 21 | Lost |
| 1991 | Edmonton | 80 | Calgary | 100 | 20 | Won |
| 1995 | NY Rangers | 47 | Quebec | 65 | 18 | Lost |
| 1994 | San Jose | 82 | Detroit | 100 | 18 | Lost |

after this season, but there's no way the Oilers will ever let it get that far. They won't risk getting nothing for him, so if they don't re-sign him by early season, they'll trade him.

Hockey Annual Rating: 7 of 26

DEFENCE: There's good reason to be optimistic about the Oilers' defence plans for this season...and there's good reason to be pessimistic.

The glass is half empty with the loss of Luke Richardson, who has been the cornerstone of an Oiler defence that hasn't been all that great anyway. His loss means the team will be depending more than they should on young players. Young players are mistake-prone, and when they're learning from each other they pick up bad habits.

On the plus side, Kevin Lowe will be back for another year, and he's like having a coach right on the ice. He was credited with bringing along Daniel McGillis and could do it with some of the others as well. On the minus side of that equation, a playing coach can lose the respect of the players he's trying to teach. Because his skill level has diminished, he's telling one thing and doing another when he's on the ice. That may or may not be the case with Lowe, but that's the danger.

Boris Mironov was the workhorse during the playoffs, and he'll be expected to carry the workload again, and contribute offensively. McGillis can contribute offensively as well, which he showed when Mironov was out with injuries.

Bryan Marchment gave everyone a scare during the playoffs when he crashed headfirst into the open penalty box door. He suffered a concussion and didn't make it back on the ice in the post-season, but should be ready for the regular season. His penalty totals declined again last season, which may or may not be a good thing. It's nice to have a looney toon back there to keep opposing players on their toes.

The Oilers used three rookie defencemen regularly in the playoffs. Besides McGillis, Greg de Vries and Drew Bannister played all the games. Bannister was a pickup at the trade deadline from Tampa Bay.

Other rookie defencemen who played for Edmonton last year included Brian Muir, Sean Brown, and Craig Millar.

All the above names could be on the Edmonton roster come opening day. Sather will probably give the young guys a chance to prove themselves, but he's never happy with his defence, so he'll be making moves to bring in veterans by about the first month of the season. They could use a little more offence from the defence as well, but would be very happy if they played solid defensive hockey.

Hockey Annual Rating: 16 of 26

FORWARD: The nice thing about the Edmonton forwards last season was that when they weren't in one of their lengthy slumps, they were scoring. Kind of a back-handed compliment, but for some reason these guys couldn't do anything right over extended periods, and then couldn't do any-

| GOALTENDER | GPI | MINS | AVG | W | L | T | EN | SO | GA | SA | SV % |
|---|---|---|---|---|---|---|---|---|---|---|---|
| BOB ESSENSA | 19 | 879 | 2.80 | 4 | 8 | 0 | 3 | 1 | 41 | 406 | .899 |
| CURTIS JOSEPH | 72 | 4089 | 2.93 | 32 | 29 | 9 | 3 | 6 | 200 | 2144 | .907 |
| EDM TOTALS | 82 | 4982 | 2.97 | 36 | 37 | 9 | 6 | 7 | 247 | 2556 | .903 |

thing wrong. And it wasn't as if the infliction only affected a few players, it was almost all of them.

So, what's the deal with that? Some of the slumpers, such as Todd Marchant and Dean McAmmond, are speedy guys. Speedy guys go into slumps more often — you can look it up. Sometimes the smaller, fast guys get stuck on the perimeter where goal scoring is difficult. They're not usually the types to bump and grind in front of the net and pick up some garbage goals, and small, fast guys aren't as important on the power play where the team can utilize their shooters and puckhandlers.

Some of the players were hampered by injuries, which can make it difficult to score when they get back. Maybe put Jason Arnott into the category.

Another thing is youth, where you can stick Arnott, Rem Murray and some of the others. Young guys are often inconsistent, and don't have the maturity level to deal with adversity. They may start to fret and lose their confidence.

Another category is the Doug Weight category. He goes into a lengthy slump every year it seems, but always comes out of it and makes up for lost time by carrying the team for a month or so. Tough to figure that one.

There is some reason to worry about almost all of the Edmonton forwards, with the exception of Weight, Kelly Buchberger and maybe Mike Grier. The value of the latter two is high, even when they're not scoring.

Others don't have similar value if they're not contributing offensively. Here are the main forwards and the worries:

Ryan Smyth - a truly outstanding season, scoring 39 goals and tying for the league lead with 20 power play markers. Duplicating those totals won't be easy.

Andrei Kovalenko - Colorado and Montreal

didn't give up on him for nothing. If he slides from 32 goals to less than 20 it won't be a big surprise.

Mariusz Czerkawksi - same deal as Kovalenko, but it was Boston who wasn't playing him anymore before the Oilers got their hands on him.

Jason Arnott - rumored to be on the trading block, and apparently almost dealt at the draft during the summer, he has to perform better. Nineteen goals from him, even though he missed 15 games, isn't enough. A good bet to turn things around this season, however.

Todd Marchant - his overtime goal to beat Dallas in the seventh game should go into the playoff goal Hall of Fame. He turned on the jets, and just blew by the defenceman. So, how come he doesn't score more often?

Rem Murray - he scored on his first two NHL shots and then added a hat-trick to score five of his 11 goals on the season in his first 10 games. That means he had just six in the team's last 72 games.

Dean McAmmond - another speedy little guy, he's coming off back surgery. He's another one who shows lots of talent, but can't become a consistent scorer.

Among the other younger players, Mats Lindgren and Steve Kelly haven't been around long enough to judge. Both look like they could be good ones. Kelly kind of fits into the Oilers mold: lots of speed, good talent, but where's the net?

Other kids who will get a good look this season are Joe Hulbig, who demonstrated his worth with Hamilton in the AHL last season; junior Boyd Devereaux, a good two-way player that the Oilers don't have enough of; Mike Watt, a college scoring star; and Dennis Bonvie, the toughest guy not playing in the NHL. Bonvie led the AHL in penalty minutes with 522.

Petr Klima won't be back. He was an interesting experiment on Sather's part. He hoped lightning would strike twice. It didn't. Louis DeBrusk has had a checkered couple of seasons with Edmonton, and his return is unlikely as well. The Oilers could be interested in Bonvie taking his place, or Bill Huard, signed as a free agent from Dallas.

While there are some excellent Oiler forwards and some excellent prospects, there's still too much to worry about. Let them prove themselves for a year and then we'll talk. One positive thing in their favor is that they have so many of the young fellers that if a couple falter, a couple more will be glad to take their place.

Hockey Annual Rating: 13 of 26

SPECIAL TEAMS: The Oilers scored exactly one more power play goal last season than they did the year before. But, that was good enough to move from 20th in the rankings to sixth. That's because power play scoring was way down all over the league. The 73 goals they popped in with the man-advantage was third best in the league.

Ryan Smyth came out of nowhere to tie Brendan Shanahan for the league lead in power play goals. Kovalenko and Arnott put the puck in the net, Weight quarterbacked from the blueline and Mironov or McGillis handled the other point.

POWER PLAY

|  | G | ATT | PCT |
|---|---|---|---|
| Overall | 73 | 406 | 18.0% (6th NHL) |
| Home | 37 | 207 | 17.9% (5th NHL) |
| Road | 36 | 199 | 18.1% (7th NHL) |

13 SHORT HANDED GOALS ALLOWED (22nd NHL)

PENALTY KILLING

|  | G | TSH | PCT |
|---|---|---|---|
| Overall | 59 | 338 | 82.5% (18th NHL) |
| Home | 28 | 165 | 83.0% (16th NHL) |
| Road | 31 | 173 | 82.1% (17th NHL) |

OILERS SPECIAL TEAMS SCORING

| Power play | G | A | PTS |
|---|---|---|---|
| WEIGHT | 4 | 35 | 39 |
| ARNOTT | 10 | 22 | 32 |
| KOVALENKO | 14 | 11 | 25 |
| SMYTH | 20 | 4 | 24 |
| MIRONOV | 2 | 16 | 18 |
| MCAMMOND | 4 | 5 | 9 |
| CZERKAWSKI | 4 | 5 | 9 |
| KLIMA | 0 | 9 | 9 |
| MCGILLIS | 2 | 5 | 7 |
| BANNISTER | 1 | 6 | 7 |
| GRIER | 4 | 1 | 5 |
| MURRAY | 1 | 3 | 4 |
| LINDGREN | 2 | 1 | 3 |
| MARCHANT | 0 | 3 | 3 |
| RICHARDSON | 0 | 2 | 2 |
| MOORE | 1 | 0 | 1 |
| MARCHMENT | 1 | 0 | 1 |
| LOWE | 0 | 1 | 1 |

| Short handed | G | A | PTS |
|---|---|---|---|
| MARCHANT | 4 | 0 | 4 |
| BUCHBERGER | 0 | 4 | 4 |
| LINDGREN | 3 | 0 | 3 |
| MCGILLIS | 1 | 0 | 1 |
| ARNOTT | 1 | 0 | 1 |
| RICHARDSON | 0 | 1 | 1 |
| MURRAY | 0 | 1 | 1 |
| MARCHMENT | 0 | 1 | 1 |
| LOWE | 0 | 1 | 1 |

COACHING AND MANAGEMENT: The decision by Peter Pocklington to sell the Oilers may cause some distraction around the team, but then again maybe it will affect nothing.

Ron Low seems to be doing the job as coach and is one of the few in which you rarely hear player complaints about.

Glen Sather is complaining less about money these days, with a little more cash to spare. He's gone and assembled the team he wants within his budget so now we'll just have to wait to see if it turns out.

Sather isn't one to get cheated in deals, holding out until he's the one in the driver seat. But, you have to wonder about some of the players he gets. It looks like he still wants to win in the old Oiler tradition of firewagon offensive hockey. At least among the forwards, you don't find many two-way defensive-minded players.

He's only kept a small core of Oilers on the team from year to year, but it looks like he could be stabilizing, with that core getting a little bigger. He gets a lot of credit for this and that and everybody's willing to give him excuses for this and that, but the fact remains the Oilers have only had one winning team in the seven years since they last won the Stanley Cup in 1990.

Hockey Annual Rating: 8 of 26

DRAFT

| Round | Sel. | Player | Pos | Team |
|---|---|---|---|---|
| 1 | 14 | Michel Riesen | LW | Switzerland |
| 2 | 41 | Patrick Dovigi | G | Erie (OHL) |
| 3 | 68 | Sergei Terkovich | D | Las Vegas (IHL) |
| 4 | 94 | Jonas Elofsson | D | Sweden |
| 5 | 121 | Jason Chimera | C | Medicine Hat (WHL) |
| 6 | 141 | Peter Sarno | C | Windsor (OHL) |
| 7 | 176 | Kevin Bolibruck | D | Peterborough (OHL) |
| 7 | 187 | Chad Hinz | C | Moose Jaw (WHL) |
| 8 | 205 | Chris Kerr | D | Sudbury (OHL) |
| 9 | 231 | A. Fomitchev | G | St. Albert (tier II) |

Michel Riesen is the highest Swiss player ever taken in the draft. For that matter, he's one of the few taken at any time. The Oilers' say he's a Jari Kurri-like player with a great shot. It's pretty much the kiss of doom to be drafted by the Oilers anyway, with few of their picks amounting to much.

PROGNOSIS: In the pre-season the Oilers are going to be a lot of people's picks to be one of the up and coming teams. Not here. They have some excellent players and others who are coming off excellent years. But, they're kidding themselves. This team is not that good. They're not ready to move up into the elite, and will be hard pressed to remain with the mediocre.

PREDICTION

Western Conference: 8th
Overall: 17th

## STAT SECTION

| Team Scoring Stats | 1996-97 | | | | | CAREER | | | | | |
|---|---|---|---|---|---|---|---|---|---|---|---|
| | GP | G | A | PTS | +/- | PIM | SH | Gm | G | A | Pts |
| DOUG WEIGHT | 80 | 21 | 61 | 82 | 1 | 80 | 235 | 425 | 102 | 276 | 378 |
| RYAN SMYTH | 82 | 39 | 22 | 61 | 7- | 76 | 265 | 133 | 41 | 31 | 72 |
| ANDREI KOVALENKO | 74 | 32 | 27 | 59 | 5- | 81 | 163 | 335 | 117 | 123 | 240 |
| JASON ARNOTT | 67 | 19 | 38 | 57 | 21- | 92 | 248 | 251 | 95 | 126 | 221 |
| M. CZERKAWSKI | 76 | 26 | 21 | 47 | 0 | 16 | 182 | 187 | 57 | 59 | 116 |
| KELLY BUCHBERGER | 81 | 8 | 30 | 38 | 4 | 159 | 78 | 661 | 72 | 137 | 209 |
| TODD MARCHANT | 79 | 14 | 19 | 33 | 11 | 44 | 202 | 209 | 46 | 53 | 99 |
| MIKE GRIER | 79 | 15 | 17 | 32 | 7 | 45 | 89 | 79 | 15 | 17 | 32 |
| BORIS MIRONOV | 55 | 6 | 26 | 32 | 2 | 85 | 147 | 241 | 31 | 120 | 151 |
| REM MURRAY | 82 | 11 | 20 | 31 | 9 | 16 | 85 | 82 | 11 | 20 | 31 |
| DEAN MCAMMOND | 57 | 12 | 17 | 29 | 15- | 28 | 106 | 166 | 33 | 55 | 88 |
| MATS LINDGREN | 69 | 11 | 14 | 25 | 7- | 12 | 71 | 69 | 11 | 14 | 25 |
| DANIEL MCGILLIS | 73 | 6 | 16 | 22 | 2 | 52 | 139 | 73 | 6 | 16 | 22 |
| DREW BANNISTER | 65 | 4 | 14 | 18 | 23- | 44 | 59 | 78 | 4 | 15 | 19 |
| BRYAN MARCHMENT | 71 | 3 | 13 | 16 | 13 | 132 | 89 | 417 | 23 | 73 | 96 |
| PETR KLIMA | 33 | 2 | 12 | 14 | 12- | 12 | 55 | 773 | 312 | 260 | 572 |
| KEVIN LOWE | 64 | 1 | 13 | 14 | 1- | 50 | 46 | 1,247 | 84 | 347 | 431 |
| LUKE RICHARDSON | 82 | 1 | 11 | 12 | 9 | 91 | 67 | 714 | 24 | 101 | 125 |
| BARRIE MOORE | 35 | 2 | 6 | 8 | 1 | 18 | 43 | 38 | 2 | 6 | 8 |
| GREG DE VRIES | 37 | 0 | 4 | 4 | 2- | 52 | 31 | 50 | 1 | 5 | 6 |
| LOUIE DEBRUSK | 32 | 2 | 0 | 2 | 6- | 94 | 10 | 228 | 19 | 12 | 31 |
| RALPH INTRANUOVO | 8 | 1 | 1 | 2 | 1- | 0 | 6 | 22 | 2 | 4 | 6 |
| CURTIS JOSEPH | 72 | 0 | 2 | 2 | 0 | 20 | 0 | | | | |
| STEVE KELLY | 8 | 1 | 0 | 1 | 1- | 6 | 6 | 8 | 1 | 0 | 1 |
| DONALD DUFRESNE | 22 | 0 | 1 | 1 | 1- | 15 | 10 | 268 | 6 | 36 | 42 |
| CRAIG MILLAR | 1 | 0 | 0 | 0 | 0 | 2 | 1 | 1 | 0 | 0 | 0 |
| SEAN BROWN | 5 | 0 | 0 | 0 | 1- | 4 | 2 | 5 | 0 | 0 | 0 |
| JESSE BELANGER | 6 | 0 | 0 | 0 | 3- | 0 | 8 | 218 | 56 | 70 | 126 |
| JOE HULBIG | 6 | 0 | 0 | 0 | 1- | 0 | 4 | 6 | 0 | 0 | 0 |
| BOB ESSENSA | 19 | 0 | 0 | 0 | 0 | 4 | 0 | | | | |

## TEAM RANKINGS

|  | | Conference Rank | League Rank |
|---|---|---|---|
| Record | 36-37-9 | 7 | 13 |
| Home | 21-16-4 | 5 | 12 |
| Away | 15-21-5 | 7 | 15 |
| Versus Own Conference | 21-28-7 | 11 | 21 |
| Versus Other Conference | 15-9-2 | 4 | 6 |
| Team Plus\Minus | -9 | 8 | 16 |
| Goals For | 252 | 4 | 7 |
| Goals Against | 247 | 9 | 16 |
| Average Shots For | 30.7 | 4 | 8 |
| Average Shots Against | 31.1 | 10 | 18 |
| Overtime | 1-6-9 | 13 | 26 |
| One Goal Games | 9-13 | 11 | 22 |
| Times outshooting opponent | 44 | 7 | 13 |

| Versus Teams Over .500 | 10-23-5 | 11 | 22 |
|---|---|---|---|
| Versus Teams Under .500 | 26-14-4 | 4 | 6 |
| First Half Record | 18-19-4 | 6 | 13 |
| Second Half Record | 18-18-5 | 8 | 13 |

## PLAYOFFS

Results:          Defeated Dallas 4-3
                      Lost to Colorado 4-1

Record: 5-7
Home: 2-3
Away: 3-4
Goals For: 32 (2.7/gm.)
Goals Against: 37 (3.1/gm)
Overtime: 3-1
Power play: 14.5% (10th)
Penalty Killing: 83.6% (9th)

|  | GP | G | A | PTS | +/- | PIM | PP | SH | GW | OT | S |
|---|---|---|---|---|---|---|---|---|---|---|---|
| DOUG WEIGHT | 12 | 3 | 8 | 11 | 0 | 8 | 0 | 0 | 0 | 0 | 54 |
| RYAN SMYTH | 12 | 5 | 5 | 10 | 4- | 12 | 1 | 0 | 2 | 1 | 48 |
| BORIS MIRONOV | 12 | 2 | 8 | 10 | 6- | 16 | 2 | 0 | 0 | 0 | 31 |
| JASON ARNOTT | 12 | 3 | 6 | 9 | 3- | 18 | 1 | 0 | 0 | 0 | 27 |
| KELLY BUCHBERGER | 12 | 5 | 2 | 7 | 1- | 16 | 0 | 0 | 1 | 1 | 19 |
| ANDREI KOVALENKO | 12 | 4 | 3 | 7 | 1 | 6 | 3 | 0 | 0 | 0 | 35 |
| TODD MARCHANT | 12 | 4 | 2 | 6 | 2 | 12 | 0 | 3 | 1 | 1 | 40 |
| DANIEL MCGILLIS | 12 | 0 | 5 | 5 | 8 | 24 | 0 | 0 | 0 | 0 | 20 |
| MIKE GRIER | 12 | 3 | 1 | 4 | 2- | 4 | 1 | 0 | 1 | 0 | 21 |
| MATS LINDGREN | 12 | 0 | 4 | 4 | 2- | 0 | 0 | 0 | 0 | 0 | 22 |
| M. CZERKAWSKI | 12 | 2 | 1 | 3 | 2- | 10 | 0 | 0 | 0 | 0 | 19 |
| REM MURRAY | 12 | 1 | 2 | 3 | 1- | 4 | 0 | 0 | 0 | 0 | 7 |
| LUKE RICHARDSON | 12 | 0 | 2 | 2 | 4- | 14 | 0 | 0 | 0 | 0 | 6 |
| JOE HULBIG | 6 | 0 | 1 | 1 | 2 | 2 | 0 | 0 | 0 | 0 | 5 |

| | | | | | | | | | | | |
|---|---|---|---|---|---|---|---|---|---|---|---|
| GREG DE VRIES | 12 | 0 | 1 | 1 | 4 | 8 | 0 | 0 | 0 | 0 | 16 |
| KEVIN LOWE | 1 | 0 | 0 | 0 | 1- | 0 | 0 | 0 | 0 | 0 | 0 |
| DONALD DUFRESNE | 3 | 0 | 0 | 0 | 0 | 0 | 0 | 0 | 0 | 0 | 0 |
| BRYAN MARCHMENT | 3 | 0 | 0 | 0 | 3- | 4 | 0 | 0 | 0 | 0 | 2 |
| BRYAN MUIR | 5 | 0 | 0 | 0 | 2- | 4 | 0 | 0 | 0 | 0 | 7 |
| PETR KLIMA | 6 | 0 | 0 | 0 | 0 | 4 | 0 | 0 | 0 | 0 | 2 |
| LOUIE DEBRUSK | 6 | 0 | 0 | 0 | 0 | 4 | 0 | 0 | 0 | 0 | 1 |
| STEVE KELLY | 6 | 0 | 0 | 0 | 1 | 2 | 0 | 0 | 0 | 0 | 2 |
| CURTIS JOSEPH | 12 | 0 | 0 | 0 | 0 | 2 | 0 | 0 | 0 | 0 | 0 |
| DREW BANNISTER | 12 | 0 | 0 | 0 | 4- | 30 | 0 | 0 | 0 | 0 | 9 |

| GOALTENDER | GPI | MINS | AVG | W | L | T | EN | SO | GA | SA | SV % |
|---|---|---|---|---|---|---|---|---|---|---|---|
| CURTIS JOSEPH | 12 | 767 | 2.82 | 5 | 7 | 1 | 2 | 0 | 36 | 405 | .911 |
| EDM TOTALS | 12 | 771 | 2.88 | 5 | 7 | 1 | 2 | 0 | 37 | 406 | .909 |

## ALL-TIME LEADERS

Goals
Wayne Gretzky 583
Jari Kurri 474
Glenn Anderson 417

Assists
Wayne Gretzky 1,086
Mark Messier 642
Jari Kurri 569

Points
Wayne Gretzky 1,669
Jari Kurri 1,043
Mark Messier 1,034

## BEST INDIVIDUAL SEASONS

Goals
Wayne Gretzky 1981-82 92
Wayne Gretzky 1983-84 87
Wayne Gretzky 1984-85 73

Assists
Wayne Gretzky 1985-86 163
Wayne Gretzky 1984-85 135
Wayne Gretzky 1982-83 125

Points
Wayne Gretzky 1985-86 215
Wayne Gretzky 1981-82 212
Wayne Gretzky 1984-85 208

## TEAM

### Last 3 years
|         | GP | W  | L  | T  | Pts | %    |
|---------|----|----|----|----|-----|------|
| 1996-97 | 82 | 36 | 37 | 9  | 81  | .494 |
| 1995-96 | 82 | 30 | 34 | 8  | 68  | .415 |
| 1994-95 | 48 | 17 | 27 | 4  | 38  | .396 |

### Best 3 regular seasons
| 1983-84 | 80 | 57 | 18 | 5  | 119 | .744 |
|---------|----|----|----|----|-----|------|
| 1985-86 | 80 | 56 | 17 | 7  | 119 | .744 |
| 1981-82 | 80 | 48 | 17 | 15 | 111 | .694 |

### Worst 3 regular seasons
| 1992-93 | 84 | 26 | 50 | 8  | 60 | .357 |
|---------|----|----|----|----|----|------|
| 1993-94 | 84 | 25 | 45 | 14 | 64 | .381 |
| 1995-96 | 48 | 17 | 27 | 4  | 38 | .396 |

### Most Goals (min. 70 game schedule)
| 1983-84 | 446 |
|---------|-----|
| 1985-86 | 426 |
| 1982-83 | 424 |

### Fewest Goals (min. 70 game schedule)
| 1995-95 | 240 |
|---------|-----|
| 1992-93 | 242 |
| 1996-97 | 252 |

### Most Goals Against (min. 70 game schedule)
| 1992-93 | 337 |
|---------|-----|
| 1980-81 | 327 |
| 1979-80 | 322 |

### Fewest Goals Against (min. 70 game schedule)
| 1996-97 | 242 |
|---------|-----|
| 1990-91 | 272 |
| 1989-90 | 283 |

# Los Angeles Kings

What a mess. What a stinkin' mess.

They may not have finished last in the standings, but they were the worst team, and have the worst prospects for improvement.

They were were so bad they would have still been bad in the AHL or IHL.

They were so bad they could have been fined by the league for "conduct detrimental to the game."

They were so bad that their leader in shots on net, Kevin Stevens, had slightly more than half the shots of Anaheim's Paul Kariya (175 compared to 340).

They were so bad that they were thinking of changing their nickname from Kings to Princes.

They were so bad that the leader in game winning goals, among those who were on the team at the end of the year, had just two.

They were so bad that their highest paid player, Kevin Stevens, received $214,115 for each goal he scored.

They were so bad that numerous injuries didn't hamper them because the players who replaced them were just as bad.

They were so bad that their farm team in Phoenix in the IHL finished dead last, and then folded.

They were so bad that they were their own worst enemy, such as when Khristich missed two weeks after having to undergo laser eye surgery when high-sticked in practice by Barry Potomski.

They were so bad that when it was revealed that because of the above incident Potomski would never play for the Kings again, many of his teammates thought it was a reward.

They were so bad that they traded the son of chief hockey operations officer, Rogie Vachon.

They were so bad that at the start of the year they said that defenceman Sean O'Donnell didn't fit into their plans as one of the top eight defencemen, and sent him to the minors. As it turned out, Larry Robinson could have suited up and been one of the top eight defencemen.

They were so bad that when festivities were held for the team's 30th anniversary, the old-timers team would have beat the current team.

They were so bad that when the best thing for them was to lose, at the end of the season to improve their lottery chances, they won.

## SHORTS

* Jan Vopat and Roman Vopat were the first brothers ever to suit up for the same game in Kings' franchise history.
* Sean McKenna, 6-8, 247, became the biggest player in NHL history when he suited up for the Kings last season.
* the penalty killing percentage of 87.2% was the best in franchise history.

* in 30 years, the Kings have only had a first round choice in 12 of them.
* the Kings' farm team in Phoenix had an almost identical record, finishing last in the IHL at 27-42-13, compared to 28-43-11 for Los Angeles.
* the Kings beat the Colorado Avalanche three times last year, in five games.
* were one of only two teams not to earn an overtime victory last year. Ottawa was the other.

## STAT ANALYSIS

Whatever was going on in Los Angeles last year, it didn't change much. In fact, it was remarkably similar to the previous season as the numbers below show.

|  | 1995-96 | 1996-97 | Change |
|---|---|---|---|
| Points | 66 | 67 | +1 |
| Home Points | 41 | 43 | +2 |
| Away Points | 25 | 24 | -1 |
| Own Conference Points | 45 | 46 | +1 |
| Other Conference Points | 21 | 21 | 0 |
| Team Plus\Minus | -46 | -55 | -11 |
| Goal Differential | -46 | -54 | -9 |
| Shot Differential | -4.1 | -4.9 | -0.8 |

## TEAM PREVIEW

GOAL: On a lot of teams, great depth in net with the likes of Stephane Fiset, Byron Dafoe and Jamie Storr would be exciting. But on this team, what does it matter?

A lot of people will say that you build a team from the goal out. Hogwash.

It's important to have good goaltending, but not before you're good at anything else.

The only goalie in the last 20 years who has made a weak team a winner is Dominik Hasek, and that was just this last season. Hasek performed miracles, but even he would have had a tough time on the Kings.

The Kings probably feel that Storr deserves a chance to show his stuff at the NHL level now, which would make Dafoe or Fiset the odd man out. But, since the position is a strength — the only strength on this team — look for them to deal one of their goaltenders and get some real players for the rest of the team.

Hockey Annual Rating: 20 of 26

DEFENCE: The Kings have one of the better defencemen in the league in Rob Blake, but the Bruins had one of the best in Ray Bourque, and all that got them was last place overall. Besides, Blake is always injured.

Larry Robinson said that he saw some positive signs from Aki-Petteri Berg and Roman Vopat. But, what do you expect him to say. He has to say something positive, even when there's no reason.

In actuality, Berg has been somewhat of a disappointment, or Robinson wouldn't be

| GOALTENDER | GPI | MINS | AVG | W | L | T | EN | SO | GA | SA | SV % |
|---|---|---|---|---|---|---|---|---|---|---|---|
| JAMIE STORR | 5 | 265 | 2.49 | 2 | 1 | 1 | 1 | 0 | 11 | 147 | .925 |
| BYRON DAFOE | 40 | 2162 | 3.11 | 13 | 17 | 5 | 4 | 0 | 112 | 1178 | .905 |
| STEPHANE FISET | 44 | 2482 | 3.19 | 13 | 24 | 5 | 4 | 4 | 132 | 1410 | .906 |
| J.C. BERGERON | 1 | 56 | 4.29 | 0 | 1 | 0 | 0 | 0 | 4 | 35 | .886 |
| L.A TOTALS | 82 | 4985 | 3.23 | 28 | 43 | 11 | 9 | 4 | 268 | 2779 | .904 |

saying he's seen positive signs, but he's still only 21-years-old and should see regular duty this season.

Mattias Norstrom was the only defence-man who played more than 60 games, so he should stick, along with Philippe Boucher, who showed some offensive promise.

Others who could play are John Slaney, Doug Zmolek, Steven Finn, Jarolslav Modry and giant Steve McKenna.

At the start of last season, Sean O'Donnell learned that he didn't fit into the team's plans and wouldn't be staying with the team as one of their top eight defencemen. This after play-ing the most games of any of their defence-men the year before as a rookie, and being one of the better rearguards. So, the news came to him as a shock. On this team, that's like saying you're not a man. To O'Donnell's credit he went to the minors for a short stint and then returned to play regularly the rest of the season. He's the toughest defencemen they have—let's rephrase that—he's the only tough defenceman they have, so he probably won't fit into the team's plans again this year.

It's fairly obvious that the Kings wanted to have a mobile defence corps. But, even if they were it didn't matter because nobody was going to score when they moved it to them anyway.

The only defenceman who could play reg-ularly on any decent team is Rob Blake. He had the worst plus-minus at -28, which illus-trates the problem with that stat. He was always on the ice against the other teams' top lines because he was one of the few hopes of stopping them. A thankless, impossible job.

One welcome addition will be Garry Galley, signed as a free agent during the sum-mer. He's 34-years-old, but should make a nice offensive contribution.

If they asked the forwards around the league which defence they'd like to play against most, Los Angeles would top most of the lists. Who wouldn't like to venture into opposing territory and not have to worry about being hit. It's easy. It's fun.

Hockey Annual Rating: 26 of 26

FORWARD: If somebody seriously thought they could win with this group of jokers, then they should be fired.

Oh, he was? Okay.

There isn't enough here to make a good second line on almost any NHL team. A third line, yes, but even that's stretching things.

You could trade this unit for that of the Detroit Vipers, or Manitoba Moose, or Long Beach Ice Dogs, and still not be much worse off.

Ray Ferraro was the only player to get at least 20 goals. For service beyond the call of duty, the Kings should have had the decency to trade him at the deadline.

Dimitri Khristich, traded for a first and a fourth round pick (the Kings also got Dafoe), led the team with a whopping 56 points. The only team that had fewer from their top scor-er was Buffalo.

Kevin Stevens was a ridiculously bad bust who would be put out to pasture except for the fact that they're paying him so much they have to use him.

Vitali Yachmenev, who discovered goals are more difficult to come by if Wayne Gretzky isn't passing to him, dropped from 19 to 10 goals.

Vladimir Tsyplakov, another of the Kings' extremely soft forwards, is a career minor-lea-guer who got a chance with the Kings because they're a minor-league team. Sixteen goals from him isn't bad.

Kai Nurminen, another softy, had 16 goals which isn't bad either, but the Kings opted not to resign him, saying they already had too many of his ilk on board. At least there is some perception now in the Kings' camp. But, if those are the reasons for not signing him, then they wouldn't sign most of their players.

Yanic Perreault is a guy who can put the puck in the net, but only played half the schedule. Double his points and he would have had 50, good for second on the team.

Craig Johnson is an exciting player, with a lot of speed, who had injury problems. If you pro-rated his goals over 82 games, though, he would still only have 11.

Glen Murray is a chronic underachiever who has been passed on by two previous teams during his short NHL tenure.

In what passes for optimism on this team, Roman Vopat had four goals in 29 games, and the Kings said they liked what they saw.

Brad Smyth, acquired in a trade with Florida, made a big entrance by piling in the goals for a couple games, but then was eventually returned to the minors.

Matt Johnson is the team's enforcer.

See anything you like?

Well, we haven't got to the good stuff yet.

Dan Bylsma, who has played for almost every single minor-league team over his career, was one of the most valuable players on the minor-league Kings. He was instrumental in penalty killing, making it the only competent area of play on this team.

Ian Laperriere was also good as a defensive forward.

Among the prospects, Pavel Rosa can step right into the lineup. Even if they think he needs minor-league experience there's no better place for that than with the Kings. He was 63-90-153 in the Quebec junior league last year.

As for other newcomers, look for somebody who has played in the minors for years. That means he has the experience to play on the Kings.

Hockey Annual Rating: 26 of 26

SPECIAL TEAMS: Absolutely no surprise that the Kings' power play was second worst in the league, but finishing third in penalty killing is shocking. It is, in fact, the only thing this team did well.

So, who's to blame for this nonsense?

Dan Bylsma and Ian Laperriere were the key forwards on the penalty killing unit, and were remarkable considering the weakness of this team. Or, it could be that since the other teams had few problems scoring at even strength, they didn't put as much priority in their power play.

The Kings' power play was brutal. That's because their power play was equivalent to other teams' third lines. Simple enough.

POWER PLAY

|  | G | ATT | PCT |
|---|---|---|---|
| Overall | 46 | 338 | 13.6% (25th NHL) |
| Home | 24 | 181 | 13.3% (T-22nd NHL) |
| Road | 22 | 157 | 14.0% (21st NHL) |

14 SHORT HANDED GOALS ALLOWED (T-23rd NHL)

PENALTY KILLING

|  | G | TSH | PCT |
|---|---|---|---|
| Overall | 45 | 352 | 87.2% (3rd NHL) |
| Home | 22 | 175 | 87.4% (T-3rd NHL) |
| Road | 23 | 177 | 87.0% (5th NHL) |

5 SHORT HANDED GOALS SCORED (T-23rd NHL)

KINGS SPECIAL TEAMS SCORING

| Power play | G | A | PTS |
|---|---|---|---|
| FERRARO | 11 | 6 | 17 |
| BLAKE | 4 | 9 | 13 |
| KHRISTICH | 3 | 6 | 9 |
| BOUCHER | 2 | 7 | 9 |
| NURMINEN | 4 | 4 | 8 |
| STEVENS | 4 | 2 | 6 |
| O'DONNELL | 2 | 4 | 6 |
| TSYPLAKOV | 1 | 5 | 6 |
| MURRAY | 3 | 2 | 5 |

| | | | |
|---|---|---|---|
| YACHMENEV | 2 | 3 | 5 |
| NORSTROM | 0 | 5 | 5 |
| SLANEY | 1 | 3 | 4 |
| SHEVALIER | 1 | 3 | 4 |
| PERREAULT | 1 | 3 | 4 |
| BERG | 2 | 0 | 2 |
| SMYTH | 0 | 2 | 2 |
| VOPAT | 1 | 0 | 1 |
| MODRY | 1 | 0 | 1 |
| JOHNSON | 1 | 0 | 1 |
| VOPAT | 0 | 1 | 1 |
| LAPERRIERE | 0 | 1 | 1 |
| BYLSMA | 0 | 1 | 1 |

| Short handed | G | A | PTS |
|---|---|---|---|
| PERREAULT | 1 | 1 | 2 |
| KHRISTICH | 0 | 2 | 2 |
| MODRY | 1 | 0 | 1 |
| LAPERRIERE | 1 | 0 | 1 |
| LAFAYETTE | 1 | 0 | 1 |
| SHEVALIER | 0 | 1 | 1 |
| O'DONNELL | 0 | 1 | 1 |
| NORSTROM | 0 | 1 | 1 |

COACHING AND MANAGEMENT: Sam McMaster did what he could and seemed to really feel the team was making progress. Probably the biggest progressive step the team made was firing him. Maybe that's not fair, because he thought the young players were going to develop over time and turn this team around.

The problem is that they're not. They're not good young players with great futures. They were almost all passed over by other teams, so what he was hoping for was a miracle.

He didn't get it, and neither will new GM Dave Taylor, at least not with this bunch. He thinks there's lots of great young talent on this team as well, so we only assume he's either dilusional, a positive thinker, or just says that in public and knows full well that this team stinks and is going nowhere.

His only hope is to be aware of that fact, and then go from there, putting a team together that has good young talent, mixed with veterans who can still play the game, and make a big push in the character area.

As for coach Larry Robinson, it is impossible to say whether he's made a sad sack team better than it is, or if the sad sack team is playing the way it should be. If he could have made them into winners then he would be the miracle the team needs. But, not bloody likely.

Hockey Annual Rating: 26 of 26

DRAFT

| Round | Sel. | Player | Pos | Amateur Team |
|---|---|---|---|---|
| 1 | 3 | Olli Jokinen | C | Finland |
| 1 | 15 | Matt Zultek | LW | Ottawa (OHL) |
| 2 | 29 | Scott Barney | C | Peterborough (OHL) |
| 4 | 83 | Joseph Corvo | D | Western Michigan |
| 4 | 99 | Sean Blanchard | D | Ottawa (OHL) |
| 6 | 137 | Richard Seeley | D | Prince Albert (WHL) |
| 6 | 150 | Jeff Katcher | D | Brandon (WHL) |
| 8 | 193 | Jay Kopischke | LW | Northern Iowa (USHL) |
| 9 | 220 | Konrad Brand | D | Medicine Hat (WHL) |

If you choose to look at it a certain way, the Kings got three first rounders in the draft. Olli Jokinen is a big strong guy who can score. He suggests his style of play is similar to that of Eric Lindros.

Their second pick in the first round, Matt Zultek is considered a good two-way prospect. His statistics show he's a goal scorer first and playmaker second. He was 27-13-40 for Ottawa in the OHL.

Second round pick, Scott Barney was a projected first rounder whose stock dropped dramatically last season. It wasn't a good time to have a poor year, but he could turn it around and have an outstanding season with Peterborough.

## PROGNOSIS:

This is the worst team in the league, bar none.

They will finish last overall. There isn't even a slight hope they can make the playoffs.

Not only do they not have a first line, they don't have a second one. How ridiculous is that?

They're weak defensively, they're too soft, they're on the minus side in character, and that's just for starters.

There is no hope for this team. None.

## PREDICTION

Western Conference: 13th
Overall: 26th

## STAT SECTION

| Team Scoring Stats | | 1996-97 | | | | | CAREER | | | | |
|---|---|---|---|---|---|---|---|---|---|---|---|
| | GP | G | A | PTS | +/- | PIM | SH | Gm | G | A | Pts |
| DIMITRI KHRISTICH | 75 | 19 | 37 | 56 | 8 | 38 | 135 | 466 | 167 | 203 | 370 |
| RAY FERRARO | 81 | 25 | 21 | 46 | 22- | 112 | 152 | 915 | 327 | 368 | 685 |
| V. TSYPLAKOV | 67 | 16 | 23 | 39 | 8 | 12 | 118 | 90 | 21 | 28 | 49 |
| KEVIN STEVENS | 69 | 14 | 20 | 34 | 27- | 96 | 175 | 588 | 278 | 319 | 597 |
| VITALI YACHMENEV | 65 | 10 | 22 | 32 | 9- | 10 | 97 | 145 | 29 | 56 | 85 |
| ROB BLAKE | 62 | 8 | 23 | 31 | 28- | 82 | 169 | 388 | 68 | 170 | 238 |
| GLEN MURRAY | 77 | 16 | 14 | 30 | 21- | 32 | 153 | 293 | 59 | 49 | 108 |
| KAI NURMINEN | 67 | 16 | 11 | 27 | 3- | 22 | 112 | 67 | 16 | 11 | 27 |
| YANIC PERREAULT | 41 | 11 | 14 | 25 | 0 | 20 | 98 | 158 | 41 | 46 | 87 |
| PHILIPPE BOUCHER | 60 | 7 | 18 | 25 | 0 | 25 | 159 | 184 | 22 | 40 | 62 |
| IAN LAPERRIERE | 62 | 8 | 15 | 23 | 25- | 102 | 84 | 171 | 27 | 40 | 67 |
| MATTIAS NORSTROM | 80 | 1 | 21 | 22 | 4- | 84 | 106 | 134 | 3 | 28 | 31 |
| BRAD SMYTH | 52 | 9 | 8 | 17 | 10- | 76 | 84 | 59 | 10 | 9 | 19 |
| SEAN O'DONNELL | 55 | 5 | 12 | 17 | 13- | 144 | 68 | 141 | 7 | 19 | 26 |
| JOHN SLANEY | 32 | 3 | 11 | 14 | 10- | 4 | 60 | 133 | 16 | 37 | 53 |
| JEFF SHEVALIER | 26 | 4 | 9 | 13 | 6- | 6 | 42 | 27 | 5 | 9 | 14 |
| ROMAN VOPAT | 29 | 4 | 5 | 9 | 7- | 60 | 54 | 54 | 6 | 8 | 14 |
| JAN VOPAT | 33 | 4 | 5 | 9 | 3 | 22 | 44 | 44 | 5 | 9 | 14 |

| | | | | | | | | | | | |
|---|---|---|---|---|---|---|---|---|---|---|---|
| DAN BYLSMA | 79 | 3 | 6 | 9 | 15- | 32 | 86 | 84 | 3 | 6 | 9 |
| AKI BERG | 41 | 2 | 6 | 8 | 9- | 24 | 65 | 92 | 2 | 13 | 15 |
| CRAIG JOHNSON | 31 | 4 | 3 | 7 | 7- | 26 | 30 | 106 | 20 | 17 | 37 |
| BRENT GRIEVE | 18 | 4 | 2 | 6 | 2- | 15 | 50 | 97 | 20 | 16 | 36 |
| JAROSLAV MODRY | 30 | 3 | 3 | 6 | 13- | 25 | 32 | 155 | 9 | 35 | 44 |
| BARRY POTOMSKI | 26 | 3 | 2 | 5 | 8- | 93 | 18 | 59 | 6 | 4 | 10 |
| STEVEN FINN | 54 | 2 | 3 | 5 | 8- | 84 | 35 | 725 | 34 | 78 | 112 |
| NATHAN LAFAYETTE | 15 | 1 | 3 | 4 | 8- | 8 | 26 | 120 | 10 | 15 | 25 |
| MATT JOHNSON | 52 | 1 | 3 | 4 | 4- | 194 | 20 | 67 | 2 | 3 | 5 |
| PAUL DIPIETRO | 6 | 1 | 0 | 1 | 2- | 6 | 10 | 192 | 31 | 49 | 80 |
| DOUG ZMOLEK | 57 | 1 | 0 | 1 | 22- | 116 | 28 | 316 | 9 | 24 | 33 |
| J.C. BERGERON | 1 | 0 | 0 | 0 | 0 | 0 | 0 | | | | |
| CHRIS MARINUCCI | 1 | 0 | 0 | 0 | 2- | 0 | 1 | 13 | 1 | 4 | 5 |
| JASON MORGAN | 3 | 0 | 0 | 0 | 3- | 0 | 4 | 3 | 0 | 0 | 0 |
| JAMIE STORR | 5 | 0 | 0 | 0 | 0 | 0 | 0 | | | | |
| STEVE MCKENNA | 9 | 0 | 0 | 0 | 1 | 37 | 6 | 9 | 0 | 0 | 0 |
| BYRON DAFOE | 40 | 0 | 0 | 0 | 0 | 0 | 0 | | | | |
| STEPHANE FISET | 44 | 0 | 0 | 0 | 0 | 2 | 0 | | | | |

## TEAM RANKINGS

| | | Conference Rank | League Rank |
|---|---|---|---|
| Record | 28-43-11 | 12 | 24 |
| Home | 18-16-7 | 8 | 16 |
| Away | 10-27-4 | 13 | 26 |
| Versus Own Conference | 19-29-8 | 13 | 25 |
| Versus Other Conference | 9-14-3 | 11 | 20 |
| Team Plus\Minus | -55 | 12 | 25 |
| Goals For | 214 | 11 | 23 |
| Goals Against | 268 | 11 | 20 |
| Average Shots For | 29.0 | 10 | 20 |

| | | | |
|---|---|---|---|
| Average Shots Against | 33.9 | 12 | 23 |
| Overtime | 0-3-11 | 12 | 24 |
| One Goal Games | 8-13 | 13 | 24 |
| Times outshooting opponent | 21 | 13 | 25 |
| Versus Teams Over .500 | 9-25-4 | 13 | 26 |
| Versus Teams Under .500 | 19-18-7 | 10 | 17 |
| First Half Record | 14-23-4 | 13 | 25 |
| Second Half Record | 14-20-7 | 11 | 22 |

## PLAYOFFS

- did not make the playoffs

## ALL-TIME LEADERS

Goals
| Marcel Dionne | 550 |
| Dave Taylor | 431 |
| Luc Robitaille | 392 |

Assists
| Marcel Dionne | 757 |
| Dave Taylor | 638 |
| Wayne Gretzky | 619 |

Points
| Marcel Dionne | 1,307 |
| Dave Taylor | 1,069 |
| Wayne Gretzky | 858 |

## BEST INDIVIDUAL SEASONS

Goals
| Bernie Nicholls | 1988-89 | 70 |
| Luc Robitaille | 1992-93 | 63 |
| Marcel Dionne | 1978-79 | 59 |

Assists
| Wayne Gretzky | 1990-91 | 122 |
| Wayne Gretzky | 1988-89 | 114 |
| Wayne Gretzky | 1989-90 | 102 |

Points
| Wayne Gretzky | 1988-89 | 168 |
| Wayne Gretzky | 1990-91 | 163 |
| Bernie Nicholls | 1988-89 | 150 |

## TEAM

Last 3 years
| | GP | W | L | T | Pts | % |
|---|---|---|---|---|---|---|
| 1996-97 | 82 | 28 | 43 | 11 | 67 | .409 |
| 1995-96 | 82 | 24 | 40 | 18 | 68 | .415 |
| 1994-95 | 48 | 16 | 23 | 9 | 41 | .427 |

Best 3 regular seasons
| 1974-75 | 80 | 47 | 17 | 21 | 105 | .656 |
| 1990-91 | 80 | 46 | 24 | 10 | 102 | .638 |
| 1980-81 | 80 | 43 | 24 | 13 | 99 | .619 |

Worst 3 regular seasons
| 1969-70 | 76 | 14 | 52 | 10 | 38 | .250 |
| 1971-72 | 78 | 20 | 49 | 9 | 49 | .314 |
| 1985-86 | 80 | 23 | 49 | 8 | 54 | .338 |

Most Goals (min. 70 game schedule)
| 1988-89 | 376 |
| 1990-91 | 340 |
| 1984-85 | 339 |

Fewest Goals (min. 70 game schedule)
| 1969-79 | 168 |
| 1968-69 | 185 |
| 1967-68 | 200 |

Most Goals Against (min. 70 game schedule)
| 1985-86 | 389 |
| 1983-84 | 376 |
| 1981-82 | 369 |

Fewest Goals Against (min. 70 game schedule)
| 1974-75 | 185 |
| 1967-68 | 224 |
| 1973-74 | 231 |

# Phoenix Coyotes

If you've ever wondered what an average NHL team looks like, look no further — it's the Phoenix Coyotes.

When the franchise was in Winnipeg it was characterized for different things over the years: they often and quickly reversed their winning and losing from year to year; were at times offensive powerhouses; were big-time losers on occasion; were big on Europeans at one time; and also were in a city that wasn't a favorite place for too many players.

Last season there wasn't much to carve out an identity for Coyotes, unless you count off-ice activities such as Bobby Smith taking over and eventually firing everyone, Keith Tkachuk being accused of gambling, Tkachuk's family in barroom brawls, or Jeremy Roenick's holdout saga and continued verbal diahrea.

On the ice they were average...and not so average.

Average: The play of Jeremy Roenick for much of the season, although he did come on towards the end of the season and in the playoffs before being injured.
Not Average: His salary demands and his and his agent's over-estimation of his value.

Average: Jeremy Roenick shooting his mouth off.
Not Average: Roenick accusing Canadian hockey writers of bias against American hockey players, and being jealous of the money they make. It's such a stupid comment that it's not worth a reply. It probably says more about the person making the comment than anything else. For the record, Canadian hockey writers are jealous of all the player salaries (see previous "not average") not just Americans.

Average: Phoenix's record of one game over .500.
Not Average: The fact that they were lousy at home (11th in conference) and very good on the road (3rd in conference).

Average: Mike Gartner's season, for him anyway. Another 30-goal year, giving him 17 for his career, three more than anyone else.
Not Average: The play of Keith Tkachuk, who led the league with 52 goals.

Average: The number of shots they had per game - 30.0 - which was 0.1 shots per game over the league average.
Not Average: That when they outshot their opponents they had a losing record (15-16-4) and when they were outshot themselves they had a winning record (21-18-3).

Average: an 18-19-4 record in the first half and 20-18-3 in the second half.
Not Average: That they were 19-23-4 before

the all-star break, but came on strong after it with a 19-14-3 mark.

Average: Fifth place finish in the conference. Not Average: Twenty games into the season they were in 12th place.

## SHORTS

* The Coyotes were the only team that did not have a goal scored by a rookie.
* Seven of eight Coyote shutouts came on the road.
* Mike Gartner scored the first goal in the team's first game as the Phoenix Coyotes. Keith Tkachuk had the first assist, Kris King the first penalty and Nikolai Khabibulin the first win.
* Seven teams have changed cities in modern NHL history. Six of them, including Phoenix, had a better record in their first season in their new city than they did in their last season in their old city.
* The Coyotes allowed the fewest goals in franchise history, but also scored the second fewest.
* Twenty-three road wins were the most in franchise history, and tied with Colorado and Dallas for the most in the league.
* Mike Gartner needs just four goals to reach the 700 mark for his career.

## STAT ANALYSIS

Three teams had better road records than home records last season — Phoenix, St. Louis and Chicago. Perhaps coincidentally, the three were in the same division and within two points of each other. Perhaps not so coincidentally, all three are playing in arenas in which they weren't a couple years ago.

Sometimes, teams play better on the road because it better suits their defensive style. In other words, they don't have to be fancy or try to put on a show. But, that's not something these three teams have in common anyway. The home-road difference rarely extends beyond one season, so watch if these three teams aren't better at home than on the road this year.

|           | Home Win% | Road Win% | Difference |
|-----------|-----------|-----------|------------|
| Phoenix   | .451      | .561      | .110       |
| Chicago   | .439      | .549      | .110       |
| St. Louis | .467      | .549      | .085       |

## TEAM PREVIEW

GOAL: Nikolai Khabibulin may be one of the premier goalies in the league, but when's he going to play like it for a full season? He got off to a poor start again last year and only the play of Darcy Wakaluk kept the Coyotes on track. Then Wakaluk got hurt and Khabibulin rose to the occasion — and rose and rose.

During one hot streak he had three shutouts in a row. On March 5, 6, and 8 he shut out Florida, Tampa Bay and Chicago, all on the road.

He finished the season by playing 47 straight games.

Some observers would suggest that type of workload doesn't make sense and would just wear him out.

Why should it?

Skaters sometimes play 82 consecutive games and rarely is it suggested that they rest by sitting out. Just what does sitting and watching a game for three hours do in terms of providing a rest anyway? Big deal.

The only other positions in professional team sports that require players to miss games in order to rest are pitchers, because of their arms, and catchers, because it's tough on the legs to squat for a couple hours at a time.

Goalies don't need to sit out games in order to rest. Maybe sitting out a practice or two might help, but not games. These guys are all in good shape, so usually the only thing they need to do is rest mentally.

But, there is one good reason to sit out number one goalies — to make sure your number two man is sharp in case there's an injury to the number one guy. In defence of the handling of Khabibulin, however, the number two man, Wakaluk, was injured for most of the season.

Hockey Annual Rating: X of 26

DEFENCE: There are two types of Phoenix defensemen: flashy and offensive, and not-flashy and not-offensive. Since those are the two types of defensemen a team needs, that's not bad.

Oleg Tverdovsky came into his own in the flashy department, scoring more last season than his first two years combined. He led the team in power play with 30, which was 55 percent of his 55 points.

Other offensive types are Teppo Numminen, who scored only half the points he did the previous season (27 from 54); Deron Quint, who came up and down from Springfield; and Norm MacIver, who was injured most of the season.

Defensive types are Gerald Diduck, Jim Johnson, Murray Baron, Jay More, and Kevin Dahl or Brent Thompson. Brad McCrimmon

hung around for his experience and leadership but didn't get to play much, so his return is unlikely. Jeff Finley became an unrestricted free agent.

The trading of Dave Manson was a curious move because he's the type of player who is far more valuable than his numbers suggest. He had a lousy plus-minus number with the Coyotes (-25) but it's pretty much a meaningless stat anyway. He has a presence on the ice. Opposing players don't want to play against him because he's a bit of a loony, much like Bryan Marchment with Edmonton. And for sure they don't want to take liberties around their net.

Manson went to Montreal for Murray Baron and Chris Murray. Murray was traded immediately to Hartford for Gerald Diduck. The Coyotes got two defensive defensemen for one.

Among the prospects, Ian Doig is expected to be a regular in the near future. He's big and tough. Dan Foht, last year's 11th draft pick overall, is even bigger at 6-6 226, but he's expected to be a couple years away.

Overall, good depth on the blueline, good experience, good offence, good defence, and some good youngsters on the way.

Overall talent, however, is only average.

Hockey Annual Rating:

FORWARD: The key to scoring success on the Coyotes is simple: get yourself a spot on

| GOALTENDER | GPI | MINS | AVG | W | L | T | EN | SO | GA | SA | SV % |
|---|---|---|---|---|---|---|---|---|---|---|---|
| PAT JABLONSKI | 2 | 59 | 2.03 | 0 | 1 | 0 | 1 | 0 | 2 | 24 | .917 |
| PARRIS DUFFUS | 1 | 29 | 2.07 | 0 | 0 | 0 | 0 | 0 | 1 | 8 | .875 |
| N. KHABIBULIN | 72 | 4091 | 2.83 | 30 | 33 | 6 | 7 | 7 | 193 | 2094 | .908 |
| DARCY WAKALUK | 16 | 782 | 2.99 | 8 | 3 | 1 | 0 | 1 | 39 | 386 | .899 |
| PHO TOTALS | 82 | 4974 | 2.93 | 38 | 37 | 7 | 8 | 8 | 243 | 2520 | .904 |

Tkachuk's line. He's going to score goals no matter what else happens so linemates will stock up on assists.

A lot of juggling went on with that number one line last season, so getting there and staying there isn't so simple. Ideally, they want to have two scoring lines, which they are perfectly capable of doing. Then they put their top offensive threats together for the power play.

Tkachuk is the top left winger on the team and one of the top two in the game (John LeClair). Craig Janney or Cliff Ronning are both acceptable centres. Janney, however is prone to slumps. Jeremy Roenick is also a centre, but might be better utilized as a winger in order to get more balance. Chad Kilger might also be ready for prime time and he might not be out of place there either. Pretty much it's a can't-fail spot as long as they can put the puck on Tkachuk's stick.

Right wing on the top line seems important to the Coyotes. If it's not Roenick, then it's Mike Gartner or Rick Tocchet, whom they signed during the summer as a free agent. Tocchet is not kid anymore, however, and has a ton of injury problems.

Gartner never seems to slow down. His style is to score in bunches and then disappear for a while, but when they total up the goals at the end of the season he's always up there. Thirty-two goals in today's lower scoring NHL is a pretty good tally.

Bob Corkum is a good centre for the checking line leaving wingers Darrin Shannon, Jim McKenzie, and Jocelyn Lemieux, to round out the forward units.

Among the prospects who will get a look are right winger Brad Isbister and centre Daniel Briere. Isbister was very impressive for Canada in the World Junior Championships, but then ran into injury problems. Briere, who has to overcome his size deficiency (5-9,

160) was 52-78-130 for Drummondville in the QMJHL. Briere will probably have to show tremendous scoring punch in the Springfield before he gets a shot at the big-time.

Hockey Annual Rating:

SPECIAL TEAMS:
The power play didn't perform very well during the playoffs, but that's not such a big deal. Every power play gets hot and cold.

The Coyotes have an excellent power play and they had excellent penalty killing last season. If not for their special teams they would not have made the playoffs because they were -21 at even strength, 19th in the league.

Oddly enough, Tkachuk, one of the best snipers in the league was only third on the team in power play goals. He had nine, but Gartner had 13 and Roenick had 10. Ronning was only one behind, with eight.

It's much better that more than one guy can pot the power play goals, because if one person gets cold another can pick up the slack.

There are plenty of bodies to play the points, starting with Tverdovsky and Numminen. Quint and MacIver are also good pointmen on the power play.

There are some good defensive forwards, especially Bob Corkum, to man penalty killing duty, but like most teams nowadays, the Coyotes aren't afraid to put out their offensive stars when down a man. They can sometimes generate shorthanded opportunites, as Roenick did with six points, and guys like Mike Gartner, not known to be a terribly good defensive player, can use their speed.

POWER PLAY

|         | G  | ATT | PCT                |
|---------|----|-----|--------------------|
| Overall | 65 | 359 | 18.1% (T-4th NHL)  |
| Home    | 34 | 193 | 17.6% (6th NHL)    |
| Road    | 31 | 166 | 18.7% (6th NHL)    |

14 SHORT HANDED GOALS ALLOWED (T-23rd NHL)

PENALTY KILLING

|         | G   | TSH | PCT              |
|---------|-----|-----|------------------|
| Overall | 47  | 334 | 85.9% (5th NHL)  |
| Home    | 27  | 162 | 83.3% (T-14th NHL) |
| Road    | 20  | 172 | 88.4% (2nd NHL)  |

9 SHORT HANDED GOALS SCORED (T-16th NHL)

COYOTES SPECIAL TEAMS SCORING

| Power play  | G  | A  | PTS |
|-------------|----|----|-----|
| TVERDOVSKY  | 3  | 27 | 30  |
| GARTNER     | 13 | 12 | 25  |
| RONNING     | 8  | 15 | 23  |
| ROENICK     | 10 | 11 | 21  |
| TKACHUK     | 9  | 10 | 19  |
| JANNEY      | 5  | 8  | 13  |
| DRAKE       | 5  | 4  | 9   |
| NUMMINEN    | 0  | 9  | 9   |
| QUINT       | 1  | 7  | 8   |
| MACIVER     | 1  | 6  | 7   |
| STAPLETON   | 2  | 3  | 5   |
| KOROLEV     | 2  | 1  | 3   |
| DIDUCK      | 1  | 2  | 3   |
| SHANNON     | 1  | 1  | 2   |
| KILGER      | 1  | 0  | 1   |
| FINLEY      | 1  | 0  | 1   |
| KING        | 0  | 1  | 1   |
| DOAN        | 0  | 1  | 1   |
| CORKUM      | 0  | 1  | 1   |
| BARON       | 0  | 1  | 1   |

| Short handed | G | A | PTS |
|--------------|---|---|-----|
| ROENICK      | 3 | 3 | 6   |
| DRAKE        | 1 | 2 | 3   |
| TKACHUK      | 2 | 0 | 2   |
| JOHNSON      | 0 | 2 | 2   |
| TVERDOVSKY   | 1 | 0 | 1   |
| GARTNER      | 1 | 0 | 1   |
| CORKUM       | 1 | 0 | 1   |
| MORE         | 0 | 1 | 1   |
| MCCRIMMON    | 0 | 1 | 1   |

| FINLEY | 0 | 1 | 1 |
|--------|---|---|---|
| BARON  | 0 | 1 | 1 |

COACHING AND MANAGEMENT: Bobby Smith is certainly a hands-on GM. But, if he puts his hands on your shoulder, chances are you're going to be fired. He fired John Paddock and Don Hay and is putting his own stamp on things.

The new coach is Jim Schoenfeld, considered a no-nonsense guy, unless you count those mattress commercials. He might be just what the team needs.

Hockey Annual Rating

DRAFT

| Round | Sel. | Player          | Pos | Amateur Team          |
|-------|------|-----------------|-----|-----------------------|
| 2     | 43   | Juha Gustafsson | D   | Finland               |
| 4     | 96   | Scott McCallum  | D   | Tri-City (WHL)        |
| 5     | 123  | Curtis Suter    | D   | Spokane (WHL)         |
| 6     | 151  | Robert Francz   | LW  | Peterborough (OHL)    |
| 8     | 207  | Alex Andreyev   | D   | Weyburn (SJHL)        |
| 9     | 233  | Wyatt Smith     | C   | U. of Minnesota       |

With no first round pick, the Coyotes selected Juha Gustafsson in the second round. He wasn't rated anywhere near as high as Phoenix took him, but they think he could be another Teppo Numminen.

PROGNOSIS

The Coyotes are still just an average team. But, they're a .500 team with more upside than downside potential. They have some good young players who have to get into the lineup, and they've got some tired old retreads no longer capable of taking Phoenix to the next level.

They're good enough to make the play-offs, that shouldn't be a problem at all, but they're not good enough to make a serious run at contending for the Cup.

PREDICTION

## STAT SECTION

| Team Scoring Stats | 1996-97 | | | | | CAREER | | | | | |
|---|---|---|---|---|---|---|---|---|---|---|---|
| | GP | G | A | PTS | +/- | PIM | SH | Gm | G | A | Pts |
| KEITH TKACHUK | 81 | 52 | 34 | 86 | 1- | 228 | 296 | 389 | 196 | 179 | 375 |
| JEREMY ROENICK | 72 | 29 | 40 | 69 | 7- | 115 | 228 | 596 | 296 | 369 | 665 |
| MIKE GARTNER | 82 | 32 | 31 | 63 | 11- | 38 | 271 | 1,372 | 696 | 612 | 1,308 |
| OLEG TVERDOVSKY | 82 | 10 | 45 | 55 | 5- | 30 | 144 | 200 | 20 | 77 | 97 |
| CRAIG JANNEY | 77 | 15 | 38 | 53 | 1- | 26 | 88 | 636 | 173 | 498 | 671 |
| CLIFF RONNING | 69 | 19 | 32 | 51 | 9- | 26 | 171 | 615 | 185 | 319 | 504 |
| DALLAS DRAKE | 63 | 17 | 19 | 36 | 11- | 52 | 113 | 309 | 75 | 110 | 185 |
| TEPPO NUMMINEN | 82 | 2 | 25 | 27 | 3- | 28 | 135 | 629 | 55 | 237 | 292 |
| DARRIN SHANNON | 82 | 11 | 13 | 24 | 4 | 41 | 104 | 448 | 85 | 151 | 236 |
| BOB CORKUM | 80 | 9 | 11 | 20 | 7- | 40 | 119 | 372 | 61 | 66 | 127 |
| MIKE STAPLETON | 55 | 4 | 11 | 15 | 4- | 36 | 74 | 443 | 45 | 79 | 124 |
| DERON QUINT | 27 | 3 | 11 | 14 | 4- | 4 | 63 | 78 | 8 | 24 | 32 |
| KRIS KING | 81 | 3 | 11 | 14 | 7- | 185 | 57 | 648 | 58 | 76 | 134 |
| GERALD DIDUCK | 67 | 2 | 12 | 14 | 7- | 63 | 80 | 770 | 48 | 141 | 189 |
| NORM MACIVER | 32 | 4 | 9 | 13 | 11- | 24 | 40 | 459 | 53 | 224 | 277 |
| SHANE DOAN | 63 | 4 | 8 | 12 | 3- | 49 | 100 | 137 | 11 | 18 | 29 |
| IGOR KOROLEV | 41 | 3 | 7 | 10 | 5- | 28 | 41 | 306 | 43 | 91 | 134 |
| JIM JOHNSON | 55 | 3 | 7 | 10 | 5 | 74 | 51 | 813 | 27 | 165 | 192 |
| JEFF FINLEY | 65 | 3 | 7 | 10 | 8- | 40 | 38 | 272 | 6 | 36 | 42 |
| JIM MCKENZIE | 65 | 5 | 3 | 8 | 5- | 200 | 38 | 425 | 26 | 21 | 47 |
| JAY MORE | 37 | 1 | 7 | 8 | 10 | 62 | 28 | 330 | 13 | 45 | 58 |
| MURRAY BARON | 79 | 1 | 7 | 8 | 20- | 122 | 64 | 480 | 23 | 50 | 73 |
| CHAD KILGER | 24 | 4 | 3 | 7 | 5- | 13 | 30 | 98 | 11 | 13 | 24 |

| | | | | | | | | | | |
|---|---|---|---|---|---|---|---|---|---|---|
| BRAD MCCRIMMON | 37 | 1 | 5 | 6 | 2 | 18 | 28 | 1,222 | 81 | 322 | 403 |
| N. KHABIBULIN | 72 | 0 | 3 | 3 | 0 | 16 | 0 | | | | |
| JOCELYN LEMIEUX | 2 | 1 | 0 | 1 | 0 | 0 | 4 | 568 | 77 | 81 | 158 |
| DARCY WAKALUK | 16 | 0 | 1 | 1 | 0 | 4 | 0 | | | | |
| PARRIS DUFFUS | 1 | 0 | 0 | 0 | 0 | 0 | 0 | | | | |
| JASON SIMON | 1 | 0 | 0 | 0 | 1- | 0 | 0 | 5 | 0 | 0 | 0 |
| BRENT THOMPSON | 1 | 0 | 0 | 0 | 1- | 7 | 0 | 121 | 1 | 10 | 11 |
| TAVIS HANSEN | 1 | 0 | 0 | 0 | 0 | 0 | 0 | 2 | 0 | 0 | 0 |
| KEVIN DAHL | 2 | 0 | 0 | 0 | 0 | 0 | 2 | 162 | 7 | 21 | 28 |
| JUHA YLONEN | 2 | 0 | 0 | 0 | 0 | 0 | 2 | 2 | 0 | 0 | 0 |
| MIKE HUDSON | 7 | 0 | 0 | 0 | 4- | 2 | 9 | 416 | 49 | 87 | 136 |
| PAT JABLONSKI | 19 | 0 | 0 | 0 | 0 | 0 | 0 | | | | |

## TEAM RANKINGS

| | | Conference Rank | League Rank |
|---|---|---|---|
| Record | 38-37-7 | 5 | 11 |
| Home | 15-19-7 | 11 | 16 |
| Away | 23-18-0 | 3 | 5 |
| Versus Own Conference | 29-24-3 | 3 | 6 |
| Versus Other Conference | 9-13-4 | 9 | 17 |
| Team Plus\Minus | -21 | 9 | 19 |
| Goals For | 240 | 9 | 11 |
| Goals Against | 243 | 8 | 15 |
| Average Shots For | 30.0 | 6 | 11 |
| Average Shots Against | 30.7 | 9 | 17 |
| Overtime | 5-4-7 | 6 | 8 |
| One Goal Games | 12-11 | 4 | 9 |
| Times outshooting opponent | 35 | 8 | 16 |
| Versus Teams Over .500 | 13-19-5 | | |
| Versus Teams Under .500 | 25-18-2 | | |

| | | | |
|---|---|---|---|
| First Half Record | 18-19-4 | 7 | 11 |
| Second Half Record | 20-18-3 | 7 | 11 |

## PLAYOFFS

Results: Lost 4-3 to Anaheim
Record: 3-4
Home: 2-1
Away: 1-3
Goals For: 17 (2.4/game)
Goals Against: 17 (2.4 game)
Overtime: 0-1
Power play: 7.5% (14th)
Penalty Killing: 78.6% (14th)

| | GP | G | A | PTS | +/- | PIM | PP | SH | GW | OT | S |
|---|---|---|---|---|---|---|---|---|---|---|---|
| CLIFF RONNING | 7 | 0 | 7 | 7 | 2 | 12 | 0 | 0 | 0 | 0 | 11 |
| KEITH TKACHUK | 7 | 6 | 0 | 6 | 2 | 7 | 2 | 0 | 0 | 0 | 37 |
| TEPPO NUMMINEN | 7 | 3 | 3 | 6 | 3 | 0 | 1 | 0 | 1 | 0 | 19 |
| JEREMY ROENICK | 6 | 2 | 4 | 6 | 6 | 4 | 0 | 0 | 0 | 0 | 16 |
| DARRIN SHANNON | 7 | 3 | 1 | 4 | 2 | 4 | 0 | 0 | 1 | 0 | 5 |
| BOB CORKUM | 7 | 2 | 2 | 4 | 1- | 4 | 0 | 0 | 1 | 0 | 9 |
| MIKE GARTNER | 7 | 1 | 2 | 3 | 1- | 4 | 0 | 0 | 0 | 0 | 17 |
| CRAIG JANNEY | 7 | 0 | 3 | 3 | 1 | 4 | 0 | 0 | 0 | 0 | 6 |
| DERON QUINT | 7 | 0 | 2 | 2 | 2 | 0 | 0 | 0 | 0 | 0 | 13 |
| DALLAS DRAKE | 7 | 0 | 1 | 1 | 2- | 2 | 0 | 0 | 0 | 0 | 12 |
| OLEG TVERDOVSKY | 7 | 0 | 1 | 1 | 0 | 0 | 0 | 0 | 0 | 0 | 10 |
| MURRAY BARON | 1 | 0 | 0 | 0 | 0 | 0 | 0 | 0 | 0 | 0 | 0 |
| JEFF FINLEY | 1 | 0 | 0 | 0 | 1- | 2 | 0 | 0 | 0 | 0 | 1 |
| IGOR KOROLEV | 1 | 0 | 0 | 0 | 0 | 0 | 0 | 0 | 0 | 0 | 1 |
| JOCELYN LEMIEUX | 2 | 0 | 0 | 0 | 0 | 4 | 0 | 0 | 0 | 0 | 2 |
| SHANE DOAN | 4 | 0 | 0 | 0 | 1- | 2 | 0 | 0 | 0 | 0 | 2 |
| JIM JOHNSON | 6 | 0 | 0 | 0 | 0 | 4 | 0 | 0 | 0 | 0 | 7 |
| GERALD DIDUCK | 7 | 0 | 0 | 0 | 2 | 10 | 0 | 0 | 0 | 0 | 8 |
| KRIS KING | 7 | 0 | 0 | 0 | 1- | 17 | 0 | 0 | 0 | 0 | 2 |
| JIM MCKENZIE | 7 | 0 | 0 | 0 | 0 | 2 | 0 | 0 | 0 | 0 | 7 |
| JAY MORE | 7 | 0 | 0 | 0 | 1 | 7 | 0 | 0 | 0 | 0 | 6 |
| MIKE STAPLETON | 7 | 0 | 0 | 0 | 1- | 14 | 0 | 0 | 0 | 0 | 5 |
| N. KHABIBULIN | 7 | 0 | 0 | 0 | 0 | 6 | 0 | 0 | 0 | 0 | 0 |

| GOALTENDER | GPI | MINS | AVG | W | L | EN | SO | GA | SA | SV % |
|---|---|---|---|---|---|---|---|---|---|---|
| N. KHABIBULIN | 7 | 426 | 2.11 | 3 | 4 | 2 | 1 | 15 | 222 | .932 |
| PHO TOTALS | 7 | 427 | 2.39 | 3 | 4 | 2 | 1 | 17 | 224 | .924 |

## ALL-TIME LEADERS

### Goals
| | |
|---|---|
| Dale Hawerchuk | 379 |
| Thomas Steen | 259 |
| Paul MacLean | 248 |

### Assists
| | |
|---|---|
| Dale Hawerchuk | 550 |
| Thomas Steen | 543 |
| Paul MacLean | 270 |

### Points
| | |
|---|---|
| Dale Hawerchuk | 929 |
| Thomas Steen | 802 |
| Paul MacLean | 518 |

## BEST INDIVIDUAL SEASONS

### Goals
| | | |
|---|---|---|
| Teemu Selanne | 1992-93 | 76 |
| Dale Hawerchuk | 1984-85 | 53 |
| Keith Tkachuk | 1996-97 | 52 |

### Assists
| | | |
|---|---|---|
| Phil Housley | 1992-93 | 79 |
| Dale Hawerchuk | 1987-88 | 77 |
| Dale Hawerchuk | 1984-85 | 77 |

### Points
| | | |
|---|---|---|
| Teemu Selanne | 1992-93 | 132 |
| Dale Hawerchuk | 1984-85 | 130 |
| Dale Hawerchuk | 1987-88 | 121 |

## TEAM

### Last 3 years
| | GP | W | L | T | Pts | % |
|---|---|---|---|---|---|---|
| 1996-97 | 82 | 38 | 37 | 7 | 83 | .506 |
| 1995-96 | 82 | 36 | 40 | 6 | 78 | .476 |
| 1994-95 | 48 | 16 | 25 | 7 | 57 | .594 |

### Best 3 regular seasons
| | | | | | | |
|---|---|---|---|---|---|---|
| 1984-85 | 80 | 43 | 27 | 10 | 96 | .600 |
| 1986-87 | 80 | 40 | 32 | 8 | 88 | .550 |
| 1989-90 | 80 | 37 | 32 | 11 | 85 | .531 |

### Worst 3 regular seasons
| | | | | | | |
|---|---|---|---|---|---|---|
| 1980-81 | 80 | 9 | 57 | 14 | 32 | .200 |
| 1979-89 | 80 | 20 | 49 | 11 | 51 | .319 |
| 1993-94 | 84 | 24 | 51 | 9 | 57 | .339 |

### Most Goals (min. 70 game schedule)
| | |
|---|---|
| 1984-85 | 358 |
| 1983-84 | 340 |
| 1992-93 | 322 |

### Fewest Goals (min. 70 game schedule)
| | |
|---|---|
| 1979-80 | 214 |
| 1996-97 | 240 |
| 1993-94 | 245 |

### Most Goals Against (min. 70 game schedule)
| | |
|---|---|
| 1980-81 | 400 |
| 1983-84 | 374 |
| 1985-86 | 372 |

### Fewest Goals Against (min. 70 game schedule)
| | |
|---|---|
| 1996-97 | 243 |
| 1991-92 | 244 |
| 1986-87 | 271 |

# San Jose Sharks

Okay, so you're stuck with the second worst team in the league — a bunch of sissy-boys who were pushed around and laughed at by everyone. One that had won just 20 games and earned 47 points.

What do you do?

Do you sit back and wait, suggesting that everyone's patience will be rewarded when the youthful potential is realized?

Or, do you recognize that it wasn't going to happen and aggressively pursue other alternatives.

San Jose General Manager, Dean Lombardi, chose Plan B. He had to improve the team and make them competitive, as well as provide hope for the future. Since the future was so bleak, immediate improvement through veterans was the only viable course of action. The other he could work on.

Under those circumstances, Lombardi was almost dealing with a first year expansion team, and while the record doesn't show great success, he did his job, and did it well.

The team needed a fresh approach and new ideas, and he provided them.

RIGHT IDEA: Tough character player veterans on defence, such as Todd Gill and Marty McSorley to help clear the front of the net, make the San Jose zone less of a vacation zone for opposing forwards, and to show some of the youngsters how it's done.

RESULT: Gill and McSorley did their jobs fine, but apparently few were paying attention. Marcus Ragnarsson was a bust, while Vlastimil Kroupa and Mike Rathje continued to play like big teddy bears.

RIGHT IDEA: More veteran defencemen, such as Doug Bodger and Al Iafrate, to contribute offensively, and again, show the youngsters the way in San Jose.

RESULT: Forget the youngsters, they're lost causes (see previous result) and since the old guys outplayed the kids, they played more often. Bodger's offensive days are behind him, but Iafrate would have been the top scoring defenceman if not for injuries.

RIGHT IDEA: Increased toughness, to make teams be on the alert for Sharks, thereby getting them off their game, and turning around from one of the league's softest teams to one of the toughest.

RESULT: Mission accomplished. The Sharks led the league with 25.3 penalty minutes per game. But, they also had the most play opportunies against, with 409, a whopping 174 more than New Jersey, which had the fewest.

RIGHT IDEA: Trading for established star goalie Ed Belfour in the hopes he could be their number one man for many years to come.

RESULT: Belfour flopped in his first partial season in San Jose, and was an unrestricted free agent at the end of the season. He signed with Dallas during the summer.

## STUFF

* Michal Sykora, later traded to Chicago, was a plus-6 in an October 6 game versus Los Angeles. That was tied for the highest in the NHL last season, and set a Sharks record.
* the Sharks set a team record with three shorthanded goals in one game versus Anaheim on October 18. They only scored six more in the other 81 games.
* Bernie Nicholls reached the 1,000 game mark last season.
* Nicholls had an eight-game assist streak, tying a club record, and tying for the second longest streak of that nature last season.
* Nolan's 31 goals were the most in team history.
* Andrei Nazarov set a team record for fastest goal from the start of a game when he did it in 15 seconds versus Vancouver on December 26.
* Ed Belfour finally got to wear #20 when he played in San Jose, which he wanted to wear to salute Vladislav Tretiak, the great Russian goalie. He was unable to get it in Chicago.

## STAT ANALYSIS

The San Jose Sharks were a team with bite last season, but it cost them. They were the most penalized team in the league.

They were shorthanded 409 times, which was 174 more than New Jersey, and 35 more than Chicago, the team with the second most power plays against. The 66 power play goals they allowed were the third most.

Let's say, for argument's sake, that the Sharks had 100 fewer penalties against. That

would put them at 309, the fifth least penalized in the league. If you use their same penalty killing percentage of 83.9%, they would have allowed a projected 50 power play goals instead of 66.

Sixteen goals over the course of a season can make a big difference, but probably not to the Sharks at this stage. They were most likely better off playing the tougher game. Who knows how many goals that saved the team.

Most Times Shorthanded:

| | |
|---|---|
| SAN JOSE | 409 |
| Chicago | 374 |
| Buffalo | 364 |
| Tampa Bay | 360 |

Fewest Times Shorthanded:

| | |
|---|---|
| New Jersey | 235 |
| Ottawa | 265 |
| Boston | 308 |
| Dallas | 308 |

## TEAM PREVIEW

GOAL: On most poor teams goaltending isn't an important issue. Once the team is in good shape on defence and forward, then goaltending becomes much more of a concern. Unless, of course, the goaltending is brutal, as it was in Arturs Irbe's final season in San Jose.

The goaltending was fine on the Sharks, with Chris Terreri and Kelly Hrudey. They didn't lose games for the team, and didn't win many. But the Blackhawks put a carrot in front of the Sharks' noses, in the name of Ed Belfour, and they bit.

Belfour wasn't entirely healthy during his stay in San Jose, but his netminding didn't make anyone else feel any better either. He was a flop, and worst of all, became a free agent at the end of the season, and turned down the Sharks', offer to sign with Dallas.

With Terreri gone to Chicago, and Wade Flaherty signed by the Islanders, that leaves Hrudey to handle the goalie chores all by himself.

Obviously, they'll find someone else, but they hadn't left any clues as of press time.

The Sharks are ranked last in goaltending, but that's not because of Hrudey who is a good NHL goalie. I kept them at the bottom of the rankings until I could see who else they got, but since they didn't get anyone else I couldn't judge them.

Hockey Annual Rating: 26 of 26

DEFENCE: A healthy Marty McSorley, Al Iafrate, Todd Gill and Doug Bodger, and you have the nucleus of an okay NHL defence. A healthy, and young, McSorley, Iafrate, Gill and Bodger and you have the nucleus of a great NHL defence.

Unfortunately, in reality, what the Sharks have from those four is a crippled, aging nucleus.

But, they have character, toughness, tenacity, experience and committment. That's the next best thing.

What the team doesn't have is any depth at this position.

The jury is still out on Mike Rathje and Vlastimil Kroupa, two big guys who play small. This season will determine whether they can play at the NHL level or not. The Sharks would dearly love to see them do that, but don't appear overly confident that it will ever happen.

Marcus Ragnarsson had an excellent rookie year, at least offensively, but last season he couldn't even get into the lineup at the start of the year. His offensive contributions were reduced to almost nothing, but he became better defensively, and that's something the Sharks would rather have.

Andrei Zyuzin, the second pick overall in last year's draft is the club's best defence prospect — check that, the only defence prospect. When he'll be ready to play in the NHL, however, is the only question. The sooner the better.

Bill Houlder, who played with Tampa Bay last season, was signed as a free agent over the summer and will help. A healthy Iafrate would help the most.

Hockey Annual Rating: 22 of 26

FORWARD: The Sharks scored the fewest goals in the league last year, so obviously there's a problem.

But, there were a lot of good things that happened with the San Jose forwards last season.

For example, Owen Nolan set a team record with 31 goals. Okay, not so great, but on this team, in a season that was way down in scoring around the league, it's not bad at all.

Jeff Friesen had his breakout season, right on time in his third year. He jumped to 62 points from 46 and has established himself as an excellent young centre.

| GOALTENDER | GPI | MINS | AVG | W | L | T | EN | SO | GA | SA | SV % |
|---|---|---|---|---|---|---|---|---|---|---|---|
| CHRIS TERRERI | 22 | 1200 | 2.75 | 6 | 10 | 3 | 4 | 0 | 55 | 553 | .901 |
| KELLY HRUDEY | 48 | 2631 | 3.19 | 16 | 24 | 5 | 4 | 0 | 140 | 1263 | .889 |
| ED BELFOUR | 13 | 757 | 3.41 | 3 | 9 | 0 | 1 | 1 | 43 | 371 | .884 |
| WADE FLAHERTY | 7 | 359 | 5.18 | 2 | 4 | 0 | 0 | 0 | 31 | 202 | .847 |
| S.J TOTALS | 82 | 4970 | 3.36 | 27 | 47 | 8 | 9 | 1 | 278 | 2398 | .884 |

Victor Kozlov finally did something. Sixteen goals and 41 points may not sound like much, but considering what he'd shown prior to last season, that's almost a miracle.

Tony Granato had an outstanding comeback season from brain surgery. Amazing really, that he could score 25 goals, or any goals for that matter. He was rewarded by winning the Masterton Trophy.

Stephen Guolla came out of nowhere to score some goals for the Sharks. He was lighting up the minors in Kentucky when he got the call, and responded with 13 goals in 43 games.

Ron Sutter came on board as a free agent and proved to be just the fourth line checking centre they needed. He's a free agent again this season, but could be signed, especially with his brother coaching. Bob Errey also helped out defensively, later in the season.

Andrei Nazarov showed himself to be the toughest Russian player yet to play in the NHL. He totaled 222 penalty minutes and even got suspended for going a little wacky. Twelve goals out of him was a bonus. A big tough European willing to scrap it out and score some goals at the same time is almost unheard of, and a good commodity. And you have to figure the guy has something going on upstairs to figure out that his hockey skills alone weren't going to keep him in the NHL.

Another positive is that the Sharks are one of the few teams that can put together two scoring lines and two checking lines.

Yet another positive is the toughness they got from their forwards. Nolan, Nazarov, Granato and Dody Wood all had more than 150 penalty minutes. That's not counting the work of enforcers Tim Hunter (free agent) and Todd Ewen.

Gee, lots of good things going on here. So, why did they stink?

Well, the thing is that while there were some good signs they weren't performing any major scoring feats. For the individuals they were good, but for a team as a whole they weren't so great. For example, 16 goals from Kozlov is great for him, but not great for the team if he's playing on one of the top two lines. Many of the players on the Sharks roster either wouldn't get a chance with other teams or would not be considered first or second line material.

As well, they might have expected more from Bernie Nicholls and Darren Turcotte, although each missed 18 games.

The Sharks picked up Shawn Burr during the summer from Tampa Bay. He's a hard-nosed winger, but won't score much.

The cupboard is pretty bare after the above-mentioned, thanks to years of stupid picks at the draft table. All kinds of wasted picks that year and previous years, because of their ridiculous scouting methods. Mostly Europeans that will never come close to making it to the NHL.

But that was a previous regime that has since been let out to pasture.

The new command is considerably smarter. Even though their top two prospects are still Europeans, they're not overrated Europeans. Zyuzin is a sure-bet at defence, and German Marco Sturm, another first-rounder from last season looks like he could be a keeper.

This year's number one draft pick, Patrick Marleau, is going to be good too, but will probably need at least one more year of junior.

Hockey Annual Rating: 5 of 26

SPECIAL TEAMS: Penalty killing was decent on the Sharks, probably because they got so much practice at it. They were shorthanded more than any other team in the league last season. That's the price you pay though, for becoming a tougher team.

Not much firepower for the power play. Nolan is one of the better snipers in the league, and Nicholls has been one of the best setup men previously, but they didn't get much help last year. Iafrate is the only one capable of being a quarterback on the power play. If he can stay healthy (doubtful) their power play should improve.

## POWER PLAY

| | G | ATT | PCT |
|---|---|---|---|
| Overall | 50 | 349 | 14.3% (20th NHL) |
| Home | 29 | 175 | 16.6% (10th NHL) |
| Road | 21 | 174 | 12.1% (24th NHL) |

11 SHORT HANDED GOALS ALLOWED (T-15th NHL)

## PENALTY KILLING

| | G | TSH | PCT |
|---|---|---|---|
| Overall | 66 | 409 | 83.9% (12th NHL) |
| Home | 33 | 189 | 82.5% (T-18th NHL) |
| Road | 33 | 220 | 85.0% (11th NHL) |

9 SHORT HANDED GOALS SCORED (T-16th NHL)

## SHARKS SPECIAL TEAMS SCORING

| Power play | G | A | PTS |
|---|---|---|---|
| NOLAN | 10 | 10 | 20 |
| NICHOLLS | 2 | 12 | 14 |
| FRIESEN | 6 | 7 | 13 |
| KOZLOV | 4 | 8 | 12 |
| HAWGOOD | 3 | 9 | 12 |
| TURCOTTE | 3 | 8 | 11 |
| GRANATO | 5 | 4 | 9 |
| IAFRATE | 3 | 4 | 7 |
| BODGER | 0 | 7 | 7 |
| RAGNARSSON | 2 | 4 | 6 |
| GILL | 0 | 5 | 5 |
| KROUPA | 2 | 2 | 4 |
| GUOLLA | 2 | 1 | 3 |
| NAZAROV | 1 | 2 | 3 |
| TANCILL | 1 | 0 | 1 |
| SUTTER | 1 | 0 | 1 |
| PELTONEN | 1 | 0 | 1 |
| RATHJE | 0 | 1 | 1 |
| MCSORLEY | 0 | 1 | 1 |

| Short handed | G | A | PTS |
|---|---|---|---|
| SUTTER | 2 | 2 | 4 |
| NICHOLLS | 1 | 3 | 4 |
| FRIESEN | 2 | 1 | 3 |
| TURCOTTE | 1 | 0 | 1 |
| MCSORLEY | 1 | 0 | 1 |
| GRANATO | 1 | 0 | 1 |
| DONOVAN | 1 | 0 | 1 |

COACHING AND MANAGEMENT: Although it may not look like it at first glance, General Manager Dean Lombardi did an outstanding job of transforming this team from hopeless losers into competitive losers. He brought in character, winning attitudes and toughness. They may lose the game, but the other team won't be prancing about without looking over their shoulders, like they used to.

Some might say he just went out and acquired a bunch of over-the-hill veterans. Well, he had to do something, because their farm system was weak from terrible drafting.

He wasn't in a position to offer much for other team's best prospects, which aren't surrendered easily anyway. So, he did the next best thing. Sure, there were older players around, but he selected them carefully. They were mostly character players with good attitudes. What else was he going to do?

The result was that they were a much-improved team. Yes, still lousy, but without the job he did, they would have been so very much worse.

There are a couple good youngsters on this team, but obviously not enough. Like most general managers, he knows the key to success is to build through the draft. That takes time, and as mentioned, many previous selections were wasted.

Another good thing Lombardi has done is

hire Darryl Sutter as coach after firing Al Sims. He just hates losing and can only make the Sharks more competitive. He will place a priority on discipline and attitude.

Hockey Annual Rating: 10 of 26

## DRAFT

| Round | Sel. | Player | Pos | Amateur Team |
|---|---|---|---|---|
| 1 | 2 | Patrick Marleau | C | Seattle (WHL) |
| 1 | 23 | Scott Hannan | D | Kelowna (WHL) |
| 4 | 82 | A. Colagiacomo | RW | Oshawa (OHL) |
| 5 | 107 | Adam Nittel | RW | Erie (OHL) |
| 7 | 163 | Joe Nusbabek | RW | Notre Dame |
| 8 | 192 | Dam Severson | LW | Prince Albert (WHL) |
| 9 | 219 | Mark Smith | C | Lethbridge (WHL) |

The interesting thing about Patrick Marleau is that if he had been born one day later he wouldn't even have been eligible for this draft. That's a pretty good indication that he's something special when he still scored 51 goals and 125 points for Seattle in the WHL.

Fourth round pick, Adam Colagiacomo, was once ranked as an early first rounder. His fall in the rankings means he has something very big to prove to everyone. Watch out for him.

PROGNOSIS: The Sharks are still a couple years away from being competitive. It's not likely they'll make a quick transition, but sometimes to make the playoffs all it takes is a couple moves and a couple surprises.

It's not likely to happen this year, but it's not a total impossibility, what with a lot of character veterans. They won't finish last though, and that's a good start.

If picking three or four possible surprise teams this season, the Sharks could be slotted in as having the fourth best chance.

## PREDICTION

Western Conference: 12th
Overall: 25th

| Team Scoring Stats | | 1996-97 | | | | CAREER | | | | | |
|---|---|---|---|---|---|---|---|---|---|---|---|
| | GP | G | A | PTS | +/- | PIM | SH | Gm | G | A | Pts |
| OWEN NOLAN | 72 | 31 | 32 | 63 | 19- | 155 | 225 | 412 | 177 | 171 | 348 |
| JEFF FRIESEN | 82 | 28 | 34 | 62 | 8- | 75 | 200 | 209 | 58 | 75 | 133 |
| BERNIE NICHOLLS | 65 | 12 | 33 | 45 | 21- | 63 | 137 | 1,057 | 469 | 710 | 1,179 |
| VIKTOR KOZLOV | 78 | 16 | 25 | 41 | 16- | 40 | 184 | 307 | 103 | 124 | 227 |
| TONY GRANATO | 76 | 25 | 15 | 40 | 7- | 159 | 231 | 571 | 216 | 217 | 433 |
| DARREN TURCOTTE | 65 | 16 | 21 | 37 | 8- | 16 | 126 | 524 | 179 | 204 | 383 |
| ANDREI NAZAROV | 60 | 12 | 15 | 27 | 4- | 222 | 116 | 129 | 22 | 27 | 49 |
| STEPHEN GUOLLA | 43 | 13 | 8 | 21 | 10- | 14 | 81 | 43 | 13 | 8 | 21 |
| TODD GILL | 79 | 0 | 21 | 21 | 20- | 101 | 101 | 718 | 59 | 231 | 290 |
| GREG HAWGOOD | 63 | 6 | 12 | 18 | 22- | 69 | 83 | 377 | 53 | 142 | 195 |

| | | | | | | | | | | | |
|---|---|---|---|---|---|---|---|---|---|---|---|
| M. RAGNARSSON | 69 | 3 | 14 | 17 | 18- | 63 | 57 | 140 | 11 | 45 | 56 |
| MARTY MCSORLEY | 57 | 4 | 12 | 16 | 6- | 186 | 74 | 832 | 102 | 235 | 337 |
| DOUG BODGER | 81 | 1 | 15 | 16 | 14- | 64 | 96 | 916 | 94 | 399 | 493 |
| SHEAN DONOVAN | 73 | 9 | 6 | 15 | 18- | 42 | 115 | 161 | 22 | 14 | 36 |
| AL IAFRATE | 38 | 6 | 9 | 15 | 10- | 91 | 91 | 778 | 150 | 304 | 454 |
| RON SUTTER | 78 | 5 | 7 | 12 | 8- | 65 | 78 | 878 | 194 | 307 | 501 |
| BOB ERREY | 66 | 4 | 8 | 12 | 5- | 47 | 72 | 824 | 168 | 204 | 372 |
| VLASTIMIL KROUPA | 35 | 2 | 6 | 8 | 17- | 12 | 24 | 103 | 4 | 18 | 22 |
| MIKE RATHJE | 31 | 0 | 8 | 8 | 1- | 21 | 22 | 147 | 3 | 31 | 34 |
| DODY WOOD | 44 | 3 | 2 | 5 | 3- | 193 | 43 | 98 | 8 | 10 | 18 |
| VILLE PELTONEN | 28 | 2 | 3 | 5 | 8- | 0 | 35 | 59 | 4 | 14 | 18 |
| CHRIS TANCILL | 25 | 4 | 0 | 4 | 5- | 8 | 20 | 132 | 17 | 31 | 48 |
| TIM HUNTER | 46 | 0 | 4 | 4 | 0 | 135 | 13 | 815 | 62 | 76 | 138 |
| RAY WHITNEY | 12 | 0 | 2 | 2 | 6- | 4 | 24 | 200 | 48 | 72 | 120 |
| TODD EWEN | 51 | 0 | 2 | 2 | 5- | 162 | 22 | 518 | 36 | 40 | 76 |
| JASON WIDMER | 2 | 0 | 1 | 1 | 1 | 0 | 0 | 7 | 0 | 1 | 1 |
| ALEXEI YEGOROV | 2 | 0 | 1 | 1 | 1 | 0 | 0 | 11 | 3 | 3 | 6 |
| IAIN FRASER | 2 | 0 | 0 | 0 | 1- | 2 | 0 | 94 | 23 | 23 | 46 |
| JAN CALOUN | 2 | 0 | 0 | 0 | 2- | 0 | 3 | 13 | 8 | 3 | 11 |
| WADE FLAHERTY | 7 | 0 | 0 | 0 | 0 | 0 | 0 | | | | |
| CHRIS LIPUMA | 8 | 0 | 0 | 0 | 2- | 22 | 4 | 72 | 0 | 9 | 9 |
| ED BELFOUR | 46 | 0 | 0 | 0 | 0 | 34 | 0 | | | | |
| KELLY HRUDEY | 48 | 0 | 0 | 0 | 0 | 0 | 0 | | | | |

## TEAM RANKINGS

| | | Conference Rank | League Rank |
|---|---|---|---|
| Record | 27-47-8 | 13 | 25 |
| Home | 14-23-4 | 13 | 26 |
| Away | 13-24-4 | 10 | 23 |
| Versus Own Conference | 23-32-1 | 12 | 23 |
| Versus Other Conference | 4-15-7 | 13 | 26 |
| Team Plus\Minus | -51 | 13 | 25 |
| Goals For | 211 | 13 | 26 |
| Goals Against | 278 | 13 | 24 |

| | | | |
|---|---|---|---|
| Average Shots For | 28.8 | 11 | 22 |
| Average Shots Against | 29.2 | 5 | 11 |
| Overtime | 3-1-8 | 3 | 5 |
| One Goal Games | 16-16 | 5 | 10 |
| Times outshooting opponent | 34 | 9 | 18 |
| Versus Teams Over .500 | 11-22-5 | 10 | 21 |
| Versus Teams Under .500 | 16-25-3 | 13 | 26 |
| First Half Record | 14-22-5 | 11 | 22 |
| Second Half Record | 13-25-3 | 13 | 25 |

## PLAYOFFS

- did not make the playoffs

## ALL-TIME LEADERS

Goals
Pat Falloon           76
Owen Nolan            60
Jeff Friesen          58

Assists
Pat Falloon           86
Johan Garpenlov       86
Kelly Kisio           78

Points
Pat Falloon           162
Jeff Friesen          133
Johan Garpenlov       132

## BEST INDIVIDUAL SEASONS

Goals
Owen Nolan        1996-97    31
Sergei Makarov    1993-94    30
Owen Nolan        1995-96    29
(with SJ only)

Assists
Kelly Kisio       1992-93    52
Johan Garpenlov   1992-93    44
Todd Elik         1993-94    41

Points
Kelly Kisio       1992-93    78
Sergei Makarov    1993-94    68
Todd Elik         1993-94    66
Johan Garpenlov   1992-93    66

## TEAM

Last 3 years

|         | GP | W  | L  | T  | Pts | %    |
|---------|----|----|----|----|-----|------|
| 1996-97 | 82 | 27 | 48 | 8  | 62  | .378 |
| 1995-96 | 82 | 20 | 55 | 7  | 47  | .287 |
| 1994-95 | 48 | 19 | 25 | 4  | 42  | .438 |

Best 3 regular seasons

| 1993-94 | 84 | 33 | 35 | 16 | 82 | .488 |
| 1994-95 | 48 | 19 | 25 | 4  | 42 | .438 |
| 1995-96 | 82 | 20 | 55 | 7  | 47 | .287 |

Worst 3 regular seasons

| 1992-93 | 84 | 11 | 71 | 2 | 24 | .143 |
| 1991-92 | 80 | 17 | 58 | 5 | 39 | .244 |
| 1995-96 | 82 | 20 | 55 | 7 | 47 | .287 |

Most Goals (min. 70 game schedule)
1995-96           252
1993-94           252
1991-92           219

Fewest Goals (min. 70 game schedule)
1996-97           211
1992-93           218
1991-92           219

Most Goals Against (min. 70 game schedule)
1992-93           414
1991-92           359
1995-96           357

Fewest Goals Against (min. 70 game schedule)
1993-94           265
1996-97           278
1995-96           357

# St. Louis Blues

Somebody stop the merry-go-round and let the Blues' fans off.

It's been a wild couple of seasons. A Mike Keenan tour of duty can accomplish that with relative ease.

Along the way there were lots of sideshows: the loss of Brendan Shanahan, Curtis Joseph and Wayne Gretzky; players in and out of the lineup as if it were a tryout camp; Brett Hull and Keenan feuds; Brett Hull and feuds with others; and financial incompetence.

Now, the Blues fans can expect a time of stability, if only to give everyone a rest — stability for stability sake, if you will.

That means you're unlikely to see Brett Hull shipped out, although it could be time. His feud with Keenan was well-publicized, but reports that teammates and new coach Joel Quenneville were tired of his act were also made known. Whether or not they're true or not is another story. For his part, Hull says he's tired of hearing things about himself in the media that are false.

Hull's jaw must also be tired though, because he seems to have lots to say about most everything. He's probably the most quoted player in the NHL, next to Gretzky.

He seems to care about the game, however, and thinks the stars should be allowed to show their skills more. The NHL has already cut down on obstruction, and whether players believe it or not, all you have to do is look at unofficial NHL summaries which note the added "obstruction charge" for restraining fouls. There are plenty of them.

There's little else they can do without hurting the integrity of the game. It's just that there are more whiners around now who think they should be running the league. In times gone by, the stars dealt with the added attention and the best ones overcame it.

Hull doesn't seem to be having a tough time of it anyway. Forty-two goals last season is like 50 in other years. What's the problem?

The game goes in cycles anyway. It's a defensive game at the moment, but either a successful all-out offensive powerhouse will come along and change attitudes, or coaches will find ways to deal with defensive schemes. Besides, there's pressure on teams that play boring styles to make things more exciting for the fans. If a team is winning and playing defensive, that's one thing, but if a team is playing defensive and losing, that's another. When they start losing fans, they'll have to change their ways.

Mike Keenan may have eventually brought a winning team to St. Louis but he was going about it in a strange way. His real success comes as a coach, battling with the GM to get the players he wants. When he also has the title of GM it makes him too aware of his fiscal responsibilities to be effective. Not that he seemed aware of them when he sprung for big bucks for free agent flops such as Joe Murphy.

Keenan's real problem was that he alienated the fans. He traded their favorites and appeared to constantly be at odds with Hull, another fave. Keenan may have thought he was the real star in St. Louis because he was going to bring them a winner, but he turned out to be the enemy. Empty seats and fan unrest sealed his fate.

Make no mistake about it though, Keenan is still one of the best coaches in the history of the game. Argue if you want, but his success speaks for itself. He hasn't taken good teams and made them win, he has taken weak teams and turned them around.

He's not perfect, however, and made lots of mistakes in St. Louis. Things don't always turn out right — even for hockey geniuses.

## SHORTS

* Hull scored his 500th goal as a St. Louis Blue, making him the 15th player to manage that feat with one team. His father also accomplished it with Chicago.
* when Craig MacTavish retired at the end of the season, he became the last helmetless player in the NHL.
* the Blues have been in the playoffs for 18 straight years, the second longest active streak behind Chicago, which is at 28.
* Al MacInnis needs just 15 games to reach the 1,000 plateau, and Geoff Courtnall needs 61.
* MacInnis is 46 away from 1,000 points, while Brett Hull is 85 points short.

## STAT ANALYSIS

The Boston Bruins broke off a string of 29 consecutive years in the playoffs when they finished with the worst record in the league last season. That moves a couple teams up the list of longest consecutive playoff appearances, including the Blues. The list below shows how rare it is now to make the playoffs for that many years.

| | |
|---|---|
| Chicago | 28 |
| ST. LOUIS | 18 |
| Detroit | 7 |
| Pittsburgh | 7 |

## TEAM PREVIEW

GOAL: Another marathon season for Grant Fuhr. He led the league in games played for the second year in a row, and third time in his career. In the last two seasons he has played 152 games.

If that's what it takes to keep him going then why not? He's 35-years-old and has a propensity to get out of shape, so there's no point saving him. He plays better the more he plays anyway.

Backup is a problem becase Jon Casey didn't do the job very well in the few times he was called on. If the Blues can sign someone else, they will. Jamie McLellan is the emergency man.

Brent Johnson was picked up from Colorado and the Blues have Scott Roche, as two youngsters who could develop.

| GOALTENDER | GPI | MINS | AVG | W | L | T | EN | SO | GA | SA | SV % |
|---|---|---|---|---|---|---|---|---|---|---|---|
| GRANT FUHR | 73 | 4261 | 2.72 | 33 | 27 | 11 | 4 | 3 | 193 | 1940 | .901 |
| JON CASEY | 15 | 707 | 3.39 | 3 | 8 | 0 | 2 | 0 | 40 | 299 | .866 |
| STL TOTALS | 82 | 4980 | 2.88 | 36 | 35 | 11 | 6 | 3 | 239 | 2245 | .894 |

Hockey Annual Rating: 23 of 26

DEFENCE: The Chris Pronger watch continues.

Will he become the player everyone expected him to be when selected second overall by Hartford in the 1993 draft?

One thing for sure is that there have been a lot of judges. And the jury is still out.

His progress has not been quick by any means, but it is there. He is showing signs of becoming a top NHL defenceman, and already is at the "very good" level.

Defencemen take longer to make their mark in the NHL. They have more to learn and their mistakes are more noticable. A forward can make mistakes, but still score a couple goals, and nobody cares. A defenceman who makes mistakes costs the team games. That just increases the pressure.

Consistency may be Pronger's last step up the ladder to respectability. At times last season he was the Blues' best defenceman, especially when Al MacInnis was out with an injury. At that time, the team thought enough of his leadership to make him an assistant captain.

MacInnis didn't have a banner year. It was the worst point production of his career, but keep in mind that goals were down everywhere, especially on the power play. The 34-year-old was still getting lots of shots, however, and even if his shot does lose some of its power, it's still among the best in the league.

Marc Begevin and Igor Kravchuk played every game last season. Dependability is what you want from those guys. Kravchuk can contribute something offensively, and Bergevin, with four assists in total, can't, although he did score a rare goal in the playoffs.

Ricard Persson won a regular spot on the blueline, but his job is by no means safe. Trent Yawney's part-time job is even further from safe.

More competition will come from youngsters, Chris McAlpine, Jamie Rivers, Rory Fitzpatrick and Libor Zabransky. All four had auditions last season, so they should be able to find something they like. McAlpine was the only one of the four who played for them in the playoffs. Rivers has shown some offensive promise, Zabransky has showed some spunk and Fitzpatrick was obtained from Montreal in the Turgeon deal. They also traded for Alexander Godynyuk from Carolina during the summer.

The Blues aren't spectacular by any means on defence, but their top four is better than many teams. Depth is a problem that they will have to address. Getting a couple solid defensive NHLers shouldn't be a problem, and they can hope one of their youngsters proves good enough to make the grade.

Hockey Annual Rating: 20 of 26

FORWARD: The Blues are going to need some help. They have a front-line centre in Pierre Turgeon, who has a rich history of scoring, slumping, scoring, slumping, getting traded, scoring, slumping and getting traded again.

The thing about Turgeon is he's almost always there at the end. If anybody ever unlocked the key to his consistency, Turgeon would be in the top five scoring every season.

Anyway you look at it, though, he's still one of the top centres in the league, and Hull is still one of the best right-wingers. It's the rest of the lineup that isn't all so great.

Geoff Courtnall got to play left wing on the top line most of the time. He and Joe Murphy have been or could be good scorers, but not consistently enough. Jim Campbell scored a lot early and then tailed off. Stephane Matteau isn't really a scorer, but he put up some decent numbers. Matteau will be gone anyway as soon as Keenan finds a team to work for and trades for him. Stephen Leach was traded to Carolina.

Harry York was a surprise find last year, but his scoring dropped off considerably. He could be a checking centre.

The rest of the Blues' forwards are retreads that don't have much going for them. Robert Petrovicky, Scott Pellerin, Craig Conroy, Pavol Dimitra are all no longer with previous teams for a reason. And the reason isn't that they were so good they could afford to let them go.

Tony Twist handles the rough stuff, with Mike Peluso gone to the Rangers as compensation for signing Larry Pleau as GM. Sergio Momesso, who scored one goal in 40 games last year, could still be around, but if he is, you have to wonder just how bad the Blues are.

The Blues weren't that low scoring a team last year, but they still have one of the weakest forward units in the league. They only have one scoring centre, and only two proven wingers they can count on to still put points on the board.

Hockey Annual Rating: 19 of 26

SPECIAL TEAMS: Mike Keenan doesn't practise the power play as a coach, which helps explain a low ranking that should have been higher. His philosophy is that if you use a set system then other teams can figure it out and stop it in the playoffs.

Maybe that logic would be okay if the Blues didn't need to worry about making the playoffs. With more teams and a lower percentages going to the post-season, it's not a given like it was a few years ago.

It's kind of like saying a goalie shouldn't play his best during the regular season because then other teams would be able to figure out his strengths, and thereby his weaknesses, and exploit them in the playoffs.

And if it were so easy to figure out other teams' power plays and stop them, Keenan teams would be better at penalty killing.

When Keenan left the Blues they were in 13th place on the power play with a 15.9% percentage. After he left, the Blues had a 14.7% effeciency percentage, and finished up 15th overall. Ironically, the penalty killing ranking rose from 25th to 14th after Keenan was replaced.

POWER PLAY

|  | G | ATT | PCT |
|---|---|---|---|
| Overall | 50 | 327 | 15.3% (15th NHL) |
| Home | 23 | 174 | 13.2% (T-24th NHL) |
| Road | 27 | 153 | 17.6% (10th NHL) |

8 SHORT HANDED GOALS ALLOWED (T-4th NHL)

PENALTY KILLING

|  | G | TSH | PCT |
|---|---|---|---|
| Overall | 55 | 332 | 83.4% (T-14th NHL) |
| Home | 31 | 168 | 81.5% (T-23rd NHL) |
| Road | 24 | 164 | 85.4% (T-9th NHL) |

9 SHORT HANDED GOALS SCORED (T-16th NHL)

BLUES SPECIAL TEAMS SCORING

| Power play | G | A | PTS |
|---|---|---|---|
| TURGEON | 5 | 22 | 27 |
| HULL | 12 | 14 | 26 |
| MACINNIS | 6 | 11 | 17 |
| PRONGER | 4 | 11 | 15 |
| COURTNALL | 4 | 10 | 14 |
| MURPHY | 4 | 7 | 11 |
| KRAVCHUK | 1 | 10 | 11 |
| CAMPBELL | 5 | 5 | 10 |
| YORK | 3 | 2 | 5 |
| RIVERS | 1 | 2 | 3 |
| DEMITRA | 2 | 0 | 2 |
| PERSSON | 1 | 1 | 2 |
| MATTEAU | 1 | 0 | 1 |
| PETROVICKY | 0 | 1 | 1 |
| PEARSON | 0 | 1 | 1 |
| MAYERS | 0 | 1 | 1 |
| LEEMAN | 0 | 1 | 1 |
| BERGEVIN | 0 | 1 | 1 |

| Short handed | G | A | PTS |
|---|---|---|---|
| MATTEAU | 2 | 1 | 3 |
| MACINNIS | 1 | 2 | 3 |
| PELLERIN | 2 | 0 | 2 |
| HULL | 2 | 0 | 2 |
| MURPHY | 1 | 1 | 2 |
| CONROY | 0 | 2 | 2 |
| CAMPBELL | 0 | 2 | 2 |
| YORK | 1 | 0 | 1 |
| YAWNEY | 0 | 1 | 1 |

COACHING AND MANAGEMENT: Okay, Keenan's departure made everybody happy, or almost everybody, but it didn't make the Blues a much better team. They had a record of 15-18-1 with Keenan, and 21-17-10 without him.

Much of the improvement came in the first 10 games or so when Quenneville took over as coach. The players were just showing their gratitude for a while before slipping back into mediocrity.

Quenneville managed to give the players a purpose, a method to their madness. They all pretty much said so.

Quenneville' problems will be more difficult to handle this year. Mostly stemming from a lack of talent on the team. Keenan was a master of getting the most out of the least, but there aren't many of that ilk around.

The Blues are on their way to becoming a better team, however, thanks to the hiring of Larry Pleau as general manager. Hired away from the Rangers, where he was vice-president of player personnel, his strength is in building a strong organization.

If ever a team needed improvement in that area it's the Blues. And not just because of Keenan. Even before him, with Ron Caron, there was never a high priority of building within the organization. If they needed players they went out and got them from somewhere else.

It is going to take Pleau some time, however, because the cupboard is pretty much bare. He can build it up and make it strong, but it's not going to help them this year.

Hockey Annual Rating: 21 of 26

DRAFT

| Round | Sel. | Player | Pos | Amateur Team |
|---|---|---|---|---|
| 2 | 40 | Tyler Rennette | C | North Bay (OHL) |
| 4 | 86 | Didier Tremblay | D | Halifax (QMJHL) |
| 4 | 98 | Jan Horacek | D | Czech Rep. |
| 4 | 106 | Jame Pollock | D | Seattle (WHL) |
| 6 | 149 | Nicholas Bilotto | D | Beauport (QMJHL) |
| 7 | 177 | Ladislav Nagy | C | Slovakia |
| 8 | 206 | Bobby Haglund | LW | Des Moines (USHL) |
| 9 | 232 | Dmitri Plekhanov | D | Russia |
| 9 | 244 | Marek Ivan | LW | Lethbridge (WHL) |

The Blues didn't have a first round pick, which isn't unusual, and didn't even know they were getting a second rounder compensatory pick for losing Gretzky as a group III free agent. With Pleau on board, it's unlikely you'll see the majority of the Blues draft picks in the later rounds anymore.

PROGNOSIS: The Blues are going down, straight out of the playoffs. Some teams have positions in which they're strong and ones in which they're weak. The Blues are weak at every position. Every single one of them.

The areas in which strengths are perceived to be are manned by old-timers whose time is running out. That includes goal with Grant

Fuhr, right wing with Brett Hull, and defence with Al MacInnis. The weakness isn't those players, however, it's the ones behind them on the depth chart.

All the signs point to disappointment, but Blues fans can take some solace in the fact that their team is being rebuilt by Pleau, and in a few years they may have an organization with budding stars and depth.

## PREDICTION

Western Conference: 9th
Overall: 20th

## STAT SECTION

| Team Scoring Stats | | 1996-97 | | | | | | CAREER | | | |
|---|---|---|---|---|---|---|---|---|---|---|---|
| | GP | G | A | PTS | +/- | PIM | SH | Gm | G | A | Pts |
| PIERRE TURGEON | 78 | 26 | 59 | 85 | 8 | 14 | 216 | 750 | 344 | 520 | 864 |
| BRETT HULL | 77 | 42 | 40 | 82 | 9- | 10 | 302 | 735 | 527 | 388 | 915 |
| GEOFF COURTNALL | 82 | 17 | 40 | 57 | 3 | 86 | 203 | 939 | 329 | 392 | 721 |
| JOE MURPHY | 75 | 20 | 25 | 45 | 1- | 69 | 151 | 597 | 186 | 239 | 425 |
| JIM CAMPBELL | 68 | 23 | 20 | 43 | 3 | 68 | 169 | 84 | 25 | 23 | 48 |
| AL MACINNIS | 72 | 13 | 30 | 43 | 2 | 65 | 296 | 985 | 261 | 693 | 954 |
| STEPHANE MATTEAU | 74 | 16 | 20 | 36 | 11 | 50 | 98 | 451 | 85 | 104 | 189 |
| CHRIS PRONGER | 79 | 11 | 24 | 35 | 15 | 143 | 147 | 281 | 28 | 76 | 104 |
| HARRY YORK | 74 | 14 | 18 | 32 | 1 | 24 | 86 | 74 | 14 | 18 | 32 |
| IGOR KRAVCHUK | 82 | 4 | 24 | 28 | 7 | 35 | 142 | 338 | 41 | 114 | 155 |
| ROBERT PETROVICKY | 44 | 7 | 12 | 19 | 2 | 10 | 54 | 126 | 17 | 24 | 41 |
| SCOTT PELLERIN | 54 | 8 | 10 | 18 | 12 | 35 | 76 | 106 | 20 | 22 | 42 |
| CRAIG CONROY | 61 | 6 | 11 | 17 | 0 | 43 | 74 | 74 | 7 | 11 | 18 |
| RICARD PERSSON | 54 | 4 | 8 | 12 | 2- | 45 | 70 | 66 | 6 | 9 | 15 |
| JAMIE RIVERS | 15 | 2 | 5 | 7 | 4- | 6 | 9 | 18 | 2 | 5 | 7 |
| CRAIG MACTAVISH | 50 | 2 | 5 | 7 | 12- | 33 | 26 | 1,093 | 213 | 267 | 480 |
| MIKE PELUSO | 64 | 2 | 5 | 7 | 0 | 226 | 37 | 435 | 38 | 52 | 90 |
| LIBOR ZABRANSKY | 34 | 1 | 5 | 6 | 1- | 44 | 26 | 34 | 1 | 5 | 6 |
| SERGIO MOMESSO | 40 | 1 | 3 | 4 | 6- | 48 | 43 | 710 | 152 | 193 | 345 |
| MARC BERGEVIN | 82 | 0 | 4 | 4 | 9- | 53 | 30 | 778 | 27 | 107 | 134 |
| PAVOL DEMITRA | 8 | 3 | 0 | 3 | 0 | 2 | 15 | 67 | 15 | 14 | 29 |
| K. SHAFRANOV | 5 | 2 | 1 | 3 | 1 | 0 | 8 | 5 | 2 | 1 | 3 |
| STEPHEN LEACH | 17 | 2 | 1 | 3 | 2- | 24 | 33 | 570 | 123 | 142 | 265 |

| | | | | | | | | | | | |
|---|---|---|---|---|---|---|---|---|---|---|---|
| ROB PEARSON | 18 | 1 | 2 | 3 | 5- | 37 | 14 | 269 | 56 | 54 | 110 |
| TONY TWIST | 64 | 1 | 2 | 3 | 8- | 121 | 21 | 322 | 7 | 11 | 18 |
| TRENT YAWNEY | 39 | 0 | 2 | 2 | 2 | 17 | 8 | 528 | 26 | 102 | 128 |
| GRANT FUHR | 73 | 0 | 2 | 2 | 0 | 6 | 0 | | | | |
| YURI KHMYLEV | 2 | 1 | 0 | 1 | 1- | 2 | 3 | 263 | 64 | 88 | 152 |
| GARY LEEMAN | 2 | 0 | 1 | 1 | 0 | 0 | 3 | 667 | 199 | 132 | 331 |
| JAMAL MAYERS | 6 | 0 | 1 | 1 | 3- | 2 | 7 | 6 | 0 | 1 | 1 |
| RORY FITZPATRICK | 8 | 0 | 1 | 1 | 4- | 8 | 6 | 50 | 0 | 3 | 3 |
| A. VASILEVSKI | 3 | 0 | 0 | 0 | 1- | 2 | 3 | 4 | 0 | 0 | 0 |
| JON CASEY | 15 | 0 | 0 | 0 | 0 | 0 | 0 | | | | |
| CHRIS MCALPINE | 15 | 0 | 0 | 0 | 2- | 24 | 3 | 39 | 0 | 3 | 3 |

## TEAM RANKINGS

| | | Conference Rank | League Rank |
|---|---|---|---|
| Record | 36-35-11 | 6 | 12 |
| Home | 17-20-4 | 10 | 21 |
| Away | 19-15-7 | 4 | 6 |
| Versus Own Conference | 27-23-6 | 4 | 10 |
| Versus Other Conference | 9-12-5 | 8 | 16 |
| Team Plus\Minus | +2 | 6 | 11 |
| Goals For | 236 | 8 | 14 |
| Goals Against | 239 | 6 | 13 |
| Average Shots For | 29.5 | 8 | 15 |
| Average Shots Against | 27.4 | 3 | 7 |
| Overtime | 1-1-11 | 7 | 13 |
| One Goal Games | 12-10 | 3 | 7 |
| Times outshooting opponent | 47 | 5 | 9 |
| Versus Teams Over .500 | 13-17-6 | 7 | 13 |
| Versus Teams Under .500 | 23-18-5 | 7 | 13 |
| First Half Record | 17-20-4 | 7 | 14 |
| Second Half Record | 19-15-7 | 5 | 8 |

## PLAYOFFS

Results: lost to Detroit 4-2
Record: 2-4
Home: 1-2
Away: 1-2
Goals For: 12 (2.0/game)
Goals Against: 13 (2.2/game)
Overtime: 0-0
Power play: 13.5% (12th)
Penalty Killing: 85.7% (7th)

| | GP | G | A | PTS | +/- | PIM | PP | SH | GW | OT | S |
|---|---|---|---|---|---|---|---|---|---|---|---|
| BRETT HULL | 6 | 2 | 7 | 9 | 4 | 2 | 0 | 0 | 0 | 0 | 25 |
| GEOFF COURTNALL | 6 | 3 | 1 | 4 | 0 | 23 | 1 | 0 | 2 | 0 | 11 |
| PAVOL DEMITRA | 6 | 1 | 3 | 4 | 3 | 6 | 0 | 0 | 0 | 0 | 8 |
| AL MACINNIS | 6 | 1 | 2 | 3 | 1- | 4 | 1 | 0 | 0 | 0 | 22 |
| PIERRE TURGEON | 5 | 1 | 1 | 2 | 0 | 2 | 1 | 0 | 0 | 0 | 8 |
| JOE MURPHY | 6 | 1 | 1 | 2 | 2- | 10 | 1 | 0 | 0 | 0 | 8 |
| CHRIS PRONGER | 6 | 1 | 1 | 2 | 0 | 22 | 0 | 0 | 0 | 0 | 19 |
| JIM CAMPBELL | 4 | 1 | 0 | 1 | 1- | 6 | 1 | 0 | 0 | 0 | 6 |
| MARC BERGEVIN | 6 | 1 | 0 | 1 | 2 | 8 | 0 | 0 | 0 | 0 | 4 |
| CHRIS MCALPINE | 4 | 0 | 1 | 1 | 1 | 0 | 0 | 0 | 0 | 0 | 6 |
| CRAIG MACTAVISH | 1 | 0 | 0 | 0 | 1- | 2 | 0 | 0 | 0 | 0 | 0 |
| IGOR KRAVCHUK | 2 | 0 | 0 | 0 | 1- | 2 | 0 | 0 | 0 | 0 | 6 |
| R. PETROVICKY | 2 | 0 | 0 | 0 | 1 | 0 | 0 | 0 | 0 | 0 | 1 |
| SERGIO MOMESSO | 3 | 0 | 0 | 0 | 0 | 6 | 0 | 0 | 0 | 0 | 0 |
| S. MATTEAU | 5 | 0 | 0 | 0 | 0 | 0 | 0 | 0 | 0 | 0 | 2 |
| MIKE PELUSO | 5 | 0 | 0 | 0 | 1- | 25 | 0 | 0 | 0 | 0 | 1 |
| HARRY YORK | 5 | 0 | 0 | 0 | 1- | 2 | 0 | 0 | 0 | 0 | 2 |
| GRANT FUHR | 6 | 0 | 0 | 0 | 0 | 4 | 0 | 0 | 0 | 0 | 0 |
| STEPHEN LEACH | 6 | 0 | 0 | 0 | 2- | 33 | 0 | 0 | 0 | 0 | 8 |
| TONY TWIST | 6 | 0 | 0 | 0 | 0 | 0 | 0 | 0 | 0 | 0 | 0 |
| CRAIG CONROY | 6 | 0 | 0 | 0 | 1- | 8 | 0 | 0 | 0 | 0 | 4 |
| SCOTT PELLERIN | 6 | 0 | 0 | 0 | 1- | 6 | 0 | 0 | 0 | 0 | 7 |
| RICARD PERSSON | 6 | 0 | 0 | 0 | 1- | 27 | 0 | 0 | 0 | 0 | 1 |

| GOALTENDER | GPI | MINS | AVG | W | L | T | EN | SO | GA | SA | SV % |
|---|---|---|---|---|---|---|---|---|---|---|---|
| GRANT FUHR | 6 | 357 | 2.18 | 2 | 4 | 0 | 2 | 0 | 13 | 183 | .929 |
| STL TOTALS | 6 | 360 | 2.17 | 2 | 4 | 0 | 2 | 0 | 13 | 183 | .929 |

## ALL-TIME LEADERS

### Goals
| | |
|---|---|
| Brett Hull | 500 |
| Bernie Federko | 352 |
| Brian Sutter | 303 |

### Assists
| | |
|---|---|
| Bernie Federko | 721 |
| Brett Hull | 364 |
| Brian Sutter | 334 |

### Points
| | |
|---|---|
| Bernie Federko | 1,073 |
| Brett Hull | 864 |
| Brian Sutter | 636 |

## BEST INDIVIDUAL SEASONS

### Goals
| | | |
|---|---|---|
| Brett Hull | 1990-91 | 86 |
| Brett Hull | 1989-90 | 72 |
| Brett Hull | 1991-92 | 70 |

### Assists
| | | |
|---|---|---|
| Adam Oates | 1990-91 | 90 |
| Craig Janney | 1992-93 | 82 |
| Adam Oates | 1989-90 | 79 |

### Points
| | | |
|---|---|---|
| Brett Hull | 1990-91 | 131 |
| Adam Oates | 1990-91 | 115 |
| Brett Hull | 1989-90 | 113 |

## TEAM

### Last 3 years
| | GP | W | L | T | Pts | % |
|---|---|---|---|---|---|---|
| 1996-97 | 82 | 36 | 35 | 11 | 82 | .506 |
| 1995-96 | 82 | 32 | 34 | 16 | 80 | .488 |
| 1994-95 | 48 | 28 | 15 | 5 | 61 | .635 |

### Best 3 regular seasons
| | | | | | | |
|---|---|---|---|---|---|---|
| 1980-81 | 80 | 45 | 18 | 17 | 107 | .669 |
| 1990-91 | 80 | 47 | 22 | 11 | 105 | .656 |
| 1994-95 | 48 | 28 | 15 | 5 | 61 | .635 |

### Worst 3 regular seasons
| | | | | | | |
|---|---|---|---|---|---|---|
| 1978-79 | 80 | 18 | 50 | 12 | 48 | .300 |
| 1977-78 | 80 | 20 | 47 | 13 | 53 | .331 |
| 1982-83 | 80 | 25 | 40 | 15 | 65 | .406 |

### Most Goals (min. 70 game schedule)
| | |
|---|---|
| 1980-81 | 352 |
| 1981-82 | 315 |
| 1990-91 | 310 |

### Fewest Goals (min. 70 game schedule)
| | |
|---|---|
| 1967-68 | 177 |
| 1968-69 | 204 |
| 1973-74 | 206 |

### Most Goals Against (min. 70 game schedule)
| | |
|---|---|
| 1981-82 | 349 |
| 1978-79 | 348 |
| 1982-83 | 316 |
| 1983-84 | 316 |

### Fewest Goals Against (min. 70 game schedule)
| | |
|---|---|
| 1968-69 | 157 |
| 1969-70 | 179 |
| 1967-68 | 191 |

# Toronto Maple Leafs

This space had been reserved to recap the insanity of last season. Little did we know, however, that there would be no off-season in the craziness department at Maple Leaf Gardens.

When Ken Dryden was hired as president everything was going to be right again in Leaf Land.

Dryden was supposed to bring a new level of intelligence to the hockey process. We've read his books, we know he has deep thoughts. Instead, with no experience in the job for which he was hired, his early work was closer in line to a bungling lunatic.

His main job (only job?) was to find a new general manager. Dryden decided his old teammate, Bob Gainey was his man. The only problem was that he was already employed by Dallas. Two winning seasons in six was was just too irresistable, however, so Dryden was willing to surrender Mathieu Schneider as compensation to the Stars for hiring Gainey.

The Leafs only have about three players who could even make the Dallas team, and Schneider was one of them. To offer that much for a GM who isn't even considered among the elite in the game, was ridiculous. Gainey ended up declining, one of the reasons being family considerations, which is fair, but probably another was that he didn't want to work for an organization that would give up a premier NHL defenceman for him.

Next in line was David Poile, ex of the Washington Capitals for many years.

More funny business there with Poile saying the job had been offered to him and that he had refused it. Dryden refuted that...maybe. He orated on the world of self-discovery and how it could be lifted to new heights by those seeking a job as a hockey general manager in Toronto. And you thought you had to go to the mountains of Tibet.

While this was going on, assistant GM to Cliff Fletcher, Bill Watters, was self-discovering that he could take care of business just fine. He signed free agents Mike Kennedy, Derek King, Kris King and Glenn Healy.

Watters kept to the party line about just filling in until a GM was hired, even when the days dragged into weeks and at least one month. Meanwhile, Dryden, whose search for self-discovery was more succesful than his search for a GM, was talking code in interviews and sounding like he was ready to crack.

At press time, Dryden had yet to start turning around on the ground like Curly of the Three Stooges, but he was probably asking himself on a daily basis what he had gotten himself into.

One thing for sure that he'll get out of this job — a whole heaping mess of self-discovery.

## STUFF

* 231 goals were the fewest since the 1971-

72 season when they had 209.
* 12 players made their NHL debuts with Toronto last season: Sergei Berezin, Fredrik Modin, David Cooper, Mike Johnson, Nathan Dempsey, D.J. Smith, Yanick Tremblay, Shayne Toporowski, Brian Wiseman, Marcel Cousineau, Jeff Ware and John Craighead.
* Jamie Macoun is 15 games away from the 1,000 mark.

## STAT ANALYSIS

Ever play the IF game? It's fun, the kind of thing you do when you have a whole season on your hands and the local team stinks.

Ready? Let's go.

IF: Steve Sullivan had played the whole season in Toronto, would he have been rookie of the year?

Sullivan had 16 points in 21 games for the Leafs. Projected over 82 games that would give him a total of 62 points. The top rookie scorer, Jarome Iginla, only had 50 points, so Sullivan would have been a clear favorite in the rookie race.

IF: Felix Potvin had played for Detroit, what would be his goals against average.

Detroit averaged 25.3 shots against last year; Toronto averaged 34.4 against.

If Potvin had faced 25.3 shots per 60 minutes instead of 34.4 he would have faced 637 fewer shots. At his save percentage of .908, it

would have resulted in 59 fewer goals against.

His revised goals against average would be 2.32. Almost a goal better than the 3.15 he earned with Toronto.

## TEAM PREVIEW

GOAL: One day Felix Potvin looks like a first team all-star, and the next day he looks like a 26th team all-star. Inconsistency has plagued him throughout his career in Toronto. The thing is, it's almost worth putting up with the bad times because the good times are, oh, so good.

One thing for certain, he's not a 70-game goalie. He needs time off just to re-focus. There's no reason why Marcel Cousineau couldn't have played more last season. He did a fine job when he got the chance, but the Leafs weren't interested. Even when it was obvious they weren't going to make the playoffs Cousineau just wasted away on the bench.

Potvin will get a challenge this year from free agent signee Glenn Healy. Healy is 35-years-old, but he's still getting the job done, and has been a perfect compliment to Mike Richter on the Rangers for a number of years. He's even outplayed Richter at times, including some playoffs. But because his role is as backup, he always reverted back.

Healy is going to have some periods during the season when the Leafs won't be able to take him out of the net. He's no threat to Potvin as the number one, but Potvin is going to have to

| GOALTENDER | GPI | MINS | AVG | W | L | T | EN | SO | GA | SA | SV % |
|---|---|---|---|---|---|---|---|---|---|---|---|
| FELIX POTVIN | 74 | 4271 | 3.15 | 27 | 36 | 7 | 6 | 0 | 224 | 2438 | .908 |
| MARCEL COUSINEAU | 13 | 566 | 3.29 | 3 | 5 | 1 | 1 | 1 | 31 | 317 | .902 |
| DON BEAUPRE | 3 | 110 | 5.45 | 0 | 3 | 0 | 1 | 0 | 10 | 60 | .833 |
| TOR TOTALS | 82 | 4966 | 3.30 | 30 | 44 | 8 | 8 | 2 | 273 | 2823 | .903 |

FELIX POTVIN and MARCEL COUSINEAU shared a shutout vs STL on Dec 3, 1996

wake up and play well consistently if he wants to maintain his status as the top guy.

Hockey Annual Rating: 12 of 26

DEFENCE: Let's get something straight here about Larry Murphy.

Toronto fans booed him unmercifully last year. That prompted analysis from every quarter: he was the scapegoat for the Leafs' lousy season or people were joining in the booing because it was the thing to do. As well, the "knowledgeable" fans in Toronto were drawn into question by certain media types, suggesting they didn't know hockey. Even Murphy, after he made good with a Stanley Cup in Detroit, suggested the same thing.

Here is the real reason he was booed so much when he a Maple Leaf. He was brutal. Good for him that he played better in Detroit, but in Toronto the fans showed how knowledgable they really were.

This is what Murphy did that knowledgable hockey fans picked up (including one 10-year-old rep hockey player). Murphy almost always moved in from his point area when the puck was in the attacking zone. Incredibly, but true, he even did this when killing penalties. Because he was so slow, opposing teams had the simple task of simply knocking it around the boards on Murphy's side, outracing him easily for the puck and (with another forward in on the plan) jaunt down the ice on a two-on-one. It happened over and over again, sometimes a couple times in one game. It was so ridiculous.

Never mind his other faults, which knowledgeable hockey fans in Toronto also knew about.

With the Wings, his mistakes were more easily covered, and in fairness to Murphy, he wasn't expected to do as much.

In Toronto, virtually everyone has exposure to hockey, apart from the NHL, in one form or another. There are more knowledgable people in Maple Leaf Gardens on any given night than anywhere in the league. If someone wants to question their knowledge of the game, then the "knowledge" of the person doing the questioning should be even more seriously challenged.

So, here's some more knowledge for you. The Leafs' best defenceman is Mathieu Schneider. He can play offence, defence, and has a mean streak. He's also one of only a couple who could play regularly for a good NHL team.

After that, there's Jason Smith, a big young player who is coming along.

After that, it's trouble.

Jamie Macoun is a veteran who could help a good team as a sixth defenceman. On the Leafs, he might have been the one booed if not for Murphy. Craig Wolanin is a big, slow guy, who doesn't play as physically as he should. Dimitri Yuskevich, went AWOL last season when he was benched. Yuskevich should be holding parties every week to thank the Leafs brass for keeping him on the team. D.J. Smith and Jeff Ware are unproven at the NHL level, as is big prospect Marek Posmyk.

The Leafs traded for Per Gustafsson from Florida during the summer. He couldn't crack the Panthers lineup because they didn't like the fact that he was unphysical and generally untalented. That makes him a good fit for the Leafs, however, and he should be a regular. He should add some offence, at least.

Overall, the Leaf defence is still brutal, but they made headway in getting rid of Dave Ellett and Murphy. The youngsters should get a lot of opportunity to play. Ideally, you want to bring the kids along slowly by pairing them with veterans and learning the game. Since the Leafs don't have anyone that youngsters should be learning from, they're on their own.

Hockey Annual Rating: 24 of 26

FORWARD: There is some hope. Not much, but some.

Mats Sundin is coming off an outstanding season. He tired in the second half, but that was from trying to carry the team the whole first half. Despite all he did, he still took some heat. Seventh in the league in scoring on one of the worst teams and still it wasn't enough.

Mats Sundin is Mats Sundin, and Wendel Clark is Wendel Clark. Clark piles in the goals for weeks at time, and then nothing for more weeks at a time. At least he's consistently inconsistent.

Sergei Berezin scored 25 goals last year, but is as clueless about the game as they come. That he could still score 25 goals is a tribute...to something.

As for the rest of the offence, there is Steve Sullivan, who had a decent rookie year after being acquired from the Devils, and there is free agent signee Derek King. He had a pretty good year, scoring 26 goals, most of them on the Islanders top line before he was traded to Hartford. He might be able to take advantage of Sundin's playmaking ability.

Assuming the Leafs can make up a decent scoring line, the rest of the roster is composed of role players. All of them are non-scorers, although Todd Warriner earned much praise for filling the nets with 12 goals.

The truth is that most of the Toronto forwards are fourth-liners, and few would have even earned that opportunity with most teams. Warriner did show something at times last year, as did Darby Hendrickson, and Tie Domi is as valuable an enforcer as there is. Free agent signee Kris King will give the Leafs some toughness and character, but he won't score. Nick Kypreos fills the same role as King, and uh, so does Kelly Chase. If nothing else, the Leafs should win some fights.

Mike Kennedy, another free agent, couldn't play on Dallas, but on Toronto he should get plenty of action.

Fredrik Modin should not have even been allowed to step into an NHL arena last season. He probably had something in his contract that wouldn't allow him to go to the minors. He Leafs were so bad, that sometimes he was even put on the top line. Every couple months, Modin would do some crashing and banging, and the pundits, trying desperately to find something positive, would jump all over themselves praising him. Modin may very well have been the worst regular forward in the NHL last season. That's not to say Modin couldn't make himself a useful NHLer. He has a good shot afterall, which he never uses, but the odds are about the same as Berezin winning the Selke trophy as best defensive forward.

As is typical with sinking ships, the blame gets handed out in strange places. Jamie Baker did exactly what he's done to make himself a valuable NHL defensive centre, but found himself being accused of underachieving, and then was banished to the press box. No wonder he let loose with some temper tantrums during the season.

Jason Podollan and especially Mike Johnson, looked good in limited time with the Maple Leafs, and Toronto has signed another Czech prospect in Martin Prochazka who will be pushed right into the lineup.

A lot of hope is resting on the shoulders of Alyn McCauley. The CHL player of the year has the right stuff to be an excellent two-way forward.

Free agents are going to help move the Toronto forward situation closer to the respectable level. But, that's about it. They are so far away from the "good" level, it's not funny.

It's good to add character players, which

they've done, but on this team that's sort of like putting icing on mud pies.

Hockey Annual Rating: 25 of 26

SPECIAL TEAMS: Hey, something the Leafs are good at. Well, not good, but hey, they're not one of the worst.

There is no reason, however to think they can improve on their rankings this season. Maybe with Schneider playing the full year, but that's not enough to compensate for the loss of Gilmour.

POWER PLAY

|  | G | ATT | PCT |
|---|---|---|---|
| Overall | 48 | 309 | 15.5% (14th NHL) |
| Home | 24 | 155 | 15.5% (14th NHL) |
| Road | 24 | 154 | 15.6% (15th NHL) |

8 SHORT HANDED GOALS ALLOWED (T-4th NHL)

PENALTY KILLING

|  | G | TSH | PCT |
|---|---|---|---|
| Overall | 59 | 328 | 82.0% (19th NHL) |
| Home | 28 | 162 | 82.7% (17th NHL) |
| Road | 31 | 166 | 81.3% (T-19th NHL) |

11 SHORT HANDED GOALS SCORED (T-9th NHL)

MAPLE LEAFS SPECIAL TEAMS SCORING

| Power play | G | A | PTS |
|---|---|---|---|
| SUNDIN | 7 | 13 | 20 |
| BEREZIN | 7 | 5 | 12 |
| CLARK | 6 | 6 | 12 |
| SULLIVAN | 3 | 5 | 8 |
| WARRINER | 2 | 5 | 7 |
| SCHNEIDER | 1 | 4 | 5 |
| COOPER | 2 | 2 | 4 |
| DOMI | 2 | 1 | 3 |
| CRAIG | 1 | 2 | 3 |
| YUSHKEVICH | 1 | 1 | 2 |
| PEDERSON | 1 | 1 | 2 |
| NEDVED | 1 | 1 | 2 |
| BAKER | 1 | 1 | 2 |
| HEWARD | 0 | 2 | 2 |
| CONVERY | 0 | 2 | 2 |
| PODOLLAN | 1 | 0 | 1 |
| HENDRICKSON | 0 | 1 | 1 |

| Short handed | G | A | PTS |
|---|---|---|---|
| SUNDIN | 4 | 3 | 7 |
| WARRINER | 2 | 0 | 2 |
| YUSHKEVICH | 1 | 0 | 1 |
| JOHNSON | 1 | 0 | 1 |
| HENDRICKSON | 1 | 0 | 1 |
| SULLIVAN | 0 | 1 | 1 |
| MACOUN | 0 | 1 | 1 |
| CONVERY | 0 | 1 | 1 |
| BAKER | 0 | 1 | 1 |

COACHING AND MANAGEMENT: It's difficult to tell if Mike Murphy is a good coach or not. The team was bad before he got there, and he was unable to perform a miracle. He did, however, gain lots of experience in trying every method imaginable. But, it was like trying to paddle across the Pacific in a canoe.

There was no GM at press time and Ken Dryden was still coming to some more "self realization" about the job. Puh-leeeeeze.

The irony in the firing of Cliff Fletcher was that after a year or two absence from the job, he resurfaced and looked to be making giant strides in the right direction. Maybe he wouldn't have had to make those strides, however, if he hadn't disappeared for a while and fallen out of touch with the game.

The new GM (Yes, I will accept the job) will have to do the following. Get the free agents as a stop-gap measure, just as Watters did during Dryden's search for truth; build up the organization with young talent, that doesn't come from Europe; and stick to a plan.

The people of Toronto can accept rebuilding. As long as they have hope, and a convenient excuse for losing.

Hockey Annual Rating: 25 of 26

## DRAFT

| Round | Sel. | Player | Pos | Amateur Team |
|---|---|---|---|---|
| 3 | 57 | Jeff Farkas | C | Boston College |
| 4 | 84 | Adam Mair | C | Owen Sound (OHL) |
| 5 | 111 | Frantisek Mrazek | C | Czech Rep. |
| 6 | 138 | Eric Gooldy | LW | Detroit (OHL) |
| 7 | 165 | Hugo Marchand | D | Victoriaville (QMJHL) |
| 7 | 190 | Shawn Thornton | RW | Peterborough (OHL) |
| 8 | 194 | Russ Barlett | C | Phillips-Exeter (USHS) |
| 9 | 221 | J. Hedstrom | W | Sweden |

Jeff Farkas is a speedy guy who needs to put on weight to be more effective. When a team doesn't draft until the third round their main concern is not letting it happen again.

## PROGNOSIS

The Leafs are still one of the worst teams in the league, but at least now they're offering some hope, if ever so slight. As for this year, forget it. They'll have some tougher players with character, but it's not near enough.

## PREDICTION

Western Conference: 11th
Overall: 24th

## STAT SECTION

| Team Scoring Stats | 1996-97 | | | | | | | CAREER | | | |
|---|---|---|---|---|---|---|---|---|---|---|---|
| | GP | G | A | PTS | +/- | PIM | SH | Gm | G | A | Pts |
| MATS SUNDIN | 82 | 41 | 53 | 94 | 6 | 59 | 281 | 529 | 232 | 326 | 558 |
| WENDEL CLARK | 65 | 30 | 19 | 49 | 2- | 75 | 212 | 636 | 282 | 209 | 491 |
| SERGEI BEREZIN | 73 | 25 | 16 | 41 | 3- | 2 | 177 | 73 | 25 | 16 | 41 |
| STEVE SULLIVAN | 54 | 13 | 25 | 38 | 14 | 37 | 108 | 70 | 18 | 29 | 47 |
| TODD WARRINER | 75 | 12 | 21 | 33 | 3- | 41 | 146 | 137 | 19 | 29 | 48 |
| TIE DOMI | 80 | 11 | 17 | 28 | 17- | 275 | 98 | 406 | 38 | 54 | 91 |
| MIKE CRAIG | 65 | 7 | 13 | 20 | 20- | 62 | 128 | 420 | 71 | 97 | 168 |
| D. HENDRICKSON | 64 | 11 | 6 | 17 | 20- | 47 | 105 | 134 | 18 | 17 | 35 |
| JAMIE BAKER | 58 | 8 | 8 | 16 | 2 | 28 | 69 | 390 | 71 | 73 | 144 |
| D. YUSHKEVICH | 74 | 4 | 10 | 14 | 24- | 56 | 99 | 340 | 20 | 81 | 101 |
| ROB ZETTLER | 48 | 2 | 12 | 14 | 8 | 51 | 31 | 418 | 4 | 48 | 54 |
| FREDRIK MODIN | 76 | 6 | 7 | 13 | 14- | 24 | 85 | 76 | 6 | 7 | 13 |

| | | | | | | | | | | |
|---|---|---|---|---|---|---|---|---|---|---|
| M. SCHNEIDER | 26 | 5 | 7 | 12 | 3 | 20 | 63 | 477 | 84 | 190 | 274 |
| JAMIE MACOUN | 73 | 1 | 10 | 11 | 14- | 93 | 64 | 985 | 75 | 265 | 340 |
| BRANDON CONVERY | 39 | 2 | 8 | 10 | 9- | 20 | 41 | 50 | 7 | 10 | 17 |
| ZDENEK NEDVED | 23 | 3 | 5 | 8 | 4 | 6 | 22 | 390 | 4 | 6 | 10 |
| JASON SMITH | 78 | 1 | 7 | 8 | 12- | 54 | 74 | 185 | 3 | 13 | 16 |
| DAVID COOPER | 19 | 3 | 3 | 6 | 3- | 16 | 23 | 19 | 3 | 3 | 6 |
| NICK KYPREOS | 35 | 3 | 2 | 5 | 1 | 62 | 18 | 442 | 46 | 44 | 90 |
| JAMIE HEWARD | 20 | 1 | 4 | 5 | 6- | 6 | 23 | 25 | 1 | 4 | 5 |
| JASON PODOLLAN | 29 | 1 | 4 | 5 | 5- | 10 | 30 | 29 | 1 | 4 | 5 |
| MIKE JOHNSON | 13 | 2 | 2 | 4 | 2- | 4 | 27 | 13 | 2 | 2 | 4 |
| MATT MARTIN | 36 | 0 | 4 | 4 | 12- | 38 | 30 | 76 | 0 | 5 | 5 |
| CRAIG WOLANIN | 38 | 0 | 4 | 4 | 6- | 21 | 43 | 685 | 40 | 133 | 173 |
| TOM PEDERSON | 15 | 1 | 2 | 3 | 0 | 9 | 23 | 240 | 20 | 49 | 69 |
| KELLY CHASE | 30 | 1 | 2 | 3 | 2 | 149 | 6 | 321 | 10 | 25 | 35 |
| FELIX POTVIN | 74 | 0 | 3 | 3 | 0 | 19 | 0 | | | | |
| NATHAN DEMPSEY | 14 | 1 | 1 | 2 | 2- | 2 | 11 | 14 | 1 | 1 | 2 |
| KELLY FAIRCHILD | 22 | 0 | 2 | 2 | 5- | 2 | 14 | 23 | 0 | 3 | 3 |
| D.J. SMITH | 8 | 0 | 1 | 1 | 5- | 7 | 4 | 8 | 0 | 1 | 1 |
| MARCEL COUSINEAU | 13 | 0 | 1 | 1 | 0 | 0 | 0 | | | | |
| SCOTT PEARSON | 1 | 0 | 0 | 0 | 0 | 2 | 0 | 290 | 56 | 41 | 97 |
| GREG SMYTH | 2 | 0 | 0 | 0 | 0 | 0 | 1 | 229 | 4 | 16 | 20 |
| DON BEAUPRE | 3 | 0 | 0 | 0 | 0 | 0 | 0 | | | | |
| BRIAN WISEMAN | 3 | 0 | 0 | 0 | 0 | 0 | 1 | 3 | 0 | 0 | 0 |
| S. TOPOROWSKI | 3 | 0 | 0 | 0 | 0 | 7 | 3 | 3 | 0 | 0 | 0 |
| YANNICK TREMBLAY | 5 | 0 | 0 | 0 | 4- | 0 | 2 | 5 | 0 | 0 | 0 |
| JOHN CRAIGHEAD | 5 | 0 | 0 | 0 | 0 | 10 | 0 | 5 | 0 | 0 | 0 |
| MARK KOLESAR | 7 | 0 | 0 | 0 | 3- | 0 | 3 | 28 | 2 | 2 | 4 |
| JEFF WARE | 13 | 0 | 0 | 0 | 2 | 6 | 4 | 13 | 0 | 0 | 0 |

## TEAM RANKINGS

|  |  | Conference Rank | League Rank |
|---|---|---|---|
| Record | 30-44-8 | 11 | 23 |
| Home | 18-20-3 | 9 | 20 |
| Away | 12-24-5 | 11 | 21 |
| Versus Own Conference | 22-29-5 | 9 | 19 |
| Versus Other Conference | 8-15-3 | 12 | 22 |
| Team Plus\Minus | -32 | 11 | 22 |
| Goals For | 230 | 9 | 17 |
| Goals Against | 273 | 11 | 21 |
| Average Shots For | 29.3 | 9 | 17 |
| Average Shots Against | 34.4 | 13 | 26 |
| Overtime | 1-1-8 | 9 | 16 |
| One Goal Games | 11-13 | 10 | 18 |
| Times outshooting opponent | 24 | 11 | 22 |
| Versus Teams Over .500 | 11-26-6 | 12 | 24 |
| Versus Teams Under .500 | 19-18-2 | 9 | 16 |
| First Half Record | 17-24-0 | 10 | 21 |
| Second Half Record | 13-20-8 | 12 | 23 |

## PLAYOFFS

- did not make the playoffs

## ALL-TIME LEADERS

Goals
Darryl Sittler    389
Dave Keon        365
Ron Ellis        332

Assists
Borje Salming    620
Darryl Sittler   527
Dave Keon        493

Points
Darryl Sittler   916
Dave Keon        858
Borje Salming    768

## BEST INDIVIDUAL SEASONS

Goals
Rick Vaive         1981-82    54
Dave Andreychuk    1993-94    53
Rick Vaive         1983-84    52

Assists
Doug Gilmour       1992-93    95
Doug Gilmour       1993-94    84
Darryl Sittler     1977-78    72

Points
Doug Gilmour       1992-93    127
Darryl Sittler     1977-78    117
Doug Gilmour       1993-94    111

## TEAM

Last 3 years

|  | GP | W | L | T | Pts | % |
|---|---|---|---|---|---|---|
| 1996-97 | 82 | 30 | 44 | 8 | 68 | .415 |
| 1995-96 | 82 | 34 | 36 | 12 | 80 | .488 |
| 1994-95 | 48 | 21 | 19 | 8 | 50 | .521 |

Best 3 regular seasons

| 1950-51 | 70 | 41 | 16 | 13 | 95 | .679 |
|---|---|---|---|---|---|---|
| 1934-35 | 48 | 30 | 14 | 4 | 64 | .667 |
| 1940-41 | 48 | 28 | 14 | 6 | 62 | .646 |

Worst 3 regular seasons

| | | | | | | |
|---|---|---|---|---|---|---|
| 1918-19 | 18 | 5 | 13 | 0 | 10 | .278 |
| 1984-85 | 80 | 20 | 52 | 8 | 48 | .300 |
| 1987-88 | 80 | 21 | 49 | 10 | 52 | .325 |

Most Goals (min. 70 game schedule)

| | |
|---|---|
| 1989-90 | 337 |
| 1980-81 | 322 |
| 1985-86 | 311 |

Fewest Goals (min. 70 game schedule)

| | |
|---|---|
| 1954-55 | 147 |
| 1953-54 | 152 |
| 1955-56 | 153 |

Most Goals Against (min. 70 game schedule)

| | |
|---|---|
| 1983-84 | 387 |
| 1985-86 | 386 |
| 1981-82 | 380 |

Fewest Goals Against (min. 70 game schedule)

| | |
|---|---|
| 1953-54 | 131 |
| 1954-55 | 135 |
| 1950-51 | 130 |

# Vancouver Canucks

If you had to pick one word to describe the Canucks last season it would be...disappointing.

Okay, need another word. How about ridiculous.

Another one? Joke.

This team should have made the playoffs. Before the season started, they weren't even on the bubble, they were in it — easily.

Hopes were high. They coulda been a contenda.

So, what went wrong?

For one thing the team lacked character. For another they lacked physical toughness. For another they lacked dedication and committment.

Their star player, Mogilny, won the award last season for "Biggest Whiner." They didn't have a centreman he liked. Awww....

Actually, they should have had one, but that's still no excuse for his lousy season. The former 76 and 55 goal scorer should have popped in more than 31 goals even if Wilt Chamberlain was his centre. Maybe a practice or two with Mark Messier will help.

The team started the season off decently enough. In late November, they were in fifth place overall with a 13-9-0 record. Optimism was running rampant. Six games later, they would be above .500 for the last time.

A good example of the kind of year it was for Vancouver came after they pummelled St. Louis 8-0 in a road game in December. In their next contest they could manage just eight shots. In case you didn't hear correctly, that was eight shots in the entire game.

Another indication of the Canucks up and down play is shown by their up and down monthly records from November through February:

|  |  |
|---|---|
| November | 8-5-0 |
| December | 3-9-1 |
| January | 8-4-1 |
| February | 4-9-0 |

Oh, there were lots of injury problems too. Pavel Bure and Trevor Linden both missed considerable time. But, the Canucks were 7-7-5 when Bure wasn't in the lineup, better than when he was, and 13-16-4 without Linden. When Mogilny wasn't up to putting on the uniform the Canucks were undefeated, with a mark of 4-0-2.

The thing that points to attitude mostly is that they played well in big games and poorly against weak ones (see stat analysis). That's a problem also reflected in the softness of their players. The top penalty minute earner among their top 13 scorers was David Roberts, with 51. Mike Ridley, a very unaggressive player, was tied for second with 42.

Gutless was another word used in reference to the Canucks last season. And one thing gutless teams have in common is losing.

## SHORTS

* Gino Odjick became the team's all-time penalty minute leader, with 1,946, passing Garth Butcher's mark of 1,668.
* Trevor Linden's ironman streak ended at 482 games when he suffered a knee injury in early December.
* Mogilny needs three goals to reach 300 for his career.
* if Linden can get 23 goals this season he will become the all-time leading Canucks goal scorer.
* Jyrki Lumme became the all-time leading defenceman goal scorer for the Canucks last season, when he passed Doug Lidster, who had 66. Lumme has 74.
* the Canucks had just eight shots in a game at home versus New Jersey, the lowest in team history.
* With 371 penalty minutes, Gino Odjick broke his own single-season team record of 370, set in 1992-93,
* In January of last season, the Canucks had eight wins, a team record for that month.
* the Canucks had five overtime wins last season. In the two seasons prior to last year, they had a total of one OT victory.
* Mike Fountain became the 19th player in league history to earn a shutout in his NHL debut.

## STAT ANALYSIS

Maybe Martin Gelinas got tired of waiting for the superstars to start filling the net, so he just started doing it himself. The list below shows goal scorers since the all-star break, last season. Gelinas had twice as many as anybody else on the Canucks, and the second most in the league, after Paul Kariya.

Vancouver Goal Scorers After The All-Star Break:

| | |
|---|---|
| Martin Gelinas | 26 |
| Alexander Mogilny | 13 |
| Markus Naslund | 11 |
| Lonny Bohonos | 7 |
| Jyrki Lumme | 7 |
| Mike Ridley | 7 |

## TEAM PREVIEW

GOAL: Before last year, goaltending was considered a trouble spot because the Canucks had two number ones. But, for most of last season they had two number two men. Not only did neither want to grab the number one spot, neither deserved it. McLean, previously considered expendable, launched a comeback of sorts and had a much better win-loss record than Hirsch, despite the fact that the rest of their stats were close to being identical. Hirsch seemed to suffer a case of the sophomore jinx, so this season will be more telling.

Injuries were also a problem, however, giving Mike Fountain a shot at the big time. He earned a shutout in his NHL debut, but the ecstacy didn't last. In his next start he was

| GOALTENDER | GPI | MINS | AVG | W | L | T | EN | SO | GA | SA | SV % |
|---|---|---|---|---|---|---|---|---|---|---|---|
| KIRK MCLEAN | 44 | 2581 | 3.21 | 21 | 18 | 3 | 3 | 0 | 138 | 1247 | .889 |
| COREY HIRSCH | 39 | 2127 | 3.27 | 12 | 20 | 4 | 2 | 2 | 116 | 1090 | .894 |
| MICHAEL FOUNTAIN | 6 | 245 | 3.43 | 2 | 2 | 0 | 0 | 1 | 14 | 135 | .896 |
| VAN TOTALS | 82 | 4972 | 3.29 | 35 | 40 | 7 | 5 | 3 | 273 | 2477 | .890 |

lifted in the second period after allowing five goals. Despite an off-season it's not really a worry area for Vancouver. Part of the blame should go to a porous defence anyway. With two seasoned performers in McLean and Hirsch, things could be a lot worse.

Hockey Annual Rating: 19 of 26

DEFENCE: Let's play a game, shall we?

It's called Where's Ohlund. The Canucks and their fans play it all the time.

Mattias Ohlund is considered by some to be the second coming, or at the very least better than all the previous Canucks defencemen combined. Others, however, are somewhat less enthusiastic in their praise.

The only problem is getting his name on the dotted line. The Canucks couldn't do it last year, when the big 6-4 Swede opted to stay in his homeland, and they couldn't do it the year before when they drafted him.

With Ohlund being a restricted free agent, and not bound by the salary cap, he wants the big money the old-fashioned way — before he's earned it. If some other team signs him the Canucks will match the offer, and then decide whether to trade him if he doesn't fit within the team's salary structure.

If nobody signs him that won't be so bad either, because then the everyone can play another season of Where's Ohlund.

Even if Ohlund isn't a wonderkind, he'd have little trouble moving to the top of the garbage heap that is the Canucks defence.

They are one of the worst units in the league, with most of them only likely to be role fillers or press box sitters on any good defensive team. Opposing forwards love to face the Canucks defenders because they know they won't get their hands dirty.

There is almost nothing to get excited about on the Canucks defense (unless Ohlund

signs, of course). Lumme is the only offensive threat of note, and he didn't exactly have a great year. Bret Hedican is one of the fastest defencemen in the league, which would make him a great partner for someone, although that someone doesn't appear to be on the Canucks. Also, there's Steve Staois, who has played 75 NHL games and has been the property of three teams. Throw in Adrian Aucoin, and Dave Babych, who will be back for another year. Chris Joseph was lost to free agency and Leif Rohlin is expected to play in Europe this season.

The Canucks did sign Grant Ledyard, who played with Dallas last season. He turns 36-years-old this year.

Minor league prospects include big 6-7 Chris McAllister and Mark Wotton who is under six feet, but plays a big game.

The Canucks need help at this position, and they need it quickly. They need a legitimate power play quarterback and some big tough guys who don't play defence like pussycats.

Hockey Annual Rating: 25 of 26

FORWARD: The Canucks can score goals, but perhaps more importantly, they can't prevent them. Blame some of that on the defence, but this group of forwards aren't very good defensively. Worst than that, they are the softest group of forwards in the league. They have almost no toughness among their scorers, relying on Gino Odjick and Donald Brashear, and sometimes Scott Walker, to handle all the rough stuff. Enter Messier, even if he has slowed down a stride or two.

The Canucks could have scored more, too, if their stars had been up to it. You never know what you're going to get from Mogilny anyway. He can be a 50-70 goal scorer or he can be a 30-goal scorer. Currently, his biggest value is that he could bring a lot in a trade.

Bure had his problems last year with a neck injury, but 23 goals from a two-time 60-goal scorer is just goofy, even if he did miss 19 games.

Mogilny and Bure together on one line and you'd figure on coming close to some scoring records. Apparently, they only play well for one game. In that one game, the two combined for nine points in an 8-0 win over St. Louis. The rest of the time forget it. They're both right wingers anyway and of course, according to Mogilny he never had a centreman.

One centreman, Mike Ridley, did do an excellent job considering his career was threatened before last season with various injuries, specifically his back. He proved to be a trooper and performed beyond expectations. His shooting percentage of 25.7 was the best in the league, although he was three shots short of what the NHL would call official. Ridley and Martin Gelinas combined for 55 goals, one more than the combined total of Mogilny and Bure. Maybe Ridley should have made a big stink about needing some better right wingers. Ridley became an unrestricted free agent during the summer.

Trevor Linden's season was a write-off. He missed 33 games, and has been consistently a 30-goal scorer, so nine goals last year isn't telling us much.

The best player on the Canucks last season was Martin Gelinas, and he didn't even start to score until after the all-star break (see stat analysis).

Returning players include Brian Noonan, utility forward; Dave Roberts, utility forward; Mike Sillinger, utility forward; and tough guys Odjick, Brashear and Troy Crowder.

Vancouver fans who blinked, missed the GREAT NEMCHINOV, who played exactly six games after being acquired from the Rangers last year. He became an unrestricted free agent and signed with the Islanders, thereby becoming just a glorious footnote in Vancouver Canuck history.

One player who made a late season impression is Lonny Bohonos. He's had some impressive minor-pro and junior scoring seasons, and didn't do badly with the Canucks with 22 points in 36 games.

There are some good young forward prospects in the Canucks system, and all have a good chance of making the team. Don't count out Larry Courville yet. He didn't impress much in 19 games with the Canucks but may turn into a decent power forward if given more time.

Dave Scatchard is a big tough centre who doesn't score much, but could be useful in a defensive role.

Peter Schaeffer is a left winger who can score. He had 123 points with Brandon last year in the OHL, and then joined Syracuse for their playoffs.

Josh Holden, last year's top Vancouver draft pick, is a centre who could make the team this year. He is getting a reputation as a loony, earning suspensions with Regina of the WHL last year for spitting and throwing a puck. The Canucks could use a loony who can score, especially at centre.

Hockey Annual Rating: 10 of 26 (potentially)

SPECIAL TEAMS: One of the few things the Canucks do well on special teams is score shorthanded goals. They had 12 last season, and 18 the year before.

That may have a direct correlation, however, to their penalty killing which was among the worst in the league. If the penalty-killers are paying more attention to scoring opportunities for themselves than they are in actually killing the penalty, then trouble follows right along with it. It's not just a Canucks thing, but often teams that score a lot shorthanded, have poor penalty killing percentages. The Rangers and Boston, for example were tied for second in shorthanded goals, with 15, and ranked 21st and 25th respectively in penalty killing percentage.

The power play was mediocre, but with the snipers they have in Mogilny, Bure and Gelinas, it should be much better. Bure once led the league with 25 power play goals, but could manage only four last year. Mogilny, who had 27 one year in Buffalo, had just seven. Their best power play goal single seasons combined add up to 52, or one less than the whole Canucks team had last year.

With the kind of firepower they have it doesn't even matter who's playing the points. Unless, of course, Mogilny points to them as the problem, and then demands to be traded unless that area improves.

POWER PLAY

|  | G | ATT | PCT |
|---|---|---|---|
| Overall | 51 | 303 | 16.8% (T-9th NHL) |
| Home | 27 | 169 | 16.0% (13th NHL) |
| Road | 24 | 134 | 17.9% (9th NHL) |

8 SHORT HANDED GOALS ALLOWED (T-4th NHL)

PENALTY KILLING

|  | G | TSH | PCT |
|---|---|---|---|
| Overall | 66 | 344 | 80.8% (24th NHL) |
| Home | 29 | 179 | 83.8% (T-10th NHL) |
| Road | 37 | 165 | 77.6% (26th NHL) |

12 SHORT HANDED GOALS SCORED (T-7th NHL)

CANUCKS SPECIAL TEAMS SCORING

| Power play | G | A | PTS |
|---|---|---|---|
| MOGILNY | 7 | 9 | 16 |
| LUMME | 5 | 10 | 15 |
| BURE | 4 | 8 | 12 |
| GELINAS | 6 | 5 | 11 |
| RIDLEY | 3 | 8 | 11 |
| JOSEPH | 2 | 8 | 10 |

| | G | A | PTS |
|---|---|---|---|
| NASLUND | 4 | 5 | 9 |
| NOONAN | 3 | 5 | 8 |
| LINDEN | 2 | 6 | 8 |
| BOHONOS | 2 | 4 | 6 |
| HEDICAN | 2 | 3 | 5 |
| SILLINGER | 3 | 1 | 4 |
| BABYCH | 2 | 2 | 4 |
| AUCOIN | 1 | 3 | 4 |
| ROBERTS | 1 | 2 | 3 |
| NEMCHINOV | 1 | 1 | 2 |
| SEMAK | 1 | 0 | 1 |
| ODJICK | 1 | 0 | 1 |
| STAIOS | 0 | 1 | 1 |
| ROHLIN | 0 | 1 | 1 |

| Short handed | G | A | PTS |
|---|---|---|---|
| SILLINGER | 3 | 1 | 4 |
| LINDEN | 2 | 1 | 3 |
| BURE | 1 | 2 | 3 |
| ROBERTS | 1 | 1 | 2 |
| NOONAN | 1 | 1 | 2 |
| MOGILNY | 1 | 1 | 2 |
| GELINAS | 1 | 1 | 2 |
| BABYCH | 0 | 2 | 2 |
| WOTTON | 1 | 0 | 1 |
| STAIOS | 0 | 1 | 1 |
| ROHLIN | 0 | 1 | 1 |
| LUMME | 0 | 1 | 1 |
| HEDICAN | 0 | 1 | 1 |

COACHING AND MANAGEMENT: Tom Renney was supposed to turn this team around. Instead, many of the players turned on him. There was talk that the players didn't respect him or his ways.

The challenge for a coach in today's game is to get the players to listen to him and to buy into his system. If the players are selfish, such as ones the Canucks have, then they won't care about the team's success as a whole. That means the coach's input will have little impact.

Give Renney credit for admitting his mistakes and being anxious to correct them. That shows a lot of smarts, but coaches who turn into babysitters and start letting the babies dictate how things should be done, don't last long.

If it looks good, is structurally sound and meets all the specifications there's no reason to think it won't work. Pat Quinn may earn an A in engineering class but he gets a D in chemistry.

It's one thing to have talent, but the talent has to be utilized properly, and intersperced with less-talented but no-less important character players. Quinn doesn't seem to do that.

And while we're at it, what's with the inability to get a top-notch centre for the Canucks? It's ridiculous.

Hockey Annual Rating: 23 of 26

## DRAFT

| Round | Sel. | Player | Pos | Amateur Team |
|---|---|---|---|---|
| 1 | 10 | Brad Ference | D | Spokane (WHL) |
| 2 | 34 | Ryan Bonni | D | Saskatoon (WHL) |
| 2 | 36 | Harold Druken | C | Detroit (OHL) |
| 3 | 64 | Kyle Freadrich | LW | Regina (WHL) |
| 4 | 90 | Chris Stanley | C | Belleville (OHL) |
| 5 | 114 | David Darguzas | LW | Edmonton (WHL) |
| 5 | 117 | Matt Cockell | G | Saskatoon (WHL) |
| 6 | 144 | Matt Cooke | LW | Windsor (OHL) |
| 6 | 148 | Larry Shapley | D | Welland (GHJHL) |
| 7 | 171 | Rod Leroux | D | Seattle (WHL) |
| 8 | 201 | Denis Martynyuk | LW | Russia |
| 9 | 227 | Peter Brady | G | Powell River (BCJHL) |

If there's one thing the Canucks need, it's toughness, and couldn't have done any better in that department than selecting Brad Ference. He had a whopping 324 penalty minutes with Spokane in the WHL last season. That included 39 fighting majors.

PROGNOSIS: It's a tough call because the Canucks could be much better than they were last season. Just about everyone had an off-year except for Gelinas, so what would happen if they all played better this season?

Interesting, but a couple things have to happen if they're going to be successful. They need more character and toughness at both forward and defence, and not just from the enforcers. And they need more talent on defence.

If you figure on the basis of injuries alone that the Canucks could have made the playoffs last year, then you have to figure they'll make it this year.

Or not. You just never know what a Canucks team is going to do.

## PREDICTION

Western Conference: 7th
Overall: 16th

## STAT SECTION

| Team Scoring Stats | 1996-97 | | | | | | | CAREER | | | |
|---|---|---|---|---|---|---|---|---|---|---|---|
| | GP | G | A | PTS | +/- | PIM | SH | Gm | G | A | Pts |
| A. MOGILNY | 76 | 31 | 42 | 73 | 9 | 18 | 174 | 726 | 297 | 327 | 624 |
| MARTIN GELINAS | 74 | 35 | 33 | 68 | 6 | 42 | 177 | 523 | 152 | 143 | 295 |
| PAVEL BURE | 63 | 23 | 32 | 55 | 14- | 40 | 265 | 346 | 203 | 185 | 388 |
| MIKE RIDLEY | 75 | 20 | 32 | 52 | 0 | 42 | 79 | 863 | 292 | 476 | 768 |
| MARKUS NASLUND | 78 | 21 | 20 | 41 | 15- | 30 | 120 | 239 | 49 | 62 | 111 |
| TREVOR LINDEN | 49 | 9 | 31 | 40 | 5 | 27 | 84 | 660 | 240 | 308 | 548 |
| MIKE SILLINGER | 78 | 17 | 20 | 37 | 3- | 25 | 112 | 296 | 47 | 94 | 141 |
| JYRKI LUMME | 66 | 11 | 24 | 35 | 8 | 32 | 107 | 580 | 76 | 239 | 315 |
| BRIAN NOONAN | 73 | 12 | 22 | 34 | 3- | 34 | 100 | 540 | 106 | 144 | 250 |
| DAVID ROBERTS | 58 | 10 | 17 | 27 | 11 | 51 | 74 | 112 | 19 | 32 | 41 |
| DAVE BABYCH | 78 | 5 | 22 | 27 | 2- | 38 | 105 | 1,101 | 140 | 566 | 706 |
| SERGEI NEMCHINOV | 69 | 8 | 16 | 24 | 9 | 16 | 97 | 424 | 107 | 123 | 230 |
| LONNY BOHONOS | 36 | 11 | 11 | 22 | 3- | 10 | 67 | 39 | 11 | 12 | 23 |
| ADRIAN AUCOIN | 70 | 5 | 16 | 21 | 0 | 63 | 116 | 120 | 10 | 30 | 40 |
| BRET HEDICAN | 67 | 4 | 15 | 19 | 3- | 51 | 93 | 304 | 13 | 69 | 82 |
| SCOTT WALKER | 64 | 3 | 15 | 18 | 2 | 132 | 55 | 138 | 7 | 24 | 31 |
| STEVE STAIOS | 63 | 3 | 14 | 17 | 24- | 91 | 66 | 75 | 3 | 14 | 17 |
| CHRIS JOSEPH | 63 | 3 | 13 | 16 | 21- | 62 | 99 | 403 | 35 | 99 | 134 |
| DONALD BRASHEAR | 69 | 8 | 5 | 13 | 8- | 245 | 61 | 170 | 11 | 12 | 23 |
| GINO ODJICK | 70 | 5 | 8 | 13 | 5- | 371 | 85 | 409 | 43 | 50 | 83 |
| LEIF ROHLIN | 40 | 2 | 8 | 10 | 4 | 8 | 37 | 96 | 8 | 24 | 32 |
| MARK WOTTON | 36 | 3 | 6 | 9 | 8 | 19 | 41 | 37 | 3 | 6 | 9 |
| DANA MURZYN | 61 | 1 | 7 | 8 | 7 | 118 | 70 | 795 | 47 | 148 | 195 |
| ALEXANDER SEMAK | 18 | 2 | 1 | 3 | 2- | 2 | 12 | 289 | 83 | 91 | 174 |
| TROY CROWDER | 30 | 1 | 2 | 3 | 6- | 52 | 11 | 150 | 9 | 7 | 16 |
| LARRY COURVILLE | 19 | 0 | 2 | 2 | 4- | 11 | 11 | 22 | 1 | 2 | 3 |
| KIRK MCLEAN | 44 | 0 | 2 | 2 | 0 | 2 | 0 | | | | |
| COREY HIRSCH | 39 | 0 | 1 | 1 | 0 | 6 | 0 | | | | |
| Y. NAMESTNIKOV | 2 | 0 | 0 | 0 | 1- | 4 | 1 | 35 | 0 | 8 | 8 |
| MICHAEL FOUNTAIN | 6 | 0 | 0 | 0 | 0 | 0 | 0 | | | | |

## TEAM RANKINGS

| | | Conference Rank | League Rank |
|---|---|---|---|
| Record | 35-40-7 | 9 | 15 |
| Home | 20-17-4 | 7 | 14 |
| Away | 15-23-3 | 7 | 16 |
| Versus Own Conference | 25-25-6 | 7 | 13 |
| Versus Other Conference | 10-15-1 | 10 | 18 |
| Team Plus\Minus | -1 | 7 | 12 |
| Goals For | 257 | 2 | 5 |
| Goals Against | 273 | 11 | 23 |
| Average Shots For | 28.0 | 13 | 24 |
| Average Shots Against | 30.2 | 7 | 14 |
| Overtime | 5-2-7 | 1 | 2 |
| One Goal Games | 13-14 | 7 | 15 |
| Times outshooting opponent | 32 | 10 | 19 |
| Versus Teams Over .500 | 17-21-2 | 5 | 11 |
| Versus Teams Under .500 | 18-19-5 | 11 | 20 |
| First Half Record | 20-20-1 | 4 | 10 |
| Second Half Record | 15-20-6 | 10 | 21 |

## PLAYOFFS

- did not make the playoffs

## ALL-TIME LEADERS

### Goals
Stan Smyl 262
Tony Tanti 250
Trevor Linden 240

### Assists
Stan Smyl 411
Thomas Gradin 353
Trevor Linden 308

### Points
Stan Smyl 673
Thomas Gradin 550
Trevor Linden 548

## BEST INDIVIDUAL SEASONS

### Goals
Pavel Bure 1993-94 60
Pavel Bure 1992-93 60
Alexander Mogilny 1995-96 55

### Assists
Andre Boudrias 1974-75 62
Andre Boudrias 1973-74 59
Thomas Gradin 1983-84 57

### Points
Pavel Bure 1992-93 110
Alexander Mogilny 1995-96 107
Pavel Bure 1993-94 107

## TEAM

### Last 3 years
| | GP | W | L | T | Pts | % |
|---|---|---|---|---|---|---|
| 1996-97 | 82 | 35 | 40 | 7 | 77 | .470 |
| 1995-96 | 82 | 32 | 35 | 15 | 79 | .482 |
| 1994-95 | 48 | 18 | 18 | 12 | 48 | .500 |

### Best 3 regular seasons
| | GP | W | L | T | Pts | % |
|---|---|---|---|---|---|---|
| 1992-93 | 84 | 46 | 29 | 9 | 101 | .601 |
| 1991-92 | 80 | 42 | 27 | 12 | 96 | .600 |
| 1974-75 | 80 | 38 | 32 | 10 | 86 | .538 |

Worst 3 regular seasons

| | | | | | | |
|---|---|---|---|---|---|---|
| 1971-72 | 78 | 20 | 50 | 8 | 48 | .308 |
| 1972-73 | 78 | 22 | 47 | 9 | 53 | .340 |
| 1977-78 | 80 | 27 | 43 | 17 | 57 | .359 |

Most Goals (min. 70 game schedule)

| | |
|---|---|
| 1992-93 | 346 |
| 1983-84 | 306 |
| 1982-83 | 303 |

Fewest Goals (min. 70 game schedule)

| | |
|---|---|
| 1971-72 | 203 |
| 1978-79 | 217 |
| 1973-74 | 224 |

Most Goals Against (min. 70 game schedule)

| | |
|---|---|
| 1984-85 | 401 |
| 1972-73 | 339 |
| 1985-86 | 333 |

Fewest Goals Against (min. 70 game schedule)

| | |
|---|---|
| 1991-92 | 250 |
| 1988-89 | 253 |
| 1974-75 | 254 |

# TOWNSEND'S ULTIMATE POOL PICKS

A strange thing happened on the way to the Stanley Cup last year — players stopped scoring goals.

There were only two 100-point getters in the lowest scoring NHL season since 1969-70.

Defensive hockey is clearly in vogue, and that is affecting poolsters.

Strategies have to be re-examined with respect to the player selection process.

Many teams are no longer able to put a decent second scoring line together. It's the all-the-eggs-in-one-basket approach for most. That means that you need players off that first line, no matter which team they're playing for. Second line players too, at worst. Third liners were scoring twenty-something points last year and popping in less than 10 goals.

Another area that showed change last year was on the power play. Power play opportunities were way down, and as a result so were power play goals. That doesn't mean power play performers are any less valuable because they're usually on the top two lines anyway, but it could mean that offensive defencemen aren't going to get as many points. We saw that last year, with just a select few high in the point parade.

There is a chart put together for each team along with our overall player rankings.

Player rankings, incidently, are carefully compiled, with the following in mind: age, power play time, career patterns, first-and second-half points, injury history, streak scoring from last season, and most importantly, where they fit on their club's depth chart.

The player rankings simply list the player's name, team, scoring stats from last year and a rating on the reliability index, which is as follows:

Reliability Index
  A: rarely hurt, in prime of career
  B: has had minor injury problems, but still in prime of career
  C: Age or injury problems could be a medium factor, or status uncertain, or has shown a lot of inconsistency from year to year.
  D: Could go for a fall or not rise at all - major injury problems or age also a major factor

Good luck with your pool and look me up during the season under "Townsend's Pool Tips" in the Hockey News Online Edition at www.thn.com.

| Player | Team | Reliability Index | 1996-97 Gms | 1996-97 Pts | Estimate Pts |
|---|---|---|---|---|---|
| Paul Kariya | Ana | B | 69 | 99 | 120 |
| Eric Lindros | Phi | B | 52 | 79 | 118 |
| Jaromir Jagr | Pit | B | 63 | 95 | 115 |
| Teemu Selanne | Ana | A | 78 | 109 | 110 |
| Joe Sakic | Col | A | 65 | 74 | 100 |
| Peter Forsberg | Col | A | 65 | 86 | 97 |
| Wayne Gretzky | NYR | B | 82 | 97 | 95 |
| John LeClair | Phi | A | 82 | 97 | 93 |
| Zigmund Palffy | NYI | A | 80 | 90 | 92 |
| Saku Koivu | Mtl | B | 50 | 56 | 87 |
| Mike Modano | Dal | B | 80 | 83 | 86 |
| Adam Oates | Wsh | B | 80 | 82 | 86 |
| Brendan Shanahan | Det | A | 81 | 88 | 85 |
| Theoren Fleury | Cgy | B | 81 | 67 | 85 |
| Keith Tkachuk | Pho | A | 81 | 86 | 84 |
| Doug Weight | Edm | B | 80 | 82 | 84 |
| Alexander Mogilny | Van | B | 76 | 73 | 84 |
| Mark Messier | Van | C | 71 | 84 | 84 |
| Mark Recchi | Mtl | A | 82 | 80 | 83 |
| Pavel Bure | Van | B | 74 | 68 | 83 |
| Vincent Damphousse | Mtl | A | 82 | 81 | 82 |
| Mats Sundin | Tor | B | 82 | 94 | 82 |
| Peter Bondra | Wsh | A | 77 | 77 | 81 |
| Alexei Zhamnov | Chi | B | 74 | 62 | 81 |
| Sergei Fedorov | Det | B | 74 | 63 | 81 |
| Brian Leetch | NYR | A | 82 | 78 | 80 |
| Pierre Turgeon | StL | B | 78 | 85 | 78 |
| Jeremy Roenick | Pho | C | 72 | 69 | 77 |
| Doug Gilmour | NJ | C | 81 | 82 | 76 |
| Robert Reichel | NYI | C | 82 | 62 | 75 |
| Jeff Friesen | SJ | B | 72 | 63 | 74 |
| Steve Yzerman | Det | C | 81 | 85 | 73 |
| Brett Hull | StL | B | 77 | 82 | 73 |
| Valeri Kamensky | Col | C | 68 | 66 | 73 |
| Alexei Yashin | Ott | B | 82 | 75 | 73 |
| Joe Nieuwendyk | Dal | C | 66 | 51 | 72 |
| Daniel Alfredsson | Ott | A | 76 | 71 | 72 |
| Brian Bradley | TB | C | 35 | 24 | 72 |
| Jason Arnott | Edm | B | 67 | 57 | 72 |
| Petr Nedved | Pit | B | 74 | 71 | 72 |
| Rod Brind'Amour | Phi | B | 82 | 59 | 71 |
| Owen Nolan | SJ | B | 82 | 62 | 71 |
| Trevor Linden | Van | B | 49 | 40 | 70 |
| Bryan Smolinski | NYI | B | 64 | 56 | 70 |
| Pat Verbeek | Dal | B | 81 | 53 | 69 |
| Andrew Cassels | Car | B | 81 | 66 | 68 |
| Sandis Ozolinsh | Col | A | 80 | 68 | 68 |
| Geoff Sanderson | Car | A | 82 | 67 | 66 |

| Player | Team | Reliability Index | 1996-97 Gms | 1996-97 Pts | Estimate Pts |
|---|---|---|---|---|---|
| Chris Gratton | TB | B | 82 | 62 | 66 |
| Dave Gagner | Fla | C | 82 | 60 | 66 |
| Claude Lemieux | Col | C | 45 | 28 | 66 |
| Ray Bourque | Bos | C | 62 | 31 | 65 |
| Adam Graves | NYR | A | 82 | 61 | 65 |
| Tony Amonte | Chi | B | 81 | 77 | 65 |
| Adam Deadmarsh | Col | B | 78 | 60 | 65 |
| Mikael Renberg | Phi | B | 77 | 59 | 65 |
| Ron Francis | Pit | B | 81 | 90 | 65 |
| Ray Sheppard | Fla | C | 68 | 60 | 65 |
| Joe Thornton | Bos | - | - | - | 63 |
| Ryan Smyth | Edm | B | 82 | 61 | 63 |
| Alexei Kovalev | NYR | C | 45 | 35 | 63 |
| Steve Sullivan | Tor | B | 54 | 38 | 63 |
| Scott Mellanby | Fla | B | 82 | 56 | 63 |
| Slava Kozlov | Det | B | 75 | 45 | 62 |
| Martin Gelinas | Van | B | 74 | 68 | 62 |
| Mikael Nylander | Cgy | C | - | - | 61 |
| Wendel Clark | Tor | C | 65 | 49 | 61 |
| Jeff Brown | Car | C | 1 | 0 | 60 |
| Geoff Courtnall | StL | B | 82 | 57 | 60 |
| Donald Audette | Buf | B | 73 | 50 | 59 |
| Keith Primeau | Car | B | 75 | 51 | 58 |
| Luc Robitaille | NYR | C | 69 | 48 | 58 |
| Rob Niedermayer | Fla | B | 60 | 38 | 58 |
| Oleg Tverdovsky | Pho | B | 82 | 55 | 58 |
| Keith Jones | Col | B | 78 | 48 | 57 |
| Bernie Nicholls | SJ | C | 65 | 45 | 57 |
| Dave Andreychuk | NJ | C | 82 | 61 | 56 |
| Derek Plante | Buf | B | 82 | 53 | 56 |
| Bill Guerin | NJ | B | 82 | 47 | 56 |
| Yogi Svejkovsky | Wsh | B | 19 | 10 | 55 |
| Brian Holzinger | Buf | B | 81 | 51 | 55 |
| Jeff O'Neill | Car | C | 72 | 30 | 55 |
| Andrei Kovalenko | Edm | C | 74 | 59 | 55 |
| German Titov | Cgy | B | 79 | 52 | 55 |
| Martin Rucinsky | Mtl | B | 70 | 55 | 54 |
| Todd Harvey | Dal | C | 71 | 31 | 54 |
| Brian Savage | Mtl | B | 81 | 60 | 53 |
| Steve Rucchin | Ana | C | 79 | 67 | 53 |
| Bryan Berard | NYI | B | 82 | 48 | 53 |
| Joe Juneau | Wsh | B | 58 | 42 | 53 |
| Dimitri Khristich | LA | B | 75 | 56 | 53 |
| Viktor Kozlov | SJ | B | 78 | 41 | 53 |
| Steve Thomas | NJ | C | 57 | 34 | 53 |
| Josef Stumpel | Bos | B | 78 | 76 | 53 |
| Jarome Iginla | Cgy | B | 82 | 50 | 52 |
| Derek King | Tor | B | 82 | 59 | 52 |

| Player | Team | Reliability Index | 1996-97 Gms | 1996-97 Pts | Estimate Pts |
|---|---|---|---|---|---|
| Phil Housley | Wsh | C | 77 | 40 | 52 |
| Craig Janney | Pho | C | 77 | 53 | 52 |
| Alexandre Daigle | Ott | C | 82 | 61 | 52 |
| Travis Green | NYI | B | 79 | 64 | 51 |
| Darren Turcotte | SJ | C | 65 | 37 | 51 |
| Mike Peca | Buf | A | 79 | 49 | 51 |
| Dino Ciccarelli | TB | C | 77 | 60 | 51 |
| Al MacInnis | StL | C | 72 | 43 | 51 |
| Stu Barnes | Pit | B | 81 | 49 | 51 |
| Ray Ferraro | LA | B | 81 | 46 | 50 |
| Bobby Holik | NJ | B | 82 | 62 | 50 |
| Nicklas Lidstrom | Det | B | 79 | 57 | 50 |
| Rick Tocchet | Pho | D | 53 | 40 | 50 |
| Dimitri Mironov | Ana | C | 77 | 52 | 50 |
| Brian Rolston | NJ | B | 81 | 45 | 49 |
| Janne Niinimaa | Phi | B | 77 | 44 | 49 |
| Anson Carter | Bos | B | 38 | 18 | 48 |
| Mike Gartner | Pho | C | 82 | 63 | 48 |
| Markus Naslund | Van | B | 78 | 41 | 48 |
| Joe Murphy | StL | B | 75 | 45 | 48 |
| Darryl Sydor | Dal | B | 82 | 48 | 48 |
| Ed Olczyk | Pit | C | 79 | 55 | 48 |
| Stephane Richer | Mtl | C | 63 | 46 | 48 |
| Marty McInnis | Cgy | B | 89 | 49 | 47 |
| Roman Hamrlik | TB | B | 79 | 40 | 47 |
| Niklas Sundstrom | NYR | B | 82 | 52 | 47 |
| Rob Zamuner | TB | B | 82 | 50 | 46 |
| Todd Bertuzzi | NYI | C | 64 | 23 | 47 |
| Darren McCarty | Det | B | 68 | 49 | 46 |
| Igor Larionov | F/A | C | 64 | 54 | 45 |
| Alexei Zhitnik | Buf | B | 80 | 35 | 45 |
| Cliff Ronning | Pho | B | 69 | 51 | 45 |
| Chris Chelios | Chi | B | 72 | 48 | 45 |
| Rob Blake | LA | C | 62 | 31 | 45 |
| Sergei Berezin | Tor | B | 73 | 41 | 45 |
| Sergei Zubov | Dal | B | 78 | 43 | 45 |
| Sergei Samsonov | Bos | - | - | - | 44 |
| Tony Granato | SJ | B | 76 | 40 | 44 |
| John MacLean | NJ | C | 80 | 54 | 44 |
| Alexander Selivanov | TB | B | 69 | 33 | 44 |
| Paul Coffey | Phi | D | 57 | 34 | 44 |
| Randy Burridge | Buf | C | 55 | 31 | 44 |
| Boris Mironov | Edm | B | 55 | 32 | 43 |
| Vladimir Malakhov | Mtl | C | 65 | 30 | 43 |
| Steve Duchesne | Ott | B | 78 | 47 | 43 |
| Mike Sillinger | Van | B | 78 | 37 | 43 |
| Steve Heinze | Bos | C | 30 | 25 | 43 |
| Robert Svelha | Fla | B | 82 | 45 | 43 |

| Player | Team | Reliability Index | 1996-97 Gms | 1996-97 Pts | Estimate Pts |
|---|---|---|---|---|---|
| Eric Daze | Chi | B | 71 | 41 | 43 |
| Kevin Hatcher | Pit | C | 80 | 54 | 43 |
| Shawn McEachern | Ott | C | 65 | 31 | 42 |
| Al Iafrate | SJ | D | 38 | 15 | 42 |
| Mike Ricci | Col | C | 63 | 32 | 42 |
| Chris Pronger | StL | B | 79 | 35 | 42 |
| Valeri Bure | Mtl | B | 64 | 35 | 42 |
| Mathieu Schneider | Tor | B | 26 | 12 | 42 |
| Dallas Drake | Pho | B | 63 | 36 | 41 |
| Daymond Langkow | TB | B | 79 | 28 | 41 |
| Greg Adams | Dal | C | 50 | 36 | 41 |
| Russ Courtnall | F/A | B | 61 | 35 | 41 |
| Jason Allison | Bos | C | 72 | 34 | 40 |
| Steve Konowalchuk | Wsh | B | 78 | 42 | 40 |
| Garry Galley | LA | B | 71 | 38 | 40 |
| Jere Lehtinen | Dal | B | 63 | 43 | 40 |
| Larry Murphy | Det | C | 81 | 45 | 40 |
| Stephen Guolla | SJ | B | 43 | 21 | 40 |
| John Cullen | TB | C | 70 | 55 | 40 |
| Trent Klatt | Phi | B | 76 | 45 | 40 |
| David Wilkie | Mtl | B | 61 | 15 | 40 |
| J. Langenbrunner | Dal | B | 76 | 39 | 40 |
| Nelson Emerson | Car | C | 66 | 38 | 39 |
| Yanic Perreault | LA | C | 41 | 25 | 39 |
| Gary Suter | Chi | D | 82 | 28 | 39 |
| Richard Smehlik | Buf | B | 62 | 30 | 38 |
| Mariusz Czercawski | Edm | C | 76 | 47 | 38 |
| Zarley Zalapski | Cgy | C | 2 | 0 | 38 |
| Matthew Barnaby | Buf | B | 68 | 43 | 37 |
| Murray Craven | Chi | D | 75 | 35 | 37 |
| Ethan Moreau | Chi | B | 82 | 41 | 37 |
| Scott Niedermayer | NJ | A | 81 | 35 | 37 |
| Martin Lapointe | Det | B | 78 | 33 | 37 |
| Dainius Zubrus | Phi | C | 68 | 21 | 37 |
| Steven Rice | Car | B | 78 | 35 | 37 |
| Teppo Numminen | Pho | B | 82 | 27 | 36 |
| Vladimir Tsyplakov | LA | B | 67 | 39 | 36 |
| Dale Hunter | Wsh | C | 82 | 46 | 36 |
| Denis Pederson | NJ | B | 70 | 32 | 36 |
| Scott Young | Col | D | 72 | 37 | 36 |
| JJ Daigneault | F/A | C | 66 | 28 | 35 |
| Dave Reid | Dal | B | 82 | 39 | 35 |
| Shayne Corson | Mtl | C | 58 | 24 | 35 |
| Chris Simon | Wsh | B | 42 | 22 | 35 |
| Jim Campbell | StL | B | 68 | 43 | 35 |
| Todd Warriner | Tor | B | 75 | 33 | 35 |
| Jyrki Lumme | Van | B | 66 | 35 | 35 |
| Kirk Muller | Fla | C | 76 | 40 | 35 |

| Player | Team | Reliability Index | 1996-97 Gms | 1996-97 Pts | Estimate Pts |
|---|---|---|---|---|---|
| Ted Donato | Bos | B | 67 | 51 | 34 |
| Radek Dvorak | Fla | B | 78 | 39 | 34 |
| Michal Grosek | Buf | B | 82 | 36 | 34 |
| Benoit Brunet | Mtl | C | 39 | 23 | 34 |
| Jason Woolley | Pit | C | 60 | 36 | 34 |
| Darren Van Impe | Ana | D | 74 | 23 | 33 |
| Kelly Buchberger | Edm | B | 81 | 38 | 33 |
| Ulf Dahlen | Chi | C | 73 | 33 | 33 |
| Andrei Nazarov | SJ | B | 60 | 27 | 33 |
| Jonas Hoglund | Cgy | B | 68 | 35 | 33 |
| Bryan McCabe | NYI | B | 82 | 28 | 33 |
| Brian Noonan | Van | B | 73 | 34 | 33 |
| Alexei Karpovtsev | NYR | B | 77 | 38 | 33 |
| Esa Tikkanen | F/A | D | 76 | 30 | 33 |
| Kevin Stevens | LA | D | 69 | 34 | 33 |
| Andreas Dackell | Ott | B | 79 | 31 | 33 |
| Don Sweeney | Bos | B | 82 | 26 | 32 |
| Todd Marchant | Edm | B | 79 | 33 | 32 |
| Ed Jovanovski | Fla | B | 61 | 23 | 32 |
| Shjon Podein | Phi | B | 82 | 32 | 32 |
| Vitali Yachmenev | LA | B | 65 | 32 | 32 |
| Miroslav Satan | Buf | C | 76 | 38 | 32 |
| Joel Otto | Phi | B | 78 | 32 | 32 |
| Kevin Dineen | Car | D | 78 | 48 | 32 |
| Eric Weinrich | Chi | C | 81 | 32 | 31 |
| Benoit Hogue | Dal | D | 73 | 43 | 31 |
| Mike Grier | Edm | B | 79 | 32 | 31 |
| Glen Murray | LA | C | 77 | 30 | 31 |
| Patrice Brisbois | Mtl | C | 49 | 15 | 31 |
| Vaclav Prospal | Phi | C | 18 | 15 | 31 |
| Lonny Bohonos | Van | C | 36 | 22 | 31 |
| Eric Lacroix | Col | B | 81 | 36 | 31 |
| Cory Stillman | Cgy | C | 58 | 26 | 31 |
| Glen Wesley | Car | C | 68 | 32 | 30 |
| Steve Chiasson | Car | C | 65 | 30 | 30 |
| Randy Cunneyworth | Ott | B | 76 | 36 | 30 |
| Dean McAmmond | Edm | C | 57 | 29 | 30 |
| Mats Lindgren | Edm | B | 69 | 25 | 30 |
| Johan Garpenlov | Fla | D | 53 | 36 | 30 |

# TOWNSEND'S STAT GRAB BAG

## EASTERN CONFERENCE

### NORTHEAST DIVISION

|                | GP | W  | L  | T  | GF  | GA  | PTS | PCTG |
|----------------|----|----|----|----|-----|-----|-----|------|
| BUFFALO (2)    | 82 | 40 | 30 | 12 | 237 | 208 | 92  | .561 |
| PITTSBURGH (6) | 82 | 38 | 36 | 8  | 285 | 280 | 84  | .512 |
| OTTAWA (7)     | 82 | 31 | 36 | 15 | 226 | 234 | 77  | .470 |
| MONTREAL (8)   | 82 | 31 | 36 | 15 | 249 | 276 | 77  | .470 |
| HARTFORD (10)  | 82 | 32 | 39 | 11 | 226 | 256 | 75  | .457 |
| BOSTON (13)    | 82 | 26 | 47 | 9  | 234 | 300 | 61  | .372 |

### ATLANTIC DIVISION

|                   | GP | W  | L  | T  | GF  | GA  | PTS | PCTG |
|-------------------|----|----|----|----|-----|-----|-----|------|
| NEW JERSEY (1)    | 82 | 45 | 23 | 14 | 231 | 182 | 104 | .634 |
| PHILADELPHIA (3)  | 82 | 45 | 24 | 13 | 274 | 217 | 103 | .628 |
| FLORIDA (4)       | 82 | 35 | 28 | 19 | 221 | 201 | 89  | .543 |
| NY RANGERS (5)    | 82 | 38 | 34 | 10 | 258 | 231 | 86  | .524 |
| WASHINGTON (9)    | 82 | 33 | 40 | 9  | 214 | 231 | 75  | .457 |
| TAMPA BAY (11)    | 82 | 32 | 40 | 10 | 217 | 247 | 74  | .451 |
| NY ISLANDERS (12) | 82 | 29 | 41 | 12 | 240 | 250 | 70  | .427 |

## WESTERN CONFERENCE

### CENTRAL DIVISION

|               | GP | W  | L  | T  | GF  | GA  | PTS | PCTG |
|---------------|----|----|----|----|-----|-----|-----|------|
| DALLAS (2)    | 82 | 48 | 26 | 8  | 252 | 198 | 104 | .634 |
| DETROIT (3)   | 82 | 38 | 26 | 18 | 253 | 197 | 94  | .573 |
| PHOENIX (5)   | 82 | 38 | 37 | 7  | 240 | 243 | 83  | .506 |
| ST LOUIS (6)  | 82 | 36 | 35 | 11 | 236 | 239 | 83  | .506 |
| CHICAGO (8)   | 82 | 34 | 35 | 13 | 223 | 210 | 81  | .494 |
| TORONTO (11)  | 82 | 30 | 44 | 8  | 230 | 273 | 68  | .415 |

PACIFIC DIVISION

|                     | GP | W  | L  | T  | GF  | GA  | PTS | PCTG |
|---------------------|----|----|----|----|-----|-----|-----|------|
| COLORADO (1)        | 82 | 49 | 24 | 9  | 277 | 205 | 107 | .652 |
| ANAHEIM (4)         | 82 | 36 | 33 | 13 | 245 | 233 | 85  | .518 |
| EDMONTON (7)        | 82 | 36 | 37 | 9  | 252 | 247 | 81  | .494 |
| VANCOUVER (9)       | 82 | 35 | 40 | 7  | 257 | 273 | 77  | .470 |
| CALGARY (10)        | 82 | 32 | 41 | 9  | 214 | 239 | 73  | .445 |
| LOS ANGELES (12)    | 82 | 28 | 43 | 11 | 214 | 268 | 67  | .409 |
| SAN JOSE (13)       | 82 | 27 | 47 | 8  | 211 | 278 | 62  | .378 |

# TEAM STANDINGS BY CONFERENCE

EASTERN CONFERENCE

|               | GP | W  | L  | T  | GF  | GA  | PTS | PCTG |
|---------------|----|----|----|----|-----|-----|-----|------|
| NEW JERSEY    | 82 | 45 | 23 | 14 | 231 | 182 | 104 | .634 |
| PHILADELPHIA  | 82 | 45 | 24 | 13 | 274 | 217 | 103 | .628 |
| BUFFALO       | 82 | 40 | 30 | 12 | 237 | 208 | 92  | .561 |
| FLORIDA       | 82 | 35 | 28 | 19 | 221 | 201 | 89  | .543 |
| NY RANGERS    | 82 | 38 | 34 | 10 | 258 | 231 | 86  | .524 |
| PITTSBURGH    | 82 | 38 | 36 | 8  | 285 | 280 | 84  | .512 |
| OTTAWA        | 82 | 31 | 36 | 15 | 226 | 234 | 77  | .470 |
| MONTREAL      | 82 | 31 | 36 | 15 | 249 | 276 | 77  | .470 |
| WASHINGTON    | 82 | 33 | 40 | 9  | 214 | 231 | 75  | .457 |
| HARTFORD      | 82 | 32 | 39 | 11 | 226 | 256 | 75  | .457 |
| TAMPA BAY     | 82 | 32 | 40 | 10 | 217 | 247 | 74  | .451 |
| NY ISLANDERS  | 82 | 29 | 41 | 12 | 240 | 250 | 70  | .427 |
| BOSTON        | 82 | 26 | 47 | 9  | 234 | 300 | 61  | .372 |

WESTERN CONFERENCE

|           | GP | W  | L  | T  | GF  | GA  | PTS | PCTG |
|-----------|----|----|----|----|-----|-----|-----|------|
| COLORADO  | 82 | 49 | 24 | 9  | 277 | 205 | 107 | .652 |
| DALLAS    | 82 | 48 | 26 | 8  | 252 | 198 | 104 | .634 |
| DETROIT   | 82 | 38 | 26 | 18 | 253 | 197 | 94  | .573 |
| ANAHEIM   | 82 | 36 | 33 | 13 | 245 | 233 | 85  | .518 |
| PHOENIX   | 82 | 38 | 37 | 7  | 240 | 243 | 83  | .506 |
| ST LOUIS  | 82 | 36 | 35 | 11 | 236 | 239 | 83  | .506 |
| EDMONTON  | 82 | 36 | 37 | 9  | 252 | 247 | 81  | .494 |
| CHICAGO   | 82 | 34 | 35 | 13 | 223 | 210 | 81  | .494 |

| | GP | W | L | T | GF | GA | PTS | PCTG |
|---|---|---|---|---|---|---|---|---|
| VANCOUVER | 82 | 35 | 40 | 7 | 257 | 273 | 77 | .470 |
| CALGARY | 82 | 32 | 41 | 9 | 214 | 239 | 73 | .445 |
| TORONTO | 82 | 30 | 44 | 8 | 230 | 273 | 68 | .415 |
| LOS ANGELES | 82 | 28 | 43 | 11 | 214 | 268 | 67 | .409 |
| SAN JOSE | 82 | 27 | 47 | 8 | 211 | 278 | 62 | .378 |

OVERALL STANDINGS

| | GP | W | L | T | GF | GA | PTS | PCTG |
|---|---|---|---|---|---|---|---|---|
| COLORADO | 82 | 49 | 24 | 9 | 277 | 205 | 107 | .652 |
| DALLAS | 82 | 48 | 26 | 8 | 252 | 198 | 104 | .634 |
| NEW JERSEY | 82 | 45 | 23 | 14 | 231 | 182 | 104 | .634 |
| PHILADELPHIA | 82 | 45 | 24 | 13 | 274 | 217 | 103 | .628 |
| DETROIT | 82 | 38 | 26 | 18 | 253 | 197 | 94 | .573 |
| BUFFALO | 82 | 40 | 30 | 12 | 237 | 208 | 92 | .561 |
| FLORIDA | 82 | 35 | 28 | 19 | 221 | 201 | 89 | .543 |
| NY RANGERS | 82 | 38 | 34 | 10 | 258 | 231 | 86 | .524 |
| ANAHEIM | 82 | 36 | 33 | 13 | 245 | 233 | 85 | .518 |
| PITTSBURGH | 82 | 38 | 36 | 8 | 285 | 280 | 84 | .512 |
| PHOENIX | 82 | 38 | 37 | 7 | 240 | 243 | 83 | .506 |
| ST LOUIS | 82 | 36 | 35 | 11 | 236 | 239 | 83 | .506 |
| EDMONTON | 82 | 36 | 37 | 9 | 252 | 247 | 81 | .494 |
| CHICAGO | 82 | 34 | 35 | 13 | 223 | 210 | 81 | .494 |
| VANCOUVER | 82 | 35 | 40 | 7 | 257 | 273 | 77 | .470 |
| OTTAWA | 82 | 31 | 36 | 15 | 226 | 234 | 77 | .470 |
| MONTREAL | 82 | 31 | 36 | 15 | 249 | 276 | 77 | .470 |
| WASHINGTON | 82 | 33 | 40 | 9 | 214 | 231 | 75 | .457 |
| HARTFORD | 82 | 32 | 39 | 11 | 226 | 256 | 75 | .457 |
| TAMPA BAY | 82 | 32 | 40 | 10 | 217 | 247 | 74 | .451 |
| CALGARY | 82 | 32 | 41 | 9 | 214 | 239 | 73 | .445 |
| NY ISLANDERS | 82 | 29 | 41 | 12 | 240 | 250 | 70 | .427 |
| TORONTO | 82 | 30 | 44 | 8 | 230 | 273 | 68 | .415 |
| LOS ANGELES | 82 | 28 | 43 | 11 | 214 | 268 | 67 | .409 |
| SAN JOSE | 82 | 27 | 47 | 8 | 211 | 278 | 62 | .378 |
| BOSTON | 82 | 26 | 47 | 9 | 234 | 300 | 61 | .372 |

TEAMS' HOME-AND-ROAD RECORD BY CONFERENCE

HOME

EASTERN CONFERENCE

|  | GP | W | L | T | GF | GA | PTS | PCTG |
|---|---|---|---|---|---|---|---|---|
| PITTSBURGH (1) | 41 | 25 | 11 | 5 | 154 | 122 | 55 | .671 |
| NEW JERSEY (2) | 41 | 23 | 9 | 9 | 119 | 85 | 55 | .671 |
| BUFFALO (3) | 41 | 24 | 11 | 6 | 139 | 107 | 54 | .659 |
| PHILADELPHIA (4) | 41 | 23 | 12 | 6 | 135 | 101 | 52 | .634 |
| FLORIDA (5) | 41 | 21 | 12 | 8 | 119 | 97 | 50 | .610 |
| HARTFORD (6) | 41 | 23 | 15 | 3 | 116 | 108 | 49 | .598 |
| NY RANGERS (7) | 41 | 21 | 14 | 6 | 139 | 110 | 48 | .585 |
| WASHINGTON (8) | 41 | 19 | 17 | 5 | 109 | 109 | 43 | .524 |
| NY ISLANDERS (9) | 41 | 19 | 18 | 4 | 141 | 125 | 42 | .512 |
| MONTREAL (10) | 41 | 17 | 17 | 7 | 128 | 138 | 41 | .500 |
| OTTAWA (11) | 41 | 16 | 17 | 8 | 122 | 117 | 40 | .488 |
| TAMPA BAY (12) | 41 | 15 | 18 | 8 | 103 | 115 | 38 | .463 |
| BOSTON (13) | 41 | 14 | 20 | 7 | 123 | 139 | 35 | .427 |
| | | | | | | | | |
| CONFERENCE TOTAL | 533 | 260 | 191 | 82 | 1647 | 1473 | 602 | .565 |

WESTERN CONFERENCE

|  | GP | W | L | T | GF | GA | PTS | PCTG |
|---|---|---|---|---|---|---|---|---|
| COLORADO (1) | 41 | 26 | 10 | 5 | 143 | 103 | 57 | .695 |
| DALLAS (2) | 41 | 25 | 13 | 3 | 137 | 103 | 53 | .646 |
| ANAHEIM (3) | 41 | 23 | 12 | 6 | 138 | 110 | 52 | .634 |
| DETROIT (4) | 41 | 20 | 12 | 9 | 115 | 84 | 49 | .598 |
| EDMONTON (5) | 41 | 21 | 16 | 4 | 124 | 117 | 46 | .561 |
| CALGARY (6) | 41 | 21 | 18 | 2 | 121 | 121 | 44 | .537 |
| VANCOUVER (7) | 41 | 20 | 17 | 4 | 126 | 123 | 44 | .537 |
| LOS ANGELES (8) | 41 | 18 | 16 | 7 | 119 | 122 | 43 | .524 |
| TORONTO (9) | 41 | 18 | 20 | 3 | 121 | 128 | 39 | .476 |
| ST LOUIS (10) | 41 | 17 | 20 | 4 | 113 | 128 | 38 | .463 |
| PHOENIX (11) | 41 | 15 | 19 | 7 | 117 | 121 | 37 | .451 |
| CHICAGO (12) | 41 | 16 | 21 | 4 | 105 | 112 | 36 | .439 |
| SAN JOSE (13) | 41 | 14 | 23 | 4 | 109 | 136 | 32 | .390 |
| | | | | | | | | |
| CONFERENCE TOTAL | 533 | 254 | 217 | 62 | 1588 | 1508 | 570 | .535 |
| HOME TOTAL | 1066 | 514 | 408 | 144 | 3235 | 2981 | 1172 | .550 |

ROAD

EASTERN CONFERENCE

| | GP | W | L | T | GF | GA | PTS | PCTG |
|---|---|---|---|---|---|---|---|---|
| PHILADELPHIA (1) | 41 | 22 | 12 | 7 | 139 | 116 | 51 | .622 |
| NEW JERSEY (2) | 41 | 22 | 14 | 5 | 112 | 97 | 49 | .598 |
| FLORIDA (3) | 41 | 14 | 16 | 11 | 102 | 104 | 39 | .476 |
| NY RANGERS (4) | 41 | 17 | 20 | 4 | 119 | 121 | 38 | .463 |
| BUFFALO (5) | 41 | 16 | 19 | 6 | 98 | 101 | 38 | .463 |
| OTTAWA (6) | 41 | 15 | 19 | 7 | 104 | 117 | 37 | .451 |
| TAMPA BAY (7) | 41 | 17 | 22 | 2 | 114 | 132 | 36 | .439 |
| MONTREAL (8) | 41 | 14 | 19 | 8 | 121 | 138 | 36 | .439 |
| WASHINGTON (9) | 41 | 14 | 23 | 4 | 105 | 122 | 32 | .390 |
| PITTSBURGH (10) | 41 | 13 | 25 | 3 | 131 | 158 | 29 | .354 |
| NY ISLANDERS (11) | 41 | 10 | 23 | 8 | 99 | 125 | 28 | .341 |
| BOSTON (12) | 41 | 12 | 27 | 2 | 111 | 161 | 26 | .317 |
| HARTFORD (13) | 41 | 9 | 24 | 8 | 110 | 148 | 26 | .317 |
| CONFERENCE TOTAL | 533 | 195 | 263 | 75 | 1465 | 1640 | 465 | .436 |

WESTERN CONFERENCE

| | GP | W | L | T | GF | GA | PTS | PCTG |
|---|---|---|---|---|---|---|---|---|
| DALLAS (1) | 41 | 23 | 13 | 5 | 115 | 95 | 51 | .622 |
| COLORADO (2) | 41 | 23 | 14 | 4 | 134 | 102 | 50 | .610 |
| PHOENIX (3) | 41 | 23 | 18 | 0 | 123 | 122 | 46 | .561 |
| ST LOUIS (4) | 41 | 19 | 15 | 7 | 123 | 111 | 45 | .549 |
| DETROIT (5) | 41 | 18 | 14 | 9 | 138 | 113 | 45 | .549 |
| CHICAGO (6) | 41 | 18 | 14 | 9 | 118 | 98 | 45 | .549 |
| EDMONTON (7) | 41 | 15 | 21 | 5 | 128 | 130 | 35 | .427 |
| VANCOUVER (8) | 41 | 15 | 23 | 3 | 131 | 150 | 33 | .402 |
| ANAHEIM (9) | 41 | 13 | 21 | 7 | 107 | 123 | 33 | .402 |
| SAN JOSE (10) | 41 | 13 | 24 | 4 | 102 | 142 | 30 | .366 |
| TORONTO (11) | 41 | 12 | 24 | 5 | 109 | 145 | 29 | .354 |
| CALGARY (12) | 41 | 11 | 23 | 7 | 93 | 118 | 29 | .354 |
| LOS ANGELES (13) | 41 | 10 | 27 | 4 | 95 | 146 | 24 | .293 |
| CONFERENCE TOTAL | 533 | 213 | 251 | 69 | 1516 | 1595 | 495 | .464 |
| ROAD TOTAL | 1066 | 408 | 514 | 144 | 2981 | 3235 | 960 | .450 |

## TEAMS' INTER-CONFERENCE RECORD AGAINST OWN CONFERENCE

EASTERN CONFERENCE

|                    | GP  | W   | L   | T   | GF   | GA   | PTS  | PCTG |
|--------------------|-----|-----|-----|-----|------|------|------|------|
| NEW JERSEY (1)     | 56  | 29  | 16  | 11  | 154  | 130  | 69   | .616 |
| BUFFALO (2)        | 56  | 30  | 19  | 7   | 164  | 135  | 67   | .598 |
| PHILADELPHIA (3)   | 56  | 29  | 19  | 8   | 187  | 156  | 66   | .589 |
| FLORIDA (4)        | 56  | 23  | 20  | 13  | 155  | 141  | 59   | .527 |
| HARTFORD (5)       | 56  | 25  | 23  | 8   | 171  | 176  | 58   | .518 |
| OTTAWA (6)         | 56  | 24  | 23  | 9   | 168  | 156  | 57   | .509 |
| NY RANGERS (7)     | 56  | 24  | 24  | 8   | 181  | 164  | 56   | .500 |
| WASHINGTON (8)     | 56  | 23  | 25  | 8   | 138  | 148  | 54   | .482 |
| PITTSBURGH (9)     | 56  | 23  | 26  | 7   | 185  | 197  | 53   | .473 |
| NY ISLANDERS (10)  | 56  | 22  | 27  | 7   | 163  | 166  | 51   | .455 |
| MONTREAL (11)      | 56  | 18  | 26  | 12  | 158  | 184  | 48   | .429 |
| TAMPA BAY (12)     | 56  | 20  | 29  | 7   | 156  | 178  | 47   | .420 |
| BOSTON (13)        | 56  | 19  | 32  | 5   | 160  | 209  | 43   | .384 |
| CONF. TOTAL        | 728 | 309 | 309 | 110 | 2140 | 2140 | 728  | .500 |

WESTERN CONFERENCE

|                    | GP   | W   | L   | T   | GF   | GA   | PTS  | PCTG |
|--------------------|------|-----|-----|-----|------|------|------|------|
| COLORADO (1)       | 56   | 35  | 17  | 4   | 198  | 142  | 74   | .661 |
| DALLAS (2)         | 56   | 32  | 18  | 6   | 171  | 141  | 70   | .625 |
| PHOENIX (3)        | 56   | 29  | 24  | 3   | 175  | 162  | 61   | .545 |
| ST LOUIS (4)       | 56   | 27  | 23  | 6   | 160  | 164  | 60   | .536 |
| ANAHEIM (5)        | 56   | 24  | 22  | 10  | 160  | 153  | 58   | .518 |
| DETROIT (6)        | 56   | 21  | 20  | 15  | 168  | 144  | 57   | .509 |
| VANCOUVER (7)      | 56   | 25  | 25  | 6   | 173  | 178  | 56   | .500 |
| CHICAGO (8)        | 56   | 22  | 26  | 8   | 153  | 149  | 52   | .464 |
| CALGARY (9)        | 56   | 22  | 29  | 5   | 144  | 166  | 49   | .438 |
| TORONTO (10)       | 56   | 22  | 29  | 5   | 158  | 181  | 49   | .438 |
| EDMONTON (11)      | 56   | 21  | 28  | 7   | 168  | 175  | 49   | .438 |
| SAN JOSE (12)      | 56   | 23  | 32  | 1   | 155  | 198  | 47   | .420 |
| LOS ANGELES (13)   | 56   | 19  | 29  | 8   | 148  | 178  | 46   | .411 |
| CONF. TOTAL        | 728  | 322 | 322 | 84  | 2131 | 2131 | 728  | .500 |
| VS. OWN CONF.      | 1456 | 631 | 631 | 194 | 4271 | 4271 | 1456 | .500 |

## AGAINST OTHER CONFERENCE

EASTERN CONFERENCE

|  | GP | W | L | T | GF | GA | PTS | PCTG |
|---|---|---|---|---|---|---|---|---|
| PHILADELPHIA (1) | 26 | 16 | 5 | 5 | 87 | 61 | 37 | .712 |
| NEW JERSEY (2) | 26 | 16 | 7 | 3 | 77 | 52 | 35 | .673 |
| PITTSBURGH (3) | 26 | 15 | 10 | 1 | 100 | 83 | 31 | .596 |
| NY RANGERS (4) | 26 | 14 | 10 | 2 | 77 | 67 | 30 | .577 |
| FLORIDA (5) | 26 | 12 | 8 | 6 | 66 | 60 | 30 | .577 |
| MONTREAL (6) | 26 | 13 | 10 | 3 | 91 | 92 | 29 | .558 |
| TAMPA BAY (7) | 26 | 12 | 11 | 3 | 61 | 69 | 27 | .519 |
| BUFFALO (8) | 26 | 10 | 11 | 5 | 73 | 73 | 25 | .481 |
| WASHINGTON (9) | 26 | 10 | 15 | 1 | 76 | 83 | 21 | .404 |
| OTTAWA (10) | 26 | 7 | 13 | 6 | 58 | 78 | 20 | .385 |
| NY ISLANDERS (11) | 26 | 7 | 14 | 5 | 77 | 84 | 19 | .365 |
| BOSTON (12) | 26 | 7 | 15 | 4 | 74 | 91 | 18 | .346 |
| HARTFORD (13) | 26 | 7 | 16 | 3 | 55 | 80 | 17 | .327 |
| CONF. TOTAL | 338 | 146 | 145 | 47 | 972 | 973 | 339 | .501 |

WESTERN CONFERENCE

|  | GP | W | L | T | GF | GA | PTS | PCTG |
|---|---|---|---|---|---|---|---|---|
| DETROIT (1) | 26 | 17 | 6 | 3 | 85 | 53 | 37 | .712 |
| DALLAS (2) | 26 | 16 | 8 | 2 | 81 | 57 | 34 | .654 |
| COLORADO (3) | 26 | 14 | 7 | 5 | 79 | 63 | 33 | .635 |
| EDMONTON (4) | 26 | 15 | 9 | 2 | 84 | 72 | 32 | .615 |
| CHICAGO (5) | 26 | 12 | 9 | 5 | 70 | 61 | 29 | .558 |
| ANAHEIM (6) | 26 | 12 | 11 | 3 | 85 | 80 | 27 | .519 |
| CALGARY (7) | 26 | 10 | 12 | 4 | 70 | 73 | 24 | .462 |
| ST LOUIS (8) | 26 | 9 | 12 | 5 | 76 | 75 | 23 | .442 |
| PHOENIX (9) | 26 | 9 | 13 | 4 | 65 | 81 | 22 | .423 |
| VANCOUVER (10) | 26 | 10 | 15 | 1 | 84 | 95 | 21 | .404 |
| LOS ANGELES (11) | 26 | 9 | 14 | 3 | 66 | 90 | 21 | .404 |
| TORONTO (12) | 26 | 8 | 15 | 3 | 72 | 92 | 19 | .365 |
| SAN JOSE (13) | 26 | 4 | 15 | 7 | 56 | 80 | 15 | .288 |
| CONF. TOTAL | 338 | 145 | 146 | 47 | 973 | 972 | 337 | .499 |
| VS. OTHER CONF. | 676 | 291 | 291 | 94 | 1945 | 1945 | 676 | .500 |

## POWER PLAY REPORT

(ADV) TOTAL ADVANTAGES (PPGF) POWER-PLAY GOALS FOR (PCTG) ARRIVED BY DIVIDING NUMBER OF POWER-PLAY GOALS BY TOTAL ADVANTAGES

| | HOME TEAM | GP | ADV | PPGF | PCTG | ROAD TEAM | GP | ADV | PPGF | PCTG | OVER ALL TEAM | GP | ADV | PPGF | PCTG |
|---|---|---|---|---|---|---|---|---|---|---|---|---|---|---|---|
| 1 | NYR | 41 | 135 | 32 | 23.7 | PIT | 41 | 169 | 41 | 24.3 | NYR | 82 | 287 | 63 | 22.0 |
| 2 | PIT | 41 | 169 | 33 | 19.5 | COL | 41 | 188 | 41 | 21.8 | PIT | 82 | 338 | 74 | 21.9 |
| 3 | COL | 41 | 215 | 42 | 19.5 | DET | 41 | 187 | 40 | 21.4 | COL | 82 | 403 | 83 | 20.6 |
| 4 | CGY | 41 | 184 | 35 | 19.0 | NYR | 41 | 152 | 31 | 20.4 | HFD | 82 | 321 | 58 | 18.1 |
| 5 | EDM | 41 | 207 | 37 | 17.9 | HFD | 41 | 159 | 30 | 18.9 | PHO | 82 | 359 | 65 | 18.1 |
| 6 | PHO | 41 | 193 | 34 | 17.6 | PHO | 41 | 166 | 31 | 18.7 | EDM | 82 | 406 | 73 | 18.0 |
| 7 | FLA | 41 | 194 | 34 | 17.5 | EDM | 41 | 199 | 36 | 18.1 | DET | 82 | 368 | 66 | 17.9 |
| 8 | HFD | 41 | 162 | 28 | 17.3 | OTT | 41 | 161 | 29 | 18.0 | CGY | 82 | 361 | 61 | 16.9 |
| 9 | ANA | 41 | 168 | 28 | 16.7 | VAN | 41 | 134 | 24 | 17.9 | ANA | 82 | 333 | 56 | 16.8 |
| 10 | S.J | 41 | 175 | 29 | 16.6 | STL | 41 | 153 | 27 | 17.6 | VAN | 82 | 303 | 51 | 16.8 |
| 11 | MTL | 41 | 171 | 28 | 16.4 | ANA | 41 | 165 | 28 | 17.0 | OTT | 82 | 336 | 56 | 16.7 |
| 12 | WSH | 41 | 167 | 27 | 16.2 | DAL | 41 | 157 | 26 | 16.6 | WSH | 82 | 322 | 51 | 15.8 |
| 13 | VAN | 41 | 169 | 27 | 16.0 | PHI | 41 | 182 | 29 | 15.9 | MTL | 82 | 337 | 53 | 15.7 |
| 14 | TOR | 41 | 155 | 24 | 15.5 | CHI | 41 | 139 | 22 | 15.8 | TOR | 82 | 309 | 48 | 15.5 |
| 15 | OTT | 41 | 175 | 27 | 15.4 | TOR | 41 | 154 | 24 | 15.6 | STL | 82 | 327 | 50 | 15.3 |
| 16 | N.J | 41 | 138 | 21 | 15.2 | WSH | 41 | 155 | 24 | 15.5 | BOS | 82 | 310 | 46 | 14.8 |
| 17 | T.B | 41 | 186 | 28 | 15.1 | MTL | 41 | 166 | 25 | 15.1 | CHI | 82 | 304 | 45 | 14.8 |
| 18 | BOS | 41 | 157 | 23 | 14.6 | BOS | 41 | 153 | 23 | 15.0 | PHI | 82 | 362 | 53 | 14.6 |
| 19 | BUF | 41 | 165 | 24 | 14.5 | CGY | 41 | 177 | 26 | 14.7 | DAL | 82 | 314 | 46 | 14.6 |
| 20 | DET | 41 | 181 | 26 | 14.4 | NYI | 41 | 179 | 26 | 14.5 | S.J | 82 | 349 | 50 | 14.3 |
| 21 | CHI | 41 | 165 | 23 | 13.9 | L.A | 41 | 157 | 22 | 14.0 | FLA | 82 | 352 | 50 | 14.2 |
| 22 | L.A | 41 | 181 | 24 | 13.3 | N.J | 41 | 150 | 19 | 12.7 | NYI | 82 | 346 | 48 | 13.9 |
| 23 | PHI | 41 | 180 | 24 | 13.3 | T.B | 41 | 154 | 19 | 12.3 | N.J | 82 | 288 | 40 | 13.9 |
| 24 | STL | 41 | 174 | 23 | 13.2 | S.J | 41 | 174 | 21 | 12.1 | T.B | 82 | 340 | 47 | 13.8 |
| 25 | NYI | 41 | 167 | 22 | 13.2 | BUF | 41 | 161 | 19 | 11.8 | L.A | 82 | 338 | 46 | 13.6 |
| 26 | DAL | 41 | 157 | 20 | 12.7 | FLA | 41 | 158 | 16 | 10.1 | BUF | 82 | 326 | 43 | 13.2 |
| | | 1066 | 4490 | 723 | 16.1 | | 1066 | 4249 | 699 | 16.5 | | 1066 | 8739 | 1422 | 16.3 |

## TEAMS' PENALTY KILLING RECORD

(TSH) TOTAL TIMES SHORT-HANDED (PPGA) POWER-PLAY GOALS AGAINST (PCTG) ARRIVED BY DIVIDING - TIMES SHORT MINUS POWER-PLAY GOALS AGAINST- BY TIMES SHORT

| | HOME TEAM | GP | ADV | PPGF | PCTG | ROAD TEAM | GP | ADV | PPGF | PCTG | OVER ALL TEAM | GP | ADV | PPGF | PCTG |
|---|---|---|---|---|---|---|---|---|---|---|---|---|---|---|---|
| 1 | COL | 41 | 167 | 20 | 88.0 | N.J | 41 | 123 | 12 | 90.2 | N.J | 82 | 235 | 28 | 88.1 |
| 2 | T.B | 41 | 187 | 23 | 87.7 | PHO | 41 | 172 | 20 | 88.4 | COL | 82 | 339 | 42 | 87.6 |
| 3 | L.A | 41 | 175 | 22 | 87.4 | PHI | 41 | 186 | 23 | 87.6 | L.A | 82 | 352 | 45 | 87.2 |
| 4 | DET | 41 | 159 | 20 | 87.4 | COL | 41 | 172 | 22 | 87.2 | DET | 82 | 346 | 46 | 86.7 |
| 5 | N.J | 41 | 112 | 16 | 85.7 | L.A | 41 | 177 | 23 | 87.0 | PHO | 82 | 334 | 47 | 85.9 |
| 6 | FLA | 41 | 166 | 25 | 84.9 | WSH | 41 | 188 | 25 | 86.7 | PHI | 82 | 342 | 49 | 85.7 |
| 7 | HFD | 41 | 153 | 24 | 84.3 | DET | 41 | 187 | 26 | 86.1 | FLA | 82 | 346 | 50 | 85.5 |
| 8 | OTT | 41 | 125 | 20 | 84.0 | FLA | 41 | 180 | 25 | 86.1 | T.B | 82 | 360 | 55 | 84.7 |
| 9 | CHI | 41 | 175 | 28 | 84.0 | STL | 41 | 164 | 24 | 85.4 | WSH | 82 | 354 | 54 | 84.7 |
| 10 | BOS | 41 | 148 | 24 | 83.8 | DAL | 41 | 157 | 23 | 85.4 | HFD | 82 | 332 | 51 | 84.6 |
| 11 | VAN | 41 | 179 | 29 | 83.8 | S.J | 41 | 220 | 33 | 85.0 | CHI | 82 | 374 | 59 | 84.2 |
| 12 | BUF | 41 | 188 | 31 | 83.5 | HFD | 41 | 179 | 27 | 84.9 | S.J | 82 | 409 | 66 | 83.9 |
| 13 | PIT | 41 | 169 | 28 | 83.4 | CGY | 41 | 176 | 27 | 84.7 | BUF | 82 | 364 | 59 | 83.8 |
| 14 | PHI | 41 | 156 | 26 | 83.3 | NYI | 41 | 168 | 26 | 84.5 | STL | 82 | 332 | 55 | 83.4 |
| 15 | PHO | 41 | 162 | 27 | 83.3 | CHI | 41 | 199 | 31 | 84.4 | NYI | 82 | 319 | 53 | 83.4 |
| 16 | EDM | 41 | 165 | 28 | 83.0 | BUF | 41 | 176 | 28 | 84.1 | DAL | 82 | 308 | 51 | 83.4 |
| 17 | TOR | 41 | 162 | 28 | 82.7 | EDM | 41 | 173 | 31 | 82.1 | CGY | 82 | 345 | 58 | 83.2 |
| 18 | WSH | 41 | 166 | 29 | 82.5 | T.B | 41 | 173 | 32 | 81.5 | EDM | 82 | 338 | 59 | 82.5 |
| 19 | S.J | 41 | 189 | 33 | 82.5 | MTL | 41 | 166 | 31 | 81.3 | TOR | 82 | 328 | 59 | 82.0 |
| 20 | ANA | 41 | 160 | 28 | 82.5 | TOR | 41 | 166 | 31 | 81.3 | OTT | 82 | 265 | 48 | 81.9 |
| 21 | NYI | 41 | 151 | 27 | 82.1 | ANA | 41 | 176 | 34 | 80.7 | BOS | 82 | 308 | 56 | 81.8 |
| 22 | CGY | 41 | 169 | 31 | 81.7 | OTT | 41 | 140 | 28 | 80.0 | ANA | 82 | 336 | 62 | 81.5 |
| 23 | STL | 41 | 168 | 31 | 81.5 | BOS | 41 | 160 | 32 | 80.0 | PIT | 82 | 338 | 64 | 81.1 |
| 24 | DAL | 41 | 151 | 28 | 81.5 | NYR | 41 | 178 | 36 | 79.8 | VAN | 82 | 344 | 66 | 80.8 |
| 25 | NYR | 41 | 166 | 33 | 80.1 | PIT | 41 | 169 | 36 | 78.7 | NYR | 82 | 344 | 69 | 79.9 |
| 26 | MTL | 41 | 181 | 40 | 77.9 | VAN | 41 | 165 | 37 | 77.6 | MTL | 82 | 347 | 71 | 79.5 |
| | | 1066 | 4249 | 699 | 83.5 | | 1066 | 4490 | 723 | 83.9 | | 1066 | 8739 | 1422 | 83.7 |

SHORT HAND GOALS FOR

| | HOME TEAM | GP | SHGF | ROAD TEAM | GP | SHGF | OVER ALL TEAM | GP | SHGF |
|---|---|---|---|---|---|---|---|---|---|
| 1 | BUF | 41 | 11 | BOS | 41 | 10 | BUF | 82 | 16 |
| 2 | NYI | 41 | 10 | T.B | 41 | 9 | BOS | 82 | 15 |
| 3 | PIT | 41 | 9 | DAL | 41 | 9 | NYR | 82 | 15 |
| 4 | MTL | 41 | 7 | NYR | 41 | 8 | COL | 82 | 14 |
| 5 | TOR | 41 | 7 | PHO | 41 | 8 | NYI | 82 | 14 |
| 6 | VAN | 41 | 7 | COL | 41 | 7 | T.B | 82 | 13 |
| 7 | NYR | 41 | 7 | DET | 41 | 7 | HFD | 82 | 12 |
| 8 | CGY | 41 | 7 | S.J | 41 | 6 | VAN | 82 | 12 |
| 9 | COL | 41 | 7 | EDM | 41 | 6 | PHI | 82 | 11 |
| 10 | HFD | 41 | 6 | PHI | 41 | 6 | TOR | 82 | 11 |
| 11 | ANA | 41 | 6 | HFD | 41 | 6 | DAL | 82 | 11 |
| 12 | STL | 41 | 5 | BUF | 41 | 5 | CGY | 82 | 11 |
| 13 | BOS | 41 | 5 | VAN | 41 | 5 | PIT | 82 | 10 |
| 14 | PHI | 41 | 5 | WSH | 41 | 5 | MTL | 82 | 10 |
| 15 | OTT | 41 | 5 | NYI | 41 | 4 | DET | 82 | 10 |
| 16 | T.B | 41 | 4 | OTT | 41 | 4 | STL | 82 | 9 |
| 17 | EDM | 41 | 3 | CHI | 41 | 4 | EDM | 82 | 9 |
| 18 | L.A | 41 | 3 | CGY | 41 | 4 | PHO | 82 | 9 |
| 19 | WSH | 41 | 3 | STL | 41 | 4 | OTT | 82 | 9 |
| 20 | S.J | 41 | 3 | TOR | 41 | 4 | ANA | 82 | 9 |
| 21 | FLA | 41 | 3 | ANA | 41 | 3 | S.J | 82 | 9 |
| 22 | DET | 41 | 3 | MTL | 41 | 3 | WSH | 82 | 8 |
| 23 | N.J | 41 | 2 | FLA | 41 | 2 | L.A | 82 | 5 |
| 24 | DAL | 41 | 2 | N.J | 41 | 2 | FLA | 82 | 5 |
| 25 | CHI | 41 | 1 | L.A | 41 | 2 | CHI | 82 | 5 |
| 26 | PHO | 41 | 1 | PIT | 41 | 1 | N.J | 82 | 4 |
| | | 1066 | 132 | | 1066 | 134 | | 1066 | 266 |

## SHORT HAND GOALS AGAINST

| | HOME TEAM | GP | SHGF | ROAD TEAM | GP | SHGF | OVER ALL TEAM | GP | SHGF |
|---|---|---|---|---|---|---|---|---|---|
| 1 | HFD | 41 | 2 | COL | 41 | 2 | BUF | 82 | 4 |
| 2 | PHI | 41 | 2 | BUF | 41 | 2 | NYR | 82 | 5 |
| 3 | NYR | 41 | 2 | ANA | 41 | 2 | BOS | 82 | 6 |
| 4 | DET | 41 | 2 | TOR | 41 | 2 | STL | 82 | 8 |
| 5 | BUF | 41 | 2 | NYR | 41 | 3 | DET | 82 | 8 |
| 6 | BOS | 41 | 3 | VAN | 41 | 3 | PHI | 82 | 8 |
| 7 | N.J | 41 | 3 | STL | 41 | 3 | TOR | 82 | 8 |
| 8 | MTL | 41 | 4 | BOS | 41 | 3 | VAN | 82 | 8 |
| 9 | CHI | 41 | 4 | NYI | 41 | 4 | NYI | 82 | 9 |
| 10 | T.B | 41 | 4 | S.J | 41 | 4 | T.B | 82 | 9 |
| 11 | STL | 41 | 5 | WSH | 41 | 4 | N.J | 82 | 9 |
| 12 | EDM | 41 | 5 | DAL | 41 | 4 | CHI | 82 | 9 |
| 13 | PIT | 41 | 5 | PHO | 41 | 5 | DAL | 82 | 9 |
| 14 | DAL | 41 | 5 | T.B | 41 | 5 | WSH | 82 | 10 |
| 15 | VAN | 41 | 5 | CHI | 41 | 5 | HFD | 82 | 11 |
| 16 | NYI | 41 | 5 | OTT | 41 | 6 | MTL | 82 | 11 |
| 17 | WSH | 41 | 6 | DET | 41 | 6 | ANA | 82 | 11 |
| 18 | TOR | 41 | 6 | N.J | 41 | 6 | S.J | 82 | 11 |
| 19 | OTT | 41 | 6 | L.A | 41 | 6 | COL | 82 | 12 |
| 20 | S.J | 41 | 7 | PHI | 41 | 6 | PIT | 82 | 12 |
| 21 | CGY | 41 | 7 | PIT | 41 | 7 | OTT | 82 | 12 |
| 22 | L.A | 41 | 8 | MTL | 41 | 7 | EDM | 82 | 13 |
| 23 | FLA | 41 | 8 | FLA | 41 | 8 | L.A | 82 | 14 |
| 24 | PHO | 41 | 9 | EDM | 41 | 8 | PHO | 82 | 14 |
| 25 | ANA | 41 | 9 | HFD | 41 | 9 | FLA | 82 | 16 |
| 26 | COL | 41 | 10 | CGY | 41 | 12 | CGY | 82 | 19 |
| | | 1066 | 134 | | 1066 | 132 | | 1066 | 266 |

## TEAM PENALTY INFORMATION

(GP) GAMES PLAYED (PEN) TOTAL PENALTY MINUTES INCLUDING BENCH MINUTES (BMI) TOTAL BENCH MINOR MINUTES (AVG) AVERAGE PENALTY MINUTES/GAME ARRIVED BY DIVIDING TOTAL PENALTY MINUTES BY GAMES PLAYED

MINUTES

| TEAM | GP | PEN | BMI | AVG |
|------|-----|-------|-----|------|
| OTT | 82 | 1087 | 10 | 13.3 |
| N.J | 82 | 1135 | 4 | 13.8 |
| DAL | 82 | 1325 | 10 | 16.2 |
| TOR | 82 | 1331 | 12 | 16.2 |
| STL | 82 | 1336 | 24 | 16.3 |
| COL | 82 | 1361 | 24 | 16.6 |
| BOS | 82 | 1369 | 4 | 16.7 |
| EDM | 82 | 1368 | 18 | 16.7 |
| CGY | 82 | 1444 | 16 | 17.6 |
| MTL | 82 | 1469 | 24 | 17.9 |
| NYR | 82 | 1481 | 14 | 18.1 |
| PIT | 82 | 1498 | 12 | 18.3 |
| HFD | 82 | 1513 | 18 | 18.5 |
| DET | 82 | 1582 | 12 | 19.3 |
| PHO | 82 | 1582 | 16 | 19.3 |
| VAN | 82 | 1607 | 22 | 19.6 |
| FLA | 82 | 1628 | 20 | 19.9 |
| L.A | 82 | 1638 | 8 | 20.0 |
| NYI | 82 | 1640 | 18 | 20.0 |
| WSH | 82 | 1652 | 28 | 20.1 |
| T.B | 82 | 1686 | 10 | 20.6 |
| PHI | 82 | 1699 | 8 | 20.7 |
| ANA | 82 | 1710 | 22 | 20.9 |
| CHI | 82 | 1763 | 14 | 21.5 |
| BUF | 82 | 1840 | 12 | 22.4 |
| S.J | 82 | 2085 | 6 | 25.4 |
| TOT | 1066 | 39829 | 386 | 37.4 |

## TEAMS' OVERTIME RECORDS

| | HOME | | | | | | ROAD | | | | | | OVERALL | | | | | |
|---|---|---|---|---|---|---|---|---|---|---|---|---|---|---|---|---|---|---|
| | GP | W | L | T | PTS | PCTG | GP | W | L | T | PTS | PCTG | GP | W | L | T | PTS | PCTG |
| NYR | 7 | 1 | 0 | 6 | 8 | .571 | 6 | 2 | 0 | 4 | 8 | .667 | 13 | 3 | 0 | 10 | 16 | .615 |
| VAN | 7 | 2 | 1 | 4 | 8 | .571 | 7 | 3 | 1 | 3 | 9 | .643 | 14 | 5 | 2 | 7 | 17 | .607 |
| ANA | 6 | 0 | 0 | 6 | 6 | .500 | 10 | 3 | 0 | 7 | 13 | .650 | 16 | 3 | 0 | 13 | 19 | .594 |
| DET | 14 | 4 | 1 | 9 | 17 | .607 | 13 | 3 | 1 | 9 | 15 | .577 | 27 | 7 | 2 | 18 | 32 | .593 |
| S.J | 6 | 2 | 0 | 4 | 8 | .667 | 6 | 1 | 1 | 4 | 6 | .500 | 12 | 3 | 1 | 8 | 14 | .583 |
| T.B | 10 | 2 | 0 | 8 | 12 | .600 | 6 | 2 | 2 | 2 | 6 | .500 | 16 | 4 | 2 | 10 | 18 | .563 |
| DAL | 7 | 2 | 2 | 3 | 7 | .500 | 8 | 2 | 1 | 5 | 9 | .563 | 15 | 4 | 3 | 8 | 16 | .533 |
| PHO | 12 | 2 | 3 | 7 | 11 | .458 | 4 | 3 | 1 | 0 | 6 | .750 | 16 | 5 | 4 | 7 | 17 | .531 |
| NYI | 7 | 2 | 1 | 4 | 8 | .571 | 10 | 1 | 1 | 8 | 10 | .500 | 17 | 3 | 2 | 12 | 18 | .529 |
| PHI | 8 | 2 | 0 | 6 | 10 | .625 | 10 | 1 | 2 | 7 | 9 | .450 | 18 | 3 | 2 | 13 | 19 | .528 |
| BUF | 10 | 2 | 2 | 6 | 10 | .500 | 11 | 3 | 2 | 6 | 12 | .545 | 21 | 5 | 4 | 12 | 22 | .524 |
| BOS | 9 | 1 | 1 | 7 | 9 | .500 | 6 | 2 | 2 | 2 | 6 | .500 | 15 | 3 | 3 | 9 | 15 | .500 |
| COL | 6 | 1 | 0 | 5 | 7 | .583 | 9 | 2 | 3 | 4 | 8 | .444 | 15 | 3 | 3 | 9 | 15 | .500 |
| WSH | 7 | 2 | 0 | 5 | 9 | .643 | 6 | 0 | 2 | 4 | 4 | .333 | 13 | 2 | 2 | 9 | 13 | .500 |
| STL | 5 | 1 | 0 | 4 | 6 | .600 | 8 | 0 | 1 | 7 | 7 | .438 | 13 | 1 | 1 | 11 | 13 | .500 |
| TOR | 3 | 0 | 0 | 3 | 3 | .500 | 7 | 1 | 1 | 5 | 7 | .500 | 10 | 1 | 1 | 8 | 10 | .500 |
| FLA | 10 | 1 | 1 | 8 | 10 | .500 | 16 | 2 | 3 | 11 | 15 | .469 | 26 | 3 | 4 | 19 | 25 | .481 |
| HFD | 7 | 3 | 1 | 3 | 9 | .643 | 11 | 0 | 3 | 8 | 8 | .364 | 18 | 3 | 4 | 11 | 17 | .472 |
| N.J | 11 | 1 | 1 | 9 | 11 | .500 | 6 | 0 | 1 | 5 | 5 | .417 | 17 | 1 | 2 | 14 | 16 | .471 |
| CGY | 7 | 2 | 3 | 2 | 6 | .429 | 9 | 1 | 1 | 7 | 9 | .500 | 16 | 3 | 4 | 9 | 15 | .469 |
| MTL | 12 | 2 | 3 | 7 | 11 | .458 | 9 | 0 | 1 | 8 | 8 | .444 | 21 | 2 | 4 | 15 | 19 | .452 |
| OTT | 10 | 0 | 2 | 8 | 8 | .400 | 7 | 0 | 0 | 7 | 7 | .500 | 17 | 0 | 2 | 15 | 15 | .441 |
| CHI | 8 | 0 | 4 | 4 | 4 | .250 | 11 | 1 | 1 | 9 | 11 | .500 | 19 | 1 | 5 | 13 | 15 | .395 |
| L.A | 8 | 0 | 1 | 7 | 7 | .438 | 6 | 0 | 2 | 4 | 4 | .333 | 14 | 0 | 3 | 11 | 11 | .393 |
| PIT | 9 | 1 | 3 | 5 | 7 | .389 | 4 | 0 | 1 | 3 | 3 | .375 | 13 | 1 | 4 | 8 | 10 | .385 |
| EDM | 8 | 1 | 3 | 4 | 6 | .375 | 8 | 0 | 3 | 5 | 5 | .313 | 16 | 1 | 6 | 9 | 11 | .344 |
| TOT | 214 | 37 | 33 | 144 | 218 | .509 | 214 | 33 | 37 | 144 | 210 | .491 | 214 | 70 | 70 | 144 | 428 | 1.000 |

## TEAM STREAKS

### CONSECUTIVE WINS - MINIMUM 3 GAMES

| GM | TEAM | FROM | TO |
|---|---|---|---|
| 7 | PHILADELPHIA | DEC. 6 | DEC. 21 |
| 7 | DALLAS | MAR. 16 | APR. 2 |
| 6 | DALLAS | OCT. 5 | OCT. 15 |
| 6 | PITTSBURGH | DEC. 4 | DEC. 13 |
| 6 | PITTSBURGH | DEC. 28 | JAN. 10 |
| 6 | COLORADO | FEB. 11 | FEB. 23 |
| 5 | NEW JERSEY | NOV. 2 | NOV. 12 |
| 5 | COLORADO | NOV. 6 | NOV. 13 |
| 5 | ST LOUIS | NOV. 8 | NOV. 17 |
| 5 | DALLAS | DEC. 13 | DEC. 21 |
| 5 | NY RANGERS | DEC. 13 | DEC. 22 |
| 5 | COLORADO | DEC. 23 | JAN. 2 |
| 5 | EDMONTON | JAN. 24 | FEB. 5 |
| 5 | CALGARY | FEB. 7 | FEB. 15 |
| 5 | LOS ANGELES | FEB. 20 | MAR. 1 |
| 5 | NEW JERSEY | FEB. 26 | MAR. 5 |
| 5 | NEW JERSEY | MAR. 27 | APR. 6 |

### CONSECUTIVE UNDEFEATED - MINIMUM 5 GAMES

| GM | TEAM | W | T | FROM | TO |
|---|---|---|---|---|---|
| 17 | PHILADELPHIA | 14 | 3 | NOV. 30 | JAN. 7 |
| 14 | PITTSBURGH | 12 | 2 | DEC. 19 | JAN. 21 |
| 13 | NEW JERSEY | 6 | 7 | JAN. 24 | FEB. 20 |
| 12 | FLORIDA | 8 | 4 | OCT. 5 | OCT. 30 |
| 12 | COLORADO | 9 | 3 | DEC. 23 | JAN. 20 |
| 12 | BUFFALO | 7 | 5 | JAN. 29 | FEB. 23 |
| 12 | ANAHEIM | 7 | 5 | FEB. 22 | MAR. 19 |
| 11 | COLORADO | 9 | 2 | OCT. 23 | NOV. 13 |
| 11 | DETROIT | 6 | 5 | FEB. 16 | MAR. 10 |
| 11 | DALLAS | 9 | 2 | MAR. 5 | APR. 2 |
| 10 | PITTSBURGH | 8 | 2 | NOV. 22 | DEC. 13 |
| 7 | DETROIT | 5 | 2 | OCT. 19 | NOV. 1 |
| 7 | NY RANGERS | 6 | 1 | NOV. 26 | DEC. 9 |

| 7 | DALLAS | 5 | 2 | DEC. 8 | DEC. 21 |
| 7 | NEW JERSEY | 5 | 2 | DEC. 10 | DEC. 23 |
| 7 | MONTREAL | 4 | 3 | DEC. 26 | JAN. 6 |
| 7 | ANAHEIM | 5 | 2 | MAR. 28 | APR. 11 # |

## CONSECUTIVE HOME WINS - MINIMUM 3 GAMES

| GM | TEAM | FROM | TO |
|---|---|---|---|
| 8 | PHILADELPHIA | NOV. 21 | JAN. 7 |
| 6 | NY RANGERS | DEC. 16 | JAN. 4 |
| 6 | PITTSBURGH | DEC. 28 | JAN. 21 |
| 5 | PITTSBURGH | OCT. 12 | NOV. 12 |
| 5 | ST LOUIS | NOV. 3 | NOV. 21 |
| 5 | EDMONTON | JAN. 12 | FEB. 5 |
| 5 | CALGARY | FEB. 7 | FEB. 15 |
| 5 | DALLAS | FEB. 14 | MAR. 7 |
| 5 | TAMPA BAY | FEB. 20 | MAR. 1 |
| 5 | NEW JERSEY | FEB. 27 | MAR. 15 |
| 5 | DALLAS | MAR. 16 | APR. 9 |

## CONSECUTIVE HOME TIES - MINIMUM 3 GAMES

| GM | TEAM | FROM | TO |
|---|---|---|---|
| 3 | TORONTO | MAR. 5 | MAR. 10 |

## CONSECUTIVE HOME UNDEFEATED - MINIMUM 5 GAMES

| GM | TEAM | W | T | FROM | TO |
|---|---|---|---|---|---|
| 15 | NEW JERSEY | 9 | 6 | JAN. 8 | MAR. 15 |
| 14 | ANAHEIM | 10 | 4 | FEB. 12 | APR. 9 # |
| 11 | BUFFALO | 7 | 4 | JAN. 29 | MAR. 5 |
| 11 | DALLAS | 10 | 1 | FEB. 14 | APR. 9 |
| 9 | PHILADELPHIA | 8 | 1 | NOV. 16 | JAN. 7 |
| 8 | COLORADO | 6 | 2 | OCT. 19 | NOV. 22 |
| 8 | BUFFALO | 7 | 1 | DEC. 18 | JAN. 22 |
| 8 | PITTSBURGH | 7 | 1 | DEC. 21 | JAN. 21 |
| 8 | DETROIT | 7 | 1 | FEB. 12 | MAR. 28 |
| 7 | NY RANGERS | 6 | 1 | DEC. 16 | JAN. 6 |
| 7 | TAMPA BAY | 6 | 1 | FEB. 15 | MAR. 1 |

CONSECUTIVE ROAD WINS - MINIMUM 3 GAMES

| GM | TEAM | FROM | TO |
|---|---|---|---|
| 6 | PITTSBURGH | NOV. 22 | DEC. 13 |
| 5 | PHILADELPHIA | OCT. 31 | NOV. 23 |
| 5 | NY RANGERS | NOV. 26 | DEC. 21 |
| 5 | NEW JERSEY | DEC. 10 | DEC. 20 |
| 5 | ST LOUIS | JAN. 15 | JAN. 30 |
| 4 | COLORADO | NOV. 6 | NOV. 13 |
| 4 | FLORIDA | NOV. 13 | DEC. 1 |
| 4 | WASHINGTON | NOV. 14 | NOV. 30 |
| 4 | DALLAS | DEC. 15 | DEC. 21 |
| 4 | PITTSBURGH | DEC. 19 | JAN. 7 |
| 4 | PHILADELPHIA | DEC. 27 | JAN. 2 |
| 4 | TAMPA BAY | JAN. 6 | JAN. 13 |
| 4 | NY RANGERS | JAN. 22 | FEB. 8 |
| 4 | COLORADO | FEB. 2 | FEB. 21 |
| 4 | PHOENIX | MAR. 5 | MAR. 14 |

CONSECUTIVE ROAD UNDEFEATED - MINIMUM 5 GAMES

| GM | TEAM | W | T | FROM | TO |
|---|---|---|---|---|---|
| 12 | PHILADELPHIA | 8 | 4 | NOV. 30 | JAN. 29 |
| 8 | HARTFORD | 4 | 4 | NOV. 12 | DEC. 5 |
| 8 | COLORADO | 5 | 3 | DEC. 18 | JAN. 20 |
| 7 | FLORIDA | 4 | 3 | OCT. 5 | OCT. 29 |
| 7 | COLORADO | 6 | 1 | OCT. 23 | NOV. 13 |
| 7 | DALLAS | 6 | 1 | NOV. 20 | DEC. 21 |
| 7 | MONTREAL | 3 | 4 | DEC. 6 | JAN. 2 |
| 7 | PITTSBURGH | 6 | 1 | DEC. 19 | JAN. 26 |
| 7 | ST LOUIS | 5 | 2 | JAN. 15 | FEB. 8 |
| 7 | DETROIT | 3 | 4 | FEB. 16 | MAR. 10 |
| 6 | PITTSBURGH | 6 | 0 | NOV. 22 | DEC. 13 |
| 6 | NEW JERSEY | 3 | 3 | JAN. 24 | FEB. 20 |
| 6 | NEW JERSEY | 4 | 2 | MAR. 9 | APR. 8 |
| 5 | CHICAGO | 3 | 2 | OCT. 5 | OCT. 29 |
| 5 | PHILADELPHIA | 5 | 0 | OCT. 31 | NOV. 23 |

| 5 | NY RANGERS | 5 | 0 | NOV. 26 | DEC. 21 |
| 5 | NEW JERSEY | 5 | 0 | DEC. 10 | DEC. 20 |
| 5 | CHICAGO | 2 | 3 | MAR. 2 | APR. 1 |

INDIVIDUAL SCORING LEADERS

| PLAYER | TEAM | GP | G | A | PTS | +/- | PIM | PP | SH | GW | GT | S | PCTG |
|---|---|---|---|---|---|---|---|---|---|---|---|---|---|
| MARIO LEMIEUX | PITTSBURGH | 76 | 50 | 72 | 122 | 27 | 65 | 15 | 2 | 7 | 1 | 327 | 15.3 |
| TEEMU SELANNE | ANAHEIM | 78 | 51 | 58 | 109 | 28 | 34 | 11 | 1 | 8 | 2 | 273 | 18.7 |
| PAUL KARIYA | ANAHEIM | 69 | 44 | 55 | 99 | 36 | 6 | 15 | 3 | 10 | 0 | 340 | 12.9 |
| JOHN LECLAIR | PHILADELPHIA | 82 | 50 | 47 | 97 | 44 | 58 | 10 | 0 | 5 | 2 | 324 | 15.4 |
| WAYNE GRETZKY | NY RANGERS | 82 | 25 | 72 | 97 | 12 | 28 | 6 | 0 | 2 | 1 | 286 | 8.7 |
| JAROMIR JAGR | PITTSBURGH | 63 | 47 | 48 | 95 | 22 | 40 | 11 | 2 | 6 | 1 | 234 | 20.1 |
| MATS SUNDIN | TORONTO | 82 | 41 | 53 | 94 | 6 | 59 | 7 | 4 | 8 | 1 | 281 | 14.6 |
| ZIGMUND PALFFY | NY ISLANDERS | 80 | 48 | 42 | 90 | 21 | 43 | 6 | 4 | 6 | 1 | 292 | 16.4 |
| RON FRANCIS | PITTSBURGH | 81 | 27 | 63 | 90 | 7 | 20 | 10 | 1 | 2 | 0 | 183 | 14.8 |
| BRENDAN SHANAHAN | HFD-DET | 81 | 47 | 41 | 88 | 32 | 131 | 20 | 3 | 7 | 2 | 336 | 14.0 |
| KEITH TKACHUK | PHOENIX | 81 | 52 | 34 | 86 | 1- | 228 | 9 | 2 | 7 | 1 | 296 | 17.6 |
| PETER FORSBERG | COLORADO | 65 | 28 | 58 | 86 | 31 | 73 | 5 | 4 | 4 | 0 | 188 | 14.9 |
| PIERRE TURGEON | MTL-STL | 78 | 26 | 59 | 85 | 8 | 14 | 5 | 0 | 7 | 1 | 216 | 12.0 |
| STEVE YZERMAN | DETROIT | 81 | 22 | 63 | 85 | 22 | 78 | 8 | 0 | 3 | 0 | 232 | 9.5 |
| MARK MESSIER | NY RANGERS | 71 | 36 | 48 | 84 | 12 | 88 | 7 | 5 | 9 | 1 | 227 | 15.9 |
| MIKE MODANO | DALLAS | 80 | 35 | 48 | 83 | 43 | 42 | 9 | 5 | 9 | 2 | 291 | 12.0 |
| BRETT HULL | ST LOUIS | 77 | 42 | 40 | 82 | 9- | 10 | 12 | 2 | 6 | 2 | 302 | 13.9 |
| ADAM OATES | BOS-WSH | 80 | 22 | 60 | 82 | 5- | 14 | 3 | 2 | 5 | 0 | 160 | 13.8 |
| DOUG GILMOUR | TOR-N.J | 81 | 22 | 60 | 82 | 2 | 68 | 4 | 1 | 1 | 1 | 143 | 15.4 |
| DOUG WEIGHT | EDMONTON | 80 | 21 | 61 | 82 | 1 | 80 | 4 | 0 | 2 | 0 | 235 | 8.9 |
| VINCENT DAMPHOUSSE | MONTREAL | 82 | 27 | 54 | 81 | 6- | 82 | 7 | 2 | 3 | 2 | 244 | 11.1 |
| MARK RECCHI | MONTREAL | 82 | 34 | 46 | 80 | 1- | 58 | 7 | 2 | 3 | 0 | 202 | 16.8 |
| ERIC LINDROS | PHILADELPHIA | 52 | 32 | 47 | 79 | 31 | 136 | 9 | 0 | 7 | 2 | 198 | 16.2 |
| BRIAN LEETCH | NY RANGERS | 82 | 20 | 58 | 78 | 31 | 40 | 9 | 0 | 2 | 0 | 256 | 7.8 |

DEFENCEMEN SCORING LEADERS

| PLAYER | TEAM | GP | G | A | PTS | +/- | PIM | PP | SH | GW | GT | S | PCTG |
|---|---|---|---|---|---|---|---|---|---|---|---|---|---|
| BRIAN LEETCH | NY RANGERS | 82 | 20 | 58 | 78 | 31 | 40 | 9 | 0 | 2 | 0 | 256 | 7.8 |
| SANDIS OZOLINSH | COLORADO | 80 | 23 | 45 | 68 | 4 | 88 | 13 | 0 | 4 | 1 | 232 | 9.9 |
| NICKLAS LIDSTROM | DETROIT | 79 | 15 | 42 | 57 | 11 | 30 | 8 | 0 | 1 | 0 | 214 | 7.0 |
| OLEG TVERDOVSKY | PHOENIX | 82 | 10 | 45 | 55 | 5- | 30 | 3 | 1 | 2 | 0 | 144 | 6.9 |
| KEVIN HATCHER | PITTSBURGH | 80 | 15 | 39 | 54 | 11 | 103 | 9 | 0 | 1 | 0 | 199 | 7.5 |
| DMITRI MIRONOV | PIT-ANA | 77 | 13 | 39 | 52 | 16 | 101 | 3 | 1 | 2 | 0 | 177 | 7.3 |
| RAY BOURQUE | BOSTON | 62 | 19 | 31 | 50 | 11- | 18 | 8 | 1 | 3 | 1 | 230 | 8.3 |
| CHRIS CHELIOS | CHICAGO | 72 | 10 | 38 | 48 | 16 | 112 | 2 | 0 | 2 | 0 | 194 | 5.2 |
| DARRYL SYDOR | DALLAS | 82 | 8 | 40 | 48 | 37 | 51 | 2 | 0 | 2 | 0 | 142 | 5.6 |
| *BRYAN BERARD | NY ISLANDERS | 82 | 8 | 40 | 48 | 1 | 86 | 3 | 0 | 1 | 0 | 172 | 4.7 |
| STEVE DUCHESNE | OTTAWA | 78 | 19 | 28 | 47 | 9- | 38 | 10 | 2 | 3 | 0 | 208 | 9.1 |
| ERIC DESJARDINS | PHILADELPHIA | 82 | 12 | 34 | 46 | 25 | 50 | 5 | 1 | 1 | 0 | 183 | 6.6 |
| ROBERT SVEHLA | FLORIDA | 82 | 13 | 32 | 45 | 2 | 86 | 5 | 0 | 3 | 0 | 159 | 8.2 |
| LARRY MURPHY | TOR-DET | 81 | 9 | 36 | 45 | 3 | 20 | 5 | 0 | 1 | 1 | 158 | 5.7 |
| *JANNE NIINIMAA | PHILADELPHIA | 77 | 4 | 40 | 44 | 12 | 58 | 1 | 0 | 2 | 0 | 141 | 2.8 |

INDIVIDUAL LEADERS

GOAL SCORING

| NAME | TEAM | GP | G |
|---|---|---|---|
| KEITH TKACHUK | PHOENIX | 81 | 52 |
| TEEMU SELANNE | ANAHEIM | 78 | 51 |
| MARIO LEMIEUX | PITTSBURGH | 76 | 50 |
| JOHN LECLAIR | PHILADELPHIA | 82 | 50 |
| ZIGMUND PALFFY | NY ISLANDERS | 80 | 48 |
| JAROMIR JAGR | PITTSBURGH | 63 | 47 |
| BRENDAN SHANAHAN | HFD-DET | 81 | 47 |
| PETER BONDRA | WASHINGTON | 77 | 46 |
| PAUL KARIYA | ANAHEIM | 69 | 44 |
| BRETT HULL | ST LOUIS | 77 | 42 |
| TONY AMONTE | CHICAGO | 81 | 41 |
| MATS SUNDIN | TORONTO | 82 | 41 |
| RYAN SMYTH | EDMONTON | 82 | 39 |
| MARK MESSIER | NY RANGERS | 71 | 36 |
| GEOFF SANDERSON | HARTFORD | 82 | 36 |
| MARTIN GELINAS | VANCOUVER | 74 | 35 |

ASSISTS

| NAME | TEAM | GP | A |
|---|---|---|---|
| MARIO LEMIEUX | PITTSBURGH | 76 | 72 |
| WAYNE GRETZKY | NY RANGERS | 82 | 72 |
| RON FRANCIS | PITTSBURGH | 81 | 63 |
| STEVE YZERMAN | DETROIT | 81 | 63 |
| DOUG WEIGHT | EDMONTON | 80 | 61 |
| ADAM OATES | BOS-WSH | 80 | 60 |
| DOUG GILMOUR | TOR-N.J | 81 | 60 |
| PIERRE TURGEON | MTL-STL | 78 | 59 |
| PETER FORSBERG | COLORADO | 65 | 58 |
| TEEMU SELANNE | ANAHEIM | 78 | 58 |
| BRIAN LEETCH | NY RANGERS | 82 | 58 |
| PAUL KARIYA | ANAHEIM | 69 | 55 |
| JOZEF STUMPEL | BOSTON | 78 | 55 |
| VINCENT DAMPHOUSSE | MONTREAL | 82 | 54 |
| MATS SUNDIN | TORONTO | 82 | 53 |
| JOE SAKIC | COLORADO | 65 | 52 |

| DINO CICCARELLI | TAMPA BAY | 77 | 35 | JAROMIR JAGR | PITTSBURGH | 63 | 48 |
|---|---|---|---|---|---|---|---|
| MIKE MODANO | DALLAS | 80 | 35 | MARK MESSIER | NY RANGERS | 71 | 48 |
| ALEXEI YASHIN | OTTAWA | 82 | 35 | STEVE RUCCHIN | ANAHEIM | 79 | 48 |
| MARK RECCHI | MONTREAL | 82 | 34 | MIKE MODANO | DALLAS | 80 | 48 |

## POWER PLAY GOALS

| NAME | TEAM | GP | PP |
|---|---|---|---|
| BRENDAN SHANAHAN | HFD-DET | 81 | 20 |
| RYAN SMYTH | EDMONTON | 82 | 20 |
| PAUL KARIYA | ANAHEIM | 69 | 15 |
| MARIO LEMIEUX | PITTSBURGH | 76 | 15 |
| ANDREI KOVALENKO | EDMONTON | 74 | 14 |
| KEITH JONES | WSH-COL | 78 | 14 |
| RAY SHEPPARD | FLORIDA | 68 | 13 |
| SANDIS OZOLINSH | COLORADO | 80 | 13 |
| MIKE GARTNER | PHOENIX | 82 | 13 |
| PETR NEDVED | PITTSBURGH | 74 | 12 |
| DINO CICCARELLI | TAMPA BAY | 77 | 12 |
| BRETT HULL | ST LOUIS | 77 | 12 |
| GERMAN TITOV | CALGARY | 79 | 12 |
| GEOFF SANDERSON | HARTFORD | 82 | 12 |

## SHORT HAND GOALS

| NAME | TEAM | GP | SH |
|---|---|---|---|
| MICHAEL PECA | BUFFALO | 79 | 6 |
| MARK MESSIER | NY RANGERS | 71 | 5 |
| TRENT KLATT | PHILADELPHIA | 76 | 5 |
| MIKE MODANO | DALLAS | 80 | 5 |
| SHELDON KENNEDY | BOSTON | 56 | 4 |
| PETER FORSBERG | COLORADO | 65 | 4 |
| PETER BONDRA | WASHINGTON | 77 | 4 |
| TODD MARCHANT | EDMONTON | 79 | 4 |
| ZIGMUND PALFFY | NY ISLANDERS | 80 | 4 |
| ADAM GRAVES | NY RANGERS | 82 | 4 |
| MATS SUNDIN | TORONTO | 82 | 4 |
| ROB ZAMUNER | TAMPA BAY | 82 | 4 |

## POWER PLAY ASSISTS

| NAME | TEAM | GP | PPA |
|---|---|---|---|
| DOUG WEIGHT | EDMONTON | 80 | 35 |
| SANDIS OZOLINSH | COLORADO | 80 | 29 |
| OLEG TVERDOVSKY | PHOENIX | 82 | 27 |
| JOE SAKIC | COLORADO | 65 | 26 |
| WAYNE GRETZKY | NY RANGERS | 82 | 25 |
| RON FRANCIS | PITTSBURGH | 81 | 24 |
| *JANNE NIINIMAA | PHILADELPHIA | 77 | 23 |
| JASON ARNOTT | EDMONTON | 67 | 22 |
| MARIO LEMIEUX | PITTSBURGH | 76 | 22 |
| PIERRE TURGEON | MTL-STL | 78 | 22 |
| NICKLAS LIDSTROM | DETROIT | 79 | 22 |
| PETER FORSBERG | COLORADO | 65 | 21 |

## SHORT HAND ASSISTS

| NAME | TEAM | GP | SHA |
|---|---|---|---|
| MARK MESSIER | NY RANGERS | 71 | 6 |
| RAY BOURQUE | BOSTON | 62 | 5 |
| ADAM OATES | BOS-WSH | 80 | 4 |
| KELLY BUCHBERGER | EDMONTON | 81 | 4 |
| ROB ZAMUNER | TAMPA BAY | 82 | 4 |
| JERE LEHTINEN | DALLAS | 63 | 3 |
| BERNIE NICHOLLS | SAN JOSE | 65 | 3 |
| PETER FORSBERG | COLORADO | 65 | 3 |
| JEREMY ROENICK | PHOENIX | 72 | 3 |
| DAVE ELLETT | TOR-N.J | 76 | 3 |
| MARIO LEMIEUX | PITTSBURGH | 76 | 3 |
| MICHAEL PECA | BUFFALO | 79 | 3 |

| NAME | TEAM | GP | |
|---|---|---|---|
| DMITRI MIRONOV | PIT-ANA | 77 | 21 |
| TEEMU SELANNE | ANAHEIM | 78 | 21 |
| BRIAN LEETCH | NY RANGERS | 82 | 21 |
| DARRYL SYDOR | DALLAS | 82 | 21 |
| DANIEL ALFREDSSON | OTTAWA | 76 | 20 |

| NAME | TEAM | GP | |
|---|---|---|---|
| BILL LINDSAY | FLORIDA | 81 | 3 |
| VINCENT DAMPHOUSSE | MONTREAL | 82 | 3 |
| DAVE GAGNER | CALGARY | 82 | 3 |
| MATS SUNDIN | TORONTO | 82 | 3 |
| *JAROME IGINLA | CALGARY | 82 | 3 |

## POWER PLAY POINTS

| NAME | TEAM | GP | PPP |
|---|---|---|---|
| SANDIS OZOLINSH | COLORADO | 80 | 42 |
| DOUG WEIGHT | EDMONTON | 80 | 39 |
| MARIO LEMIEUX | PITTSBURGH | 76 | 37 |
| JOE SAKIC | COLORADO | 65 | 36 |
| BRENDAN SHANAHAN | HFD-DET | 81 | 35 |
| PAUL KARIYA | ANAHEIM | 69 | 34 |
| RON FRANCIS | PITTSBURGH | 81 | 34 |
| JASON ARNOTT | EDMONTON | 67 | 32 |
| TEEMU SELANNE | ANAHEIM | 78 | 32 |
| DANIEL ALFREDSSON | OTTAWA | 76 | 31 |
| WAYNE GRETZKY | NY RANGERS | 82 | 31 |

## SHORT HAND POINTS

| NAME | TEAM | GP | SHP |
|---|---|---|---|
| MARK MESSIER | NY RANGERS | 71 | 11 |
| MICHAEL PECA | BUFFALO | 79 | 9 |
| ROB ZAMUNER | TAMPA BAY | 82 | 8 |
| PETER FORSBERG | COLORADO | 65 | 7 |
| MIKE MODANO | DALLAS | 80 | 7 |
| MATS SUNDIN | TORONTO | 82 | 7 |
| RAY BOURQUE | BOSTON | 62 | 6 |
| JEREMY ROENICK | PHOENIX | 72 | 6 |
| ADAM OATES | BOS-WSH | 80 | 6 |
| ZIGMUND PALFFY | NY ISLANDERS | 80 | 6 |
| ADAM GRAVES | NY RANGERS | 82 | 6 |

## GAME WINNING GOALS

| NAME | TEAM | GP | GW |
|---|---|---|---|
| PAUL KARIYA | ANAHEIM | 69 | 10 |
| MARK MESSIER | NY RANGERS | 71 | 9 |
| MIKE MODANO | DALLAS | 80 | 9 |
| BILL GUERIN | NEW JERSEY | 82 | 9 |
| TEEMU SELANNE | ANAHEIM | 78 | 8 |
| MATS SUNDIN | TORONTO | 82 | 8 |

## GAME TYING GOALS

| NAME | TEAM | GP | GT |
|---|---|---|---|
| ADAM GRAVES | NY RANGERS | 82 | 5 |
| THEOREN FLEURY | CALGARY | 81 | 3 |
| STU BARNES | FLA-PIT | 81 | 3 |

## 22 PLAYERS WITH TWO SHOTS

| NAME | TEAM | GP | S |
|---|---|---|---|
| PAUL KARIYA | ANAHEIM | 69 | 340 |
| THEOREN FLEURY | CALGARY | 81 | 336 |
| BRENDAN SHANAHAN | HFD-DET | 81 | 336 |
| MARIO LEMIEUX | PITTSBURGH | 76 | 327 |
| JOHN LECLAIR | PHILADELPHIA | 82 | 324 |

## SHOOTING PERCENTAGE (MIN 82 SHOTS)

| NAME | TEAM | GP | G | S | PCTG |
|---|---|---|---|---|---|
| MIROSLAV SATAN | EDM-BUF | 76 | 25 | 119 | 21.0 |
| JAROMIR JAGR | PITTSBURGH | 63 | 47 | 234 | 20.1 |
| MARTIN GELINAS | VANCOUVER | 74 | 35 | 177 | 19.8 |
| ANDREI KOVALENKO | EDMONTON | 74 | 32 | 163 | 19.6 |
| TEEMU SELANNE | ANAHEIM | 78 | 51 | 273 | 18.7 |

## PLUS/MINUS

| NAME | TEAM | GP | +/- |
|---|---|---|---|
| JOHN LECLAIR | PHILADELPHIA | 82 | 44 |
| MIKE MODANO | DALLAS | 80 | 43 |
| VLAD. KONSTANTINOV | DETROIT | 77 | 38 |
| DAVE ANDREYCHUK | NEW JERSEY | 82 | 38 |
| DARRYL SYDOR | DALLAS | 82 | 37 |

## CONSECUTIVE SCORING STREAKS
## GOALS SCORED IN 5 OR MORE CONSECUTIVE GAMES

| GM | PLAYER | TEAM | FROM | TO | G |
|---|---|---|---|---|---|
| 9 | JAROMIR JAGR | PITTSBURGH | Nov 21 | Dec 10 | 14 |
| 7 | MARIO LEMIEUX | PITTSBURGH | Dec 17 | Dec 30 | 12 |
| 6 | JAROMIR JAGR | PITTSBURGH | Oct 24 | Nov 08 | 9 |

| | | | | | |
|---|---|---|---|---|---|
| 6 | PETER BONDRA | WASHINGTON | Dec 23 | Jan 03 | 8 |
| 6 | BRETT HULL | ST LOUIS | Jan 23 | Feb 01 | 8 |
| 6 | MIKE MODANO | DALLAS | Jan 21 | Jan 31 | 7 |
| 6 | PETER FORSBERG | COLORADO | Mar 03 | Mar 14 | 7 |
| 5 | VINCENT DAMPHOUSSE | MONTREAL | Dec 29 | Jan 06 | 9 |
| 5 | BRENDAN SHANAHAN | HFD-DET | Feb 08 | Feb 17 | 9 |
| 5 | ZIGMUND PALFFY | NY ISLANDERS | Mar 27 | Apr 05 | 9 |
| 5 | KEITH TKACHUK | PHOENIX | Mar 12 | Mar 20 | 8 |
| 5 | TONY AMONTE | CHICAGO | Nov 17 | Nov 27 | 7 |
| 5 | PAVEL BURE | VANCOUVER | Jan 02 | Jan 10 | 7 |
| 5 | ERIC LINDROS | PHILADELPHIA | Dec 10 | Dec 19 | 6 |
| 5 | MARTIN RUCINSKY | MONTREAL | Jan 30 | Feb 06 | 6 |
| 5 | ADAM OATES | BOSTON | Jan 11 | Jan 22 | 5 |
| 5 | TEEMU SELANNE | ANAHEIM | Jan 03 | Jan 12 | 5 |
| 5 | RYAN SMYTH | EDMONTON | Apr 03 | Apr 12 | 5 |
| 5 | *DANIEL GONEAU | NY RANGERS | Oct 12 | Oct 20 | 5 |
| 5 | *HARRY YORK | ST LOUIS | Oct 30 | Nov 08 | 5 |

## ASSISTS AWARDED IN 5 OR MORE CONSECUTIVE GAMES

| GM | PLAYER | TEAM | FROM | TO | A |
|---|---|---|---|---|---|
| 14 | ADAM OATES | BOSTON | Jan 22 | Feb 20 | 16 |
| 8 | VINCENT DAMPHOUSSE | MONTREAL | Jan 30 | Feb 12 | 14 |
| 8 | KEVIN HATCHER | PITTSBURGH | Nov 30 | Dec 13 | 12 |
| 8 | DOUG WEIGHT | EDMONTON | Jan 11 | Jan 29 | 10 |
| 8 | DOUG WEIGHT | EDMONTON | Feb 26 | Mar 13 | 10 |
| 8 | STEVE YZERMAN | DETROIT | Oct 21 | Nov 04 | 9 |
| 8 | BERNIE NICHOLLS | SAN JOSE | Oct 24 | Nov 08 | 8 |
| 7 | MARIO LEMIEUX | PITTSBURGH | Jan 02 | Jan 15 | 19 |
| 7 | WAYNE GRETZKY | NY RANGERS | Dec 09 | Dec 22 | 14 |
| 7 | BRENDAN SHANAHAN | HFD-DET | Dec 12 | Dec 26 | 9 |
| 7 | BRIAN LEETCH | NY RANGERS | Nov 16 | Dec 01 | 8 |
| 7 | BRYAN SMOLINSKI | NY ISLANDERS | Mar 16 | Apr 02 | 8 |
| 6 | STEVE YZERMAN | DETROIT | Nov 15 | Nov 27 | 11 |
| 6 | STEVE YZERMAN | DETROIT | Feb 08 | Feb 19 | 11 |
| 6 | ERIC LINDROS | PHILADELPHIA | Mar 09 | Mar 22 | 10 |
| 6 | MARK RECCHI | MONTREAL | Oct 26 | Nov 06 | 9 |
| 6 | PAUL KARIYA | ANAHEIM | Dec 30 | Jan 10 | 9 |
| 6 | MATS SUNDIN | TORONTO | Oct 29 | Nov 09 | 8 |

| | | | | | | |
|---|---|---|---|---|---|---|
| 6 | *JAMIE LANGENBRUNNE | DALLAS | Jan 29 | Feb 08 | 8 | |
| 6 | STEVE RUCCHIN | ANAHEIM | Feb 05 | Feb 17 | 7 | |
| 6 | KEVIN DINEEN | HARTFORD | Jan 25 | Feb 08 | 6 | |
| 6 | CORY STILLMAN | CALGARY | Oct 13 | Oct 24 | 6 | |

## POINTS GAINED IN 5 OR MORE CONSECUTIVE GAMES

| GM | PLAYER | TEAM | FROM | TO | G | A | PTS |
|---|---|---|---|---|---|---|---|
| 20 | ADAM OATES | BOSTON | Jan 07 | Feb 20 | 7 | 21 | 28 |
| 17 | ERIC LINDROS | PHILADELPHIA | Nov 30 | Jan 07 | 13 | 16 | 29 |
| 15 | MARIO LEMIEUX | PITTSBURGH | Dec 17 | Jan 21 | 15 | 23 | 38 |
| 15 | WAYNE GRETZKY | NY RANGERS | Oct 06 | Nov 04 | 7 | 15 | 22 |
| 14 | BRIAN LEETCH | NY RANGERS | Oct 30 | Dec 01 | 6 | 14 | 20 |
| 13 | JAROMIR JAGR | PITTSBURGH | Nov 16 | Dec 13 | 15 | 9 | 24 |
| 12 | WAYNE GRETZKY | NY RANGERS | Nov 27 | Dec 22 | 5 | 19 | 24 |
| 12 | BRETT HULL | ST LOUIS | Jan 05 | Feb 01 | 11 | 8 | 19 |
| 12 | TEEMU SELANNE | ANAHEIM | Dec 30 | Jan 27 | 9 | 10 | 19 |
| 12 | PAUL KARIYA | ANAHEIM | Mar 19 | Apr 11 | 10 | 9 | 19 |
| 12 | BRETT HULL | ST LOUIS | Feb 22 | Mar 23 | 8 | 9 | 17 |
| 11 | MATS SUNDIN | TORONTO | Nov 13 | Dec 06 | 7 | 9 | 16 |
| 11 | ANDREI KOVALENKO | EDMONTON | Dec 12 | Jan 07 | 8 | 7 | 15 |
| 10 | PETER FORSBERG | COLORADO | Mar 01 | Mar 21 | 9 | 11 | 20 |
| 10 | MARK MESSIER | NY RANGERS | Jan 12 | Feb 08 | 8 | 9 | 17 |
| 10 | BOBBY HOLIK | NEW JERSEY | Jan 14 | Feb 08 | 5 | 10 | 15 |
| 10 | PETER BONDRA | WASHINGTON | Dec 23 | Jan 13 | 12 | 2 | 14 |
| 10 | DOUG WEIGHT | EDMONTON | Feb 26 | Mar 19 | 3 | 11 | 14 |

## INDIVIDUAL ROOKIE SCORING LEADERS

| PLAYER | TEAM | GP | G | A | PTS | +/- | PIM | PP | SH | GW | GT | S | PCTG |
|---|---|---|---|---|---|---|---|---|---|---|---|---|---|
| JAROME IGINLA | CALGARY | 82 | 21 | 29 | 50 | 4- | 37 | 8 | 1 | 3 | 0 | 169 | 12.4 |
| BRYAN BERARD | NY ISLANDERS | 82 | 8 | 40 | 48 | 1 | 86 | 3 | 0 | 1 | 0 | 172 | 4.7 |
| JANNE NIINIMAA | PHILADELPHIA | 77 | 4 | 40 | 44 | 12 | 58 | 1 | 0 | 2 | 0 | 141 | 2.8 |
| JIM CAMPBELL | ST LOUIS | 68 | 23 | 20 | 43 | 3 | 68 | 5 | 0 | 6 | 1 | 169 | 13.6 |
| SERGEI BEREZIN | TORONTO | 73 | 25 | 16 | 41 | 3- | 2 | 7 | 0 | 2 | 0 | 177 | 14.1 |
| JAMIE LANGENBRUNNE | DALLAS | 76 | 13 | 26 | 39 | 2- | 51 | 3 | 0 | 3 | 0 | 112 | 11.6 |
| STEVE SULLIVAN | N.J-TOR | 54 | 13 | 25 | 38 | 14 | 37 | 3 | 0 | 3 | 1 | 108 | 12.0 |
| JONAS HOGLUND | CALGARY | 68 | 19 | 16 | 35 | 4- | 12 | 3 | 0 | 6 | 1 | 189 | 10.1 |
| MIKE GRIER | EDMONTON | 79 | 15 | 17 | 32 | 7 | 45 | 4 | 0 | 2 | 0 | 89 | 16.9 |

| | | | | | | | | | | | | | | |
|---|---|---|---|---|---|---|---|---|---|---|---|---|---|---|
| HARRY YORK | ST LOUIS | 74 | 14 | 18 | 32 | 1 | 24 | 3 | 1 | 3 | 0 | 86 | 16.3 |
| DENIS PEDERSON | NEW JERSEY | 70 | 12 | 20 | 32 | 7 | 62 | 3 | 0 | 3 | 0 | 106 | 11.3 |
| ETHAN MOREAU | CHICAGO | 82 | 15 | 16 | 31 | 13 | 123 | 0 | 0 | 1 | 1 | 114 | 13.2 |
| ANDREAS DACKELL | OTTAWA | 79 | 12 | 19 | 31 | 6- | 8 | 2 | 0 | 3 | 0 | 79 | 15.2 |
| REM MURRAY | EDMONTON | 82 | 11 | 20 | 31 | 9 | 16 | 1 | 0 | 2 | 0 | 85 | 12.9 |
| WADE REDDEN | OTTAWA | 82 | 6 | 24 | 30 | 1 | 41 | 2 | 0 | 1 | 0 | 102 | 5.9 |

## RECORD OF GOALTENDERS

ALL GOALS AGAINST A TEAM IN ANY GAME ARE CHARGED TO THE GOALTENDER OF THAT GAME FOR PURPOSES OF AWARDING THE BILL JENNINGS TROPHY

WON-LOST-TIED RECORD IS BASED UPON WHICH GOALTENDER WAS PLAYING WHEN THE WINNING OR TYING GOAL WAS SCORED

OVERALL RANKING IS BASED ON GOALS AGAINST AVERAGE,
(MINIMUM OF 900 MINUTES PLAYED)

EMPTY-NET GOALS ARE NOT COUNTED IN PERSONAL AVERAGES BUT ARE INCLUDED IN THE TEAM TOTAL

(GPI) GAMES PLAYED IN          (MINS) MINUTES PLAYED          (AVG) 60 MINUTE AVERAGE
(ENG) EMPTY-NET GOALS AGAINST  (SO) SHUTOUTS                  (GA) GOALS AGAINST
(SA) SHOTS AGAINST             (SV %) SAVE PERCENTAGE          (RNK) OVERALL RANKING

| RNK | SW# | GOALTENDER | GPI | MINS | AVG | W | L | T | EN | SO | GA | SA | SV% | G | A | PIM |
|---|---|---|---|---|---|---|---|---|---|---|---|---|---|---|---|---|
| 1 | 30 | MARTIN BRODEUR | 67 | 3838 | 1.88 | 37 | 14 | 13 | 5 | 10 | 120 | 1633 | .927 | 0 | 4 | 8 |
| 11 | 1 | *MIKE DUNHAM | 26 | 1013 | 2.55 | 8 | 7 | 1 | 1 | 2 | 43 | 456 | .906 | 0 | 0 | 2 |
| 35 | | JEFF REESE | 3 | 139 | 5.61 | 0 | 2 | 0 | 0 | 0 | 13 | 65 | .800 | 0 | 0 | 0 |
| N.J TOTALS | | | 82 | 4999 | 2.18 | 45 | 23 | 14 | 6 | 13 | 182 | 2160 | .916 | | | |

MARTIN BRODEUR and MIKE DUNHAM shared a shutout vs NYI on Nov 9, 1996

| | | | | | | | | | | | | | | | | |
|---|---|---|---|---|---|---|---|---|---|---|---|---|---|---|---|---|
| 31 | | *KEVIN HODSON | 6 | 294 | 1.63 | 2 | 2 | 1 | 0 | 1 | 8 | 114 | .930 | 0 | 1 | 0 |
| 6 | 30 | CHRIS OSGOOD | 47 | 2769 | 2.30 | 23 | 13 | 9 | 3 | 6 | 106 | 1175 | .910 | 0 | 2 | 6 |
| 9 | 29 | MIKE VERNON | 33 | 1952 | 2.43 | 13 | 11 | 8 | 1 | 0 | 79 | 782 | .899 | 0 | 0 | 35 |
| DET TOTALS | | | 82 | 5031 | 2.35 | 38 | 26 | 18 | 4 | 7 | 197 | 2075 | .905 | | | |

| | | | | | | | | | | | | | | | | |
|---|---|---|---|---|---|---|---|---|---|---|---|---|---|---|---|---|
| 1 | | ROMAN TUREK | 6 | 263 | 2.05 | 3 | 1 | 0 | 0 | 0 | 9 | 129 | .930 | 0 | 0 | 0 |
| 2 | 35 | ANDY MOOG | 48 | 2738 | 2.15 | 28 | 13 | 5 | 0 | 3 | 98 | 1121 | .913 | 0 | 1 | 12 |
| 19 | 32 | ARTURS IRBE | 35 | 1965 | 2.69 | 17 | 12 | 3 | 3 | 3 | 88 | 825 | .893 | 0 | 2 | 8 |
| DAL TOTALS | | | 82 | 4979 | 2.39 | 48 | 26 | 8 | 3 | 6 | 198 | 2078 | .905 | | | |

| | | | | | | | | | | | | | | | |
|---|---|---|---|---|---|---|---|---|---|---|---|---|---|---|---|
| 5 | 34 | J. VANBIESBROUCK | 57 | 3347 | 2.29 | 27 | 19 | 10 | 3 | 2 | 128 | 1582 | .919 | 0 | 2 | 8 |
| 8 | 30 | MARK FITZPATRICK | 30 | 1680 | 2.36 | 8 | 9 | 9 | 4 | 0 | 66 | 771 | .914 | 0 | 1 | 13 |
| FLA TOTALS | | | 82 | 5041 | 2.39 | 35 | 28 | 19 | 7 | 2 | 201 | 2360 | .915 | | | |
| | | | | | | | | | | | | | | | | |
| 7 | 33 | PATRICK ROY | 62 | 3698 | 2.32 | 38 | 15 | 7 | 3 | 7 | 143 | 1861 | .923 | 0 | 1 | 15 |
| 15 | 1 | CRAIG BILLINGTON | 23 | 1200 | 2.65 | 11 | 8 | 2 | 2 | 1 | 53 | 584 | .909 | 0 | 2 | 2 |
| 30 | | *MARC DENIS | 1 | 60 | 3.00 | 0 | 1 | 0 | 1 | 0 | 3 | 26 | .885 | 0 | 0 | 0 |
| COL TOTALS | | | 82 | 4980 | 2.47 | 49 | 24 | 9 | 6 | 8 | 205 | 2477 | .917 | | | |
| | | | | | | | | | | | | | | | | |
| 4 | 39 | DOMINIK HASEK | 67 | 4037 | 2.27 | 37 | 20 | 10 | 3 | 5 | 153 | 2177 | .930 | 0 | 3 | 30 |
| 31 | | *STEVE SHIELDS | 13 | 789 | 2.97 | 3 | 8 | 2 | 2 | 0 | 39 | 447 | .913 | 0 | 0 | 4 |
| 30 | | ANDREI TREFILOV | 3 | 159 | 3.77 | 0 | 2 | 0 | 1 | 0 | 10 | 98 | .898 | 0 | 0 | 0 |
| BUF TOTALS | | | 82 | 5003 | 2.49 | 40 | 30 | 12 | 6 | 5 | 208 | 2728 | .924 | | | |
| | | | | | | | | | | | | | | | | |
| 3 | 31 | JEFF HACKETT | 41 | 2473 | 2.16 | 19 | 18 | 4 | 2 | 2 | 89 | 1212 | .927 | 0 | 1 | 6 |
| 23 | 40 | CHRIS TERRERI | 7 | 429 | 2.66 | 4 | 1 | 2 | 1 | 0 | 19 | 192 | .901 | 0 | 0 | 0 |
| 28 | 20 | ED BELFOUR | 33 | 1966 | 2.69 | 11 | 15 | 6 | 4 | 1 | 88 | 946 | .907 | 0 | 0 | 26 |
| 29 | | JIM WAITE | 2 | 105 | 4.00 | 0 | 1 | 1 | 0 | 0 | 7 | 58 | .879 | 0 | 0 | 0 |
| CHI TOTALS | | | 82 | 5000 | 2.52 | 34 | 35 | 13 | 7 | 3 | 210 | 2415 | .913 | | | |
| | | | | | | | | | | | | | | | | |
| 10 | 30 | GARTH SNOW | 35 | 1884 | 2.52 | 14 | 8 | 8 | 2 | 2 | 79 | 816 | .903 | 0 | 1 | 30 |
| 12 | 27 | RON HEXTALL | 55 | 3094 | 2.56 | 31 | 16 | 5 | 4 | 5 | 132 | 1285 | .897 | 0 | 0 | 43 |
| PHI TOTALS | | | 82 | 4995 | 2.61 | 45 | 24 | 13 | 6 | 7 | 217 | 2107 | .897 | | | |
| | | | | | | | | | | | | | | | | |
| 13 | 37 | OLAF KOLZIG | 29 | 1645 | 2.59 | 8 | 15 | 4 | 6 | 2 | 71 | 758 | .906 | 0 | 0 | 4 |
| 42 | 30 | BILL RANFORD | 18 | 1009 | 2.74 | 8 | 7 | 2 | 1 | 0 | 46 | 412 | .888 | 0 | 1 | 7 |
| 35 | 30 | JIM CAREY | 40 | 2293 | 2.75 | 17 | 18 | 3 | 2 | 1 | 105 | 984 | .893 | 0 | 0 | 2 |
| WSH TOTALS | | | 82 | 4977 | 2.78 | 33 | 40 | 9 | 9 | 3 | 231 | 2163 | .893 | | | |
| | | | | | | | | | | | | | | | | |
| 14 | 30 | GLENN HEALY | 23 | 1357 | 2.61 | 5 | 12 | 4 | 2 | 1 | 59 | 632 | .907 | 0 | 0 | 4 |
| 17 | 35 | MIKE RICHTER | 61 | 3598 | 2.68 | 33 | 22 | 6 | 9 | 4 | 161 | 1945 | .917 | 0 | 0 | 4 |
| NYR TOTALS | | | 82 | 4974 | 2.79 | 38 | 34 | 10 | 11 | 5 | 231 | 2588 | .911 | | | |
| | | | | | | | | | | | | | | | | |
| 16 | 31 | GUY HEBERT | 67 | 3863 | 2.67 | 29 | 25 | 12 | 2 | 4 | 172 | 2133 | .919 | 0 | 1 | 4 |
| 30 | 35 | M. SHTALENKOV | 24 | 1079 | 2.89 | 7 | 8 | 1 | 4 | 2 | 52 | 539 | .904 | 0 | 0 | 4 |
| 1 | | MICHAEL O'NEILL | 1 | 31 | 5.81 | 0 | 0 | 0 | 0 | 0 | 3 | 10 | .700 | 0 | 0 | 0 |
| ANA TOTALS | | | 82 | 4994 | 2.80 | 36 | 33 | 13 | 6 | 6 | 233 | 2688 | .913 | | | |
| | | | | | | | | | | | | | | | | |
| 22 | 1 | DAMIAN RHODES | 50 | 2934 | 2.72 | 14 | 20 | 14 | 2 | 1 | 133 | 1213 | .890 | 0 | 2 | 2 |
| 24 | 31 | RON TUGNUTT | 37 | 1991 | 2.80 | 17 | 15 | 1 | 2 | 3 | 93 | 882 | .895 | 0 | 1 | 0 |

# 1997-98 HOCKEY ANNUAL

| No | No | Name | GP | MIN | AVG | W | L | T | EN | SO | GA | SA | SV% | — | — | PIM |
|----|----|------|----|-----|-----|---|---|---|----|----|----|----|-----|---|---|-----|
| 35 | | *MIKE BALES | 1 | 52 | 4.62 | 0 | 1 | 0 | 0 | 0 | 4 | 18 | .778 | 0 | 0 | 0 |
| | | OTT TOTALS | | 82 | 5001 | 2.81 | 31 | 36 | 15 | 4 | 4 | 234 | 2117 | .889 | | |
| 20 | 31 | RICK TABARACCI | 7 | 361 | 2.33 | 2 | 4 | 0 | 0 | 1 | 14 | 155 | .910 | 0 | 0 | 0 |
| 27 | 37 | TREVOR KIDD | 55 | 2979 | 2.84 | 21 | 23 | 6 | 4 | 4 | 141 | 1416 | .900 | 0 | 2 | 16 |
| 29 | 30 | DWAYNE ROLOSON | 31 | 1618 | 2.89 | 9 | 14 | 3 | 2 | 1 | 78 | 760 | .897 | 0 | 0 | 2 |
| | | CGY TOTALS | | 82 | 4990 | 2.87 | 32 | 41 | 9 | 6 | 6 | 239 | 2337 | .898 | | |
| 21 | 31 | GRANT FUHR | 73 | 4261 | 2.72 | 33 | 27 | 11 | 4 | 3 | 193 | 1940 | .901 | 0 | 2 | 6 |
| 30 | | JON CASEY | 15 | 707 | 3.39 | 3 | 8 | 0 | 2 | 0 | 40 | 299 | .866 | 0 | 0 | 0 |
| | | STL TOTALS | | 82 | 4980 | 2.88 | 36 | 35 1 | 1 | 6 | 3 | 239 | 2245 | .894 | | |
| 39 | | PAT JABLONSKI | 2 | 59 | 2.03 | 0 | 1 | 0 | 1 | 0 | 2 | 24 | .917 | 0 | 0 | 0 |
| 1 | | PARRIS DUFFUS | 1 | 29 | 2.07 | 0 | 0 | 0 | 0 | 0 | 1 | 8 | .875 | 0 | 0 | 0 |
| 26 | 35 | N. KHABIBULIN | 72 | 4091 | 2.83 | 30 | 33 | 6 | 7 | 7 | 193 | 2094 | .908 | 0 | 3 | 16 |
| 43 | | DARCY WAKALUK | 16 | 782 | 2.99 | 8 | 3 | 1 | 0 | 1 | 39 | 386 | .899 | 0 | 1 | 4 |
| | | PHO TOTALS | | 82 | 4974 | 2.93 | 38 | 37 | 7 | 8 | 8 | 243 | 2520 | .904 | | |
| 30 | | BOB ESSENSA | 19 | 879 | 2.80 | 4 | 8 | 0 | 3 | 1 | 41 | 406 | .899 | 0 | 0 | 4 |
| 32 | 31 | CURTIS JOSEPH | 72 | 4089 | 2.93 | 32 | 29 | 9 | 3 | 6 | 200 | 2144 | .907 | 0 | 2 | 20 |
| | | EDM TOTALS | | 82 | 4982 | 2.97 | 36 | 37 | 9 | 6 | 7 | 247 | 2556 | .903 | | |
| 93 | | DAREN PUPPA | 6 | 325 | 2.58 | 1 | 1 | 2 | 1 | 0 | 14 | 150 | .907 | 0 | 0 | 2 |
| 20 | 31 | RICK TABARACCI | 55 | 3012 | 2.75 | 20 | 25 | 6 | 5 | 4 | 138 | 1415 | .902 | 0 | 1 | 12 |
| 34 | 32 | *COREY SCHWAB | 31 | 1462 | 3.04 | 11 | 12 | 1 | 2 | 2 | 74 | 719 | .897 | 0 | 1 | 10 |
| 35 | | *DEREK WILKINSON | 5 | 169 | 4.26 | 0 | 2 | 1 | 1 | 0 | 12 | 72 | .833 | 0 | 0 | 0 |
| | | T.B TOTALS | | 82 | 4984 | 2.97 | 32 | 40 | 10 | 9 | 6 | 247 | 2365 | .896 | | |
| 30 | | TOMMY SODERSTROM | 1 | 0 | .00 | 0 | 0 | 0 | 0 | 0 | 0 | 0 | .000 | 0 | 0 | 0 |
| 25 | 35 | TOMMY SALO | 58 | 3208 | 2.82 | 20 | 27 | 8 | 7 | 5 | 151 | 1576 | .904 | 0 | 1 | 4 |
| 36 | 1 | *ERIC FICHAUD | 34 | 1759 | 3.10 | 9 | 14 | 4 | 1 | 0 | 91 | 897 | .899 | 0 | 0 | 2 |
| | | NYI TOTALS | | 82 | 4988 | 3.01 | 29 | 41 | 12 | 8 | 5 | 250 | 2481 | .899 | | |
| 18 | 1 | SEAN BURKE | 51 | 2985 | 2.69 | 22 | 22 | 6 | 6 | 4 | 134 | 1560 | .914 | 0 | 2 | 14 |
| 46 | 29 | JASON MUZZATTI | 31 | 1591 | 3.43 | 9 | 13 | 5 | 1 | 0 | 91 | 815 | .888 | 0 | 1 | 18 |
| 47 | | *J SEBASTIEN GIGUE | 8 | 394 | 3.65 | 1 | 4 | 0 | 0 | 0 | 24 | 201 | .881 | 0 | 0 | 0 |
| | | HFD TOTALS | | 82 | 4996 | 3.07 | 32 | 39 | 11 | 7 | 4 | 256 | 2583 | .901 | | |
| 1 | | *JAMIE STORR | 5 | 265 | 2.49 | 2 | 1 | 1 | 1 | 0 | 11 | 147 | .925 | 0 | 0 | 0 |
| 37 | 34 | BYRON DAFOE | 40 | 2162 | 3.11 | 13 | 17 | 5 | 4 | 0 | 112 | 1178 | .905 | 0 | 0 | 0 |

| 40 | 35 | STEPHANE FISET | 44 | 2482 | 3.19 | 13 | 24 | 5 | 4 | 4 | 132 | 1410 | .906 | 0 | 0 | 2 |
|----|----|----|----|----|----|----|----|----|----|----|----|----|----|----|----|----|
| 32 |    | J.C. BERGERON | 1 | 56 | 4.29 | 0 | 1 | 0 | 0 | 0 | 4 | 35 | .886 | 0 | 0 | 0 |
| L.A TOTALS | | | 82 | 4985 | 3.23 | 28 | 43 | 11 | 9 | 4 | 268 | 2779 | .904 | | | |

| 41 | 1 | KIRK MCLEAN | 44 | 2581 | 3.21 | 21 | 18 | 3 | 3 | 0 | 138 | 1247 | .889 | 0 | 2 | 2 |
|----|----|----|----|----|----|----|----|----|----|----|----|----|----|----|----|----|
| 44 | 31 | COREY HIRSCH | 39 | 2127 | 3.27 | 12 | 20 | 4 | 2 | 2 | 116 | 1090 | .894 | 0 | 1 | 6 |
| 30 |    | *MICHAEL FOUNTAIN | 6 | 245 | 3.43 | 2 | 2 | 0 | 0 | 1 | 14 | 135 | .896 | 0 | 0 | 0 |
| VAN TOTALS | | | 82 | 4972 | 3.29 | 35 | 40 | 7 | 5 | 3 | 273 | 2477 | .890 | | | |

| 38 | 29 | FELIX POTVIN | 74 | 4271 | 3.15 | 27 | 36 | 7 | 6 | 0 | 224 | 2438 | .908 | 0 | 3 | 19 |
|----|----|----|----|----|----|----|----|----|----|----|----|----|----|----|----|----|
| 31 |    | *MARCEL COUSINEAU | 13 | 566 | 3.29 | 3 | 5 | 1 | 1 | 1 | 31 | 317 | .902 | 0 | 1 | 0 |
| 33 |    | DON BEAUPRE | 3 | 110 | 5.45 | 0 | 3 | 0 | 1 | 0 | 10 | 60 | .833 | 0 | 0 | 0 |
| TOR TOTALS | | | 82 | 4966 | 3.30 | 30 | 44 | 8 | 8 | 2 | 273 | 2823 | .903 | | | |

FELIX POTVIN and MARCEL COUSINEAU shared a shutout vs STL on Dec 3, 1996

| 31 | 41 | JOCELYN THIBAULT | 61 | 3397 | 2.90 | 22 | 24 | 11 | 5 | 1 | 164 | 1815 | .910 | 0 | 0 | 0 |
|----|----|----|----|----|----|----|----|----|----|----|----|----|----|----|----|----|
| 60 |    | *JOSE THEODORE | 16 | 821 | 3.87 | 5 | 6 | 2 | 0 | 0 | 53 | 508 | .896 | 0 | 0 | 0 |
| 39 |    | PAT JABLONSKI | 17 | 754 | 3.98 | 4 | 6 | 2 | 0 | 0 | 50 | 438 | .886 | 0 | 0 | 0 |
| 37 |    | *TOMAS VOKOUN | 1 | 20 | 12.00 | 0 | 0 | 0 | 0 | 0 | 4 | 14 | .714 | 0 | 0 | 0 |
| MTL TOTALS | | | 82 | 5008 | 3.31 | 31 | 36 | 15 | 5 | 1 | 276 | 2780 | .901 | | | |

| 23 | 40 | CHRIS TERRERI | 22 | 1200 | 2.75 | 6 | 10 | 3 | 4 | 0 | 55 | 553 | .901 | 0 | 0 | 0 |
|----|----|----|----|----|----|----|----|----|----|----|----|----|----|----|----|----|
| 39 | 32 | KELLY HRUDEY | 48 | 2631 | 3.19 | 16 | 24 | 5 | 4 | 0 | 140 | 1263 | .889 | 0 | 0 | 0 |
| 28 | 20 | ED BELFOUR | 13 | 757 | 3.41 | 3 | 9 | 0 | 1 | 1 | 43 | 371 | .884 | 0 | 0 | 8 |
| 31 |    | WADE FLAHERTY | 7 | 359 | 5.18 | 2 | 4 | 0 | 0 | 0 | 31 | 202 | .847 | 0 | 0 | 0 |
| S.J TOTALS | | | 82 | 4970 | 3.36 | 27 | 47 | 8 | 9 | 1 | 278 | 2398 | .884 | | | |

| 33 | 40 | *PATRICK LALIME | 39 | 2058 | 2.94 | 21 | 12 | 2 | 3 | 3 | 101 | 1166 | .913 | 0 | 0 | 0 |
|----|----|----|----|----|----|----|----|----|----|----|----|----|----|----|----|----|
| 30 |    | *PHILIPPE DE ROUVI | 2 | 111 | 3.24 | 0 | 2 | 0 | 1 | 0 | 6 | 66 | .909 | 0 | 0 | 0 |
| 43 | 31 | KEN WREGGET | 46 | 2514 | 3.25 | 17 | 17 | 6 | 6 | 2 | 136 | 1383 | .902 | 0 | 1 | 6 |
| 35 |    | TOM BARRASSO | 5 | 270 | 5.78 | 0 | 5 | 0 | 1 | 0 | 26 | 186 | .860 | 0 | 0 | 0 |
| PIT TOTALS | | | 82 | 4969 | 3.38 | 38 | 36 | 8 | 11 | 5 | 280 | 2812 | .900 | | | |

| 31 |    | TIM CHEVELDAE | 2 | 93 | 3.23 | 0 | 1 | 0 | 1 | 0 | 5 | 33 | .848 | 0 | 0 | 0 |
|----|----|----|----|----|----|----|----|----|----|----|----|----|----|----|----|----|
| 45 | 35 | *ROBBIE TALLAS | 28 | 1244 | 3.33 | 8 | 12 | 1 | 1 | 1 | 69 | 587 | .882 | 0 | 0 | 0 |
| 42 | 30 | BILL RANFORD | 37 | 2147 | 3.49 | 12 | 16 | 8 | 0 | 2 | 125 | 1102 | .887 | 0 | 0 | 0 |
| 39 |    | *SCOTT BAILEY | 8 | 394 | 3.65 | 1 | 5 | 0 | 2 | 0 | 24 | 181 | .867 | 0 | 0 | 0 |
| 35 | 30 | JIM CAREY | 19 | 1004 | 3.82 | 5 | 13 | 0 | 2 | 0 | 64 | 496 | .871 | 0 | 0 | 0 |
| 1 |    | *PAXTON SCHAFER | 3 | 77 | 4.68 | 0 | 0 | 0 | 1 | 0 | 6 | 25 | .760 | 0 | 0 | 0 |
| BOS TOTALS | | | 82 | 4982 | 3.61 | 26 | 47 | 9 | 7 | 3 | 300 | 2431 | .877 | | | |

GOALTENDING LEADERS
(MIN. 25 GPI)

GOALS AGAINST AVERAGE

| GOALTENDER | TEAM | GPI | MINS | GA | AVG |
|---|---|---|---|---|---|
| MARTIN BRODEUR | NEW JERSEY | 67 | 3838 | 120 | 1.88 |
| ANDY MOOG | DALLAS | 48 | 2738 | 98 | 2.15 |
| JEFF HACKETT | CHICAGO | 41 | 2473 | 89 | 2.16 |
| DOMINIK HASEK | BUFFALO | 67 | 4037 | 153 | 2.27 |
| J. VANBIESBROUCK | FLORIDA | 57 | 3347 | 128 | 2.29 |

WINS

| GOALTENDER | TEAM | GPI | MINS | W | L | T |
|---|---|---|---|---|---|---|
| PATRICK ROY | COLORADO | 62 | 3698 | 38 | 15 | 7 |
| MARTIN BRODEUR | NEW JERSEY | 67 | 3838 | 37 | 14 | 13 |
| DOMINIK HASEK | BUFFALO | 67 | 4037 | 37 | 20 | 10 |
| MIKE RICHTER | NY RANGERS | 61 | 3598 | 33 | 22 | 6 |
| GRANT FUHR | ST LOUIS | 73 | 4261 | 33 | 27 | 11 |

SAVE PERCENTAGE

| GOALTENDER | TEAM | GPI | MINS | GA | SA | SPCTG | W | L | T |
|---|---|---|---|---|---|---|---|---|---|
| DOMINIK HASEK | BUFFALO | 67 | 4037 | 153 | 2177 | .930 | 37 | 20 | 10 |
| MARTIN BRODEUR | NEW JERSEY | 67 | 3838 | 120 | 1633 | .927 | 37 | 14 | 13 |
| JEFF HACKETT | CHICAGO | 41 | 2473 | 89 | 1212 | .927 | 19 | 18 | 4 |
| PATRICK ROY | COLORADO | 62 | 3698 | 143 | 1861 | .923 | 38 | 15 | 7 |
| GUY HEBERT | ANAHEIM | 67 | 3863 | 172 | 2133 | .919 | 29 | 25 | 12 |
| J. VANBIESBROUCK | FLORIDA | 57 | 3347 | 128 | 1582 | .919 | 27 | 19 | 10 |

SHUTOUTS

| GOALTENDER | TEAM | GPI | MINS | SO | W | L | T |
|---|---|---|---|---|---|---|---|
| MARTIN BRODEUR | NEW JERSEY | 67 | 3838 | 10 | 37 | 14 | 13 |
| PATRICK ROY | COLORADO | 62 | 3698 | 7 | 38 | 15 | 7 |
| N. KHABIBULIN | PHOENIX | 72 | 4091 | 7 | 30 | 33 | 6 |
| CHRIS OSGOOD | DETROIT | 47 | 2769 | 6 | 23 | 13 | 9 |
| CURTIS JOSEPH | EDMONTON | 72 | 4089 | 6 | 32 | 29 | 9 |
| RON HEXTALL | PHILADELPHIA | 55 | 3094 | 5 | 31 | 16 | 5 |
| TOMMY SALO | NY ISLANDERS | 58 | 3208 | 5 | 20 | 27 | 8 |
| RICK TABARACCI | CGY-T.B | 62 | 3373 | 5 | 22 | 29 | 6 |
| DOMINIK HASEK | BUFFALO | 67 | 4037 | 5 | 37 | 20 | 10 |